Iran's Intellectual Revolution

Since its revolution in 1978–79, Iran has been viewed as the bastion of radical Islam and a sponsor of terrorism. The focus on its volatile internal politics and its foreign relations has, according to Mehran Kamrava, distracted attention from more subtle transformations which have been taking place there in the intervening years. With the death of Ayatollah Khomeini, a more relaxed political environment opened up in Iran, which encouraged intellectual and political debate between learned elites and religious reformers about the nature of Iranian society, its traditions, and its principles. What emerged from these interactions were three competing ideologies which Kamrava categorizes as conservative, reformist, and secular, and which he illustrates with reference to particular thinkers. As the book aptly demonstrates, these developments, which amount to an intellectual revolution, will have profound and far-reaching consequences for the future of the Islamic Republic, its people, and very probably for countries beyond its borders. This thought-provoking account of the Iranian intellectual and cultural scene will confound stereotypical views of Iran and its mullahs.

Mehran Kamrava is the Director of the Center for International and Regional Studies at Georgetown University School of Foreign Service in Qatar. His recent publications include *The Modern Middle East: A Political History since the First World War* (2005) and *The New Voices of Islam: Rethinking Politics and Modernity* (ed., 2006).

Iran's Intellectual Revolution

Mehran Kamrava

Georgetown University

CAMBRIDGE UNIVERSITY PRESS
Cambridge, New York, Melbourne, Madrid, Cape Town, Singapore,
São Paulo, Delhi

Cambridge University Press
The Edinburgh Building, Cambridge CB2 8RU, UK

Published in the United States of America by Cambridge University Press,
New York

www.cambridge.org
Information on this title: www.cambridge.org/9780521725187

First published 2008

Printed in the United Kingdom at the University Press, Cambridge

A catalogue record for this publication is available from the British Library

Library of Congress Cataloguing in Publication data
Kamrava, Mehran, 1964–
    Iran's intellectual revolution / Mehran Kamrava.
      p.   cm. – (Cambridge Middle East studies; no. 29)
    Includes bibliographical references and index.
    ISBN 978-0-521-89799-0 (hardback)
    1. Iran – Intellectual life – 20th century.   2. Iran – Intellectual life – 21st
    century.   3. Iran – History – 1979–1997.   4. Iran – History – 1997–
    I. Title.   II. Series.
    DS266.K35 2008
    305.5′520955–dc22   2008023228

ISBN 978-0-521-89799-0 hardback
ISBN 978-0-521-72518-7 paperback

To Melisa, Dilara, and Kendra

Contents

Tables

Acknowledgments

I could not have possibly written this book had it not been for the generous assistance of a number of organizations and individuals. Grateful acknowledgment goes to the United States Institute of Peace for a generous grant covering 2003 to 2005 (SG-036-02F) that allowed for the purchase of books, the hiring of research assistants, and extensive travels to and within Iran and elsewhere for work on the book. Additional funding support was provided by the College of Social and Behavioral Sciences at California State University, Northridge, and by the American Institute for Iranian Studies. The present book would simply not have been possible without such generous financial support.

During the time it took to complete this work, I came across many extraordinarily kind and considerate individuals. On numerous occasions, I personally experienced the warmth and beauty of the hospitality for which Iranians are so famously known. In the process I made many lasting friendships and had the opportunity to renew old ones. I am especially thankful to those friends and family members who graciously put up with my frequent impositions and with what no doubt must have been seen as the eccentricities of an inquisitive social scientist.

I am also grateful to the numerous individuals and scholars who selflessly gave me their time and advice, and, in many cases, helped guide me to important additional sources or to other useful contacts. There are far too many of these generous souls to individually mention. Nevertheless, here is a brief list of some: Saeed Hajjarian, Rohullah Hoseinian, Shahram Pazouki, Mas'oud Pedram, Mohammad Kazem Rahmati, Mohammad Rozati, 'Eesa Saharkhiz, Hosein Seifzadeh, Mahmoud Shafi'i, and Hosein Zare'. Seyyed Mostafa Shahraeeni, at the International Center for Dialogue of Civilizations, was particularly instrumental in facilitating contacts and arranging meetings with numerous thinkers and intellectuals. Mehdi Zakerian, at the Center for Scientific Research and Middle East Strategic Studies, was always generous with his time and his vast knowledge of Iranian politics. Mujtaba Zarvani was kind enough to organize a roundtable discussion on the topic of this book with his colleagues at the Faculty of Theology and Islamic Studies of the University of Tehran in July 2004, which I found most rewarding. I also benefited tremendously from subsequent meetings in January and July 2005. Equally fruitful were two similarly in-depth meetings, in July 2004 and January 2005, organized by Ali Mirmoosavi, head of the Political Science Department at Qom's Mofid University and himself a scholar with truly impressive insight into the topics discussed here. Mostafa Mehraeen, another gifted social scientist, has also been a source of invaluable support and critical input throughout the work on this project.

I also benefited tremendously from the efforts of two capable research assistants. In Iran, Maryam Sarrafpour collected bibliographical data and other relevant background information on many of the thinkers and political activists mentioned in this book. Back in the US, Arjang Sayari proofread and commented on earlier drafts of many of the chapters. I am thankful for their efforts and their great enthusiasm for this project.

Through professional collaboration, many of the scholars named here became personal friends, and I remain thankful for their friendship, their kindness, and their hospitality during my many, often intrusive visits. There were countless other individuals who either directly or indirectly helped my research. My apologies to those whose names I may have inadvertently left out. No one, of course, bears responsibility for the book's omissions and shortcomings but myself.

Work on the book required that I spend long periods away from home. This was difficult for me and for my family both emotionally and practically. During these frequent periods of absence, my wife Melisa went about the challenging task of running our household with her radiant smile and her usual gusto. Although she was often alone in looking after our beautiful daughters, she never wavered in her enthusiastic support for my research, sending me off on my many research trips to Iran with enthusiasm and much needed moral support. At home, her love and support sustained me through many long, sleepless nights and endless solitary hours behind the computer. On countless days and nights she provided the loving, supportive environment that allowed me to research for and to work on this project. I literally could not have written this book had it not been for Melisa, and for that I owe her a tremendous debt of gratitude.

A final, personal note. The Iran that I grew up with saw far too many torments – a repressive dictatorship, a mass-based revolution, a bloody and needlessly prolonged war, indiscriminate repression, political instability and uncertainty, economic woes, and more. For those Iranians who, unlike me, had the courage to stay in the country as these tragedies unfolded, the trauma was grave and the toll personally exacting. Today's Iran is not nearly as tormented as it was not too long ago, but, as this book attests, it is still far from at peace with itself. I write in the hope that my young daughters grow up with a happier Iran than the one I did.

1 Introduction

There is a new revolution brewing in Iran. It is not a political revolution, although it was caused by one. And it is not necessarily an economic or cultural revolution, although its consequences certainly reach into both economics and culture. It is a revolution of ideas, a mostly silent contest over the very meaning and essence of Iranian identity, and, more importantly, where Iran and Iranians ought to go from here. Amid all the chaos and turmoil it caused, the Iranian revolution of 1978–79 has unleashed a far more subtle and complex, and quiet, revolution, a revolution in the Iranians' views of themselves, their surrounding world, its meaning, and its essence.

This silent – and at times not-so-silent – revolution has been under-way for over two decades now and is being fought over three principal, romanticized identities: an identity rooted in traditionalist conceptions of Islam; another inspired by Islamic reformism; and a third in which neither Islam nor the weight of tradition should encumber the quest for modernity. The intellectual quest to define – or, more accurately, show the path to – an idealized identity, and the resulting contest that has been unleashed in the process, has given rise to three broad discourses in today's Iran. This book looks at each discourse, how and why it came about, what the discourse argues, and, ultimately, where it might be headed. Context, as we shall see shortly, is crucially determinative of a discourse's rise and spread, and the book will also examine the broader contexts within which each of the three contemporary discourses are being articulated.

Insofar as today's Iran is concerned, much of its "context" – political or otherwise – is shaped and influenced by the historic revolution of 1978–79. The revolution left few aspects of life in the country unchanged, with its aftermath continuing to have significant domestic, regional, and international consequences to this day. In relation to the country's intellectual life, by far the biggest consequence of the revolution was to set off three distinct yet overlapping discourses. The revolution's political success led to the emergence of an officially sanctioned, and subsequently conservative, Islamist discourse. Ever since its emergence, this conservative religious discourse has sought to theoretically justify the continued dominance of the traditionalist clergy over the entire political system and the cultural life of the country. The discourse has sought to strengthen the theoretical foundations and the practical powers of the absolutist institution of the Supreme Religious Guide, the *Velayat-e Faqih*.

Out of this discourse, and in reaction to it, has emerged an alternative interpretation of political Islam, one that seeks not necessarily to separate Islam from the political process but instead to reform what it sees as an increasingly intolerant and opportunistically motivated interpretation of the religion. This discourse of Islamic reformism is articulated primarily by intellectuals who were themselves once key figures within the post-revolutionary establishment. Once devoted to its ideals, these reformers became disenchanted by its excesses and its increasingly authoritarian tendencies. For just under a decade or so, from 1997 to 2005, the proponents of this discourse found a highly supportive political environment which allowed them unprecedented latitude to articulate, nurture, refine, and publicize their ideas. Unexpectedly, but quite happily, the discourse of Islamic reformism found itself in political tandem with "the reform movement," and for a good number of years the two seemed to be riding high. But the often-bumpy road of the reform movement hit a dead-end in 2005, and the political fortunes of the reformist Muslim discourse have suffered a precipitous decline ever since. Today, the reform movement is only barely alive. In many ways, it is searching for ways to theoretically resuscitate and revive itself. And, when it does, it will once again find a ready intellectual ally in the discourse of religious reformism.

In the meanwhile, the last decade or so have seen the articulation of a new discourse – or the revamping and re-articulating of an old one – with its central foci being modernity and secularism. Still in the process of formation and somewhat embryonic, the exact contours of this secular-modernist discourse are not yet fully clear, and neither is the degree to which the educated middle classes are willing to accept and internalize it. Nevertheless, articulated in direct response to the state's perceived theocratic excesses and the political ineptitude of religious reformers, the secular-modernist discourse could indeed become an intellectual force for the state to contend with in the relatively near future. Only time will tell. What is certain for now is that Iran's 1978–79 revolution has unleashed three vibrant, and often competing, discourses.

Before developing these introductory arguments in subsequent chapters, several of the key concepts that are used throughout the book need to be defined and operationalized. Given the focus of the book, starting out with a definition of "discourse" seems only befitting. Broadly, I have taken discourse to mean a general body of thought, based on a series of assumptions, about the nature of things as they are and as they ought to be. Discourse is meant to articulate and explain a worldview, to critically examine and decipher the present and to show signposts for the future. As such, it serves the same purpose and function as ideology. But discourse goes beyond ideology. If we take ideology to simply mean "a blueprint for political thought and action," then discourse is the larger framework of ideas that informs it. Discourse often entails several parallel or overlapping ideologies, which all coalesce into forming the same "discursive field." Robert Wuthnow's definition of discourse is most useful here:

Discourse subsumes the written as well as the verbal, the formal as well as the informal, and the gestural and the ritual as well as the conceptual. It occurs, however, within communities in the broadest sense of the word: communities of competing producers, of interpreters and critics, of audiences and consumers, and of patrons and other significant actors who become the subject of discourse itself. It is only in these concrete living and breathing communities that discourse becomes meaningful.[1]

Along the same lines, a discursive field "provides the fundamental categories in which thinking can take place. It establishes the limits of discussion and defines the range of problems that can be addressed."[2]

As we shall see in the following chapters, the three different discourses under study here are being articulated in Iran principally through books and journal articles, and, on a few occasions, through speeches and sermons, most of which are then printed as articles or book chapters and are published and distributed. In either case, it is primarily through the written word that the three discourses are being articulated. This overwhelming reliance on the print medium is not without its consequences. Those who follow the discourses and for whose consumption they are primarily produced are urban members of the middle and upper middle classes; they invariably have post-secondary or university degrees; they follow political developments and debates with interest; and, even if in the private sector, for them the state and its countless agencies are an everyday presence in their lives.

---

[1] Robert Wuthnow, *Communities of Discourse: Ideology and Social Structure in the Reformation, the Enlightenment, and European Socialism* (Cambridge, MA: Harvard University Press, 1989), p. 16.

[2] Ibid., p. 13.

It is extremely difficult, if not altogether impossible, to determine the voracity and strength of each discourse among its intended audiences and among the middle classes at large. If the palpable excitement and enthusiasm with which so-called "reformist" publications are met is any indication, however, at least the two discourses of religious reformism and secular-modernism have considerable following among the throngs of educated, urban Iranians. And, adversely, because some state institutions and agencies are often used to try to institutionalize the conservative religious discourse, its popularity and appeal are extremely difficult to gauge and open to serious question. I will return to this point more fully in chapter 7.

Dependence on print journalism and book publication has its political and economic costs as well, exposing the architects of the two non-state sanctioned discourses to changes in state policy and fluctuations in the market. As we shall see in the chapters to come, periodic arrests of authors and journalists are quite common in Iran, as are newspaper closures, official and unofficial forms of censorship, and various types of political or economic harassment. Some intellectuals have taken their message to the Internet by posting essays and treatises on the World Wide Web, thus getting around some of the restrictions on publishing. But that still does not make them immune from political harassment, thus invariably influencing the premise and content of the discourse they are seeking to articulate.

It goes without saying, of course, that in any setting there is a complex, nuanced relationship between prevailing political and historical environments and the general types and nature of the discourses that initially become prevalent among scholars and the learned literati. This interaction between reality and discourse is likely to take two broad forms. At times a particular discourse may simply be a reflection of commonly perceived realities, shaped by circumstances which it in turn reinforces by bestowing on them theoretical and ideological justification. At other times, discourse may be more of a blueprint for a utopian ideal that is not yet at hand but is seen to be within grasp. These types of discourses often have ideological and theoretical foundations that are based on perceptions of prevailing circumstances. These two different types of discourses may not necessarily be mutually exclusive. In fact, they can and often do coexist alongside one another within any one given set of circumstances.

All discourses, to borrow Wuthnow's terminology, undergo somewhat distinct processes of production, selection, and institutionalization, whereby they are, respectively, formed and articulated, begin to favor some genres and neglect others, and, steadily, become "a relatively stable feature of the institutional structure of a given society."[3] In today's Iran, two of the three dominant discourses – those of religious reformism and secular-modernism – are still in embryonic stages of formation. Neither has been around long enough to go through the processes of selection or institutionalization. The third discourse, that of religious conservatism, may have been institutionalized *politically* in the sense that it has the support and endorsement of a number of powerful actors within the state, but its *social* institutionalization is seriously debatable. Only time will tell which of the three discourses discussed here will become institutionalized in the manner that Wuthnow describes. For now, the best we can do is to analyze the circumstances and the dynamics that have facilitated the production of each discourse.

Anyone with even a cursory knowledge of contemporary Iranian political history knows that the three discourses discussed in this book are by no means novel to modern times and have, in fact, been a recurrent, if not persistent, feature of Iran since the early 1900s. The Constitutional Revolution of 1905–11 saw the two discourses of Islamic reformism and traditionalism compete for greater political space and popular appeal as articulated especially by Ayatollahs Mirza Hosein Na'ini and Fazlullah Nouri respectively. Within one or two decades, both of these discourses had largely given way to a new, politically supported discourse, this one featuring secularism, the embracing of modernity, economic development, and statism. Although the secular-modernist discourse of the 1990s places a strong emphasis on democracy and civil society instead of statism, in most other areas it overlaps significantly and has important commonalities with its earlier variety.

Given their long histories in Iran, then, what is so special about these discourses now? The answer to this important question is found throughout the book. It can be briefly summarized as follows: the articulation of, and the interplay between, each of the three discourses of religious conservatism, religious reformism, and secular-modernism in contemporary Iran, especially since the death of Ayatollah Khomeini in 1989, are unique – and also highly significant – for two main reasons. First, despite having important elements and features in common with previous, parallel discourses, today's discourses address themes and issues that in many cases did not exist in the past and are unique to the predicaments and circumstances of post-revolutionary, post-Khomeini Iran. Insofar as the religious conservative discourse is concerned, for example, some of the themes it tackles have long informed the worldview of its architects: ultimate authority belonging to

---

[3] Ibid., pp. 9–10.

God; conceptions of *ijtihad* and *taqlid*; literalist interpretations of the Qur'an; and the like. But the question of whether a *Vali-ye Faqih* should or should not also be a *Marja'* is something that has come directly out of the experiences of the Islamic Republic in general and the post-Khomeini era in particular. Moreover, while the predecessors to today's religious reformist discourse also addressed issues such as *ijtihad* and hermeneutics, as well as constitutional government in Ayatollah Na'ini's case, notions such as civil society, dialogue among civilizations, and "theo-democracy" (see chapter 5) are inventions of the latest version of the discourse. The differences between today's secular-modernist discourse and its intellectual ancestors tend to be even more stark, with democracy seen as the centerpiece of modernity today rather than the statism that was praised, or at least tolerated, in the 1920s and the 1930s.

Second, and even more important than the differences in the intellectual contents of the three discourses of today, is the actual *context* within which they are being articulated now and are competing with one another. Today Iran finds itself at a historical juncture that is unique in its recent past. Today's Iran is the product of a mass-based, religiously inspired and directed revolution, a theocracy featuring the rule of a supreme jurist, a bloody war that is still very much alive in the collective memory of Iranians, a highly politically charged population with widespread access to the latest forms of communication technology, and almost unprecedented levels of domestic and international political tensions. Since structures and environments affect the shape and direction of discourse, the discourses of today differ from those of the past in important ways. More significantly, today's discourses address wider and intellectually more sophisticated audiences, they have different goals and different "targets" for change, and they define themselves in relation or in opposition to a theocratic political system. For the first time in the history of modern Iran, worldviews about politics and the individual's role and place in it are being articulated at a time when Islam informs the official guidelines of public policy. Moreover, globalization, information technology, and the diffusion of norms, values, and ideas across national boundaries have never had the ease and the speed with which they travel today. The resulting consequences for the ideas that are formulated and expressed today as compared to twenty or thirty years ago are far-reaching. For the first time, each of the three discourses find themselves in competition with one another within a theocratic political system that lacks ideological and often institutional cohesion, frequently opting to support the conservative discourse but at times giving timid backing to the reformists as well. The very fact that Iran is a young theocracy with institutions that seem not to have taken their final shape yet is bound to affect state–religion relations in the coming decades. Whether it becomes a bastion of some idealized, conservative Islam, or alternatively one of a reformed and supposedly modernized Islam, or whether it remains a theocracy at all, in name or in actual substance, depends as much on the depth and resilience of each discourse as on political and institutional developments. What is certain is that the silent revolution of ideas underway in Iran today is bound to have consequences for the Iranian polity for decades to come. In short, the discourses under discussion here are both different and unique in themselves and are also being articulated within unique historical circumstances. As such, their study both in terms of what they say and what they mean for their intended audiences, as well as the unintended consequences they might have on the larger polity, are key to a better understanding of contemporary Iran.

I should also clarify my use of the term "intellectual." Below, in chapter 3, I offer a rather detailed definition of intellectuals as defined and operationalized by Iranian thinkers themselves. For my own usage here, in line with the arguments of Edward Shils and most other observers of intellectuals, I do not draw distinctions between *intellectuals* and the *intelligentsia* as two distinct social categories.[4] Some scholars have argued that there are a number of important differences between the two groups. In general terms, the argument goes, the intelligentsia is made up of the learned elites who are distinguished from the general population by virtue of their higher levels of learning and their philosophical expositions on the nature of the surrounding world. Intellectuals, on the other hand, are active critics of the social and political orders, thinkers for whom thought alone is insufficient and must be actively propagated and be made to understood by larger audiences.[5]

At least for the purposes of this book, I conceptualize intellectuals and the intelligentsia as being the same social group: learned men and women – made up mostly of academics, writers, and journalists – whose

---

[4] See, for example, Edward Shils, *The Intellectuals and the Power and Other Essays* (Chicago, IL: University of Chicago Press, 1972), and the collection of essays in S. N. Eisenstadt and S. R. Grubard, eds., *Intellectuals and Tradition* (New York, NY: Humanities Press, 1973).

[5] While not necessarily distinguishing them from the intelligentsia, Lewis Feuer defines intellectuals as "that section of the educated class which had aspirations to political power either directly by seeking to be society's political rulers or indirectly by directing its conscience and decisions ... Always the intellectual regarded himself as somewhat chosen; he had a mission conferred upon him as a modern Moses by history. And this sense of mission is intrinsic to the consciousness of the intellectual ... The intellectual is an amalgam of the prophet and the philosopher-king." Lewis Feuer. "What Is an Intellectual?", in Alexander Gella, ed., *The Intelligentsia and the Intellectuals: Theory, Methods, and Case Study* (London: Sage, 1976), pp. 49–51.

primary function is to reflect on their surroundings and, by doing so, encourage the emergence of intentional or unintentional worldviews and discourses. At times, as the opportunity arises, the two groups may become separated from each other by their passion and their conviction with regard to ideas, and by the means and methodology through which they convey those ideas to their intended audiences. There are entirely different dynamics at work when someone gives a speech in a public square to a large audience gathered to hear him, as compared to when one reads a book or an essay in the quiet of one's house. The key here is context and circumstance. In certain contexts, which often occur during extraordinary times, the intelligentsia may be defined as a larger social group of learned elites from whom a smaller group of intellectuals emerge and advocate certain ideals with uncharacteristic enthusiasm and determination. In specific relationship to Iran, such circumstances may have existed in the years immediately preceding and following the 1978–79 revolution, but not anymore today, more than a quarter century later. Not surprisingly, as discussed in chapter 3, the "revolutionary" intellectuals of the 1970s have today turned into what one Iranian scholar calls "discourse" intellectuals. As such, distinguishing between intellectuals and the intelligentsia in today's Iran is somewhat meaningless.

There is already a rich body of literature in English that examines intellectual trends in modern Iran, though none, to my knowledge, focuses specifically on the post-Khomeini era.[6] This literature has added immensely to our knowledge of contemporary Iranian intellectuals' efforts to come to grips with such vexing issues as modernity, authenticity, identity, and the like. Not surprisingly, the primary consumers and beneficiaries of this literature have been Western academics and

---

[6] A notable sample of such works include, among others, Mehrzad Boroujerdi, *Iranian Intellectuals and the West: The Tormented Triumph of Nativism* (Syracuse, NY: Syracuse University Press, 1996); Daniel Brumberg, *Reinventing Khomeini: The Struggle for Reform in Iran* (Chicago, IL: Chicago University Press, 2001); Hamid Dabashi, *Theology of Discontent: The Ideological Foundations of the Islamic Revolution in Iran* (New York: NYU Press, 1993); Ali Gheissari, *Iranian Intellectuals in the Twentieth Century* (Austin, TX: University of Texas Press, 1998); Forough Jahanbakhsh, *Islam, Democracy and Religious Modernity in Iran (1953–2000)* (Leiden: Brill 2001); Ali Mirsepassi, *Intellectual Discourse and the Politics of Modernization: Negotiating Modernity in Iran* (Cambridge: Cambridge University Press, 2000); Roy Mottahedeh, *The Mantle of the Prophet: Religion and Politics in Iran* (New York: Pantheon, 1985); Negin Nabavi, *Intellectuals and the State in Iran: Politics, Discourse, and the Dilemmas of Authenticity* (Gainesville, FL: University Press of Florida, 2003); Negin Nabavi, ed., *Intellectual Trends in Twentieth Century Iran: A Critical Survey* (Gainesville, FL: University Press of Florida, 2003); Behzad Yaghmaian, *Social Change in Iran: An Eyewitness Account of Dissent, Defiance, and New Movements for Rights* (Albany, NY: SUNY Press, 2002); and Farzin Vahdat, *God and Juggernaut: Iran's Intellectual Encounter with Modernity* (Syracuse, NY: Syracuse University Press, 2002).

scholars. My goal here has been to look specifically at those Iranian intellectuals who have had the greatest impact in shaping ideas and perceptions inside Iran, many of whom, at one point or another, have lived, or studied, or even written and published outside of Iran. Nevertheless, the primary focus and target of their intellectual endeavors have been inside the country.

I have sought to portray here as thorough and accurate a picture of the three discourses as possible. Despite my best efforts to have access to the widest and most representative spectrum of books and articles from each discursive field, however, I would not be surprised at all if some of the key publications with significant impact in each discourse have slipped by or fallen below my radar screen. Also, the fact that the discourses discussed here are still in the process of formation – that this round of discourse-making is still an on-going process rather than a historical episode belonging to a distant past – adds a further layer of difficulty to their study. Mindful of these challenges, I have taken as my central task here the presentation of a snapshot of the life and goals of each discourse from its birth in the 1980s up until the present. Perhaps years from now, at some point in the future, a more reflective work can assess the long-term successes or failures of the three discourses. For my part, the best that I can do at this point, as I have tried in chapter 7, is to offer some educated guesses about potential future trends based on present evidence.

In laying out the arguments of the book, I start in chapter 2 with an examination of the political and historical contexts within which the three discourses have emerged, looking specifically at developments in post-revolutionary Iran, especially after the consolidation of the Islamic Republic became fairly certain in 1988–89, and how these events have influenced the intellectual endeavors and outlooks of the country's thinkers. Chapter 3 offers an examination of the country's current crop of intellectuals, looking specifically at how they see their roles and responsibilities, what informs their definitions of what an intellectual is, and how they go about constructing idealized visions of the future. The three following chapters examine each of the discourses, beginning with the conservative religious discourse in chapter 4, the reformist religious discourse in chapter 5, and the secular-modernist discourse in chapter 6. The book concludes with chapter 7, which assesses the relative strengths and weaknesses of each discourse and ends with some thoughts on possible scenarios for the future. In the end, I hope to have made a modest contribution to our collective understanding of contemporary Iran, a fascinating and maddeningly complex country.

2   Emerging Iranian discourses

For nearly three decades now, Iran has attracted much of the world's attention as a supposed bastion of radical Islam, a key player in the global war on terrorism, and a central force in – and often an alleged cause of – turmoil in one of the most unstable regions of the world. The considerable focus thus directed at Iran's volatile internal politics and its foreign relations has all too often overshadowed attention to more subtle developments unfolding inside the country, particularly among its learned elites and opinion makers. That these unfolding dynamics are of profound and long-term cultural and intellectual consequences makes detailed and careful attention to them all the more imperative.

This chapter argues that the evolving direction of Iran's 1978–79 revolution, from its inception up to the present, and the trials and travails of Iranians as a whole over the last quarter century have given rise to three competing worldviews, three discourses, each of which advance their own interpretations of the present and the ideal path to follow in the future. In broad terms, these discourses can be categorized as religious conservative, religious reformist, and secular-modernist.

The religious conservative discourse can be most readily identified with the religio-political establishment that came to power after the revolution's success. It seeks to explain the world, and more specifically its vision of the ideal social and political order, in terms that it claims most closely reflect the letter and the spirit of the arguments of the regime's founder, Ayatollah Rohullah Khomeini. The protagonists of the religious conservative discourse maintain that Iran's cherished Islamic tradition and heritage provide the perfect blueprint for its political system, its social order, and its cultural values and aspirations. Translated into reality, this means the institutionalization of the theological notion of the Absolute Jurisconsult (*Velayat-e Mutlaq-e Faqih*) in the political realm, and the protection of the country's Islamic norms and values against the corrupting and corroding influences of Western modernity.

Although often closely linked with the Islamic Republican state, the religious conservative discourse operates parallel to, but separate from, the state's official policies. No state is perfectly unison and cohesive, and the Islamic Republican state has at times been especially fractured and factionalized. This factionalization of the state became particularly manifest beginning in the late 1980s, as the long and bloody war with Iraq was drawing to a close and as Ayatollah Khomeini's charismatic authority disappeared when he died in 1989. Competing interpretations of the Ayatollah Khomeini's legacy and the right course to follow in the future were, in large measure, products of more profound developments within what by now had become official Shi'a jurisprudence.

Specifically, a number of prominent Shi'a jurists began to openly offer alternative interpretations of Islam's proper role in the political order. The curiosity and interest they generated, at least in learned and intellectual circles, was deepened by the excesses of the state on the one hand and a growing sense of disillusionment and unease by some of the regime's own key former supporters on the other. Nevertheless, the stern political realities of the "second republic" – coupled with the continued need to recover from the shocks of the war, and the embryonic nature of the alternative worldview itself – prevented the emergence of a serious challenge to the officially sanctioned and supported religious conservative discourse. It was not until 1997, when the surprise election of Mohammad Khatami to the presidency ushered in a "third republic," that a reformist religious discourse found room within the public sphere.

Similar to the President who supported it and was generally perceived to be one of its patrons and architects, the religious reformist discourse was initially met with much excitement and enthusiasm among most urban middle-class Iranians. Articulated mostly by learned jurists and respected public intellectuals, the reformist religious discourse has sought to strike a balance between Islam and modernity. More specifically, the principal goal of the reformist religious discourse has been to distinguish between Islam as a revealed religion and the hermeneutics of Islam as popularly understood over time. It has also sought to synchronize this hermeneutics with such beneficial offerings of modernity as civil society, personal choice, and democracy.

There is a third discourse that has gained prominence among a growing number of Iranian thinkers of late – more accurately, it has *re*gained the prominence it once had – and that is the secular-modernist discourse. The modern world, this discourse's proponents claim, is no place for politicized religion. It is, instead, a world in which religion needs to be privatized and politics needs to be secularized, where civil society and globalization must become the norm rather than the exception, and where democracy needs to reign supreme. None of this means blindly thrusting one's self into the embrace of the West, or abandoning what makes Iranians who they are. It simply means reorienting one's vision and values with the prevailing realities of the modern world, welcoming the forces of change, and internalizing the values of democracy and respect for the rights of political opponents. Only then, claim the likes of the philosopher Ramin Jahanbegloo and a host of others, can Iran and Iranians truly realize the full potential of their rich civilization and their culture.

To better understand the underlying causes for the birth – or rebirth – of each discourse and its subsequent evolution, it is important to have a detailed understanding of the larger political and institutional contexts of the Iranian polity in the aftermath of the revolution. This chapter traces the birth of each of the three discourses, looking at how developments with the body politic have facilitated the conditions for the emergence of each discourse. In doing so I will briefly sketch the political history of the Islamic Republic, in broad brushstrokes, so as to present the context for the rise of each discourse. Then the chapter looks more specifically at the emergence of developments that facilitated the birth of what came to be known as "the reform movement," culminating in and in turn expedited by the presidential elections of 1997. Today, within the span of a decade, what transpired in 1997 may already be dead as a *political* movement – it is certainly deadlocked – but its longer-term intellectual and jurisprudential significance is bound to impact Iranian history for some time.

History and discourse

The success of the 1978–79 revolution was followed by the relatively speedy institutionalization and consolidation of political power by an increasingly narrow circle of revolutionaries led by Ayatollah Khomeini. Before long, the broadly based coalition of revolutionary groups whose combined efforts had brought about the collapse of the monarchy was reduced to a largely single group of Islamists who were more or less united in their endorsement of Khomeini's concept of *Velayat-e Faqih* (Supreme Jurisconsult), accepted him as their *Marja'-e Taqlid* (Source of Emulation), and were largely in sync with his traditionalist interpretations of Shi'a principles and his efforts to remake Iranian society accordingly. Not surprisingly, the official discourse became one of Shi'a traditionalism and political conservatism, backed by the full force of a highly repressive state that was being hardened by war, international condemnation, and the successive loss of its leaders to assassinations and terrorist attacks.[1]

For all of Khomeini's revolutionary zeal, his religious traditionalism, and his political conservatism, in many ways he actually turned out to be a moderating force in both the unfolding of events in the critical, early years of the revolution, and in the official, theological discourse that was beginning to gain increasing currency among both the public and the learned elites. "Imam" Khomeini's stature as both a widely recognized *Marja'* and an undisputed political leader enabled him to withstand challenges from even more traditionalist clerics in Qom to move further to the Right in political practice as well as in doctrine. Khomeini's blunt and very public condemnation of revolutionary excesses in December 1982 is a case in point. At a time when the Revolutionary Committees were wreaking havoc with the lives of ordinary citizens by administering revolutionary justice in the streets, Khomeini pointedly reminded the government of the urgent need to have qualified judges, respect the people's civil rights, ensure fair and equal treatment for the accused, and take measures to ensure that the sanctity of private residences was not violated.[2] Other examples included Khomeini's rejection of the suggestion to formally segregate male and female students in the country's universities; his prohibition on the involvement of military personnel in politics; his refusal to approve the use of chemical weapons in the war with Iraq; and his willingness to allow limited political participation by some of the old Islamic political groupings such as the Liberation Movement and the National Front.[3]

---

[1] Numerous superb studies of the Iranian revolution have appeared since that historic event. A very small sample of such publications includes: Shaul Bakhash, *The Reign of the Ayatollahs: Iran and the Islamic Revolution* (London: I. B. Tauris, 1985); Dabashi, *Theology of Discontent*; Vanessa Martin, *Creating an Islamic State: Khomeini and the Making of a New Iran* (London: I. B. Tauris, 2003); Roy Mottahedeh, *The Mantle of the Prophet: Religion and Politics in Iran* (New York: Pantheon, 1985); and Robin Wright, *The Last Great Revolution: Turmoil and Transformation in Iran* (New York: Vintage, 2001).

[2] Khomeini's edict comprised eight specific points on the need to observe the people's civil and judicial rights. The text of the edict appeared in the widely circulated *Keyhan* newspaper on December 21, 1982.

[3] A number of these trends have been reversed in recent years: some of the high-ranking officials in the armed forces have become very vocal in domestic and foreign policy issues; members of the Liberation Movement are barred from open political activism and are often harassed; and the *Velayat-e Faqih* has generally moved further to the Right under Khamenei as compared to Khomeini. In his last will and testament, in fact, Khomeini expressly reminded the regime's leaders to "remember to be servants of the masses" (p. 31), cautioned future *Velayat-e Faqih*s to remain humble (p. 43), reminded members of the executive branch that "acting against people's interests is religiously forbidden" (pp. 45–47), and emphatically forbade any members of the armed forces from participating in politics (p. 53). Rohullah Khomeini, *Sahife-ye Enqelab-e*

Taken together, the corpus of Ayatollah Khomeini's actions as a political leader, from the time of his ascent to formal political power in 1979 until his death a decade later, depict a political leader with a highly calculated sense of political timing, acting out of strategic radicalism at some points and deliberate moderation at some points.[4] The ascendancy of the so-called "fundamentalist Islamic Republicans"[5] throughout the first half of the 1980s was as much a product of Khomeini's carefully crafted maneuvers against former allies and new opponents as it was a result of his ideological preferences. Ultimately, in significant ways, within the context of the highly polarized revolutionary polity of the time, Khomeini often moderated the tempo and tenor of the prevailing discourse.

The second half of the 1980s saw the process of political institutionalization of the Islamic Republic move in new, much deeper directions. Shortly prior to his death on June 3, 1989, Ayatollah Khomeini set into motion several dynamics aimed at strengthening the institutional cohesion of the system he had founded. As early as December of the previous year, key figures within the regime had openly talked about the need to reform and amend the 1979 constitution, which, they maintained, was proving inadequate in dealing with the country's evolving political circumstances. With Khomeini's blessing, a process of constitutional review was undertaken and a new document was soon drafted. What followed was nothing short of a fundamental overhauling of the primary political institutions of the Islamic Republic. The new constitution featured, among other things, a greater concentration of power in the hands of an executive President, the dismantling of the office of the Prime Minister, codification of the mediatory Expediency Council (as an arbitrator between the Majles and the Guardian Council), and removal of the provision for a Leadership Council in the absence of consensus on a *Faqih*. Perhaps most significantly, the 1989 constitution also removed the requirement that the *Faqih* must also be a *Marja'*.[6]

Eslami: Vasiyat Nameh-e Elahi-Siyasi-e Rahbar-e Mo'azzam-e Enqelab-e Eslami-e Iran (The Book of Islamic Revolution: The Religion-Political Will and Testament of the Great Leader of the Islamic Revolution) (Tehran: Aryaban, 1378/1999).

[4] For an insightful study of Khomeini's nuanced approach to politics over time see, Ervand Abrahamian, *Khomeinism: Essays on the Islamic Republic* (Berkeley, CA: University of California Press, 1993), especially pp. 17–59.

[5] Anoushiravan Ehteshami, *After Khomeini: The Iranian Second Republic* (London: Routledge, 1995), p. 7.

[6] Ibid., pp. 34–41. For an in-depth discussion of the drafting of both the original and the amended versions of the constitution see, Asghar Schirazi, *The Constitution of Iran: Politics and the State in the Islamic Republic*, trans. John O'Kane (London: I. B. Tauris, 1998), especially chapters 1–12.

The overhauling of the constitution was accompanied by a series of other significant initiatives that signaled a shift in the Islamic Republic's overall posture and priorities. Earlier, in July 1988, the regime's senior leadership had accepted UN Security Council Resolution 598 calling for a ceasefire in the war with Iraq. The ceasefire option had long been discussed and hotly debated among the Islamic Republic's civilian and military leadership, with many civilian politicians advocating an end to the war while some high-ranking Commanders of the Revolutionary Guards called for its continued pursuit. According to a secret letter that Ayatollah Khomeini wrote to the regime's top officials, however, he had been finally convinced that the country's military capabilities were depleted and continuing the war would be futile. Referring to a letter he had received earlier from the Commander of the Revolutionary Guards, he wrote,

We have no chance for victory for another five years, and [it is estimated that] by the end of the fourth year we may have the necessary capabilities to conduct the war successfully at that point. This would include having 350 infantry divisions, 2,500 tanks, 3,000 cannons, 300 jet fighters, 300 helicopters, and access to atomic and laser weapons, which will be necessary for warfare at that point. [The Commander] says that we need to increase the power of the Revolutionary Guards seven-fold and that of the Army two-fold.

Ever the pragmatist, Ayatollah Khomeini knew full-well that these hopes were beyond reach.

The Prime Minister, speaking on behalf of the Ministers of Economy and Budget, have told me that government's financial predicament is below zero. Those responsible for the war tell me that the cost of the weapons we have lost in recent defeats equals the combined budget of the Army and Revolutionary Guards for the current year. Political figures tell me that people have realized we will not achieve victory anytime soon, and that their enthusiasm for going to the battlefront has diminished lately.[7]

He thus relented, "drank from the poison cup" of ceasefire, as he later told Iranians, and accepted peace with Iraq.

Finally, on March 28, 1989, as one of his last acts as the country's paramount leader, Khomeini ordered the removal from office of Ayatollah Hoseinali Montazeri, his former pupil and trusted aide, who up until then had been designated as Khomeini's successor. Montazeri's

---

[7] This letter was released by the office of Ayatollah Rafsanjani in September 2006 as a way to undermine his opponents at the time, one of whom included Mohsen Rezai, the Revolutionary Guards Commander to whom Khomeini refers, who in the late 1980s was one of the few voices calling for the continuation of the unpopular war. The text of the letter is widely available on the Internet, the quotations here being from the version on www.iran-emrooz.net, available as of October 1, 2006.

repeated, open calls for an end to the excesses of the government, and especially his vocal objection to the mass executions that followed soon after the end of the war, had irked Khomeini.[8]

Ayatollah Montazeri's abrupt and public removal from all official positions, and his subsequent house arrest beginning in 1997, exposed deep fissures at the highest levels of the state. Nevertheless, with Montazeri out of the way, the "second republic" became dominated by two of the revolutionary leadership's key original figures. On June 5, 1989, Hojjatoleslam Ali Khamenei, who had served as the Islamic

---

[8] The friction between Ayatollahs Khomeini and Montazeri reached breaking point in July 1988, when the regime engaged in the massacre of political prisoners shortly after an abortive attempt by the Mujahedeen-e Khalq Organization (MKO), at the time the main armed opposition to the regime, to militarily invade Iran following the conclusion of the war with Iraq. In a *fatwa* reportedly issued some time between July 22 and 25, 1988, Khomeini decreed that "those who are in prison throughout the country and who remain loyal to their hypocritical conviction [meaning the Mujahedeen], are waging war on God and are condemned to execution." Ayatollah Montazeri is said to have issued a sharp rebuttal on July 31, 1988, arguing, among other things, that a mass execution can result in the mistaken deaths of many innocent prisoners and warning that such "murders and acts of violence" can be counterproductive. Nevertheless, in the weeks that followed, thousands of political prisoners suspected of links with the MKO were reportedly executed. The full text of both Khomeini's *fatwa* and Montazeri's rebuttal in English can be found in Wilfried Buchta, *Taking Stock of a Quarter Century of the Islamic Republic of Iran* (Islamic Legal Studies Program, Harvard Law School, Occasional Publications 5, June 2005), pp. 17–21. In a letter that later surfaced and whose authenticity is often questioned, Ayatollah Khomeini is said to have written the following to his former protégé:

Since it is evident that after me you intend to hand over this beloved country and our Islamic Revolution to liberals and Hypocrites [the regime's codeword for members of the MKO], you have lost the legitimacy and the qualification to assume the leadership of the system. In many of your speeches, your letters, and your pronouncements, you have revealed your belief that liberals and Hypocrites ought to rule the country, and your positions are so obviously dictated by the Hypocrites that I do not see them as worthy of response ...

I give you the following advice in the hope that you know what is best for you:

1. Try to change the key figures in your inner circle so that the tithing paid to you do not go to the benefit of Hypocrites and liberals.
2. Since your are naïve and gullible and easily manipulated, you should not interfere in any political matters. The Almighty takes pity and forgives your sins.
3. Do not write any more letters to me, and also do not allow the Hypocrites to pass national secrets to our enemies.
4. The letters and speeches of the Hypocrites that find their way to the media through you inflict blows to Islam and the revolution and are acts of high treason against our soldiers in arms and our martyrs. Repent now so that you will not burn in hell.

From the very beginning, I was opposed to your appointment [as the designated successor] since I saw you as a naïve and gullible, fit for seminary studies but not for administration and management. If you do not cease these sorts of activities, I have another obligation that I must perform, and you know that I will not back away from it.

The full text of the letter is quoted in 'Abdollah Nouri, *Shoukaran-e Eslah* (Hemlock for Advocate of Reform) (Tehran: Tarh-e No, 1379/2000), pp. 289–91. Nouri's doubts about the letter are raised in pp. 180–81.

Republic's President for two terms since 1981, was elected as the new *Faqih* by the Assembly of Experts and was simultaneously elevated to the rank of Ayatollah. A few weeks later, Hojjatoleslam Hashemi Rafsanjani, who up until then had been the Speaker of the Majles, was elected to the presidency. A new era, characterized by new policy priorities and new agendas, started in the life of the Islamic Republic.

Whereas the central focus of the first republic was the consolidation of the revolutionary order, the second republic's main preoccupation became one of economic reconstruction. A decade into the revolution's success, and after a bloody war for eight years, the economic promises of the revolution could no longer be sidestepped, nor could the country's crumbling infrastructure be ignored. The mantra of the state became one of development – the "Reconstruction Crusade," to be more exact – and President Rafsanjani, presiding over a cabinet of technocrats, started reveling in the moniker "Commander of Reconstruction" (*Sardar-e Sazandegi*). The developmental posture of the state notwithstanding, the government's social policies changed relatively little as compared with earlier periods, with the official emphasis on revolutionary orthodoxy and "cultural authenticity" (*esalat-e farhangi*) continuing largely unabated. In fact, it was during the second republic, some time beginning in 1990–91, according to the author and journalist 'Emadeddin Baqi, when the phrase "red lines" became part of the political parlance in Iran.[9] These "red lines," Baqi maintains, began referring to political subjects or topics that "could not be questioned or criticized," where trespassers were certain to face "danger."[10]

Throughout the first and second republics, the heightened repression of the state was complemented by an increasingly conservative, mournful official discourse that the state's narrow circle of leaders articulated. The discourse was conveyed to the public through Friday Prayer sermons in the capital and in provincial towns, through the country's vast network of existing and newly constructed mosques, and through both the print and the electronic media. Designed to instill the virtues of the Islamic Republic and to maximize its ability to mobilize resources and manpower for the war effort, the official discourse emphasized the political glories of early Shi'ism – especially the martyrdom of Imam Hosein – and cast suspicious eyes on globalization, modernity, and urban life in general, all of which were portrayed as

---

[9] 'Emadeddin Baqi, *Hoquq-e Mokhalefan: Tamrin-e Demokrasi baraye Jame'h Irani* (The Rights of Opponents: Practicing Democracy in Iranian Society) (Tehran: Saraee, 1381/ 2002), p. 142.
[10] Ibid., p. 170.

corrupting and potentially anti-Islamic.[11] At the same time, mourning and austerity were upheld as exalted forms of public expression, and self-sacrifice and self-cleansing were promoted as virtues to which all must aspire. Martyrdom was hailed as the highest form of earthly accomplishment.

The 1978–79 revolution had unleashed unprecedented explosions in both intellectual fervor and political energy, and the Islamic Republic had been able to bring them under control only after resort to unfathomable levels of repression. Between July and December 1981 alone, Amnesty International recorded some 2,444 executions, and some 470 in 1985, numbers that the organization admitted were "far from exhaustive."[12] Throughout the 1980s, the official media reported on hundreds of executions every year, with the actual number being closer to the thousands. There were also reports of widespread use of torture in Iranian prisons, including severe beatings and rapes, as well as thousands of arrests, summary trials, and executions.[13] Altogether, by 1985, at the height of a reign of terror that lasted from 1981 to 1988, an estimated 12,500 Iranians were executed.[14] The prison population grew by the thousands; exactly how many, no one knows. Countless others lost their jobs in the civil service through frequent purges, and millions of Iranians from all walks of life left the country.

The post-revolutionary terror and the war with Iraq had halted the intellectual fervor of the early days of the revolution. But they did not eradicate it altogether. In fact, as a result of these experiences, and the concomitant, successful institutionalization of the Islamic Republic order, new intellectual currents were taking shape, although they were not yet being articulated and expressed. Rafsanjani's presidency and the Construction Crusade temporarily extended the eclipse of the new

[11] Mehrdad Mashayekhi, "Degardisi Mabani-ye Siyasat va Roshanfekri-ye Siyasi" (Changes in Political Principles and Political Intellectuals), *Aftab*, No. 28 (1382/ 2003), p. 9.

[12] Amnesty International, *Iran: Violations of Human Rights* (London: Amnesty International, 1987), p. 42.

[13] There is no shortage of reports cataloguing the human rights violations of the Islamic Republic in the 1980s. In addition to Amnesty International's Annual Report – which, for example, in 1989 reported 1,200 known executions in Iran – AI published periodic reports on the Islamic Republic's human rights abuses. See, for example, Amnesty International. *Iran: Violations of Human Rights 1987–1990* (London: Amnesty International, 1990); and Amnesty International, *Iran: Imprisonment, Torture and Execution of Political Opponents* (London: Amnesty International, 1992).

[14] Ervand Abrahamian, *Tortured Confessions: Prisons and Public Recantations in Modern Iran* (Berkeley, CA: University of California Press, 1999), p. 129. Abrahamian quotes figures from the Mujahedeen-e Khalq Organization that put the number of their dead at 12,028 by 1985. For Abrahamian's chilling account of the massacre see, ibid., pp. 209–28.

intellectual currents and the non-governmental discourse that was emerging. Nevertheless, with the overarching and unchallengeable presence of Ayatollah Khomeini gone, multiple interpretations of his legacy and his intentions began to emerge, exposing small cracks in the ideological cohesion of the ruling clerical class. Rafsanjani and Khamenei in particular resorted to "cleverly using" Khomeini's legacy for political ends while careful not to betray it, frequently arguing "that only certain privileged people had the requisite grasp of Khomeini's life to elucidate this complex legacy."[15] Not surprisingly, their attempts to monopolize interpretations of the Imam's legacy were less than fully successful. Before long, contending visions of the future course of the revolution were being articulated within the ranks of the ruling clerical establishment itself. Simultaneously, an emerging, non-governmental discourse, having now had some two decades to percolate and mature, began finding more opportunities for expression.

By the mid-1990s, through scattered articles and interviews published in existing and newly established journals, an increasing number of academics and social scientists began to lay the foundations for an alternative, non-official discourse. Then, in June 1997, a dark-horse candidate in the person of Hojjatoleslam Mohammad Khatami, whose relative liberalism had brought about his forced resignation as the Minister of Culture in 1993, won the presidency in a landslide and shocking victory. The second republic now gave way to a third republic.

Khatami's election victory, and the larger social and political under-currents that made it possible, were a product of larger processes of social change that touched on nearly every aspect of the Iranian polity. It is difficult to isolate the causes of these tectonic changes to one or even a few dynamics. Nevertheless, developments in three broad areas of the polity, all of them related and mutually reinforcing, converged to result in what at the time appeared to be a historic moment in the life of the Islamic Republic. First, there was broad public consensus on the need to change the general posture and direction of the polity, and to do so at a pace that was measured and relatively moderate. The urban middle classes, in other words, saw the *reform* of the system as both necessary and desirable.

Second, some time in the latter half of the second republic, a slight opening appeared for a new generation of public intellectuals to have their views and thoughts heard through an increasing number of newly founded journals and newspapers. In fact, it was largely because of facilitating this relatively more relaxed intellectual atmosphere that the

---

[15] Brumberg, *Reinventing Khomeini*, p. 158.

responsible Cabinet Minister at the time, Mohammad Khatami, had been forced to resign by the more hardline elements within the regime.

Third was the critical role that Khatami himself played in the election campaign process. He gave focused expression to popular sentiments for temperate change on the one hand, and bridged the gap between what the intellectuals were saying and what the people wanted on the other hand. With an ever-present smile and pleasant demeanor, Khatami, the intellectual-politician, represented a radical departure from the type of political figure Iranians had grown accustomed to in the post-revolutionary era.

A number of developments had prepared the public mood for a moderate change in the country's political direction. The biggest factors appear to have been rising political expectations following relatively rapid economic growth in the Rafsanjani years; a yearning for a measure of normalization of life after some two decades of revolutionary mass mobilization; and, following unprecedented growth rates in the size of the country's population, the emergence of a generation gap between the leaders of the revolution – now the elites of the state – and an expansive, increasingly young population with at best a faint memory of the revolution itself.

The developmentalism that had characterized the Rafsanjani presidency had resulted in rising expectations on the part of the urban middle classes both politically as well as economically. A public opinion survey conducted in 1995, six years into Rafsanjani's two-term presidency, demonstrated conclusively that a vast majority of urban Iranians viewed the non-economic aspects of their "quality of life" as more important than economic ones.[16] The public's pervasive, though unspoken, thirst for greater political responsiveness and accountability crystallized itself in the popular perception of Khatami as an outsider and a non-establishment candidate.[17] At the same time, Khatami's candidacy was nothing like what the public had seen before, especially not from someone approved by the archconservative Guardian Council.[18] Unlike those before him,

---

[16] Abbas 'Abdi and Mohsen Godarzi, *Tahavvolat-e Farhangi dar Iran* (Cultural Transformations in Iran) (Tehran: Ravesh, 1378/1999), p. 2.

[17] Ahmad Bokharaee, *Demokrasi va Doshmananash dar Iran* (Democracy and its Enemies in Iran) (Tehran: Gam-e No, 1381/2002), p. 14.

[18] Though not specified in the constitution, one of the functions that the Guardian Council (GC) has assumed is to vet candidates for the parliament and the presidency by determining whether or not they are qualified to run. This has generated great controversy in recent years, especially after the GC deemed many sitting parliamentary deputies in the reformist camp as unqualified to run for re-election to the Seventh Majles in the February 2004 elections. For more on the role and significance of the GC in the Iranian political system see Mehran Kamrava and Houchang Hassan-Yari,

Khatami actually campaigned and made stump speeches. His campaign speeches revolved around the themes of tolerance, moderation, civil society, and pluralism. And, perhaps most shockingly, he almost always smiled, exuding a calm, confident air of tranquility about him. After having been told to be mournful and to celebrate martyrdom, to sacrifice and to fight on, Iranians found Khatami's persona and his message soothing, reassuring, hopeful. After his victory one Iranian observer went so far as to claim that Khatami's election "helped avert an impending social *explosion* in the Islamic Republic."[19] Warning of an "impending social explosion" is perhaps an exaggeration. But it does present an insight into how the election campaign and the subsequent victory were seen by a majority of urban Iranians. At the very least, voting for Khatami was a form of "quiet protest" against the order of things.[20]

Reinforcing the changing mood of the public were changes in the make-up and composition of Iranian society itself. Because of both state policies and natural demographic trends, the composition of the voting urban classes had changed greatly from the time of the revolution until the end of the second republic. Overall, Iran's population expanded dramatically in the intervening two decades, became highly educated, remained overwhelmingly young, and became increasingly concentrated in urban areas. In 1976, the year before the revolutionary movement got underway, the country's population was estimated at slightly fewer than 34 million. By 1996 it had expanded to more than 60 million.[21] A staggering 74.4 percent of the population remained below the age of thirty-five, and a full 35 percent was made up of those between the ages of fifteen to thirty-four. In the meanwhile, the percentage of the urban population in the country went from 54.3 in 1986 to 61.3 in 1996, and the number of cities with a population of 250,000 or more went from sixteen to twenty-three during the same period.[22]

In the meanwhile, the percentage of Iranians with a formal education went from 26.5 percent in 1979 to 79.5 percent in 1996.[23] In this area

"Suspended Equilibrium in Iran's Political System," *The Muslim World*, Vol. 94, No. 4 (October 2004), pp. 504–08.

[19] Bokharaee, *Demokrasi va Doshmananash dar Iran* (Democracy and its Enemies in Iran), p. 14. Original emphasis.

[20] Khashayar Deihimi and Hamidreza Jalaeepour, "Jameʻhshenasi-ye Siyasi-e Eslahat" (Political Sociology of Reforms), *Aftab*, No. 18 (1381/2002), p. 5.

[21] Unless otherwise indicated, the population statistics in this section come from the website of the Statistical Center of Iran, at www.sci.org.ir, accessed on April 23, 2005.

[22] The total number of cities throughout the country went from 496 in 1986 to 614 in 1996, and Iranian cities of all sizes experienced growths in numbers except those with less than 5,000, which went from 84 to 83 in the same period.

[23] Mohammad Javad Chitsaz Qomi, "Gosast-e Nasli dar Iran: Afsaneh ya Vaqeʻiyyat" (Generational Rupture in Iran: Myth or Reality), in ʻAli Akbar ʻAlikhani, ed., *Negahi beh*

women made by far the biggest gains. For about two decades, from 1972
to 1991, women consistently made up around only 30 percent of those
who passed the national university entrance exam. The decades of the
1990s saw drastic changes in this arena, with the percentage of women
passing the dreaded exam jumping to 40 percent in 1995 and then
improving for every year thereafter: 43 percent in 1996, 52 percent in
1998, 56 percent in 1999, and 60 percent in 2000.[24] Women also made
up 62 percent of the country's university graduates.[25] Although statistics
on the level of women's participation in politics are not available, it is
reasonable to assume that with increased university education a greater
percentage of them developed stronger political sentiments and greater
awareness of issues affecting their lives. According to a field survey
conducted shortly before Khatami's election, of the 150 women polled,
all viewed politics as the most significant factor in "improving" their
social conditions.[26] At the same time, throughout this period, the position of the conservative clerical establishment, both in and out of the
state, on women's status in society changed little, remaining wrapped in
traditional, often archaic values. Most saw no need for "improvement."[27]
Not surprisingly, women voted for Khatami in droves.

These demographic and educational trends inevitably affected cultural norms and values. The 1995 public opinion poll alluded to earlier
concluded that urban Iranians were becoming more formal and con-
tractual in their social relationships, more protective of their privacy, and

---

Padideh-ye Gosast-e Nasl-ha (A Look at the Phenomenon of the Rupture of Generations)
(Tehran: Pazhoheshkaeh-e 'Oloom-e Ensani va 'Ejtema'i, 1382/2003), p. 321.

[24] Hamid 'Abdollahian, "Taq'irat-e Farhangi va Shekaft-e Nasl-ha dar Iran" (Cultural
Changes and the Rupture of Generations in Iran), in 'Alikhani, ed., *Negahi beh Padideh-
ye Gosast-e Nasl-ha* (A Look at the Phenomenon of the Rupture of Generations),
pp. 257–58.

[25] Chitsaz Qomi, "Gosast-e Nasli dar Iran: Afsaneh ya Vaqe'iyyat" (Generational Rupture
in Iran: Myth or Reality), p. 326.

[26] Nasrin Mosaffa, *Mosharekat-e Siyasi-e Zanan dar Iran* (Women's Political Participation
in Iran) (Tehran: Vezarat-e Omoor-e Kharejeh, 1375/1996), p. 177.

[27] The issue of the position of women according to orthodox Shi'a interpretations is a vast
topic that is well beyond the scope of this study. Nevertheless, a quote from one of the
most prominent, conservative clerics in Iran, Ayatollah Javadi Amoli, illustrates the
point:

In Islamic thought, women are more vulnerable than men, and they are also more
successful in the ways of the heart. They can therefore reach their goals faster. Women
have an easier time mourning, shedding tears, and wailing, and we know that the ways
of the heart are more successful than the ways of the mind … That is why Islam
encourages women to become mothers and to nurture humanity. Imam Ali's beautiful
words guide us to this truth: "Woman is a beautiful-smelling flower, not a hero of
warfare."

'Abdullah Javadi Amoli, *Falsafeh-ye Hoquq-e Bashar* (The Philosophy of Human Rights)
(Qom: Isra, 1375/1996), p. 235.

more likely to be members of nuclear as opposed to extended families.[28] Democratic values regarding the equal rights of men and women in decision-making and in earning money were on the rise, and, perhaps most significantly, violence was increasingly seen as an undesirable means to achieving ends.[29]

At the same time, an overwhelming majority of the country's youth, particularly those in their twenties, were too young to have had any direct experience in the revolution and the war. In fact, all indications were that the state's relentless political socialization efforts through the school system and through other official means had failed to deepen conservative religious values among the youth.[30] On the contrary, radical changes in overall perspective on the one hand and the revolutionizing effects of information technology on the other hand led to a decline in the importance of such traditional reference groups as the family and the clergy and instead facilitated the emergence of new ones.[31] If anything, the excesses of the regime in the name of religion, the stifling political atmosphere it had created, and its cultural and social rigidity combined to significantly erode the pervasiveness of religious values among the urban middle classes. "Social problems" and emerging "values and interests" had combined to result in a serious "crisis of legitimacy" for the system.[32]

Results from other public opinion surveys conducted in the mid-1990s confirm these conclusions. According to one poll, the percentage of respondents who indicated a "fondness for the clergy" declined from 86.7 percent in 1986 to 32.3 percent in 1992, and then to 29.2 percent in 1994. Between 1986 and 1992, the percentage of those indicating "respect for women wearing the chador" also declined from 81.8 to 36.8, and, conversely, the percentage of those considering "lack of *hijab* wrong" went from 86.2 to 41.5.[33] There were precipitous declines in other indicators of religiosity as well, including in areas such as

[28] 'Abdi and Godarzi, *Tahavvolat-e Farhangi dar Iran* (Cultural Transformations in Iran), pp. 52–53.

[29] Ibid., p. 53.

[30] Chitsaz Qomi, "Gosast-e Nasli dar Iran: Afsaneh ya Vaqe'iyyat" (Generational Rupture in Iran: Myth or Reality), p. 326.

[31] Hadi Semati, "Sharayet va Zamineh-haye Gosaste-e Nasli dar Iran" (The Conditions and Context of Generational Gap in Iran), in 'Alikhani, ed., *Negahi beh Padideh-ye Gosast-e Nasl-ha* (A Look at the Phenomenon of the Rupture of Generations), p. 187.

[32] Abbas Mohammadi Asl, "Bohran-e Mashro'iyat dar Jomhuri-ye Eslami Iran va Rah-e Hall-e An" (Legitimacy Crisis in the Islamic Republic of Iran and Way to Solve It), *Gozaresh*, No. 140 (1381/2002), p. 36.

[33] Mohammad Reza Sharif, *Enqelab-e Aram: Daramadi bar Tahavvol-e Farhang-e Siyasi dar Iran* (The Quiet Revolution: A Look at the Changes to Political Culture in Iran) (Tehran: Rouzaneh, 1381/2002), p. 154.

attendance to mosques, holding special prayer sessions, paying tithings, attending Friday Prayer ceremonies, and making religious vows.[34]

Reflecting on the glaring generational gap between Iran's policy-makers and the urban middle classes, especially the youth, one Iranian social scientist concluded that political reform was not just a necessity, it was an inevitability:

In our society, social, political, and cultural structures of power are held by members of the previous generation. But the new generation has demands that the existing structures cannot fulfill. Thus the old generation has no alternative but to accept reforms. It must accept that on occasion present structures must be modified in order to survive and not be swept away.

Referring to the constitutional revision of 1989, he continued:

Even after the constitution of the Islamic Republic of Iran was drafted and became the blueprint for the actions and policies of the country's leaders, Imam Khomeini accepted its revision and reform. The revision of the constitution kept its essence unchanged but reformed many of its details. Similar reforms, which ought to be repeated again, can reduce the gap between the generations, provide solutions to many lingering difficulties, and reduce the potential of dangerous ruptures.[35]

Social scientists were not alone in their advocacy of the need to reform the system. Reinforcing the general public mood of accepting the need for political reforms were similar calls from many of the country's well-known intellectuals and activists. Thanks largely to Culture Minister Khatami, in the early 1990s a number of journals and weekly magazines devoted to in-depth discussions of contemporary social issues were licensed, chief among which were *Adineh* (Friday), *Donya-ye Sokhan* (World of Talk), *Farhang va Tose'h* (Culture and Development), *Negah-e No* (New Outlook), *Jame'h Salem* (Healthy Society), and, slightly later on, *Goftego* (Dialogue).[36] Some of the existing publications also changed their focus by devoting greater attention to some of the social, cultural, and philosophical issues that they considered to be of public relevance. Both out of political prudence and due to ideological conviction, the tone and tenor of these new publications were all "reformist." The scholarly discussions they hosted and the articles they printed were devoted to

---

[34] Ibid., p. 155.

[35] Mohammad Mansournezhad, "Shekaf va Goftego-ye Nasl-ha ba Ta'keed bar Iran" (Gap and Discourse between the Generations with Emphasis on Iran), in 'Alikhani, ed., *Negahi beh Padideh-ye Gosast-e Nasl-ha* (A Look at the Phenomenon of the Rupture of Generations), p. 209.

[36] Mashayekhi, "Degardisi Mabani-ye Siyasat va Roshanfekri-ye Siaysi" (Changes in Political Principles and Political Intellectuals), p. 10.

exploring prevailing social problems and, if appropriate, offering solutions to them within the bounds of the Islamic Republic; none advocated radical action or anything deemed intolerable to the regime's censors.[37] This subtle advocacy of reforms as opposed to revolution or radicalism sat well with the general public mood prevailing at the time.

At the same time, the appearance of these publications provided a forum for the middle classes to get to know the names and the faces, as well as the arguments, of a new generation of public intellectuals. Abdolkarim Soroush, for example, who had long been active in the cultural field in the post-revolutionary regime, started becoming a household name only in the early to the mid-1990s, largely because of the appearance of these new publications. Soroush and others like him found new life after Khatami was elected (more of which below), but their initial appearance near the end of the Rafsanjani presidency – or, more accurately in some instances, their re-appearance – was instrumental in laying the groundwork for the political victory of what was becoming the "reform movement," namely Khatami's election.

The reform movement in general and Khatami's election victory in particular were also products of evolving generational dynamics within the Islamic Republic. The broad, religiously oriented coalition that initially comprised the Islamic Republic's core at first included traditionalist clerics and their conservative allies, left-leaning, radical students, and moderate activists such as Mehdi Bazargan (1907–95), a co-founder of the Liberation Movement (*Nehzat-e Azadi*) and the post-revolutionary government's Provisional Prime Minister, and Abolhasan Banisadr (b. 1933), who was elected as the new Republic's first President in 1980 but was forced out of office the following year.

Under Khomeini's stewardship, the traditionalist clerics and their conservative allies first eliminated the moderates: Bazargan resigned in protest over the storming of the US embassy in Tehran on November 4, 1979, and Banisadr was impeached in June 1981 and went into hiding, later to surface in Paris. They were the lucky ones; scores of their like-minded collaborators, chief among them Sadeq Qotbzadeh, "Khomaini's ardent promoter during the long years of exile, his aide and confidant in Paris, his foreign minister in Tehran,"[38] were arrested and

---

[37] Interestingly, Persian equivalents for terms such as democracy (*mardomsalari*) became increasingly more popular and commonplace around this time. According to one account, for example, the term *shahrvandi*, meaning "citizenship", was first introduced into Iran's social science literature in 1995 and gained currency beginning in 1997. 'Emadeddin Baqi, *Gofteman-haye Dini-ye Mo'aser* (Contemporary Religious Discourses) (Tehran: Saraee, 1382/2003), p. 322.

[38] Bakhash, *The Reign of the Ayatollahs*, p. 223.

executed. This was done largely with the unwitting collusion of younger, more militant heirs of the revolution, many of whom had taken part in the attack on the US embassy in 1979 and the taking of US diplomats hostage. Throughout the 1980s, many of these left-leaning individuals, by then mostly in their early thirties and holding technical degrees, acquired positions in the state bureaucracy. Many, in fact, became influential directors and policymakers in the cabinet of Prime Minister Mirhosein Musavi (1981 to 1988), many of whose statist policies often ran afoul of the traditionalist clerics and more conservative members of the parliament. By the late 1980s and the early 1990s, however, the conservative-dominated Majles was able to push most of these techno-crats out. They, in turn, turned to universities, where many pursued doctorates and other postgraduate degrees, this time mostly in the social sciences. Others busied themselves in low-profile research in one or another of the think tanks and research institutes tied to the various organs of the state, the Presidency's Center for Strategic Studies chief among them. And still others became writers and journalists.[39] Steadily but surely, a new reference group was emerging in Iranian society – committed to the revolution, forged in war and post-revolutionary tur-moil, desirous of a less chaotic future.[40] As we shall see in chapter 5, these former revolutionaries formed the nucleus of the so-called "religious intellectuals."

By the mid-1990s, there was a whole crop of Ph.D.s, social scientists, and journalists hungry for an opportunity to put their ideas into action. Most in their late thirties and early forties, many had modified and moderated their tactics and their *modus operandi* if not necessarily their vision of the revolution's ideals and its future. Through the years, many had continued their professional and intellectual association with some of the regime's more scholarly figures, especially with individuals such as Culture Minister Mohammad Khatami and Attorney General Mohammad Musavi-Khoiniha. The 1997 presidential election offered precisely the kind of possible political opening these and other activists like them were looking for. As we shall see later, for many, their past activities turned out to be as much of a liability as they were an asset.[41]

---

[39] Hosein Salimi, *Kalbodshekafi-e Zehniyyat-e Eslahgarayan* (Anatomy of the Reformists' Mindset) (Tehran: Gam-e No, 1384/2005), pp. 13–14.

[40] Mas'oud Pedram, *Roshanfekran-e Dini va Moderniteh dar Iran Pas az Enqelab* (Religious Intellectuals and Modernity in Iran after the Revolution) (Tehran: Gam-e No, 1382/2003), p. 66.

[41] Some of the better-known personalities among this group of individuals include Mohammad Ali Abtahi, Saeed Hajjarian, 'Ataollah Mohajerani, and Mostafa Tajzadeh, all of whom went on to become highly influential political and/or intellectual figures within the reformist movement. For an insightful analysis of the professional careers

Relatively soon after the end of the war, a number of these emerging public intellectuals had started to question some of the dominant premises of the prevailing official Islam.[42] In some ways, the reformist discourse that became so pervasive and influential during the Khatami presidency actually had its beginnings in the latter half of the Rafsanjani era. Khatami's ten-year tenure as the Minister of "Culture and Islamic Guidance" signaled the development of differing interpretations in the official Islam of the system. Other lesser luminaries were quick to follow in advocating change and reform. The following quotation, from Hojjatoleslam Mohammad Javad Hojjati Kermani, later one of Khatami's vocal supporters, is an example: "You cannot wash blood with blood, and it is impossible to create tranquility in society through radicalism! Those who want to foster social stability and peace cannot do so through violent speech, nor can they advocate social harmony through extremist writings."[43] Even figures known for their intellectual and political affinity with the religious Right started advocating moderation in conduct and methodology on the part of all political actors. The views of Mohammad Javad Larijani, a former diplomat and a respected thinker with close ties to Khamenei, are representative of this line of thought. "We must observe four primary principles," he emphasized in a journal interview. These include tolerating criticisms directed at all levels of the state; tolerating different approaches to and understandings of religion; tolerating non-religious and non-Islamic phenomena that are designed to help the development of society; and observing the rights of non-Muslim religious minorities.[44]

Also crucial in Khatami's election win, which in turn catapulted the reform movement to political victory, was the style and personality of Khatami himself and the manner in which he conducted his election campaign. For some time, the more moderate elements within the regime had tried to draft Khatami to run for the presidency, and the public – remembering his tenure in the Culture Ministry and vaguely familiar with some of his writings[45] – greeted his eventual candidacy with considerable excitement. The sharp reactions of some of the

and ideas of these and other such personalities see, Salimi, *Kalbodshekafi-e Zehniyyat-e Eslahgarayan* (Anatomy of the Reformists' Mindset), especially pp. 11–37.

[42] Mashayekhi, "Degardisi Mabani-ye Siyasat va Roshanfekri-ye Siaysi" (Changes in Political Principles and Political Intellectuals), p. 10.

[43] Quoted in Seyyed Ebrahim Nabavi, *Goftegohaye Sarih* (Frank Talk) (Tehran: Rowzaneh, 1378/1999), p. 78.

[44] Quoted in, Ibid., pp. 172–73.

[45] Khatami had written two books prior to his election to the presidency, though it is difficult to determine the extent to which they were popular before 1997. The books are: *Beem-e Mowj* (Fear of Wave) (Tehran: Seema-ye Javan, 1372/1993); and *Az Donya-ye*

regime's known hardliners – accusing "certain candidates" of "surrounding themselves with people questioning divinity in their writings"[46] – only helped enhance Khatami's stature and popularity among the electorate.

Even more instrumental were the contents and themes of Khatami's speeches, which emphasized reforms, pluralism, the importance of civil society, and the need to respect civil rights and to engage in dialogue. Crisscrossing the country, he built his campaign on the need to foster greater openness and to reform the system, all the meanwhile careful to voice his allegiance to the core principles of the Islamic Republic system, including the institution of the *Velayat-e Faqih*. His campaign speeches, greeted enthusiastically by expanding throngs of supporters, hit on similar themes:

Diversity in political views does not cause social instability.[47]

It is only natural to have different perspectives on religion.[48]

We must have an inclusive political system that utilizes the talents of all Iranians.[49]

The country's progress requires the political participation of the people, and only then can we have a strong civil society.[50]

In the West, civil society took shape in opposition to and in place of religion. In Iran, however, it was religion and the Shi'a clergy that gave shape to our nationality and to civil society.[51]

More specifically, Khatami *explained* and elaborated on the concepts and phenomena to which he devoted his speeches – phenomena such as civil society, democracy, liberty, and the clergy's social and political responsibilities.[52] He did not simply stop at using these notions as campaign slogans. In many ways, his presidential campaign was as philosophical and discourse-oriented in nature as it was political. As one observer has noted, Khatami took issues heretofore marginal in Iranian

---

Shahr ta Shahr-e Donya (From the World of the "City" to the City of the "World") (Tehran: Ney, 1376/1997).

[46] Quoted in Ali Mohammad-Pour and Karim Jalil Nezhad Mamqani, eds., *Dovvom-e Khordad Hammaseh-eh-e Beyad Mandani* (Second of Khordad, A Memorable Legend) (Tehran, Resanesh, 1378/1999), p. 49. This invaluable source lists the major newspaper headlines and selected quotes from their articles in the run-up to the 1997 presidential elections. It provides highly useful documentary evidence of the presidential election campaign.

[47] Mohammad-Pour and Mamqani, eds., *Dovvom-e Khordad Hammaseh-e Beyad Mandani* (Second of Khordad, A Memorable Legend), p. 66.

[48] Ibid.   [49] Ibid., pp. 97–98.   [50] Ibid., p. 229.   [51] Ibid., p. 232.

[52] See, for example, his speech on the clergy's roles and responsibilities delivered to a group of clergymen and seminary students at the Yazd Howzeh, excerpts from which are quoted in Ibid., pp. 234–35.

politics and put them at the center of the public debate.[53] This was critical in bringing the highbrow discourse of the intellectuals to the urban classes, making it accessible and giving it widespread currency.

Not surprisingly, Khatami's election victory was more than just a political event. In fact, the political victory of the reform movement has been highly ephemeral, prone to frequent bouts of reversal, and, at best, unsteady and with an uncertain future. At the time of his election and for a good few years thereafter, the public viewed Khatami's election as a major turning point in the political history of the Islamic Republic.[54] Contrary to popular expectations, however, Khatami's presidency ended in 2005 with a whimper rather than a bang, with the reform movement he had helped nurture politically all but dead. Within six to eight years, an Iranian press hailing the glory of reforms began writing its obituary, clamoring to figure out "what went wrong."[55] That, of course, was the press that was not banned or whose editors were not jailed or, worse, killed.[56]

Popular perceptions notwithstanding, the real significance of Khatami's election – and the real victory of the reform movement – lay elsewhere. Khatami's election facilitated the thriving of a new, post-revolutionary discourse of reformism, one that had started emerging shortly before his election. The political victory of the reform movement, however temporary, opened the floodgates for the emergence of a new discourse, one that is nearly impossible to stop or to reverse. New journals were published; new public intellectuals became famous; new thought became prevalent. Even new politicians were elected to the Majles, and municipal and local elections more closely reflected the country's ethnic make-up and diversity.[57]

---

[53] Majid Mohammadi, *Rah-e Doshvar-e Eslahat* (Reform's Difficult Road) (Tehran: Iran-e Emrouz, 1379/2000), p. 302.

[54] Bokharaee, *Demokrasi va Doshmananash dar Iran* (Democracy and its Enemies in Iran). p. 12.

[55] For a sophisticated analysis of the causes of the "defeat" of the reform movement see, Saeed Hajjarian, *et al.*, *Eslahat dar Barabar-e Eslahat* (Reforms against Reforms) (Tehran: Tarh-e No, 1382/20030), pp. 39–57.

[56] As one author has observed, "it was as if the hard-liners in the Intelligence Ministry wanted to send a message to the dissidents that President Khatami might continue giving verbal assurances to the Muslim intellectuals, but until the Supreme Leader was in power, there could be no safe place for the outspoken secularists in Iran." Reza Afshari, *Human Rights in Iran: The Abuse of Cultural Relativism* (Philadelphia, PA: University of Pennsylvania Press, 2001), p. 211. Afshari also presents an insightful examination of what came to be known in Iran as the "serial killings" of noted cultural and literary figures in 1998 and the attempted assassination of Sa'id Hajjarian, one of the reform movement's most respected theoreticians (pp. 211–32). Also see, Bokharaee, *Demokrasi va Doshmananash dar Iran* (Democracy and its Enemies in Iran), pp. 255–66.

[57] Mostafa Tajzadeh, *Siyasat, Kakh va Zendan* (Politics, Palace, and Prison) (Tehran: Zekr, 1381/2002), p. 8.

Before long, the reform movement reached a political dead-end. Speculation abounds as to why a movement of such popular depth and magnitude came to such spectacular halt. Many in the middle classes, the very people once enamored with Khatami, now blamed him and accused him of being a duplicitous "member of the system" who allegedly claimed to reform it in order to prevent its implosion. The reform movement, according to some, was nothing but a "ploy" designed to ensure the system's longevity by making it appear more moderate.[58] Others claimed that Khatami simply lacked the courage and the conviction to see his reforms through. To redeem himself, many claimed, the least that Khatami could do was to resign.[59] Khatami himself was repentant. In an open letter to the Iranian youth, published in the form of a booklet fully a year before his presidency came to a close, he acknowledged his own sense of disappointment and the anger of those who had voted for him, promising to reveal more details about "this crucial moment in Iran's history" at a later time.[60] Some commentators did blame the conservative hardliners, who, they claimed, were buoyed by the tough rhetoric coming out of the United States following the September 11 tragedy and managed to turn the tide of events in their own favor.[61] Most of the criticism, however, especially at the popular level, was directed at Khatami himself.[62]

<hr>

[58] Mohammad Behzadi, "Eslahtalabi dar Kocheh-ye Bonbast" (Reformism in a Dead-End Alley), *Nameh*, No. 23 (1382/2003), p. 3.

[59] For a discussion of the resignation debate see Tajzadeh. *Siyasat, Kakh va Zendan* (Politics, Palace, and Prison), pp. 28–32.

[60] Mohammad Khatami, *Nameh-ee baraye Farda* (A Letter for Tomorrow) (Tehran: Mo'asseseh-e Khaneh-e Farhang-e Khatami, 1838/2004), p. 5.

[61] There is considerable truth to this assertion, especially after President George Bush branded Iran as a member of an "axis of evil" in January 2002. See, for example, Kaveh Ehsani. "High Stakes for Iran," *Middle East Report*, No. 227 (Summer 2003), pp. 38–41.

[62] Especially in tenuous democracies, meteoric rises and falls in the popularity of certain political figures are relatively common. These "heroes of the hour" emerge in conditions where democratic practices and institutions are comparatively fragile and the democratic system has not yet fully become consolidated. In the absence of established traditions of party politics and democratic governance, factors such as charisma, rhetoric, and slogans come to play an especially important role in mobilizing the voters and generating popular euphoria. When, for whatever reason, the elected hero cannot deliver on the promises given during the campaign – or cannot fulfill the promises popularly ascribed to him – his fall from popularity tends to be equally meteoric. Besides Khatami, other examples include Presidents Alberto Fujimori and Hugo Chavez in Peru and Venezuela respectively. Guillermo O'Donnell has pointed to the prevalence of this phenomenon in "delegative democracies," in which "whoever wins the election is thereby entitled to govern as he or she sees fit, constrained only by the hard facts of existing power relations and by the constitutionally limited term of office. The President is taken to be the embodiment of the nation and the main custodian and definer of its interests" (Guillermo O'Donnell, "Delegative Democracies," *Journal of Democracy*, Vol. 5, No. 2 [January 1994], pp. 59–60). Since in these types of

Apart from individual initiatives, or lack thereof, the demise of the reform movement was facilitated by a number of structural factors as well. Although reformist political figures were steadily finding their way into the executive and the legislative branches, conservative hard-liners still controlled some of the more powerful levers of the state, chief among which were the office of the *Faqih* (*Bonyad-e Rahbari*), the judiciary, many publications and the state-controlled radio and television network (IRTV), and many of the economic foundations (*Bonyads*) in charge of the commanding heights of the economy. The Special Court for the Clergy, formally set up by Ayatollah Khomeini in March 1987 to help "protect the dignity of the clergy and the seminaries," became an especially effective instrument in the Right's efforts to silence those clerics considered to be non-conformist.[63] A number of prominent clerics associated with the reformist camp were summoned before the Special Court and were sentenced to terms in prison because of their writings in reformist papers or their speeches before university audiences. Many others were informally harassed, often prevented from teaching in one of the Qom seminaries and, in some cases, confined to house arrest.[64] Also, as Leader, Ayatollah Khamenei appointed his own representative to the various organs of the state. The conservatives simply could not idly stand by and see power slip away from them; "the closed system," as one observer has commented, "must necessarily have stayed closed, or all would be lost."[65]

Amid the euphoria of Khatami's successive landslide victories and hopes of the system's impending openness, many middle-class urbanites

democracies there is a "higher likelihood of gross mistakes, of hazardous implementation, and of concentrating responsibility for the outcomes on the president," these presidents "tend to suffer wild swings in popularity: one day they are acclaimed as providential saviors, and the next they are cursed as only fallen gods can be" (p. 62). Although Iran cannot be classified as a delegative democracy, Khatami's fate does parallel those of presidents in these particular type of democratic systems.

[63] ʿEmadeddin Baqi, *Rouhaniyyat va Qodrat: Jameʿhshenasi-e Nahad-haye Dini* (The Clergy and Power: Sociology of Religious Institutions) (Tehran: Saraee, 1382/2003), p. 259. Baqi presents a useful historical account of the Special Court for the Clergy in pp. 254–61.

[64] ʿEmadeddin Baqi lists the names of twelve prominent clerics, some of them very closely associated with Ayatollah Khomeini at various points in the revolution, who by 2003 were harassed, ridiculed in the press, or somehow subject to various official restrictions because of their differences with the official orthodoxy. Some of the more prominent names include Ayatollahs Khoi, Seyyed Mohammad Shirazi, Seyyed Sadeq Rouhani, Montazeri, Mousavi Ardebili, and Sadeq Khalkhali, the former revolutionary judge who in the early years of the revolution was referred to in the Western press as the "hanging judge" due to the mass executions that followed in the immediate aftermath of the revolution. See ibid., pp. 186–91.

[65] Behzadi, "Eslahtalabi dar Kocheh-ye Bonbast" (Reformism in a Dead-End Alley), p. 4.

underestimated – or simply did not grasp – the depth of the institutional resentment to the Khatami phenomenon. What many Iranians did not realize is that their political system is not simply *political*; it is *religio-political*, deeply and profoundly dependent on the conservative wing of the Shi'a clerical hierarchy that is concentrated in Qom. As chapters 4 and 6 will demonstrate, those elements within the clerical hierarchy that are not supportive of the ultraconservatives' agendas have either been politically silenced – such as Grand Ayatollah Montazeri – or themselves have chosen to be silent. Whether elected or appointed, an overwhelming majority of the country's political figures only wield technical, administrative power in certain well-defined areas of activity, in all of which ultimate authority rests with none other than the Leader, the *Vali-ye Faqih* and his narrow inner circle. Even many of the policy making purviews of these politicians are limited and are subject to final approval by the Leader, especially in key areas such as the economy, foreign and national security policy, and the like. At the same time, in addition to his "representatives" throughout the state bureaucracy – a sort of "clerical commissars" corps[66] – Khamenei has surrounded himself with a "shadow cabinet" of sorts comprised of former high-ranking officials affiliated with the conservative camp who now serve as his "advisors," with former Commander of the Revolutionary Guards Mohsen Rezai and former Foreign Mininster Ali Akbar Velayati being prime examples.[67]

Both by design and through institutional path dependence, the current Iranian political system is fractured along multiple lines of authority, all of which lead to the same supreme arbiter, the Leader. Lacking *Marja'* status on his own and thus unable to act as a "Source of Emulation" (*Marja'-e Taqlid*), the current leader, Khamenei, considers himself especially beholden to the more traditional, conservative wing of the clerical hierarchy and acts accordingly.[68] Not surprisingly, Khamenei has tended to be far more conservative as Leader than he was as President in the 1980s. Although he has followed Khomeini's lead in not becoming directly involved in many of the factional fights for which the Iranian system became famously known in the 1990s, during the Khatami presidency he did emerge as the primary pillar of the

---

[66] Wilfried Buchta, *Who Rules Iran? The Structure of Power in the Islamic Republic* (Washington, DC: Washington Institute for Near East Policy, 2000), p. 47. This source offers unique insight into the complex maze of power in Iran.

[67] In the 2005 presidential elections, along with Rafsanjani, Rezai ran unsuccessfully against Ahmadinejand.

[68] I am thankful to a colleague in Iran for bringing this cause of Khamenei's "practical conservatism" to my attention. For an examination of some of the current theological justifications for the *Vali-ye Faqih* not being a *Marja'-e Taqlid* see below, chapter 4.

conservative Right. Not only did he not support Khatami in many of the President's reformist initiatives, he frequently cautioned against "adventurism" and often issued subtle – and at times not-so-subtle – warnings to the reformists. His cues were in turn picked up by strategically located actors throughout the whole system – from provincial Friday Prayer Imams all the way to local mosque preachers, newspaper publishers, and even sympathizers in the civil service – who turned the Leader's veiled messages to blunt and stinging attacks on Khatami and the reformists. These attacks did more than merely poison the political arena. They caused many reformist policy agendas to grind to a halt, at the very least slowed and at worst completely obstructed and reversed at the highest echelons of power.

The sociologist and author Hamidreza Jalaeepour was right on the mark when he pointed to the institutional nature of the Islamic Republic as one of the primary reasons for the failure of the Khatami presidency's reformist promises. "The principal problem that the reform movement faces is that its opposition accepts neither its methodology nor its modes of operation." "The main problem is not necessarily the rightists or the conservatives, but the hidden government – those who have a governmental budget, governmental facilities, and governmental opportunities. They have the certitude of an official government, and they continue to stand firm against the reformist movement."[69] The reformists were committed to gradualism as a methodology for reforming the system, but their opponents were unwilling to play by the reformists' rules of the game. These opponents, in fact, would not hesitate to resort to brutal force if that is what it took for them to maintain the status quo and to stay in power.[70]

To most in the middle classes, none of this seemed to matter, institutional analysis not being the layman's strong suit. What seemed blatantly obvious was that Khatami simply lacked the courage to implement many of his promised reforms and to go as far he could. Many came to view him as "just another one of them," his smile being the only difference. The blame was entirely his and his coteries'.

This is not to say that there was no introspective analysis on the part of Iranian thinkers and intellectuals, many of whom were members of the reformist camp themselves. In fact, beginning in 2001–02, coinciding roughly with the start of Khatami's second term, much of the pages of reformist publications such as *Aftab*, *Nameh*, and *Jame'h Salem* were

---

[69] Deihimi and Jalaeepour, "Jame'hshenasi-ye Siyasi-e Eslahat" (Political Sociology of Reforms), p. 7.
[70] Ibid., p. 8.

devoted to exploring the shortcomings of the reformist movement itself. Significantly, this process of self-examination and soul-searching introduced new dimensions into the reformist discourse and gave it directions it would not have had otherwise. More specifically, the political failure of the religious reform movement cost its accompanying religious reformist discourse a good deal of luster and popular appeal. In the process, a competing, secular discourse with modernity as its focal point started gaining momentum.

Before exploring the contours of the emerging discourses – broadly in the next section and in more depth in the following chapters – it is helpful to highlight some of the main features of the self-critical explanations given by Iranian thinkers about the failure of the reformist movement. These critical self-examinations tend to fall into four broad categories. First, the reformist movement, it is often argued, is – or, for those writing its obituary, was – fundamentally elitist and lacking in social basis. Second, it suffered from theoretical and philosophical poverty. Third, it lacked effective organizational structure and leadership. And, fourth, from the beginning the movement found it advantageous to advocate only minor, mostly cosmetic reforms.

One of the biggest criticisms that is often levied against the reformist movement by thinkers and commentators who are themselves generally supportive of its goals is the movement's chronic weaknesses in terms of organization, tactics and strategies, and leadership. The "movement" was made up of a coalition of three or four groupings that share broad characteristics and goals but have their own corporate identities and specific agendas (more on this below). It was never fully clear exactly who or which group represented the movement.[71] Moreover, the coalition comprising the movement was organizationally and structurally weak from the beginning, never fully developing the internal cohesion that would have enhanced its political efficacy within the system and its organizational appeal among the public. Given the recency of the reformist phenomenon, the various reformist groups never fully developed organic links to one another, nor, more importantly, a mutual sense of trust that would have facilitated cooperation and sharing of goals and resources.[72] Even Khatami's charisma, which began to wane anyway after the start of his second presidency, was not enough to compensate for this internal organizational exigency.[73]

---

[71] 'Alireza 'Alavi-Tabar and Morad Saqafi, "Eslahat va Shiveh-haye Eslahtalabaneh" (Reforms and Reformists' Methods), *Aftab*, No. 17 (1381/2002), p. 9.

[72] Ibid., p. 8.

[73] Deihimi and Jalaeepour, "Jame'hshenasi-ye Siyasi-e Eslahat" (Political Sociology of Reforms), p. 5.

According to Mostafa Tajzadeh, one of the key political strategists of the reform movement, the reformists could pursue one of four strategies.[74] They could embark on "quiet activism," which meant engaging their opponents and impressing upon them the need for and the benefits of reforming the system. Alternatively, they could engage in "active obstructionism," grinding the system to a halt through obstruction and lack of cooperation until their opponents took note and accommodated their demands. A third option would have been to resign *en masse* once confronted with the intransigence of the conservatives, vacating the executive and legislative branches as well as the municipal and village councils to which they had been elected. Finally, they could engage in "civic disobedience," which would have required mass mobilization and, ultimately, confrontation. For a variety of reasons, the reformists chose the first option, and, Tajzadeh admitted, were not quite successful at it. According to Tajzadeh, the 1997 election victory took the reformists themselves by surprise, most not having had adequate time to study and devise well-thought-out strategies. Finding themselves in an unexpected position of relative power, most failed to develop meaningful organizational support structures and devised strategies that were, at best, rushed and hurried.[75]

Strategic and tactical weaknesses were equally harmful to the furtherance of the reformists' political goals. According to Khashayar Deihimi, the reformists showed no flexibility in their tactics and their strategies, keeping their methods and their objectives constant in the face of changing, often fluid and quite volatile, circumstances.[76] They kept on advocating the same things – which basically boiled down to a call for observing the rule of law – and did so at the same pace, at a time when the conservatives both defined and controlled the law and kept expanding their hold over other levers of power. This forced the reformists into a constantly reactive as opposed to a proactive posture. This was particularly the case in terms of the presidency's relationship with an overly active Fifth Majles, which remained dominated by the conservatives, where few of the President's agendas were introduced as bills. Instead, the conservatives kept introducing a variety of legislative initiatives aimed at furthering their own interests and agendas.[77] Not

---

[74] Mostafa Tajzadeh, "Chahar Rahbord-e Jonbesh-e Eslahat" (The Four Methodologies of the Reform Movement), *Aftab*, No. 11 (1380/2001), p. 14.
[75] Ibid., pp. 19–20.
[76] Deihimi and Jalaeepour, "Jame'hshenasi-ye Siyasi-e Eslahat" (Political Sociology of Reforms), p. 10.
[77] Baqi, *Hoquq-e Mokhalefan* (The Rights of Opponents), p. 328.

surprisingly, this did not help the reformists' cause before the restless middle classes.

Perhaps even more detrimental was the reformists' failure to broaden their coalition and to include within them groups who generally shared their vision but who had hitherto been excluded from the political process. This somewhat deliberate insularity tended to reinforce negative perceptions of the reformists among the public and to typecast them as power-hungry and self-interested.[78] More fundamentally, it bespoke of an innate elitism that has characterized the whole reformist project. Many Iranian analysts see this absence of social depth, and a lack of meaningful, substantive networks that could generate and articulate support among the urban middle classes, as one of the reformists' most fundamental flaws.[79] There has been a marked absence from the reform movement of contributions by syndical groups and other social organizations that are politically autonomous, self-organized, and wield social or political influence. This has limited the reform movement in scope to more of a project that is spearheaded by some intellectuals, civil servants, and perhaps even a few policymakers, none of whom, ultimately, has much power and influence.[80]

The basic emphasis of the reformist politicians has been to bring about reforms "from above," at the level of the state. Made up mostly of social scientists who are impressed by the epistemology of Descartes, the critical rationalism of Kant, and the political philosophy of Hobbes, the reformists saw the state as the primary agent for and the arena within which reforms ought to take place.[81] This led them to neglect social dynamics and groups and to instead concentrate all their efforts and energies on the state.[82] More specifically, the reformists failed to grasp the importance of "social capital" as "a prerequisite for democracy" and sought instead to deepen whatever political capital they could muster.[83] Political bargaining, therefore, took the place of establishing and

[78] 'Alavi-Tabar and Morad Saqafi, "Eslahat va Shiveh-haye Eslahtalabaneh" (Reforms and Reformists' Methods), p. 6.

[79] See, for example, 'Ali Hajiqasemi, "Bohran-e Jonbesh-e Eslahtalabi" (The Crisis of the Reform Movement), *Aftab*, No. 28 (1382/2003), pp. 14–19.

[80] Ibid., p. 15.

[81] Habibollah Peyman, "Tangna-haye Nazari va Rahbordi-e Jonbesh-e Eslah-talabi" (Methodological and Ideological Shortcomings of the Reform Movement), *Aftab*, No. 34 (1383/2004), p. 9.

[82] Ibid., p. 10.

[83] 'Abdolmohammad Kazemipour, "Rah-e Tey Shodeh, Rah-e Pishro: Tarh-i baraye Tajdid-e Sazman-e Ejtema'i-e Eslahat" (The Path Traversed, the Path Ahead: A Plan for Renewing the Social Organization of Reforms), *Aftab*, No. 23 (1381/2002), p. 5.

nurturing solid, organic ties to the urban middle classes.[84] In the process, reformist politicians and activists made themselves increasingly less relevant to people's daily lives as a competing, "third front" emerged. Made up of ordinary middle classes, this third front simply wanted to improve its daily life and to reform the social and cultural aspects of the prevailing system.[85]

Another related problem with the reformist movement was its shallow theoretical and philosophical basis. From the beginning, the reformists pursued strategies based on the assumption that the people could not be trusted and that the reformists themselves knew best what to do on behalf of the masses at large.[86] To the average person, this assumption was not only identical to that of the conservatives, it was not necessarily appealing. In fact, most found it downright insulting.[87]

A related but more fundamental criticism was that the reformists never quite clarified what their goals and their theoretical objectives were. Perhaps they did so deliberately, not wanting to publicly expose – or to have to resolve – some basic contradictions in their thinking. For example, as one commentator pointed out, how could the reformists advocate the democratization of the system from within while the constitution remains fundamentally undemocratic?[88] Even more elementally, they never offered a sound theoretical analysis of the history, characteristics, and needs of Iranian society, nor did they clarify the meaning of many of the terms and concepts they used repeatedly in their speeches and their writings – terms such as civil society, "citizen and citizenship," and "organic cohesion."[89] Although most portrayed themselves as – or were popularly portrayed as – thinking politicians, few indeed bothered to reflect on the deeper meaning of their endeavor or

---

[84] Ali Yusofian, "Farhang-e Siyasi-e Iranian va Entekhabat-e Dorehye Haftom" (The Iranians' Political Culture and the Seventh Elections), *Aftab*, No. 33 (1382/2004), p. 25.

[85] Ibid.

[86] S. Bana, "Tarh-i Baraye Taharrok-e Eslahat ya Tarh-i az Tafakkor-e Eslahtalaban" (A Plan for Moving Reforms or a Plan Based on the Reformist's Thoughts), *Aftab*, No. 23 (1381/2002), p. 118.

[87] Literally all of the authors cited here criticize this aspect of the reformists' strategy and thinking.

[88] Mehdi Rajabi, "Post-reformism va Jonbesh-e Mardomsalari-Khahi" (Post-reformism and the Democratization Movement), *Aftab*, No. 34 (1383/2004), p. 20.

[89] Parviz Piran, "Za'f-e Nazari; Pashneh-ye Ashil-e Jonbesh-e Eslahtalabi" (Theoretical Weakness; The Achilles' Heel of the Reform Movement), *Aftab*, No. 33 (1382/2003), p. 53. Along similar lines, Mas'oud Pedram argues that the reformists presented at best superficial conceptions of such basic terms as equality, justice, pluralism, and consensus. See Mas'oud Pedram, "Daramadi bar Mabani-ye Nazari-ye Jonbesh-e Dovvom-e Khordad" (A Look at the Theoretical Principles of the Second of Khordad Movement), *Aftab*, No. 14 (1381/2002), pp. 6–7.

the underlying premises of what they advocated.[90] They were mostly politicians and not thinkers. As it turned out, they were not very good politicians either.

This preoccupation with politics was perhaps inevitable given that the reformists advocating moderation and reforms were themselves, as discussed earlier, the radicals of yesteryears, "those," as many Iranians derogatorily call them, "who used to climb up embassy walls."[91] In fact, some of the most vocal proponents of the system's reform beginning in the 1990s were the very figures who stormed the US embassy in Tehran on November 4, 1979 and took many of its diplomats hostage for 444 days. In some ways, this should not be surprising: the young, "radical leftists" of the 1970s, middle aged by the 1990s, had mostly become "reformist moderates."[92] Their allegiance to the revolutionary system is intact; only their methods and strategies have changed.

For these latter-day reformists, the system's reform did not mean refutation of or the dismantling of the *Velayat-e Faqih*, which to this day remains as the system's most undemocratic hallmark, and, for most in the middle classes, its most unpopular feature.[93] With their genealogy suspect, their political credibility as genuine reformists was open to doubt, as were their real intentions.[94] More specifically, a number of observers openly wondered whether Khatamiite reformists, who were themselves the beneficiaries of the system's marginal openness, did not want things too radically altered for fear of losing what they had gained.[95] Even if Khatami had loudly protested that he did not want to become Iran's Gorbachev and thus deliberately followed a slow pace of reforms, he would have found few takers. The public, by and large, blamed him and his accomplices for losing a golden opportunity to change things. Echoing widespread sentiments among reform-minded

[90] Peyman, "Tangna-haye Nazari va Rahbordi-e Jonbesh-e Eslah-talabi" (Methodological and Ideological Shortcomings of the Reform Movement), p. 13.

[91] Some of the most notable individuals from among the "Students Following the Imam's Path" – the name the hostage takers gave themselves – who later emerged as principal figures within the reform movement include the activists Abbas 'Abdi and 'Emadeddin Baqi, along with Ma'soumeh Ebtekar, Khatami's Vice President for Environmental Affairs and the only female member of a post-revolutionary cabinet so far.

[92] Salimi, *Kalbodshekafi-e Zehniyyat-e Eslahgarayan* (Anatomy of the Reformists' Mindset), p. 11.

[93] Mas'oud Pedram, "Tahavvol-e Soratbandi-ye Oposision dar Iran" (Changes in the Composition of Opposition in Iran), *Nameh*, No. 22 (1382/2003), p. 37.

[94] See, for example, Abbas 'Abdi, "Tabar-shenasiye Eslahtalaban, Naqsh-ha va Karkardha" (Genealogy of Reformists, Roles, and Functions), *Nameh*, No. 16 (1381/ 2002), pp. 3–11; and Mohammad Javad Gholamreza Kashi. "Tabar-shenasi; Bi 'Etebari-ye Bonyadha-ye Rangbakhteh" (Genealogy; The Illegitimacy of Colorless Foundations), *Nameh*, No. 16 (1381/2002), pp. 12–17.

[95] Behzadi, "Eslahtalabi dar Kocheh-ye Bonbast" (Reformism in a Dead-End Alley), p. 4.

middle classes, the journalist and author 'Emadeddin Baqi, himself one of the most prominent figures in the reform movement, wrote at the time: "This is a weak and timid government. It is a government that is fundamentally incapable of moving in a pace consistent with the potential of society. It is an incoherent and incongruent government."[96]

Amid a flood of recrimination and dark clouds of suspicion, the reform movement began a steady ascent into the abyss beginning sometime in late 2001. Within a year or two, its political death was all but final. A system once seen as being on the threshold of take-off and meaningful democratization was now seen as morbidly ill, in dire need of rescue and resuscitation by some of its original architects. Ironically, it was none other than the old, wily Rafsanjani to whom the establishment turned. In May 2005, Rafsanjani claimed that "the most difficult decision of my political career" led him to enter the presidential race scheduled for the following month in order to serve the best interests of the nation. In a communiqué announcing his candidacy, Rafsanjani claimed he hoped his presidency would reverse "the spread of frictions and difficulties" in the country, stamp out "the growth of radical tendencies," heal "the atmosphere of indifference and the decline of values," and, "most importantly," put a stop to "the questioning of the efficacy of the system of the Islamic Republic."[97] The Reconstruction Commander of the 1980s was now seen by many middle-and upper-class Iranians as the political savior of a new era in the Islamic Republic's life. But even Rafsanjani, ever the master survivor, who was now billing himself as the last remaining hope of what remained of the reform movement, could not generate enough public support to make a comeback. Public apathy and middle-class mistrust kept many reform-minded voters away from the polls, and Rafsanjani found himself in an unprecedented run-off with Tehran's largely unknown mayor, Mahmoud Ahmadinejad, who was generally considered to be a radical hard-liner. In a stunning turn of events, Rafsanjani only garnered 36 percent of the popular vote as compared to Ahmadinejad's 63 percent.[98]

---

[96] Baqi, *Hoquq-e Mokhalefan* (The Rights of Opponents), p. 329.

[97] www.hashemirafsanjani.ir/manifest/manifest.shtml, accessed on June 10, 2005.

[98] Official statistics put the total number of Iranians who participated in the first round elections at about 63 percent of the total (of approximately 47 million eligible voters) and only about 48 percent in the second round. The election itself offered a textbook example of the tactical and strategic failures of reformists, who at first talked about boycotting the elections – and many did – and then could not decide between three competing candidates, none of whom was particularly appealing to the electorate. In a crowded field of six candidates, only Rafsanjani and Ahmadinejad were able to slip into the second round, during which Ahmadinejad's campaign proved far more adept at mobilizing and exciting his base, made up overwhelmingly of ultraconservative

If anyone ever thought there was any political life left to the reform movement, the June 2005 presidential elections definitively proved otherwise.

Significantly, however, the political death of the reform movement did not mean its intellectual death as well. Journals and newspapers could be banned; outspoken editors and journalists could be jailed; reformist politicians could be sidelined. But the doors to the new thought that had long been percolating and was now finding ways to express itself could not be closed. Two new discourses, one of religious reformism and another of secular-modernism, had by now emerged and had acquired lives and momentum of their own. There was – and there remains – precious little that the political system, and even the most hardline conservatives within it, can do to stop them.

Three discourses

By the start of the new millennium, the new discourse of religious modernism was well on its way to becoming firmly established within the Iranian intellectual tradition. Its basic tenets were simple and straightforward. In broad terms, it accepted the premises and promises of the Islamic revolution, particularly insofar as the vital role of religion in politics is concerned. More specifically, it endorsed and expanded on the relationship between the two central pillars of the Islamic Republic, namely Islam and republicanism. But whereas Ali Shariati and other "third generation" intellectuals sought to *revolutionize* political Islam, the articulators of the new discourse set out to *modernize* it. In keeping with the tenor and mood of the times, they also sought to moderate what by now had become an ideology of extremism. This was a discourse of Shi'a reformism, much more temperate in tone and more rigorous in theoretical construction and philosophical underpinning than its predecessors.

Before long, the new discourse, pregnant with political subtext and theologically significant beyond initial glance, was accompanied by yet another discourse, this one also "reformist" but virulently secular. The first few years of the Khatami presidency were a time of tremendous intellectual excitement, with a slew of new journals hitting the newsstands, featuring articles from a seemingly new breed of thinkers, and

supporters from the lower socioeconomic rungs of Iranian society. Rafsanjani's own overconfidence and the limiting of his campaign efforts to mobilizing well-to-do Tehranis who wore fashionable campaign outfits and passed out campaign bumper stickers written in English – while at the same time ignoring less affluent Iranians who felt slighted by the man reported to be the country's wealthiest individual – was also a major factor in his defeat.

tackling subjects few had dared to discuss before.[99] By far the most
influential journal in this category was *Kiyan* (Universe), followed later
by *Nameh* (Letter), *Andisheh-ye Jame'h* (Thought of Society), and *Aftab*
(Sunshine). By and large, the articles these and other similar journals
published fell within the religious reformist discourse. In between articles exploring the nexus between Islam and modernity, there slowly
appeared pieces that dropped all references to Islam and simply explored
the tenets of modernity. Many of these articles, in fact, were based on
premises that had little or nothing to do with Islam, or, alternatively, saw
little room for it in the project of modernity. Some even went so far as to
suggest that religion ought to be isolated to the private sphere since its
public manifestation, they claimed, is inimical to modernity.

Essentially, what was happening was the birth of a discourse within a
discourse, with a discourse of secular-modernism growing out of, and
because of, the discourse of religious reformism. It is perhaps more than
coincidental that the rise of the religious reformist discourse corres-
ponded roughly with the ascent of reformist politicians, and the rise of
the secular-modernist discourse paralleled their decline. The more
influential the reformist politicians became, the more pervasive the
religious reformist discourse became. By the same token, as their
influence and political clout began to diminish, there was an inverse rise
in the secular-modernist discourse.

Why did this occur? The answer seems to lie in the steady expansion
and opening of political space in Iran. A slight opening in the latter
1990s allowed Khatamiites into the political system and, more importantly, created intellectual opportunities for the articulation and later
criticism of religious reformist activism and thought. Despite the prot-
estations of the conservative Right, and despite its continued hold on
real power and its frequent – and often brutal – persecution of reformist
activists and writer-journalists, the depth and breadth of philosophical
and intellectual thought in Iran continued to grow. In fact, irrespective

---

[99] Despite the subsequent closure of nearly fifty publications, altogether the number of the
newspapers and magazines published in Iran jumped tenfold during Khatami's first
term in office. One author researching the contents of the Iranian press before and after
Khatami's election discovered that in 1999 there were approximately ten times more
articles exploring "sensitive and critical issues" as compared to 1994, with a shift
occurring to the frequency of these articles from magazines to newspapers, thus making
them more broadly accessible. Also, from 1997 to 2001, the number of articles that
engaged in critical analyses of intellectual issues and political theories multiplied by
eight times. 'Ali Bahrampour, "Tahavvol-e Mohtavai-ye Matbo'at Pas az Dovvom-e
Khordad" (Changes of the Contents of the Press after the Second of Khordad). *Aftab*,
No. 10 (1380/2001), pp. 48–53. For more on the role and the trials of the Iranian press
before and after Khatami's election see, 'Emaddedin Baqi, *Bahar-e Rokn-e Chaharom*
(Spring of the Fourth Column) (Tehran: Saraee, 1381/2002).

of the risks involved, by the late 1990s and the early years of the new century, the intellectual scene in Iran had become fascinatingly exciting, uncontrollably vibrant, and, perhaps most importantly, was becoming increasingly diversified and complex.

Within this context, the very fact that the Islamic Republic state had to resort to repression in order to suppress intellectual thought meant that it had lost much if not all of its ideological legitimacy among both the articulate as well as the popular classes. In essence, what the state had done was to start an intellectual wildfire by opening the doors of electoral politics ever so slightly in 1997. Ever since then, its orthodox and conservative elements have tried to reverse "the damage" by whatever means possible – arrests, bans, assassinations, etc. – but they have not had any precipitous, lasting success. And, at every successive election ever since then, they have shot themselves in the foot, either through mass disqualifications of popular candidates or by creating conditions that have resulted in lower and lower voter turn out. To reverse all this, and to salvage whatever legitimacy remained for the system, in 2005, candidate Rafsanjani built his presidential platform around the themes of political participation, the legalization of parties, and the empowerment of the youth – themes very close to those of Khatami in 1997. Ironically, during Rafsanjani's first stint in the presidency in the 1980s, the political arena remained closed and highly restrictive. It is doubtful that the veteran politician had undergone a democratic conversion in the intervening decade or so. More likely, the state he sought to head had become weaker in the interim and could not help but to give more concessions to society in return for its support or, at the very least, its political quiescence.

It is important to note that the two discourses of religious reformism and secular-modernism were – and still are – articulated not only in response to and within the context of the prevailing body politic but also in reaction to the accompanying official discourse that today underlies and represents the Islamic Republic. This was particularly the case with the discourse of religious reformism, many of whose articulators were directly or indirectly part of the political status quo – Khatami being a prime example. Structurally, the political ascent of Khatami and lesser luminaries in 1997 did indeed represent the Islamic Republican system's loss of ideological and institutional cohesion. There was, nevertheless, a powerful current of thought, with an even greater degree of political power at its disposal, which sought to maintain and conserve what it viewed as the purity of the revolutionary system. Just as Khomeini's death allowed his past legacy and future hopes to be viewed in more liberal and progressive terms, it also allowed them to be interpreted in more radical, fundamentalist ways. The ensuing conservative religious discourse became the mainstay of the official orthodoxy, its theoretical frame of reference, and its ideological blueprint.

Before delving into the details of each of the three discourses in subsequent chapters, I want to elaborate more fully on the architects of discourse in general in the country, namely Iranian intellectuals. More specifically, I believe it is important to examine the current pre-occupations of the country's crop of intellectuals and opinion-makers – especially in regards to their notions of the self and of Iran's larger place and predicament in the world – in order to better understand each of the discourses and the larger context within which they are being articulated, expressed, and received. It is to the exploration of these topics that the next chapter turns.

3   Theorizing about the world

Since the beginning of their appearance as a social class, Iranian intellectuals have been concerned with defining, internalizing, and, for some, indigenizing notions of modernity. Over time, the role and social composition of Iranian intellectuals have changed, as have their conceptions of and attitudes toward modernity. Thus it is important to first examine how the current generation of Iranian intellectuals looks at its predecessors and defines itself in relation – or in opposition – to each of the previous generations, all the while continuing the intellectual preoccupation with modernity. This lays the groundwork for a more detailed analysis in the following chapters of the dominant discourse to which these intellectuals have given rise. For now, it is important to explore the question of how contemporary Iranian intellectuals see and define themselves.

A brief note of clarification on the thrust of the chapter's focus may be useful. My concern in this chapter is to explore the question of how Iranian intellectuals and thinkers see themselves, and how they frame their contributions accordingly. As much as possible, I have deliberately avoided looking at them from the outside and analyzing them through the prism of (Western) social science theory, in relation to, for example, Western notions of and theories about modernity, Enlightenment, civil society, and the like. In other words, my focus here is on the perceptions of "the self" prevalent *within* Iran's intellectual circles.

As such, I am not setting out to present an analysis of the intellectuals' roles and functions within the Iranian polity and history per se. A number of scholars have already provided very sound sociological and political analyses of Iran's intellectual encounter with modernity.[1] Given the prevalence and speed of translations of Western-language

---

[1] One of the best representatives of this genre of literature is Vahdat's insightful *God and Juggernaut*. See also Mirsepassi, *Intellectual Discourse*; Ali Gheissari, *Iranian Intellectuals in the Twentieth Century* (Austin, TX: University of Texas Press, 1998); and Boroujerdi. *Iranian Intellectuals and the West.*

publications in Iran, and the fact that many of the scholars writing in French or English on the subject of modernity in Iran are first generation Iranian immigrants themselves, the dichotomy between "Western" and "Iranian" scholarship on modernity does not always apply.[2] Nevertheless, there is a subtle but unmistakable distinction between being a part of the discourse on modernity itself versus standing out of it and critically analyzing it. Often times, the outside critical analysis itself becomes part of the discourse. In the few cases when that has happened, I have again focused on the discourse itself rather than examine it against the parameters set by social science theory.

The Fourth Generation

In grappling with the larger dilemmas posed by the phenomenon of modernity, contemporary Iranian thinkers and intellectuals have posed and sought to answer a number of key questions. The first question involves discovering the very nature of the problem, or, more specifically, recognizing that modernity – understood not only in an economic and industrial sense, but, more fundamentally, also as a cultural and civilizational condition – is indeed one of the central challenges facing Iran. More specifically, they are interested in understanding the causes for the delayed introduction of modernity into Iranian culture and society. Simply stated, they want to know "why are we in our current predicament and how did we get here?"

A second question is more basic and fundamental. It has to do with the very nature and essence of modernity. "What does it indeed mean," they ask, "to be modern?" On the surface, this is a simple question with a seemingly straightforward and uncomplicated answer. In reality, however, particularly in the context of contemporary Iran, it is far more vexing than it appears. Implicit in it is a more subtle, and more charged, question: "Given what we are culturally and where we are historically, how do we become modern?" Or, more accurately, "what are the most feasible and appropriate ways that we can become modern without losing all that has gone into making us what we are?"

A profitable starting point for finding answers to these questions is to look to Iran's past intellectual history itself. Significantly, much scholarly attention has been directed of late at reaching a critical understanding of

---

[2] Complicating matters further is the publication in English or French of works by intellectuals and thinkers living in Iran. Although this is not a widespread phenomenon, it does occur on occasion. See, for example, Ramin Jahanbegloo, ed., *Iran: Between Tradition and Modernity* (Lanham, MD: Lexington, 2004).

the history of intellectual endeavors and dispositions in the country. Many authors, in fact, chief among them Ramin Jahanbegloo, subscribe to the thesis that there have historically been four generations of Iranian intellectuals so far, and that the current, Fourth Generation has a unique and fundamental preoccupation with modernity.[3]

Briefly, the thesis argues that since their emergence as a distinctively identifiable social group in the mid- to the late 1800s, Iranian intellectuals (*roshanfekran*) can be clustered into four general groups, each corresponding to one of the recent eras in Iranian history. The first and second generations, as well as the Fourth Generation, have all been "modernists," although for each generation the perception and meaning of "modernity" has been quite different. The primary concern of the third generation, meanwhile, was revolution, or, more pointedly, the radical transformation of social and political arrangements of society.

The first generation of intellectuals emerged immediately prior to the Constitutional Revolution and was instrumental in articulating its goals and objectives. The second generation followed the establishment of the Pahlavi dynasty in the mid-1920s and lasted up until the late 1960s and the 1970s. Conceptualizing of modernity in largely economic and industrial terms, these second generation intellectuals became the unwitting – and at times very deliberate – accomplices of the authoritarian political establishment in power at the time. The third generation emerged in the charged decades of the 1960s and the 1970s and enunciated what became many of the Islamic revolution's slogans and aspirations. This "revolutionary generation" of intellectuals was represented most compellingly by Jalal Al-e Ahmad (1923–69) and Ali Shariati (1933–77), who became the spiritual – if not actual – ideologues of the 1978–79 revolution. Finally, today, we see the rise of a Fourth Generation of Iranian intellectuals, whose birth dates back to about a decade after the success of the revolution, at a time when changing political dynamics began making intellectual activism once again possible.

---

[3] See, for example, Ramin Jahanbegloo, *Mowj-e Chaharom* (The Fourth Wave), trans. Mansour Goodarzi (Tehran: Ney, 1381/2002); and Ali Asghar Haqdar, *Faraso-ye Postmoderniteh* (Beyond Post-Modernity) (Tehran: Shafi'ee, 1380/2001), pp. 51–54. In her perceptive and in-depth study, Jamileh Kadivar divides the evolution of Shi'a political discourse up until the 1978–79 revolution into seven categories, each corresponding to a specific era within the life of Shi'ism: from the start of the period of Occultation until the beginning of the Safavid era; the Safavid era; from the end of the Safavid period until the establishment of the Qajars; from the start of the Qajar era until the Constitutional Revolution; the constitutional era; the Pahlavi era up until the efforts to overthrow it; and the period lasting from the preparatory groundwork to the success of the revolution. Jamileh Kadivar, *Tahavvol-e Gofteman-e Siyasi-e Shi'a dar Iran* (The Development of Shi'a Political Discourse in Iran) (Tehran: Tarh-e No, 1379/2000), p. 15.

First generation Iranian intellectuals date back to the nineteenth century, at a time when Qajar monarchs sought to consolidate their powers and to initiate some limited administrative reforms. Not surprisingly, as the era when Iran's entanglement with modernity first began, the Qajar period has received considerable attention in recent Iranian scholarship.[4] As the gifted political scientist Sadeq Zibakalam (b. 1948) notes, the Qajar era was one of profound and lasting changes to the Iranians' approach to and understanding of modernity.[5] This was a product of subjective factors such as the introduction of European political ideals and ideologies as well as objective factors arising out of Iran's demographic changes and the expansion of its commercial relations with the outside world.[6] The cumulative results of these changes may not have led to the ultimate establishment of a viable democratic polity. But they did forever alter long-held popular notions about the place and position of the King, the need for limits on political power within the framework of law, the people's right to self-determination, and the right to free opinion and free speech.[7]

It was within this context that the first generation of Iranian intellectuals emerged. The need for reforms had been impressed upon the political and educated elites of the Qajar period through two successive and utterly devastating military defeats to Russia, first in 1812 and again in 1828. These defeats were seen not just in military terms but as evidence of the superiority of modern science and rationality over traditional approaches to warfare, politics, and life in general.[8] These "painful encounters" with the West led a small minority of "enlightened thinkers" (*monnavarolfekran*) to search for the root causes of their nation's collective malaise. At the same time, they looked for cures for the morass, and, perhaps not surprisingly, found these also within the West.[9] The humiliating terms under which Iran was made to surrender territory to Russia, coupled with what a small number of courtiers and other notables had seen and experienced in Russia and in the Ottoman

---

[4] Examples include Mashallah Ajodani, *Mashroteh-ye Irani* (Iranian Constitutionalism) (Tehran Akhtaran, 1382/2003); Sadeq Zibakalam, *Sonnat va Modernism* (Tradition and Modernity) (Tehran: Rouzaneh, 1377/1998); Kadivar, *Tahavvol-e Gofteman-e Siyasi-e Shi'a dar Iran* (The Development of Shi'a Political Discourse in Iran), pp. 185–337; and 'Abbas Milani, *Tajaddod va Tajaddod-Setizi dar Iran* (Modernity and Modernity-Fighting in Iran) (Tehran: Akhtaran, 1382/2003), pp. 127–45, 317–29.

[5] Zibakalam, *Sonnat va Modernism* (Tradition and Modernity), p. 8.

[6] Ibid., p. 14.   [7] Ibid., p. 16.

[8] Jahanbegloo, *Mowj-e Chaharom* (The Fourth Wave), p. 144.

[9] Jamshid Behnam, *Iranian va Andisheh-ye Tajaddod* (Iranians and the Idea of Modernity) (Tehran: Farzan Rouz, 1375/1996), p. 5.

territories, prompted them to look critically at the circumstances inside Iran and to seek for alternatives.[10]

By the mid-1800s, an increasing number of influential men of letters were advocating the establishment of a meaningful legal framework throughout the country, some going so far as to call for the wholesale revision of the Farsi alphabet, as was the case with Mirza Fathali Akhondzadeh. Some went even further, calling for the modernization and reformation of Islam, as Mirza Malkom Khan and Seyyed Jamaladdin Assadabadi did.[11] At the same time, many equated modernity with industrialization, advocating, as Malkom did, extensive foreign investment in the country's economy.[12] Not surprisingly, and particularly given the fact that the opposition to these intellectuals – and the trends they advocated and represented – came from both the royal court as well as many of the traditional, and very influential, ulama, in the final decades of the Qajar period the two notions of "liberty" and "modernity" were seen as synonymous.[13]

It is not lost on any of the contemporary Iranian thinkers that their intellectual genealogy dates back to Iran's first encounters with the "modern" West, encounters that were, nonetheless, often unceremonious and all too frequently humiliating. As the sociologist Jamshid Behnam (b. 1928) argues, the cultural significance of Iran's encounter with the West ranks only second to the country's encounter with Islam.[14] In fact, Behnam argues, the very phenomenon of contemporary Iranian intellectualdom as we know it today owes its genesis to Iran's encounter with the West.[15] Reza Shah greatly expanded the number of students who were sent to study in various European universities, a privilege previously limited mostly to Qajar princes. As these students started returning home, and as their ranks were joined by the graduates of Tehran University, they started forming an "educated elite" whose prime social objective was to replicate in Iran some of the main features

[10] Jamshid Behnam, *Iranian va Andisheh-ye Tajaddod* (Iranians and the Idea of Modernity) (Tehran: Farzan Rouz, 1375/1996), pp. 19–20.

[11] Ajodani, *Mashroteh-ye Irani* (Iranian Constitutionalism), pp. 219–20.

[12] Kamran Dadkhah, "Andisheh-ye Eqtesadi va Roshanfekran-e Irani" (Economic Theories and Iranian Intellectuals), *Aftab*, No. 16 (1381/2002), pp. 22–27. As Dadkhah demonstrates, the intellectual currents that were dominant beginning in the 1890s up to the 1960s all featured a strong attention to economic thought.

[13] Ajodani, *Mashroteh-ye Irani* (Iranian Constitutionalism), p. 250.

[14] Behnam, *Iranian va Andisheh-ye Tajaddod* (Iranians and the Idea of Modernity), p. 14.

[15] Jamshid Behnam and Ramin Jahanbegloo, *Tamaddon va Tajaddod* (Civilization and Modernity) (Tehran: Markaz, 1382/2003), p. 23. This collaborative work by the two authors is in the form of a "conversation" between Behnam and Jahanbegloo. Since their arguments and assertions at times differ from each other, in the text of the chapter I will specify which one of the authors is being quoted.

and premises of Western civilization. Numbering in the thousands and occupying key positions in the state bureaucracy, in schools and universities, and in various artistic and cultural institutions, some of these elites began perceiving of themselves, and being popularly perceived as, "intellectuals." More importantly, they began identifying themselves with the same social strata in the West.[16] At least ideationally and subjectively, the earliest generations of Iranian intellectuals saw themselves as organically linked with Western intellectuals.

This is echoed, among others, by Taghi Azadarmaki (b. 1957), a US-trained professor of sociology at the University of Tehran. From the beginning of their emergence as a social class, Azadarmaki maintains, the most central question preoccupying Iranian intellectuals has revolved around "the existence and identity of the West and Iran's relationship with it."[17]

To the extent that the country's scholars have analyzed and elaborated on this existence and identity, they have defined "Iranian intellectualism" in relation to "global intellectualism." Based on conceptions of the self, the other (West), and the relationship between the two, the Iranian intellectual has produced a particular social construct in which he, and he alone, can live.[18]

It is within this overwhelming presence of the West – or, more accurately, in its ever-present shadow – that the four generations of Iranian intellectuals have emerged. Whereas the first generation sought to reform and in some respects fundamentally alter the social and political milieus within which they found themselves, most second generation intellectuals found themselves in tacit agreement and even cooperation with Reza Shah's tireless efforts aimed at reconstructing Iran's social and cultural identity and building a supposedly new polity. Towards the end of the constitutional era, a number of the educated elites had grown disenchanted and disillusioned with the political infighting and incompetence of the various constitutionalist factions. According to the political scientist Nader Entekhabi, it was in reality only around this time that a distinct social class emerged in Iran that could be classified as "intellectuals."[19] Having read Voltaire, Rousseau, and Montesquieu, this small, educated elite began to collectively yearn

---

[16] Ibid., p. 23.
[17] Taghi Azadaramaki, *Moderniteh-e Irani* (Iranian Modernity) (Tehran: Ejtema', 1380/ 2001), p. 63.
[18] Ibid.
[19] Quoted in Ramin Jahanbegloo, *Iran va Moderniteh* (Iran and Modernity) (Tehran: Goftar, 1380/2001), pp. 30–31.

for progress, order, and freedom. Together they formed an odd collection of political liberals, romantic nationalists, religious patriots, and Europeanized activists. What they did share was their frustration with the slow pace of social and political reforms, the politicians' frequent disregard for parliamentary procedures, the central government's inability to establish law and order across the country, Russian and British machinations in the north and south respectively, and the lawlessness and agitation of the country's various tribes.[20] As one of the newspapers published around the time put it: "It is not enough that we collect a bunch of well-meaning but ignorant clerics and merchants and ask them to implement a 'constitution' that was invented by the British and the French and is based on the thoughts of Rousseau and Montesquieu."[21]

With the country slipping deeper into chaos, and faced with the real danger of losing all the political gains of the Constitutional Revolution, many intellectuals embraced the new Pahlavi regime in the hope that it would give substance and direction to their aspirations. As it turned out, they were only partially correct.

This tacit agreement with the political establishment was particularly the case with those intellectuals who equated modernity and progress with Europeanization and secularization.[22] More importantly, this generation of intellectuals advocated familiarity with European scientific methodology and perspectives.[23] Consequently, many translated major European works into Farsi and gave frequent speeches to interested and like-minded audiences. Gradually but steadily, the ideas expounded by this second generation of intellectuals converged into what Entekhabi calls a discourse of "civilizing nationalism," the hallmarks of which were Eurocentrism, anti-religiosity, and centralized political and cultural powers.[24] "The nation" (*mellat*) was to replace religion (*din*) as the primary bond within the country's social fabric, in one stroke relegating Islam to the private sphere and also paving the nexus of Iranian identity to Europe.[25]

A soldier at heart his whole life, Reza Khan, the founder of the new dynasty, never had much patience for men of letters, whom he tolerated

---

[20] Ibid., pp. 33–34.   [21] Quoted in ibid., p. 33.

[22] Ibid., p. 22. Jahanbegloo goes on to maintain, however, that what the two Pahlavi monarchs sought to initiate in Iran was at best an incomplete or pseudo-modernity that did not extend into the realm of politics.

[23] Jahanbegloo, *Mowj-e Chaharom* (The Fourth Wave), p. 147.

[24] Quoted in Jahanbegloo, *Iran va Moderniteh* (Iran and Modernity), pp. 34–35.

[25] Quoted in ibid., p. 35.

only so long as they opposed neither him nor his ideas. But in unexpected ways he did find a convenient set of allies in the form of Iran's new crop of intellectuals, whose ideas and writings gave academic legitimacy and ideological focus to what the state was seeking to do by force. And force Reza was not loathe to use, a point not lost on anyone, much less on the intellectuals. It is important to remember that much of the intellectual endeavors of the time took place within the limits of a highly restrictive and authoritarian polity; Shakespeare's *Othello* and *The Merchant of Venice* were welcomed translations, as were works on ancient Persia and its glories, but the works of Kafka and Proust were not.[26]

Nevertheless, despite the manifold restrictions it faced, the prevailing intellectual discourse became deeper and more substantive, no longer centering around the simple question of whether or not to remain Iranian or to become wholly Western, but instead tackling issues of cultural and civilizational progress. The writer Dehkhoda sought to dichotomize between material and spiritual civilizations. Kazemsadeh talked of *zeitgeist*. And Mohammad Ali Foroughi advocated the adoption of Darwin's evolutionary theories as models for fostering social and scientific progress in Iran.[27]

Another important difference between this and the previous generation of intellectuals was their relatively wider social spectrum. This was a direct product of the expansion of educational opportunities at home and the dispatch of increasing numbers of university students abroad, as well as expedited urbanization, the spread of the printed media, the equalizing consequences of compulsory service in the armed forces by all Iranians, greater attempts to integrate women into the social and economic mainstreams, and the growth of the modern state bureaucracy.[28] While still members of a distinct sociopolitical elite, the backgrounds from which second generation intellectuals come tended to be more varied. Members of this generation included such diverse figures as the literary giant Sadeq Hedayat (1903–51), the academic and politician Mohammad Ali Foroughi, the one-time Justice Minister Ali Akbar Davar, the author Mohammad Ali Jamalzadeh, and the scholar and historian Hasan Taqizadeh.

By and large, second generation intellectuals advocated *étatism* and nationalism, which, in many ways, reflected trends and influences prevalent in the historical period in which they lived. However, by the

---

[26] Ibid., pp. 117–19.
[27] Behnam and Jahanbegloo, *Tamaddon va Tajaddod* (Civilization and Modernity), pp. 18–19.
[28] Behnam, *Iranian va Andisheh-ye Tajaddod* (Iranians and the Idea of Modernity), pp. 58–63.

early 1950s, and especially after the 1953 coup that reaffirmed Pahlavi authoritarianism in power, most members of this generation and the ideals they represented had died off. In fact, the next decade saw the emergence of a new crop of Iranian intellectuals, this time with strong revolutionary convictions and passionately anti-modernist. This third generation of Iranian intellectuals – of whom the most notable were men like Al-e Ahmad, Shariati, and Daryush Shayegan – were once praised as the ideologues and philosophers of the revolution. Today, there are few intellectuals who do not fault them and their ideas and for leading Iran's intellectual tradition astray at a critical juncture in the country's history. Even Shayegan, one of the only intellectuals of this generation who is still alive, has fundamentally changed his intellectual outlook since the revolution.[29]

There are two pervasive, interrelated themes in the criticism that the current, Fourth, Generation of Iranian scholars voice against those who preceded them. First, the arguments of the third generation scholars are said to suffer from a striking lack of theoretical depth and accurate understanding of their stated subject of study, namely the ominous threat of Western cultural and economic domination. They are seen mostly as "guerrilla intellectuals" who excelled in verbal snipes and demagoguery and are not viewed as serious thinkers with substantive thoughts to offer.[30] Both Al-e Ahmad and especially Shariati are seen as assembling together largely unrelated arguments offered by others – by the likes of the Orientalist Louis Massignon, Jean-Paul Sartre, and Frantz Fanon – in order to turn Islam into the primary source of defense against Western capitalism and Soviet communism.[31] They saw themselves as Permuthian "social engineers" who would move the masses toward some supposed revolutionary nirvana.[32] Their self-ascribed responsibility was to bring about revolutions and social change. They idolized the masses but inadequately understood them, and damned those in power regardless of what they did or did not do.[33] Today these individuals are seen more as "ideologues" rather than as intellectuals, approaching issues of concern, particularly the phenomenon of modernity, from rigid ideological lenses rather than reflecting on them

---

[29] Ali Asghar Haqdar, *Daryush Shayegan va Bohran-e Ma'naviyyat-e Sonnati* (Daryush Shayegan and the Crisis of Traditional Spirituality) (Tehran: Kavir, 1382/2003), p. 18.
[30] Behnam and Jahanbegloo, *Tamaddon va Tajaddod* (Civilization and Modernity), p. 24.
[31] Behnam, *Iranian va Andisheh-ye Tajaddod* (Iranians and the Idea of Modernity), p. 126.
[32] Milani, *Tajaddod va Tajaddod-Setizi dar Iran* (Modernity and Modernity-Fighting in Iran), p. 268.
[33] Morteza Moridiha, "Mordeh Rig-e Sonnat-e Roshanfekri" (The Dead Stone of Intellectual Tradition), *Aftab*, No. 27 (1382/2003), p. 82.

objectively and philosophically.[34] This line of critique is particularly directed at Shariati, who is said to have seen his role and the role of other intellectuals as one of waking the sleeping masses and leading them away from their present miseries.[35]

Second, their arguments essentially pointed in the wrong historical direction, calling on Iranians to look inward – under the auspices of "return to the self" – instead of where they actually ought to have looked, in the direction of modernity. Musa Ghaninezhad (b. 1951), a French-trained professor of economics, has directed some of his sharpest criticisms at Al-e Ahmad, whose "ignorance of the realities of Western civilization," he maintains, is "truly astounding."[36] Al-e Ahmad advocated the adoption of Western technology but not its norms or its social and human sciences. What he and others like him failed to realize, however, is that the West's technological advances would not have been possible had it not been for its values and cultural norms. "Technology and the humanities are two sides of the same coin and cannot be separated from each other," according to Ghaninezhad. "The science and technology that come out of modern civilization are themselves products of the new person, and this new person is a product of new thinking and new values."[37] Al-e Ahmad's proposition that our salvation lies within us – in our heritage and our culture – and that we can pick and choose from the West what we deem necessary and appropriate, "set us back" immeasurably.[38]

The importance of this collective criticism of intellectuals of a generation ago cannot be overemphasized. This is where the heart of the current, prevailing intellectual discourse lies, in the "deconstruction," in the words of the eminent contemporary philosopher Shayegan, of the discourse of the previous generation.[39] In the process, an alternative, fundamentally modernist, discourse is being constructed. It would not be an exaggeration to claim that contemporary Iranian thinkers in large measure define themselves as polar opposites of their intellectual fathers.

Let us look more closely at the arguments of some of the "Fourth Generation" intellectuals in the deliberate efforts to not only distance themselves from their immediate predecessors but to also rectify what

---

[34] Jahanbegloo, *Mowj-e Chaharom* (The Fourth Wave), p. 149.

[35] Hosein Kaji, *Kisti-ye ma az Negah-e Roshanfekran-e Irani* (Our Existence from the Perspective of Iranian Intellectuals) (Tehran: Rowzaneh, 1378/1999), p. 55.

[36] Musa Ghaninezhad, *Tajaddod Talabi va Touse'h dar Iran-e Mo'aser* (Modernism and Development in Contemporary Iran) (Tehran: Markaz, 1377/1998), p. 55.

[37] Ibid.   [38] Ibid.

[39] Kaji, *Kisti-ye ma az Negah-e Roshanfekran-e Irani* (Our Existence from the Perspective of Iranian Intellectuals), p. 96.

they see as past mistakes. One such intellectual is Musa Ghaninezhad, who says this of the ideologies that held sway in Iran in the years leading up to the revolution:

In reality, from the very beginning, the familiarity of Iranians with Western civilization and modernity, similar to that of other non-Western societies, took on the form of an involuntary competition and struggle. This forced familiarity with the West was inevitably accompanied with resentment. Since it was not out of our volition and desire that we opened our doors to the West, our curiosity about its civilization has a narrow and particular conception. We never really sought to understand the values and thoughts of this new civilization, but from the very beginning focused on its material and mechanical accomplishments.

Inattention to the philosophical foundations of the new world has been a huge catastrophe for us, and it has kept us away from the knowledge of the causes, principles, and products of modernity. Consequently, we have always directed our attention to the apparent manifestations of the new civilization – its material and mechanical progress – and have not considered the reasons for the appearance of this civilization, namely changes in its philosophy and value. This inattention, which is one of the most important and consistent features of Iranian thought from the very beginning of its familiarity with the West, is one of the most important reasons for the absence of an intellectual framework that would foster development.[40]

In specific relation to Al-e Ahmad and Shariati, Ghaninezhad criticizes their arguments as theoretically uninformed and scientifically invalid. This is particularly the case with Al-e Ahmad, he claims, who had maintained that from its very inception the West had conspired against Islam and the East.[41] Al-e Ahmad had no real understanding of the social sciences and rejected any attempt to understand the West or modernity as yet another manifestation of "Westoxication" (*gharbzadegi*).[42] Ghaninezhad claims that Shariati's arguments were similarly based on a linear understanding of history and were deeply imbued with socialist ideals. This was most clearly demonstrated by Shariati's belief that capitalism – and by implication modernity – would eventually come to an end. Due to his religious beliefs, however, his arguments had a strongly Islamic tone.[43]

---

[40] Ghaninezhad, *Tajaddod Talabi va Touse'h dar Iran-e Mo'aser* (Modernism and Development in Contemporary Iran), pp. 12–13.

[41] Akbar Ganji, *Sonnat, Moderniteh, Post-modern* (Tradition, Modernity, Post-Modern) (Tehran: Sarat, 1375/1996), p. 241.

[42] Ibid., pp. 208–9. *Gharbzadegi* has been alternatively translated into English as "West Struckedness" or "Occidentosis." Throughout this book I have used "Westoxication" as a preferred translation both in reference to Jalal Al-e Ahmad's highly influential book with the same title and the phenomenon of inebriation with things Western.

[43] Ibid., p. 207.

Ghaninezhad maintains that modernity will not come to an end but is, in fact, a goal to desire and strive for. Contemporary societies cannot be run on the basis of anything other than the project of modernity.[44] Embarking on this project requires overcoming two obstacles: one is "the hermeneutic (*ma'refet-shenakhti*) approach we take to religion and tradition"; the other is what Ghaninezhad labels as "developmentalist ideology."[45] "Our conception of society as an organic whole must change to one based on a complex order that includes personal liberty."[46] The project of modernity will not come to fruition unless Iranians critique holistic conceptions of society that are responsible for undermining personal freedoms and individualist values. These two essential ingredients of modernity have long been challenged by an odd but powerful combination of traditionalists and socialists, thus making their spread and acceptance in Iranian society all the more difficult.

There has also been a tendency to assume that modern science and technology can be adopted and understood without an internalization of their underlying intellectual, subjective premises. Ghaninezhad maintains that the ensuing "developmentalist ideology" in reality calls for some form of an "inverse" or "reactive" modernity. It reduces modernity merely to its technological components and stripping it of the normative framework that gave rise to it in the first place.[47] "Developmentalist ideology," he writes,

creates an intellectual and social set of relations that make it appear as if there is a connection or consistency between tradition and modernity. In reality, however, it undermines tradition without replacing it with anything meaningful and viable alternatives. It appears that under current circumstances, developmentalist ideology is the most formidable obstacle toward modernity and therefore objective and scientific development. It can be stated, therefore, that the most essential step in eliminating the intellectual obstacles to development, is a critique of developmentalist ideology.[48]

The philosopher Daryush Ashouri (b. 1938) criticizes the arguments of Shariati and Al-e Ahmad on similar grounds. They perceived contemporary society as afflicted and in need of repair, he argues, and as

---

[44] Ibid., p. 185.

[45] Ghaninezhad, *Tajaddod Talabi va Touse'h dar Iran-e Mo'aser* (Modernism and Development in Contemporary Iran), p. 58.

[46] Ganji, *Sonnat, Moderniteh, Post-modern* (Tradition, Modernity, Post-Modern), p. 205.

[47] Ghaninezhad, *Tajaddod Talabi va Touse'h dar Iran-e Mo'aser* (Modernism and Development in Contemporary Iran), p. 93.

[48] Ibid., pp. 93–4.

cure they advocated return to an ideal but undefined past.[49] Both of these ideologues maintained that Iranian society is gripped with self-alienation and suffers from the imperialism of a monolithic West. Its salvation rests in return to an authentic self. But they have an incomplete and incorrect understanding of both the West's and Iran's past, "simply spinning their wheels without offering a meaningful way out."[50]

Essentially, Ashouri claims, the thesis of "Westoxication" is a continuation of the Western intellectual tradition and the transference of Western ideas to the non-Western world. But its proponents do not realize this truism, and do not have any grasp of the philosophical underpinnings of the Western intellectual tradition.[51] "Westoxication" might be an effective and appealing political weapon for mass mobilization. But its essence is philosophically hollow and vacuous, full of internal contradictions and yet blissfully ignorant of them. "If we are to rid ourselves of this dark world of intellectual void that confronts the West and Western thought so superficially," Ashouri writes, "we must engage in deep, substantive study of the essence and meaning of modernity and its relationship with us."[52]

Daryush Shayegan (b. 1934), no doubt one of Iran's most celebrated philosophers, also faults third generation intellectuals for making traditionalism, and ultimately, fundamentalism, fashionable.[53] Importantly, Shayegan himself was once considered part of the third generation, and the transformation of his own intellectual perspectives represents larger paradigmatic shifts in how Iranian thinkers today interpret the world and Iran's position within it. Shayegan did not necessarily advocate a "return to the self" in the same way that Shariati and Al-e Ahmad were doing. For Shayegan – whose thoughts at that time were deeply influenced by the arguments of the French Orientalist Henry Corbin – what was key was the Iranian spirit. He called on his countrymen to rely on the spiritual and aesthetic (*ma'navi*) essence of Iranian identity. This spirit, he maintained, was profoundly dynamic and, in keeping with the general tenor of the times, even revolutionary. Invoking the memory of some of the personalities in Iranian history who in the 1970s were hailed for their revolutionary spirit, in 1977 he wrote,

The aesthetic and wisdom-filled essence (*arefaneh*) of Iranian civilization can serve as a source of anger and rebellion, and it can even take the form of a religious revolt. Rebellion has deep roots in pre-Islamic religions, and it is one of

---

[49] Daryush Ashouri, *Ma va Moderniteh* (Us and Modernity) (Tehran: Sarat, 1377/1998), pp. 134–5.
[50] Ibid., p. 139.   [51] Ibid., p. 140.   [52] Ibid., p. 141.
[53] Haqdar, *Faraso-ye Postmoderniteh* (Beyond Post-Modernity), p. 26.

the notable characteristics of the Iranian spirit. Anticipating the end of time, perceiving of one's self as an agent of day of judgment, and equating earthly revolutions with the ultimate resurrection, these are all the notable features of this perspective, which has been handed down to the Iranian nation from Zoroaster to Mazdak and Mani and then to the Ismailites and ultimately to Bab.[54]

In his earlier writings, Shayegan's criticism of the West focused not so much on its colonial encroachment or material exploitation of the East but on the depth and meaningfulness of Eastern civilizations. This was a product of Shayegan's own early studies of Indian philosophy and civilization. His concurrent attraction to the philosophies of Heidegger and Nietzsche earlier in his intellectual career had much to do with his sharply critical outlook toward the West.[55] While Shayegan continues to maintain his thesis that Iranian society is gripped with cultural schizophrenia, for the last decade or so he has drastically altered his views on the utility and manifest benefits of Western civilization and all that it has to offer. More specifically, he has been highlighting the essence and important contributions of Western philosophical thought, at the same time criticizing what he sees as the superficial critiques of the likes of Al-e Ahmad. Western thought is "very rich and is unrivalled in the diversity of its principles and the breadth of the subjects it covers."[56] "We tend to forget that Western civilization is the richest, most diverse, and most dynamic civilization on the planet Earth. Since it questions all cultural and scientific axioms that underpin it, and has not left any areas of life untouched, we can no longer approach it superficially and only with slogans."[57]

At the same time as praising its offerings, Shayegan is careful to point to the hazards of a superficial appreciation of the West at the expense of the native intellectual tradition. This, he laments, has already happened. An insufficient, superficial understanding of the West has caused Asians in general and Iranians in particular to become inebriated with the West. "Westoxication means ignorance toward the West," he writes.

It means unfamiliarity with the intellectual elements that now constitute the most dominant and aggressive worldview currently in existence on planet Earth . . . Westoxication bespeaks of an unawareness of the real essence of

<hr>

[54] Quoted in Haqdar, *Daryush Shayegan va Bohran-e Ma'naviyyat-e Sonnati* (Daryush Shayegan and the Crisis of Traditional Spirituality), p. 146.
[55] Kaji, *Kisti-ye ma az Negah-e Roshanfekran-e Irani* (Our Existence from the Perspective of Iranian Intellectuals), pp. 72–3.
[56] Daryush Shayegan, *Asia darbarabar-e Gharb* (Asia Faces the West) (Tehran: Amir Kabir, 1378/1999), p. 234.
[57] Ibid., p. 301.

Western civilization, and this unawareness draws us to a superficial encounter whereby we think of the West as an industrial giant and ignore its rich intellectual underpinnings.[58]

Not only is the drunkard entranced with the West, but he also ignores the richness and the potentials of his own heritage and civilization. The solution Shayegan seems to suggest is to approach the West with greater sobriety while continuing to maintain an appreciative eye toward native tradition.

We become mesmerized and paralyzed by what the West has to offer, losing our own intellectual creativity. This deadlock prevents us from seeing the nexus between Western thought on the one hand and native thought on the other. This leaves us unable to grasp the essence of Western thought but to also neglect of our own intellectual and native heritage at the same time.[59]

Iranian identity, he has mused with devastating poignancy, resembles a puzzle made up of forty-odd incongruent pieces. Ultimately, it has paralyzed Iranian thought and robbed it of its creativity and its ability to rid itself of its self-contradictory predicament.[60]

It is not quite clear what remedies Shayegan proposes for ending this schizophrenia and self-alienation – a state, as he calls it, of "being neither here nor there."[61] In broad, philosophical terms, he advocates a rediscovery of Iran's rich tradition, history, and heritage. This should not take a mournful form reminiscent of a funeral, but it needs to be done with a discerning eye toward rediscovering the contributions made to Iranian history and heritage and their potentials for the future. The two other pillars of Asia besides Iran – China and India – have so far failed to do so and are plagued by the same sense of schizophrenia that entangles Iran, and, despite its successful absorption of Western technology, the same fate has also befallen Japan, Asia's fourth cultural pillar.[62]

The steady transformation of Shayegan's ideas over the last two decades or so represents a larger, generational shift in the intellectual life of Iran. In fact, a fourth, post-revolutionary class of Iranian intellectuals has come to the fore whose ideas and theories are qualitatively different from those of previous generations in general and the third generation of intellectuals in particular. The social scientist Ali Asghar Haqdar (b. 1965) sees this generation change as a result of different approaches to modernity, as articulated and manifested in the West, over time.

---

[58] Ibid., p. 56.   [59] Ibid., p. 57.

[60] Haqdar, *Daryush Shayegan va Bohran-e Ma'naviyyat-e Sonnati* (Daryush Shayegan and the Crisis of Traditional Spirituality), pp. 76–77.

[61] Shayegan, *Asia darbarabar-e Gharb* (Asia Faces the West), p. 57.   [62] Ibid., p. 61.

Earlier intellectuals – those in the first and second generations – discovered the West and recognized its superiority. Then, with the third generation, came the era of disgust with the West and hatred toward it. Currently, there is a period of intellectual reflection, self-discovery, and learning from Western philosophy.[63]

Introspective self-reflection is also seen as one of the defining characteristics of post-revolutionary, post-war Iranian intellectuals by the sociologist Azadaramaki. The experiences of the revolution and the war were critical in shaping the preferences and perspectives of the current generation of Iranian intellectuals, Azadaramaki claims. They were forced to look inward and to turn away from the violent perspectives of the past, concentrating instead on the construction of "social and hermeneutical conditions" that would facilitate integration into a new, global arena.[64] Today's intellectual, he writes, is building a new social construction and a new worldview based on his experiences.

The new worldview is no longer simplistic, easy to reach, homogeneous, conveniently dichotomized into black and white, absolutist, or devotional. The experiences of the past century, coupled with the prevailing elements of modern life, have given this worldview much more flexibility in interpreting its past and its present. The new worldview has emphatically renounced its past methods and its previous orientations. If once again it enters into conflict with its classical adversaries, it will not opt for those modes of defense and combat it once so eagerly sought. If it gets a chance to overthrow the existing system, revolution is no longer its preferred method of operation or its objective. And if it finds itself sitting in judgment of the other, first it will internalize the other and will then engage in an internalized process of evaluation . . . The new worldview, in other words, is self-reflective and self-critical, but unlike its past iterations, it is not self-destructive.[65]

As noted earlier, nowhere have the emergence of this new worldview and the generation of intellectuals spearheading it been more fully articulated than in Ramin Jahanbegloo's writings, particularly in his book *The Fourth Wave.* "The intellectual trend underway supports pluralism, democratic individualism, and modern philosophy," he emphatically states.

I think one of the most important traits of Iran's fourth intellectual wave is its acceptance of discourse and dialogue. This generation does not think in ideological terms anymore and instead wants to enter into a dialogue with the three layers of Iranian identity, namely Islam, ancient Iran, and modernity and Western civilization. This is a totally new outlook that differs a great deal from

---

[63] Haqdar, *Daryush Shayegan va Bohran-e Ma'naviyyat-e Sonnati* (Daryush Shayegan and the Crisis of Traditional Spirituality), p. 12.
[64] Azadaramaki, *Moderniteh-e Irani* (Iranian Modernity), pp. 28–29.   [65] Ibid., p. 29.

the ideas of Shariati and Al-e Ahmad. It is an outlook that wants to explore issues without prejudging them.[66]

In further elaborating on the characteristics of the Fourth Generation, he points out that

This is a generation that started with the [1978–79] revolution, especially near the end of the decades of the 1980s. It is a younger generation, which today is between 35 to 50 years old, and includes individuals like Seyyed Javad Taba-taba'i, Babak Ahmadi, Sadeq Zibakalam, and me. It is a generation that thinks in thoroughly non-utopian and non-ideological terms. It is pluralist and looks at issues at a much deeper level than the other generation of intellectuals did . . . Literally all members of the Fourth Generation engage in some form of dialogue with the West. They read books, know foreign languages, and do not perceive of the West as some sort of evil with which they must fight.[67]

These intellectuals are not as interested in "positive freedom" as were previous generations of intellectuals and instead emphasize negative conceptions of freedom. For them, democracy does not necessarily mean the freedom to rebel; it means an absence of authoritarianism and arbitrariness. By the same token, they eschew ideological partisanship and do not advocate the active engagement of intellectuals in social engineering.[68] The central question today is not to identify and to get to know "the enemy" but to engage in rational discourse and exchange of ideas. What defines today's generation of Iranian intellectuals is no longer "antagonism" bur rather "agonism."[69]

Jahanbegloo clearly sees these Fourth Generation "discourse intellectuals" as important agents of democratization. In fact today's Iranian intellectual has a well-defined responsibility, Jahanbegloo maintains, to "discover and defend a critical and rational discourse of democracy . . . The responsibility here is to stand in opposition to *a priori* forms of consensus by first constructing and then institutionalizing a critical discourse" that would support the emergence of a democratic polity.[70]

We must recognize that the most basic and fundamental problem facing us is not only "instrumentalist rationality." It is, rather, the steady spread and deepening among us of a democratic rationality in all of our political structures and thoughts in a way that would allow us to live together despite our differences. A desire to spread pluralism and negative conceptions of democracy is the only way that we can mobilize our resources to defend the freedom of individuals and groups. In order for this sense of responsibility to be maintained over time, Iranian intellectuals need to have a global worldview. This global worldview does

---

[66] Jahanbegloo, *Mowj-e Chaharom* (The Fourth Wave), p. 266.
[67] Ibid., pp. 267–68.   [68] Ibid., p. 141.   [69] Ibid.   [70] Ibid., p. 86.

not mean an awareness of the self as compared to "others." But it means an acceptance of the plurality of views that currently exist in Iranian society.[71]

There is near unanimity among contemporary Iranian thinkers that the biggest challenge facing the country – politically, socially, culturally, and economically – is the issue of modernity. Iran's basic problem, they argue, is its partial and incomplete exposure to modernity. Why this exposure has been so skewed and incomplete will be discussed below. For now, it is important to realize its manifold consequences for Iranian thinking and Iranian identity. As Abbas Milani (b. 1949) maintains, Iranian society has experienced many of the facets of modernity, and has accepted many of its more superficial and even some of its more fundamental premises. But the force and strength of tradition persist, and it continues to cast a shadow over the cultural life and social structure of communities and individuals alike.[72] The end result has been "pseudo modernity," giving rise to a plethora of confusions about what it means to be modern, or a citizen, or even an urbanite.[73]

"Why has our predicament degenerated into what it is?" asks Farhang Rajaee (b. 1952), one of a number of Iranian thinkers living abroad but influential in shaping scholarly thought and discourse inside the country.[74] For nearly three centuries, he argues, Iranians have been trying to figure out how to become active and productive players in the global production of thought, creativity, culture, wealth, and power, all to no avail. "Is there a correct path in front of us?" he muses. "If we put an end to our self-destruction and our self-mutilation, which principles would we follow?"[75]

Jahanbegloo (b. 1956) sums up nicely what many other Iranian thinkers maintain. "We currently live in a condition of purgatory," he argues. "Our traditional culture, which was more in tune with our daily lives and our dispositions, has been destroyed. We live in a modern reality and we use modern technologies. But our outlook and our perspective remain traditional. We have come across a fundamental

---

[71] Ibid., p. 142.

[72] Milani, *Tajaddod va Tajaddod-Setizi dar Iran* (Modernity and Modernity-Fighting in Iran), p. 155.

[73] Parviz Piran, "Ta'sir-e Shebhe Modernism bar Jonbesh-haye Ejtama'i dar Iran" (The Influence of Pseudo-Modernism on Social Movements in Iran), *Aftab*, No. 16 (1381/ 2002), pp. 36–37.

[74] Farhang Rajaee, *Moshkeleh-e Hoviyyat-e Iranian-e Emrouz: Eefa-ye Naqsh dar 'Asr-e Yek Tamaddon va Chand Farhang* (The Problematic of Contemporary Iranian Identity: Participating in the World of One Civilization and Many Cultures) (Tehran: Nashr-e Ney, 1382/2003), p. 23.

[75] Ibid.

inconsistency in our lives, and we must reform it to the extent possible."[76]

Rajaee frames the issue in civilizational terms and links it to the question of Iranian identity. "The reality is that the Iranians' problem is not political, economic, or even cultural," he writes, "but a lack of civilizational production. From a civilizational perspective they are in a situation of crisis or even regression. This predicament has been eroding the material and intellectual forces of production for some time now."[77]

The question then becomes, "How did we get here?" Why has our exposure to, our understanding of, and our immersion into modernity been so distorted and incomplete? What explains our predicament? Is this a product of centuries of despotic rule, or is it a function of Iran's position in the larger global system and its chronic industrial under-development? Or, alternatively, have there been flaws in the character of Iran's intellectual tradition itself that have deepened the malaise that has so gripped the country's entanglement with modernity?

Not surprisingly, the answers offered involve all or a combination of these hypotheses. But, significantly, the most common thread in literally all of the expositions in this regard is a sharp critique of Iran's intellectual tradition from its inception in the late 1800s up until very recently. In essence, the current generation of Iranian intellectuals has been funda-mentally deconstructionist – deconstructing the arguments of intellectuals in past generations – and only then constructing their own, fundamentally different, theoretical frame of reference. And, again unlike any other time in recent Iranian history, this theoretical frame of reference revolves around notions of modernity and all that it entails – secularism, pluralism, rationalism, relativism, abstention from ideological endeavors, and the adoption of a critical outlook toward the past.[78]

This does not, of course, absolve the responsibility of the encroaching West or, for that matter, those individuals in positions of political power and influence who feared that, if left unchecked, modernity might erode their powers. Criticisms of the West and its efforts throughout history to plunder or to at least underdevelop the rest of the world are nothing new. This is a is well-accepted fact of history, and in recent decades it was most passionately articulated and explained to Iranian audiences by the iconic Al-e Ahmad and Shariati. Few Iranians today, or other peoples in the rest of the developing world for that matter, doubt the

---

[76] Quoted in Ashouri, *Ma va Moderniteh* (Us and Modernity), p. 282.
[77] Rajaee, *Moshkeleh-e Hoviyyat-e Iranian-e Emrouz* (The Problematic of Contemporary Iranian Identity), p. 29.
[78] Haqdar, *Faraso-ye Postmoderniteh* (Beyond Post-Modernity), p. 54.

veracity of the claim that the developed world has systematically underdeveloped their societies and their polities over time.[79] Daryush Ashouri, one of Iran's most respected philosophers, writes:

The Westerners captured the lands of other civilizations by force, and with coercion and contempt and insult made slaves of the souls of those they had conquered. The Westerners either uprooted other civilizations or dried them up, and turned peoples with deep histories and civilizations into some sort of historyless savages. Civilizations that for centuries were rich in art, literature, and philosophy, and had given birth to culture and science and learning, found themselves in regression and impotent in the face of the dominant Western civilization.[80]

Western underdevelopment of the non-Western world has gone hand in hand with domestic despotism bent on either preventing the spread of modernity altogether, or, at best, channeling it into venues that sustain existing political institutions and practices. From the very beginning, many of the efforts in the developing world aimed at achieving political liberation and the rule of law were struggles for the attainment of modernity. In Iran, this dates back to the start of the Constitutional Revolution in 1905. The bitter fight to force the Qajar Shahs to abide by a Basic Law that, among other things, would principally curb their arbitrary powers, was a contest between the forces of modernity on the one side and traditionalism on the other.[81] Eventually, the Qajars did accede to a Basic Law, but constitutionalism never triumphed in Iran. The Qajars never quite recovered from the wounds inflicted on them by the forces of the constitutional movement. But, within a few years, a reinvigorated authoritarianism found expression in the person of Reza Khan, soon to become Reza Shah Pahlavi. And, with the speedy demise of constitutionalism and political liberties, so declined the fortunes of modernity.

This was no accident. From the very beginning, the conception of modernity in Iran was skewed and incomplete. Nassereddin Shah Qajar (r. 1848–96) was infatuated with the West and retained an eagerness throughout his reign to see the modern world up close and personal. Three times in his long reign he and his extensive entourage traveled to Europe to learn more about the modern world, and, of course, enjoy its

---

[79] One of the most articulate and effective proponents of this line of thinking was Andre Gunder Frank, whose classic *Development of Underdevelopment* (Indianapolis, IN: Bobbs-Merrill, 1969) informed successive generations of students of Third World politics. See also Sing C. Chew and Robert A. Denemark, eds., *The Underdevelopment of Development: Essays in Honor of Andre Gunder Frank* (London: Sage, 1999).

[80] Ashouri, *Ma va Moderniteh* (Us and Modernity), p. 6.

[81] Ajodani, *Mashroteh-ye Irani* (Iranian Constitutionalism), p. 385.

worldly pleasures, each time plunging the country's depleted treasury deeper into debt. And his modernizing Chancellor, Mirza Hosein Khan Sepahsalar (1870–80), was eager to point out to the monarch the benefits of such trips. In a letter to the King encouraging him to undertake the trip, he wrote:

The benefits and meanings of such a royal journey are not clear to everyone . . . Tourism is not the royal intent. This is a great pathway to the progress of Iran. In this trip the King does not travel abroad alone. In reality, the entire government of Iran goes to save this land by learning about the world.[82]

That the efforts of Mirza Hosein Khan, and before him those of Nassereddin Shah's other great premier, Mirza Taqi Khan Amir Kabir (1848–51), both ended in failure is not seen as much of a surprise. After all, why would the Qajars or even the Pahlavis for that matter voluntarily and knowingly embrace a phenomenon that would undermine the very basis of their hold on political power? The men in power, after all, were dictators and made little or no effort at hiding their true nature. It is not the dictator's responsibility to welcome modernity. This is the task, indeed the very *raison d'être*, of intellectuals. Modernity's absence in Iran is not simply a product of Western machinations or the archaic mindset of successive political leaders. It is, more fundamentally, a product of the chronic failure of Iranian intellectuals to properly understand modernity and in turn introduce it to and spread it in Iranian society. It is, in fact, to this failure and its causes and consequences that most contemporary Iranian thinkers devote considerable attention.

Once again, Jahanbegloo's criticism is the sharpest. "We have closed our eyes and our ears to our own history," he laments.

We seem condemned not to have learned from the lessons of the past and so we keep repeating them. Perhaps this is because we have sought to create a nexus between tradition and modernity through political ideologies and not through philosophical endeavors . . . There has been no philosophical conversation in Iran between tradition and modernity but only ideological clashes and collisions.[83]

Behnam agrees. For 150 years, Iranian intellectuals have reacted to the West in a variety of ways, from being enamored with it to viewing it as satanic, having collectively called for its "adoration," "imitation," "criticism," and even "denial" at various junctures in the country's

---

[82] Quoted in Milani, *Tajaddod va Tajaddod-Setizi dar Iran* (Modernity and Modernity-Fighting in Iran), pp. 129–30.

[83] Behnam and Jahanbegloo, *Tamaddon va Tajaddod* (Civilization and Modernity), pp. 15–16.

history.[84] Within such a context, he maintains, reasoned discourse, particularly one sustained over time, has become exceedingly difficult.

Despite a preponderance of modernist tendencies among Fourth Generation intellectuals, there are still some contemporary thinkers for whom modernity is not a normative preoccupation. The most articulate example of this group is Reza Davari Ardekani, philosophy professor at the University of Tehran. Following in the footsteps of his old teacher Ahmad Fardid, Ardekani is an ardent fan of Heidegger's critical post-modernism.[85] Born in 1933, Davari is literally of an earlier generation, belonging more or less in the same category as Al-e Ahmad, Shariati, and the earlier Shayegan, though his arguments are philosophically much richer than Al-e Ahmad's or Shariati's ever were. And, perhaps again a product of his generation and his times, his arguments closely mirror those of Martin Heidegger, though with a strong religious tinge. "I am not a disciple of Heidegger," he disclaims, "but his thoughts contain important elements against which supporters of the West fight." Heidegger, he maintains, "is a revolutionary, modest, noble, and solid thinker who prepares the philosophical groundwork for passage from the age of the West and modernity, and with reminding us of the sense of Western alienation, and with sign language and the language of signs, calls the attention of our eyes and our souls to future horizons."[86]

For Davari, the West is an outlook in addition to an actual geographic presence, one that began in Europe some four hundred years ago and continues to this day. Looking at the surrounding universe as an object, "the West has given the world and its past new meaning, and anyone looking at the world and at history, regardless of time and place, sees things from the viewpoint of West. One of the most damaging aspects of Westoxication is the mechanical approach to and conception of life and the perception of this approach as absolute and perfect."[87]

At the heart of this outlook has been the placement of humanity at the center of the universe. "Humanism has been the pivotal axis of Western history . . . In the new terminology of today, humanism is defined as the human condition that sees humanity as independent and free of

---

[84] Ibid., p. 20.

[85] Pedram, *Roshanfekran-e Dini va Moderniteh dar Iran Pas az Enqelab* (Religious Intellectuals and Modernity in Iran after the Revolution), pp. 99–100. Ahmad Fardid (1909–94) was a philosophy professor at the University of Tehran whose ideas were deeply influenced by Martin Heidegger. Although he left behind next to no published works, Fardid's legacy continues to loom large in Iranian academic circles. It was also Fardid who first coined the term "Westoxication" which Al-e Ahmad later popularized.

[86] Ganji, *Sonnat, Moderniteh, Post-modern* (Tradition, Modernity, Post-Modern), p. 149.

[87] Reza Davari Ardekani, *Falsafeh-ye Tatbiqi* (Comparative Philosophy) (Tehran: Saqi, 1383/2004), p. 14.

anything above and beyond it."[88] It is in this very centrality accorded to humanism that the West's fundamental flaw lies. The new age might indeed be one of humanity's supreme reign, but it is also one of "oppression, rape, and pillage," "despotic rule," "humanity's loss in a meaningless world," "slavery to machines," and "a period of decline for divine thought and human alienation."[89] In today's West, he claims, "the air is depressing, doors are shut, heads are confused, hands are hidden, breaths are cloudy, hearts are heavy and tired, trees are skeleton-like, the earth is barren, the sky is dusty and confining."[90]

For Davari, the West and modernity are synonymous.[91] His definition of modernity is eerily close to how he defines the West: "a system of thought in which humanity is the center and axis of everything, gives everything a human face, and human will and power appears everywhere in politics, and rule, judgment, and science, and teachings, and school, and everything else."[92] Modernity, he maintains, is "a condition in which man considers himself worthy of conquest over all other beings, and he assumes that with his willpower and his rationality he can bestow order on everything."[93]

No system based on flawed premises can sustain itself indefinitely, and the West is no exception. "The crisis of the current world is the crisis of Western thought. In this thought humanity has reached a stage where there is no hope or refuge outside of the self."[94] Nevertheless, "the era of the West, and the eclipse in the history of sacred thought and the alienation of man, will come to an end," he states emphatically.[95] Exactly when this will happen is not clear, but it will ultimately happen. Referring to the likes of Heidegger and other post-modernists, Davari maintains that "a history and an era in which its very prophets and elites have no faith cannot last."[96] In fact, he explicitly points to post-modernity – or, more specifically, to post-modern thought – as proof of the crisis of modernity and its linchpin of humanism. The very vigorous and at times violent defense that the proponents of modernity have

[88] Quoted in Kaji, *Kisti-ye ma az Negah-e Roshanfekran-e Irani* (Our Existence from the Perspective of Iranian Intellectuals), p. 107.

[89] Ibid., p. 108.   [90] Quoted in ibid.

[91] Reza Davari Ardekani, *Darbareh-ye Gharb* (Concerning the West) (Tehran: Hermes, 1379/2000), p. ix.

[92] Quoted in Pedram, *Roshanfekran-e Dini va Moderniteh dar Iran Pas az Enqelab* (Religious Intellectuals and Modernity in Iran after the Revolution), p. 81.

[93] Davari, *Darbareh-ye Gharb* (Concerning the West), p. ix.   [94] Ibid., p. 54.

[95] Quoted in Kaji, *Kisti-ye ma az Negah-e Roshanfekran-e Irani* (Our Existence from the Perspective of Iranian Intellectuals), p. 111.

[96] Quoted in Pedram, *Roshanfekran-e Dini va Moderniteh dar Iran Pas az Enqelab* (Religious Intellectuals and Modernity in Iran after the Revolution), p. 82.

mounted against post-modern thought, he claims, bespeaks of their insecurity and steady decline.[97]

Through his criticism of modernity and the West, Davari constructs and proposes an alternative ideal, one in which religion appears to play a strong though somewhat indeterminate role. The West might be omnipresent, but its gravitational pull is not inescapable, he claims.[98] Davari does not quite articulate the details of his proposed alternative. In broad terms, what he seems to endorse is an Islamic system that revolves around the two key axes of freedom and justice, both of which he conceptualizes through thickly religious lenses. To begin with, religion is an innate aspect of human nature, but from the true meaning of which man has become more and more distanced as he has drawn himself closer to science.[99] A religious society offers the best chance of salvation from the dark West.

The conception of freedom that Davari employs has little in common with the Western, liberal sense of the term. It does not revolve around notions of individualism, or individual choice and rationality. Instead, it has more to do with traditions and sensibilities rooted in religious thought.[100] Freedom must be free of human machinations. In other words, freedom can neither be summed up through or be dependent on the legal provisions that humans create. True freedom becomes possible only when divine rules and directives are obeyed. Freedom in Islam will not be attained unless people rid themselves of the legal restrictions that they or others have made for them, and instead make themselves subject to divine directives. When that happens, there will be no oppression, and the observance of religious precepts and *hudud* (canonical punishments) will foster the satisfaction of the people.[101]

Davari's notion of justice is similarly imbued with Islamic precepts, though somewhat less explicitly. In order to create a just and equitable society, he maintains, a group of people need to be schooled in notions of justice, or others must have internalized more abstract notions of justice within themselves, so that their beliefs in justice and their deeds become one and the same. In a true Islamic society, justice will not be guaranteed by a man-made social contract of sorts. Instead, justice will

---

[97] Ganji, *Sonnat, Moderniteh, Post-modern* (Tradition, Modernity, Post-Modern), p. 119.

[98] Pedram, *Roshanfekran-e Dini va Moderniteh dar Iran Pas az Enqelab* (Religious Intellectuals and Modernity in Iran after the Revolution), p. 86.

[99] Ganji, *Sonnat, Moderniteh, Post-modern* (Tradition, Modernity, Post-Modern), p. 123.

[100] Pedram, *Roshanfekran-e Dini va Moderniteh dar Iran Pas az Enqelab* (Religious Intellectuals and Modernity in Iran after the Revolution), p. 91.

[101] Ibid., p. 92.

be based on and sustained by Islamic values that also satisfy people's needs and demands.[102]

This brings Davari extremely close to an outright endorsement of the philosophical underpinnings and the institutional make-up of the Islamic Republic's political system. In modern constitutions, he argues, one of the key principles is to place the locus of sovereignty with the people. In reality, however, sovereignty is that of God, and the religiously learned should be entrusted with executing the divine will. The intellectual notion that religion and politics should be separated is devoid of meaning and religion should form the basis on which rules governing politics and national affairs are based.[103] In fact, Davari explicitly endorses the notion of *Velayat-e Faqih*, the guardianship of the Supreme Jurisconsult, which is the hallmark of the Islamic Republic's political system and Ayatollah Khomeini's most important political contribution to *ijtihad*.[104] "In our religion," he states emphatically, "*velayat* is inherent to rule."[105] But there is one important, though somewhat vague, caveat to this endorsement. The *velayat* does not necessarily have to be that of the clergy and can be carried out by non-clerical, enlightened, and educated classes.[106] Beyond that Davari does not elaborate.

It is difficult to ascertain the popularity of Davari's arguments among learned circles in Iran and the degree to which his thoughts hold sway among the educated classes. His thoughts are, no doubt, written about and discussed in various scholarly publications and articles. At the same time, commentators point to some basic tensions within his positions that are yet to be resolved. For example, his damning criticism of the West seems at odds with his admission that that is where the path to development lies.[107] Along the same lines, he cautions against following the path to development pursued by Japan – one of acquiring Western technology while maintaining national identity – since, he maintains, "Japan has become just like the West."[108] A similar contradiction appears to belie his stated refusal to comment on political issues while at the same time endorsing the politically charged notion of *Velayat-e Faqih*.[109] His steadfast refusal to tackle substantive issues – the most

---

[102] Ibid., p. 92.   [103] Ibid., p. 98.

[104] See Rohullah Khomeini, *Velayat-e Faqih, Jehad-e Akbar* (Supreme Jurisconsult, the Great Struggle) (Tehran: Seyyed Jamal, n.d.).

[105] Quoted in Pedram, *Roshanfekran-e Dini va Moderniteh dar Iran Pas az Enqelab* (Religious Intellectuals and Modernity in Iran after the Revolution), p. 96.

[106] Ibid., p. 98.

[107] Ganji, *Sonnat, Moderniteh, Post-modern* (Tradition, Modernity, Post-Modern), p. 157.

[108] Davari, *Darbareh-ye Gharb* (Concerning the West), p. 64.

[109] Ganji, *Sonnat, Moderniteh, Post-modern* (Tradition, Modernity, Post-Modern), p. 157.

pressing of which is commonly perceived to be the perennial "what is to be done?" – leaves his readers and commentators unsatisfied with his ambiguous, overly philosophical expositions.[110] This is particularly the case in relation to the issue of the reformist religious discourse, for which Davari is widely and publicly known to have little patience. Without much elaboration, he criticizes religious reformism through oblique references and accusations, such as its alleged treatment of society as if it were a "mechanical mechanism."[111]

The Iranian intellectual

All of this begs the question of precisely what category of individuals can be classified as "intellectuals." More specifically, given the tectonic changes in Iran due to and since the 1978–79 revolution, precisely who is an intellectual, and, more importantly, what is the nature of his or her role in and responsibility toward the larger polity? Does the emergence of the so-called Fourth Generation of intellectuals portend more fundamental changes to the role and responsibilities of intellectuals as a distinct social formation? And, along the same lines, is there a shift in the perceptions that the urban middle classes have toward those whom they generally consider to be "intellectuals"?

Given that so much of the intellectual focus has been directed at exploring the notion and phenomenon of modernity, and also, as we will see shortly, given that most Iranian authors assume there to be an inextricable link between modernity on the one hand and intellectualdom on the other, recent years have seen a proliferation of scholarly works concerning the identity and predicament of intellectuals.[112] This is in sharp contrast to the years before the revolution, when Al-e

---

[110] See, for example, Kaji, *Kisti-ye ma az Negah-e Roshanfekran-e Irani* (Our Existence from the Perspective of Iranian Intellectuals), pp. 120–23.

[111] Davari, *Darbareh-ye Gharb* (Concerning the West), p. 50.

[112] The citations in the coming paragraphs should demonstrate the scope of the discussion on the topic of intellectuals in some of Iran's most notable scholarly journals, especially *Aftab, Nameh,* and *Jame'h No.* In addition to these and numerous other articles on the topic, some of the books that have dealt with the subject include: 'Alireza 'Alavi-Tabar, *Roshanfekri, Dindari, Mardomsalari* (Intellectualism, Religiosity, Democracy) (Tehran: Farhang-o Andisheh, 1379/2000); Hosein Amanian, *Kalbodshekafi-e Jaryan-haye Roshanfekri va Eslahtalabi dar Iran* (Autopsy of Intellectual and Reformist Trends in Iran) (Tehran: Porseman, 1382/2003); Mas'oud Razavi, *Roshanfekran, Ahzab, va Manaf'e Melli* (Intellectuals, Parties, and National Interests) (Tehran: Farzan-e Ruz, 1379/2000); Ramin Jahanbegloo, *Moderniteh, Demokrasi va Roshanfekran* (Modernity, Democracy and Intellectuals) (Tehran: Markaz, 1374/1995); and Yahya Yathrebi, *Majara-ye Qamangiz-e Roshanfekri dar Iran* (Tragic Adventure of Enlightenment in Iran) (Tehran: Danesh va Andisheh Mo'aser, 1379/2000).

Ahmad's *On the Service and Treason of Intellectuals* long remained as one of the only works on the subject.[113] One might even speculate that it was perhaps the most widely read work on the subject.

In broad terms, the burgeoning literature on intellectuals and intellectualdom falls into two general categories, one more definitional in nature and the other more critical. The first category of literature presents a political history of intellectualism in Iran, defines the cultural positions that intellectuals have historically occupied in the country, and seeks to clarify and analyze the identity of intellectuals as a distinct social class.[114] More specifically, this genre of literature examines the roles and responsibilities of intellectuals in relation to society, seeking to answer questions such as whether or not an intellectual ought to be merely a social and political critique or a prophet promising to deliver the masses from misery. Literally every single author, whether religious or secular, modernist or traditional, defines intellectuals as an innately critical class whose most pressing social responsibility is to pose questions about the order of things. That this questioning revolves more around the profane than the sacred will be discussed more fully below.

There is another, equally copious volume of literature devoted to criticizing the social and political roles and the scholarly outputs of Iranian intellectuals over the last few decades. Although much of this critical literature echoes the criticisms that Ramin Jahanbegloo has articulated in relation to the "third generation" of Iranian intellectuals – as having been, among other things, ideological and dogmatic – in some respects it goes beyond the ideological/non-ideological divide and is directed at the writings and philosophical outputs of the so-called "Fourth Generation" itself.

There is general consensus over the definition of intellectuals as a distinct social and cultural class. The authors writing on the subject agree that the intellectual is someone whose primary task is to critique the prevailing social and political orders.[115] According to Behnam, "the

---

[113] Jalal Al-e Ahmad. *Dar Khedmat va Khiyanat-e Roshanfekran* (On the Service and Treason of Intellectuals), Volumes I–II (Tehran: Kharazmi, 1357/1978).

[114] Examples of some of the books that specifically examine the political history of intellectuals and intellectualism in Iran over the last century or so include Amanian, *Kalbodshekafi-e Jaryan-haye Roshanfekri va Eslahtalabi dar Iran* (Autopsy of Intellectual and Reformist Trends in Iran); Hamid Ahmadi and Mohammad Hosein Fatehian, eds., *Jaryan-e Roshanfekri va Roshanfekran dar Iran* (The Trend of Intellectuals and Intellectualism in Iran) (Qom: Beh Bavaran, 1379/2000); and Yathrebi, *Majara-ye Qamangiz-e Roshanfekri dar Iran* (Tragic Adventure of Enlightenment in Iran), among others.

[115] Amanian, *Kalbodshekafi-e Jaryan-haye Roshanfekri va Eslahtalabi dar Iran* (Autopsy of Intellectual and Reformist Trends in Iran), p. 138.

central responsibility of the intellectual is to be aware of the surrounding world and to keep abreast of developments in science and technology." "The intellectual must know the world and also his own culture and society. He cannot seek after personal or corporate gains, but must instead advocate that which benefits his society. Since people tend to respect the intellectual, his prime responsibility is to be honest and frank with them."[116]

Ali Mirsepassi, who teaches at New York University but whose writings in Persian are popular in Iranian academic circles, similarly defines an intellectual as someone who poses more questions than provides answers, in the process entering into a public dialogue with a society's traditional culture.[117] "The intellectual is not a specialist telling people how to live but is instead both a teacher and a student," looking at social and political issues from all relevant angles and posing searching questions before the public.[118] The author Habibollah Peyman is equally emphatic in the intellectual's charge: critical thinking, a relentless search for truth about one's own self and one's society, and the establishment of a symbiotic relationship with society whereby self-growth reinforces the growth of society.[119] Hamid 'Azadanlou (b. 1948), who teaches political science at Tehran's Azad University, goes one step further. Even before producing knowledge that constructs the future, he maintains, the intellectual's primary responsibility is to critically understand the past and to also strike "a relationship between himself and his invention on the one hand and with the present (modernity) on the other."[120] The intellectual, therefore, plays a crucial role in the era of modernity. His task is to constantly change the present and to permanently create a new world.[121]

The important connection between *intellectuals* and *modernity* will be explored more fully below, in the next chapter. Suffice it to say here that the significance of the link between the two phenomena is a prominent theme in the writings of Ramin Jahanbegloo as well. For his part, Jahanbegloo traces the origins of the development of the "intellectual" to Emile Zola's *J'Accuse* (1898), an open letter written by the French

[116] Behnam and Jahanbegloo, *Tamaddon va Tajaddod* (Civilization and Modernity), p. 26.
[117] Ali Mirsepassi. *Demokrasi ya Haqiqat: Rasale-ee Jame'h-shenakhti dar bab-e Roshanfekri-ye Irani* (Democracy or Truth: A Sociological Study on Iranian Intellectuals) (Tehran: Tarh-e No, 1381/2002), p. 128.
[118] Ibid., p. 128.
[119] Habibollah Peyman, "Estebdad-e Roshanfekri" (Intellectual Autocracy), *Jame'h No*, Vol. 2, No. 14 (1382/2003), p. 6.
[120] Hamid 'Azadanlou, *Gofteman va Jame'h* (Discourse and Society) (Tehran: Ney, 1380/2001), p. 115.
[121] 'Azadanlou, *Gofteman va Jame'h* (Discourse and Society), p. 115.

novelist (1840–1902) as an indictment of the trumped up charges against Captain Alfred Dreyfus in the infamous Dreyfus Affair. The intellectual, Jahanbegloo asserts, must therefore necessarily have a conscience and a strong sense of moral and political responsibility.[122] Moreover, the intellectual is "a free-thinking citizen who is not concerned with mythologizing and myth-making. The modern intellectual is not a maker of idols but one who breaks them, one who looks at the world objectively and not subjectively and with emotions."[123]

The intellectual is one who thinks, and at the same time transfers his thoughts to others. From this perspective he is one who tries to serve the greater good, and by so doing maintains an intimate relationship with it . . . If the intellectual thinks about his society, it is because he feels a responsibility toward "others", all the while as society negates his true value and his rights as a thinking citizen. At the same time, since the ruling establishment seeks to separate the intellectual from the larger society, most intellectuals assume an oppositional posture. He is not necessarily an opponent of power. But, inasmuch as he assumes the right to sit in judgment, he guards his right to independently criticize political institutions and centers of power.[124]

There is, in fact, a direct relationship between the intellectual as a social class and democratic pluralism as a political phenomenon. The absence of ideological or normative lenses through which intellectuals see the world makes them receptive to a plurality of political and philosophical perspectives. They welcome discourse and do not see the world in terms of friends and enemies. These "discourse intellectuals" serve as catalysts for democracy and civic values.[125]

Saeed Razavi Faqih, a prominent student activist affiliated with the University of Tehran, is equally explicit in outlining the duties and responsibilities of intellectuals:

The intellectual class is made up of diverse social groups such as academics, writers, artists, and others who, regardless of their profession or political perspectives or cultural views, have a critical outlook toward their cultural and intellectual heritage and are inherently critical of their own social predicament . . . An intellectual is critical of tradition and power. Since tradition and power have a symbiotic and reinforcing relationship with one another, whichever one the intellectual criticizes leads him to a critique of the other one as well.[126]

---

[122] Jahanbegloo, *Moderniteh, Demokrasi va Roshanfekran*, p. 65.   [123] Ibid., p. 70.
[124] Jahanbegloo. *Modern-ha* (The Moderns), pp. 19–20.
[125] Jahanbegloo, *Moderniteh, Demokrasi va Roshanfekran* (Modernity, Democracy and Intellectuals), p. 70.
[126] Saeed Razavi Faqih, "Mafhoum-e Roshanfekri-ye Dini" (The Meaning of Religious Intellectualism), *Aftab*, No. 27 (1382/2003), p. 78.

The author and academic Manochehr Ashtiani goes one step further and attributes four specific characteristics to intellectuals: enlightenment; critical thinking; humanism; and a global outlook.[127] Ashtiani admits that "humanism" has been maligned in Iran due to its perceived opposition to or negation of religion. The real essence and spirit of humanism, he maintains, is not innately anti- or even non-religious but is, in fact, deeply concerned with casting aside pre-existing social bonds and with ensuring the wellbeing of humans.[128] Along similar lines, Mohtaram Rahmani maintains that the intellectuals' primary responsibility is to first get to know their own selves and then to devise ways of establishing meaningful nexus with the larger population, an endeavor in which, he claims, Iranian intellectuals have so far failed.[129] Intellectuals must not content themselves with the mere consumption of ideas, claims sociologist Hasan Mahdasi. They must learn from existing ideas to come up with new ones, becoming creators instead of remaining as imitators.[130]

Another general point of consensus revolves around the relationship between intellectualism and modernity. Modernity, the general argument goes, has facilitated the spread of ideas and the growth of public opinion, both of which play key roles in the constitution of power, not only in the West but also in "peripheral societies" as well. The modern construction of power has to rely on the manipulation or suppression of ideas, and, as such, intellectuals, who trade in ideas, have emerged as fundamentally important in the modern era.[131] Even Davari, who is generally perceived to hold "anti-modernist" views, maintains that there is a direct relationship between modernity as a phenomenon and the birth and the mission of intellectuals as a social class.[132] When modernity – which for Davari is the same as Westernization – resulted in a separation of religion and politics, it opened the door to a flourishing of secular ideas that sought to make sense of the universe and the order of

---

[127] Razavi, *Roshanfekran, Ahzab, va Manaf'e Melli* (Intellectuals, Parties, and National Interests), pp. 6–10, 20.

[128] Ibid., p. 10.

[129] Mohtaram Rahmani, "Roshanfekr Tolidkonandeh Ast" (The Intellectual Is a Producer), *Jame'h No*, Vol. 1, No. 9 (1381/2002), pp. 16–17.

[130] Hasan Mahdasi, "Roshanfekr Masraf-konandeh Nist" (Intellectual is not a Consumer), *Jame'h No*, No. 9 (1381/2002), p. 19.

[131] Mohammad Javad Gholamreza Kashi, "Danesh-Qodrat va Prozhe-ye Roshanfekri dar Iran" (Knowledge-Power and the Intellectual Project in Iran), *Jame'h No*, Vol. 1, No. 7 (1381/2002), p. 9.

[132] Reza Davari Ardekani. "Roshanfekri va Roshanfekran" (Intellectualism and Intellectuals), in Ahmadi and Fatehian, eds., *Jaryan-e Roshanfekri va Roshanfekran dar Iran* (The Trend of Intellectuals and Intellectualism in Iran), p. 15. Not surprisingly, as will be explored more fully below, Davari generally does not hold intellectuals in high esteem.

things, thus giving rise to the intellectual classes.[133] In a country like Iran, which, as Jahanbegloo maintains, is in a transitional stage, the role of the intellectual is all the more pivotal in critiquing, questioning, and exploring the meanings of modernity, identity, and national as well as universal, global heritage.[134]

Perhaps not surprisingly, there has also been considerable criticism directed at the current nature and the evolution of intellectualism in Iran. This criticism has come primarily from two camps that may be broadly grouped into the traditionalists and modernists. In broad terms, the modernists subscribe to Jahanbegloo's notion of a discourse-orientated Fourth Generation but criticize Iran's intellectual tradition for its philosophical poverty, its social and cultural elitism, and its lack of courage in tackling substantive issues revolving around matters such as national identity, modernity, and democratic pluralism. The tradition-alists, on the other hand, by and large continue to perceive of intellec-tuals in the same vein as Al-e Ahmad did, seeing them as inebriated with all things new and Western and far too eager to abandon anything smacking of tradition. The most prominent of these thinkers is – not surprisingly – Reza Davari.[135]

Observing social etiquette, most of the contemporary writers eschew naming the individuals whose arguments they criticize, except, of course, Al-e Ahmad and Shariati, both of whom have long been dead. This makes it difficult at times to determine whether the criticism is directed at the so-called third generation intellectuals or at other con-temporaries. Although these are at best conjectures, several consider-ations prompt me to think that the criticism is directed more at present colleagues and authors than at past theorists and ideologues. To begin with, most contemporary writers appear to have little or no difficulty mentioning the names of Al-e Ahmad and Shariati when blaming them

---

[133] Ibid.

[134] Ramin Jahanbegloo, "Roshanfekr-e Nasl-e Chaharom va Haqiqat-i Faratar az Ideolozhi" (Fourth Generation Intellectual and a Truth Bigger than Ideology), *Jame'h No*, Vol. 2, No. 16 (1382/2003), p. 9.

[135] The "modernist" and "traditionalist" categorizations of the critiques of intellectuals are ideal types into which not all writers on the subject fit. For example, Ali Yusofian criticizes Iranian intellectuals for having consistently failed to grasp the essence of the esoteric existence of Iranians and the knowledge (*ma'refat*) that has underwritten it. Iranian society, he argues, is still governed by pre-modern philosophical notions that support a vertical, hierarchical arrangement of society stretching from the executive-religious hierarchies at the top to the masses below. Advocacy of horizontal, pluralist perspectives is doomed to failure so long as this pre-modern mentality is not understood and theorized about. See Ali Yusofian, "Bohran-e Roshanfekri va Tajdid-e Nezam-e Selseleh-maratedi" (Crisis of Intellectualism and Renewal of the Hierarchical System), *Aftab*, No. 34 (1383/2004), pp. 78–81.

for having laid the wrong intellectual foundation for the Iran of today. Instead, the general language used in the literature uses the generic "intellectual" (*roshanfekr*) or, at times, in the self-deprecating style commonplace in Iran, "us intellectuals" (*ma roshanfekran*). It is hard to view the intellectuals' criticism as directed at any group other than their own contemporaries.

Some of the most biting criticisms against intellectuals have come from the author Habibollah Peyman. Iranian intellectuals, he maintains, have consistently failed to produce original thought and have, from the very beginning of their appearance, simply imported views and ideas from the outside through translated books and articles.[136] They only superficially understand critical notions and phenomena such as "social capital," "democracy," and "civil society."[137] This has resulted in their weakness as a viable and effective social group and, more fundamentally, has made them intolerant of others with differing views. Iranian intellectuals may be willing to suffer all sorts of physical and economic hardships because of their ideals and their beliefs, but they are seldom willing to tolerate other intellectuals whose views may be different from theirs.[138] Out of a deep sense of insecurity and intolerance, each individual intellectual sees others in the same category as either ignorant and misled or a personal nuisance, at best negated whenever necessary or at least avoided if at all possible. This has perpetuated the persistent lack of philosophical depth in Iran's intellectual tradition and has obstructed the growth of various types of intellectual discourse in the country.[139]

Although less personal and blunt in the tone of their criticism, a number of other writers have been equally critical of the Iranian intellectuals' lack of intimate familiarity with the essence and heritage of their own society. Hosein Ansari, for example, maintains that Iranian intellectuals have been unable to strike a "dialectical relationship" with their tradition, thus finding themselves confronted with a national heritage and a society which they understand little.[140] While this has been particularly the case with secular intellectuals, the appearance of a number of "religious intellectuals" after the revolution – such as Soroush and Mojtahed Shabestari – is beginning to somewhat remedy this

---

[136] Peyman, "Estebdad-e Roshanfekri" (Intellectual Autocracy), p. 7.
[137] Habibollah Peyman, "Roshanfekran Zir-e Tigh-e Naqd" (Intellectuals under Critical Blade), *Jame'h No*, Vol. 2, No. 15 (1382/2003), p. 10.
[138] Peyman, "Estebdad-e Roshanfekri" (Intellectual Autocracy), pp. 7–8.
[139] Ibid., p. 9.
[140] Hosein Ansari, "Roshanfekri-ye Irani va Eslah az Daroun" (Iranian Intellectualism and Reform from Within), *Aftab*, No. 27 (1382/2003), p. 86.

deficiency.[141] Nevertheless, today there are still those who espouse post-modernist ideas (that may have relevance for the West) for a society that is still in the midst of passage to modernism.[142]

Rahmani similarly laments the continuing cultural and communication chasm between intellectuals on the one hand and the urban middle classes on the other.[143] Rahmani divides Iran's intellectual currents into three – secular, Marxist, and religious – and maintains that none have properly understood Iranian culture and society and have therefore been unable to maintain a meaningful nexus with it. This has been particularly the case with Marxist and secular intellectual trends; it is still far too early to determine the success or failure of religious intellectuals.[144] This lack of success is partly a product of the intellectuals' own hurried embrace of theoretical models that are meant to liberate their society. It is also partly a product of the larger predicaments within which Iran and its intellectuals find themselves:

The phenomenon of the West, the crisis of colonialism, and other political and social crises, both big and small, have not given a chance to Iranian intellectuals to critically examine their own selves. Passage from one crisis to another, and their subsequent efforts to continually adapt to new and changing circumstances, have robbed these intellectuals of the ability to have the effect and the presence that their efforts would otherwise warrant. Intellectual trends in Iran are born into crisis, have to contend with crisis, and fade into crisis.[145]

Most of these and other similar criticisms levied against the current state of intellectualism in Iran come from individuals who maintain a rather pronounced and deliberate distance from Al-e Ahmad's overtly ideological position on the subject. They see Al-e Ahmad – as well as Shariati – as belonging to a generation whose time has passed, and whose revolutionary condemnation of the West and ideological celebration of tradition is largely irrelevant today. As mentioned previously, the self-described "discourse intellectuals" of today have little tolerance for their revolutionary predecessors of a generation ago.

But this is not always the case. For a substantial segment of the country's academics and learned elite who may be classified as comparatively "traditional," the legacy of the thoughts of Al-e Ahmad and Shariati still looms large. This is particularly the case in relation to the role and function of intellectuals, whose alleged tendency to blindly imitate the West was the subject of some of Al-e Ahmad's most

---

[141] Ibid., pp. 87–88.   [142] Ibid., p. 88.
[143] Mohtaram Rahmani, "Aseeb-shenasi-ye Jaryan-haye Roshanfekri dar Iran" (Studying the Flaws of Intellectual Trends in Iran), *Aftab*, No. 27 (1382/2003), p. 96.
[144] Ibid., p. 96.   [145] Ibid., p. 97.

blistering attacks.[146] Perhaps the most influential of this crop of authors is Reza Davari, who openly acknowledges his debt to Al-e Ahmad's thoughts on the subject.[147] According to Davari, Al-e Ahmad's thoughts on intellectuals were basically correct; the problem was that he simply criticized them without placing them and the phenomenon they represented in a larger theoretical and philosophical context.[148] Not surprisingly, Davari does not hold Iranian intellectuals in very high esteem, viewing them as opportunistic and, worse, Westoxicated.

In sharp contrast to the avowedly non-ideological intellectuals of the Fourth Generation, Davari maintains that the basic task of the intellectual is to propagate an ideology and to engage in ideological debates.[149] This means that those with true religious beliefs cannot be intellectuals, as religious beliefs are different – and are above and beyond – ideological positions.[150] This is, on the one hand, a not-too-subtle rebuttal of the arguments of Soroush and other religious intellectuals for whom Davari is known to have little patience. On the other hand, it bespeaks of the extent to which Davari's own philosophical positions are imbued with conceptions of religion that seek to separate the sacred and the profane into distinct – and perhaps only remotely related – arenas. Insofar as the intellectual is concerned, he ought to content himself with ideological endeavors and leave religious theorizing to religious specialists, by whom Davari appears to imply the clergy (as Al-e Ahmad had done earlier). Iranian intellectuals, at any rate, have only left behind a sorry legacy of failures and misguided contributions.

The intellectual, who has become familiar with the modern science and especially with the social sciences and the humanities, is unfamiliar with his own house and is alienated from it. While assuming he knows the sciences and that everyone else is ignorant, it is the intellectual himself who suffers from the most ignorance. He neither understands the people's language, nor do the people understand the artificial language he speaks. He only repeats some of what is said in Western intellectual circles. If he writes a book, it is generally a repetition of some of the thoughts he has picked up from the West, although his work is devoid of the spirit of Western scholarship. Despite what he claims, our intellectual is unfamiliar with his own historical predicament, and his feet are not firmly grounded in reality. The intellectual is Westoxicated, and it is not surprising that Al-e Ahmad wrote about both intellectualism and Westoxication.[151]

---

[146] See, for example, Yathrebi, *Majara-ye Qamangiz-e Roshanfekri dar Iran* (Tragic Adventure of Enlightenment in Iran), pp. 122–23.

[147] Reza Davari Ardekani, "Roshanfekri va Roshanfekran" (Intellectualism and Intellectuals), pp. 13–15.

[148] Ibid., pp. 16–17.   [149] Ibid., p. 15.   [150] Ibid., pp. 15, 20.   [151] Ibid., pp. 24–25.

Westoxication, Davari maintains, has been an integral feature of Iranian history for the last hundred years or so, and inattention to this truth means falling into the trap of Westoxication itself.[152] "Our intellectuals have failed to grasp the reality of the West," he laments, "and, in the process of acquiring a superficial understanding of it, have become its devotees."[153] The spirit of their scholarship is one of imitation and superficiality, devoid of philosophical depth and substance. What the Iranian intellectual ideally ought to do is to rediscover Islam, Davari argues without much elaboration.[154] "The pairing of Islam with any ideology, regardless of where that ideology may be from, and the conception of Islam and the Islamic revolution with any non-Islamic ideology or philosophy, is both detrimental to Islam and the Islamic revolution and detracts from the truth of the religion."[155]

Conclusion

The ferocity of their convictions notwithstanding, the arguments of Davari are not widely shared in many of the more scholarly journals and magazines that in today's Iran have wide readership. The intellectual trend currently gathering steam in Iran places Davari and other philosophical "traditionalists" in a clear minority. This is an intellectual current that is deeply and profoundly aware of itself, its social and political environments, and the discourse it is constructing. This intellectual current is constructing a discourse that has "changed" and "evolved" into what it is today, one that articulates itself consciously and is mindful of its past – a past it seeks more to negate rather than to validate. The ensuing discourse is one born out of life in the post-revolutionary period, war and mass mobilization, reconstruction and repression, deflation and excitement, tradition and modernity. What is ensuing is a uniquely Iranian discourse.

[152] Ibid., p. 26.   [153] Ibid., p. 29.   [154] Ibid., p. 33.   [155] Ibid., p. 34.

4   The conservative religious discourse

Recent years have seen a proliferation of studies on the ideological and political divides that today mark the Islamic Republican political system in Iran.[1] These ideological divides became especially acute after the emergence of the so-called second republic that followed the end of the war with Iraq in 1988 and the death of Ayatollah Khomeini the following year, when the post-revolutionary system lost some of the institutional and ideological cohesion. There have also been a few works on the appearance of "reformist" political figures within the Islamic Republic, and, more significantly, on Shi'a thinkers whose theories present alternative interpretations of religion's role in the polity – figures such as Abdolkarim Soroush, Mohsen Kadivar, and Mohammad Mojtahed Shabestari.[2] There have, however, been very few treatments of the theoretical dispositions of Iran's more conservative Shi'a ulama and thinkers in the post-Khomeini era, with most of the studies on the subject either being dated by now or, alternatively, concentrating on larger social and cultural issues.[3]

This chapter offers a preliminary examination of some of the main characteristics and major themes in the conservative religious discourse in Iran over the last decade or so.[4] More specifically, the chapter looks at the multiple layers and the changing political contexts within which the conservative religious current articulates its positions and reproduces itself, as well as the characteristics and positions of some main figures

---

[1] See, for example, Ehteshami, *After Khomeini*; Buchta, *Who Rules Iran?*; Brumberg, *Reinventing Khomeini*; and Mehdi Moslem, *Factional Politics in Post-Khomeini Iran* (Syracuse, NY: Syracuse University Press, 2002).

[2] See Mahmoud Sadri and Ahmad Sadri, *Reason, Freedom, and Democracy in Islam: The Essential Writings of Abdolkarim Soroush* (Oxford: Oxford University Press, 2000); and Mehran Kamrava, "Iranian Shiism under Debate," *Middle East Policy*, Vol. 10, No. 2 (2003), pp. 102–12.

[3] A recent example includes Juan Cole's insightful *Sacred Space and Holy War: The Politics, Culture and History of Shi'ite Islam* (London: I. B. Tauris, 2002).

[4] In Iran, the conservatives are often collectively referred to as "the Right," and the two labels are used interchangeably here.

involved in the discourse. This requires also an examination of the larger features of the Right's discourse in relation to the Iranian polity, especially as it compares with the "leftist", "reformist" religious discourse with which it competes. Finally, the chapter analyzes some of the more specific themes that the discourse tackles, and offers some thoughts about the discourse's possible future prospects.

I argue here that the conservative religious discourse eschews theoretical and doctrinal innovativeness unless doing so is made absolutely necessary by evolving political circumstances. Instead, it prefers to focus on reinforcing theological notions that have either long been accepted within mainstream Iranian Shi'a *fiqh*, or, alternatively, have become an accepted and integral part of the official theological discourse since the establishment of the Islamic Republic. Not surprisingly, the Right's theoretical emphasis has been on interpreting, and then preserving and strengthening, those jurisprudential notions within Shi'ism that legitimize the conservative clergy's continued hold on political power. At the same time, there has been a somewhat belated and reluctant recognition of some of the "problems" associated with the phenomenon of modernity – civil society, pluralism, civil rights, globalization, and the like – and, as a result, there have been certain defensive responses by the architects of the conservative discourse. Despite a number of external stimuli for change, however, the conservative discourse is unlikely to change or modify direction in the foreseeable future in any discernible measure barring major shifts in Iranian politics, an unlikely event given recent political developments in the country.

Before proceeding further, the use of the term *discourse* as employed here needs to be clarified. This is especially important in light of the question of whether or not the conservative body of religious thought examined here indeed constitutes a *discourse* at all. In Iran, in both scholarly and lay circles, the designation of discourse (*gofteman*) is used frequently to refer to on-going intellectual efforts to strike synchronicity between Shi'a jurisprudence and notions of modernity.[5] Reformist thinkers, in fact, often see their writings and publications as deliberate and self-conscious efforts to contribute to an evolving discourse that inheres a relatively deep level of theoretical consistency. This is not the case in relation to the writings of conservative thinkers, who see their contributions more as a reflection of the actual essence of Shi'a jurisprudence rather than as how it ought to be. As will be argued shortly, although conservative thinkers do not openly call for an end to

---

[5] Kadivar, *Tahavvol-e Gofteman-e Siyasi-e Shi'a dar Iran* (The Development of Shi'a Political Discourse in Iran), pp. 40–43.

independent reasoning (*ijtihad*), they see themselves as its guardians. And, indeed, they have been strict in their guardianship.

While the conservative religious thinkers themselves may prefer avoiding the term "discourse" in referring to their theoretical positions, it does appear that these positions and arguments, as articulated in an expansive body of literature, indeed do constitute a discourse. Conservative religious thought has a basic narrative, a set of propositions, and relatively consistent themes of analysis – all elements that constitute a "discourse."[6]

Contextualizing the Right

Given the current composition and structure of the Iranian political system, there is an intimate set of ideological and institutional connections between highly conservative, high-ranking Shi'a clerics, all senior Ayatollahs, and the most significant political office in the land, namely the Leader (*Rahbar*). These organic links between the two are institutionalized through the Assembly of Experts, a popularly elected body of senior Ayatollahs who in turn select the Leader. The primary concern of both the Assembly of Experts and the current Leader, Ayatollah Ali Khamenei, has been to preserve the doctrinal and institutional legacy of the regime's founder, Ayatollah Khomeini. Consequently, in the current system *political* and *religious* conservatism have assumed a symbiotic, mutually reinforcing relationship, often overlapping and completing one another. Much of the current religious conservative thought, therefore, is directed toward sustaining the prevailing political arrangements as designed by Khomeini. Nevertheless, as we shall see below, there are important strands within the conservative theological current – as, for example, represented by Ayatollah Hoseinali Montazeri – that are parallel to but remain very much outside of the political establishment. At the same time, in addition to political issues, most conservative clerics continue to pay attention to those issues on which they have focused traditionally, such as morality (*akhlaq*) and ethics.[7] Nonetheless, the current convergence of religious and political conservatism under the broader institutional umbrella of the Islamic Republic has resulted in an ever-greater level of attention being paid to political issues by the more conservative clergy both practically and theoretically.

---

[6] Norman Fairclough, *Discourse and Social Change* (Cambridge: Polity, 1993), pp. 40–41.

[7] See, for example, Mojtaba Mesbah, *Faslafeh-ye Akhlaq* (Moral Philosophy) (Qom: Mo'asseseh-e Amozeshi va Pazhoheshi-e Emam Khomeini, 1378/1999).

Religious and political conservatives in Iran are often collectively referred to as "the Right,"[8] and the two labels are at times used interchangeably here. Nevertheless, the Right does need to be disaggregated since it includes a diverse array of political and doctrinal persuasions. There are a number of ways to classify the different groups and individuals who collectively comprise the Right, and various typologies based on theological arguments, institutional affiliations, or political alignments are likely to yield differing though equally valid classifications.[9] One reason for this is the fluid institutional and ideological contexts within which these groups operate and their changing political and doctrinal positions over time. Adding to the difficulty in deciphering their orientation and significance is the fact that some groups are at times politically eclipsed, or cease operations altogether, only to re-emerge with renewed vigor at a later point.[10] Moreover, most of these groups maintain deep, organic ties to one another, thus making clear and consistent distinctions between them difficult and not always applicable.[11]

Despite these difficulties, in order to better understand its doctrinal outputs, it is important to distinguish between the main tendencies that comprise the Right. At the broadest level, the Right may be divided into the radicals and the conservatives (Table 1). Within this broad radical–conservative spectrum, four general categories may be distinguished, beginning with the extremist radical rightists, followed by rightist, traditionalist clerics, the Islamic councils, and, finally, neo-conservative thinkers and scholars. Of these four groups, only two – the traditionalist clergy and the neo-conservative thinkers – may be said to engage in the serious production of ideology. The radical Right, whose members are often generically referred to as the Hezbollah, prefers local activism to in-depth theorizing. This activism often takes the form of disrupting

---

[8] Mohammad Heidari, "Rastgarayan Iran-e Emrouz" (Rightists in Today's Iran), *Nameh*, No. 19 (1381/2002), p. 15.

[9] For some of these typologies see, for example, Heidari, "Rastgarayan Iran-e Emrouz" (Rightists in Today's Iran), pp. 15–19; 'Alireza 'Alavi-Tabar, "No-Andishane Rast" (The Right's New Thinkers), *Nameh*, No. 19 (1381/2002), pp. 4–5; and K. Azad, "Marz-banidye Rast-e Sonnati va Shabakeh-ye Vahshat" (The Position of the Traditional Right and the Network of Terror), *Cheshmandaz-e Iran*, Vol. 1, No. 4 (1379/2000), pp. 62–63.

[10] The Hojjatiyeh Society, for example, which is known for its staunch belief in the free market and its opposition to the concept of the *faqih*, became extremely influential in the early years of the revolution until Ayatollah Khomeini disbanded it. While still technically banned, occasional uncorroborated reports at times maintain that many of the group's sympathizers continue to hold key positions throughout the various institutions of the state.

[11] Azad, "Marz-banidye Rast-e Sonnati va Shabakeh-ye Vahshat" (The Position of the Traditional Right and the Network of Terror), p. 62.

Table 1 *Disaggregating the Right*

Radicals		Conservatives	
Radical Right	Traditionalist clergy	Islamic councils	Neo-conservative thinkers
Former Fadaiyan-e Islam members, traditionalist bazaaris, former and present Baseej members, as well as members of the Hey'at-e Mo'talefeh, former Hojjatiyeh Society, and the loosely organized Hezbollah groups	Politically influential conservative clerics based in Tehran, Qom, and the provinces, affiliated with the Howzeh 'Elmiyyeh, the Imam Khomeini Education and Research Institute, the Assembly of Experts, and the Rouhaniyyat-e Mobarez group. Includes most Friday Prayer Imams and the "Leader's Representatives" on various state bodies	Active on university campuses and among certain professional groups, such as engineers	Lay and clerical scholars and thinkers generally supportive of the Islamic Republican system, though some calling for modifications to its *modus operandi* and certain institutional features
Notable figures: 'Asgar-Oladi Badamchian	Ay. Mesbah Yazdi Ay. Javadi Amoli Ay. Jannati Hoj. Nateq-Nouri Ay. Yazdi		Ay. Montazeri Prof. Davari Ardekani

speeches and meetings featuring secular or religious reformist thinkers, holding rallies and demonstrations in support of the *Rahbar*'s edicts, harassing women in the streets with poor *hijab*, and, in a few instances, attacking university dormitories after student protests.[12] Not surprisingly, the radical Right is fervently ideological, having cemented many of its core beliefs during the early years of post-revolutionary consolidation and the war with Iraq, for which many willingly volunteered. "Fundamentalist" (*osulgara*) in the true sense of the word, the radical Right often exhibits a fanatical devotion to the personality and ideas of "Imam" Khomeini and the position and statements of the current *Rahbar*, Ayatollah Khamenei. While the radical Right's rhetoric and slogans contain frequent references to notions such as "imperialism," "oppression," "class," and "cultural authenticity," its preferred method of operation is through violent attacks on supposed agents of moral and political corruption and enticing fear among them rather than engaging in cultural and ideological activism.[13]

Somewhat more benign but no less doctrinaire are some of the Islamic Associations (*Shoura-ye Eslami*) that are found on various university campuses and among professional associations and the state bureaucracy. The primary task of these Associations is to ensure the compliance of civil society with the regime's official doctrine and to keep a watchful eye on the potentially troublesome university professors and students. Again, these associations engage in little or no doctrinal production of their own, acting instead more as guardians and enforcers of the official orthodoxy.

The real task of articulating the conservative religious discourse falls on the remaining two groups – namely the traditionalist clergy and neo-conservative thinkers and *foqaha* (plural of *faqih*). In general terms,

---

[12] A number of university dormitories in Tehran were attacked between July 9 and 13, 1999, for example, following student agitations against persistent political repression. Many of the news reports and communiqués that were issued during those fateful five days were later published in Mohammad Ali Zakariaee, *Koy-e Daneshgah be Ravayat-e Rasaneh-ha* (University Dorm as Told by the Media) (Tehran: Kavir, 1378/1999). More analytical reflections on the "student movement" and its aftereffects can be found in 'Alireza 'Alavi-Tabar, "Molahezat-e Rahbordi dar barabar-e Jonbesh-e Daneshjo-i" (Methodological Considerations concerning the Student Movement), *Aftab*, No. 7 (1380/2001), pp. 10–13; and Mas'oud Razavi, "Chera-iye Yek Gosast: Hoviyyat-yabie Jonbesh-e Daneshjoee" (Analysis of a Rupture: The Identity of the Student Movement), *Nameh*, No. 24 (1382/2003), pp. 33–36.

[13] 'Alavi-Tabar, "No-Andishane Rast" (The Right's New Thinkers), p. 5. For a concise review of the radical Right's self-criticism of its tactics and strategies, especially insofar as "cultural activities" versus street events are concerned, see Mohammad Rahbar, "Hezbollah va Enteqad az Khod" (Hezbollah and Self-Criticism), *Jame'h No*, Vol. 1, No. 7 (1381/2002), p. 7.

whereas the traditionalist clergy are the primary articulators of the conservative religious discourse as adopted and officially espoused by the state, the neo-conservative thinkers form the loyal opposition, or at least as much of an opposition as the state allows. The *neo-conservatives* are not *reformist*, and they consciously abstain from too close an association with thinkers widely considered to be in the religious reformist camp. With Ayatollah Montazeri as their primary intellectual spokesperson, they embrace the overall jurisprudential underpinnings of the Islamic Republic but advocate modifications to some of its specific features and, if possible, criticize the conduct of its officials. Admittedly, given the strong ideological connotation of the label "neo-conservative" in the United States in recent years, I am somewhat uncomfortable with this designation. Nevertheless, within the Iranian context, the label succinctly sums up the doctrinal and jurisprudential positions of many who fall within its umbrella.

For their part, the traditionalist clergy's doctrinal output forms the backbone of the Islamic Republic's official ideology and discourse. It is among this group of clerics where the primary doctrinal pillars of the theocratic state are first articulated, then internally circulated, and ultimately transmitted to the larger society. I will explain this process more fully below. Before that, however, a few words on the traditionalist clergy's larger doctrinal orientations are in order.

To begin with, the traditionalist clergy's politico-religious outlook is what one Iranian observer has called "*shari'at*-centric," with *fiqh* as the primary arena within which solutions to contemporary social, political, and even economic issues are found.[14] They advocate the protection of traditional institutions such as the family, the bazaar, commercial ownership, and ritualized forms of worship.[15] Most importantly, as we shall see presently, they are staunch advocates of the concept of *Velayat-e Mutlaq-e Faqih*, or the Absolute Jurisconsult, which was enshrined in the constitution when the document was extensively revised in 1989. Perhaps the most notable intellectual figure representing the traditionalist clergy is Ayatollah Mohammad Taqi Mesbah Yazdi, both a prolific scholar and a most vocal – and often combative – advocate of the conservative religious current.

As mentioned earlier, there are three levels at which the traditionalist clergy's discourse is articulated: a scholarly one, emanating mostly out of Qom-based research institutes, the *Howzeh*, and the Assembly of Experts; an intermediate one, through which the Leader (Khamenei) and other high-ranking functionaries of the state, such as Rafsanjani,

---

[14] 'Alavi-Tabar, "No-Andishane Rast" (The Right's New Thinkers), p. 4.   [15] Ibid.

enunciate their priorities and the general outlines of state policy; and a populist one, whereby, largely through the medium of the pulpit, state policies and priorities are outlined for the public. Most of the jurisprudential positions taken by the traditionalist wing of the conservative religious discourse are first articulated by a professional cadre of theologians whose primary responsibility appears to be research and writing on issues of doctrinal import. Based mostly in Qom, these researchers tend to be affiliated with either the Imam Khomeini Educational and Research Institute, which is headed by Ayatollah Mesbah Yazdi and is closely linked to the *Howzeh*, the Qom *Howzeh* itself, or the research arm of the Assembly of Experts. All three institutions are based in Qom and most of their professional research staff is made up of clerics in the early stages of their clerical careers, except, of course, the teaching staff at the *Howzeh*, which is comprised of largely senior clerics. All three concentrate on the provision of facilities and resources for in-depth research on Shi'a jurisprudence, the end results of which are often published as books and journal articles. For its part, the research unit of the Assembly of Experts publishes the journal *Hokumat-e Eslami* (Islamic Government), whose rigorously crafted articles have turned it into one of the most important and influential forums for the articulation of the conservative religious discourse.

It is difficult to determine the exact readership of *Hokumat-e Eslami* and other similar journals and books. Anecdotal evidence suggests, however, that such publications have highly limited circulations and are read mostly by select *fiqh* specialists only.[16] Their primary purpose, therefore, appears to be the production and reproduction of theological doctrines and jurisprudential arguments that coalesce into the officially dominant conservative religious discourse.

Significantly, recent years have witnessed consistent efforts by the clerical establishment to revamp and modernize the curriculum of the *Howzeh* and other institutions of Islamic learning. For some time now, dating to the years before the revolution, a number of senior clerics have been keenly aware of the exigencies and shortcomings of the curriculum of *Howzeh*, particularly in relation to innovations in research methodology and familiarity with new information technologies. Efforts to remedy the problem have taken several complementary forms, ranging from sending seminary students abroad on educational scholarships to

---

[16] *Hokumat-e Eslami*, for example, is all but impossible to find in Tehran and in other provincial towns, and only one major bookshop in Qom carries it. It is, nevertheless, available on the World Wide Web (www.nezam.org), thus increasing its potential readership.

establishing modern universities that concentrate on the social sciences inside the country, with Qom's Mofid University, established by Ayatollah Mousavi Ardebili, being a case in point. Other efforts designed to compensate for the archaic nature of *Howzeh* curriculum include the recent proliferation of "scientific" research centers (*marakez-e 'elmi*), the forging of deeper ties with established universities through joint scholarly efforts, adjunct teaching positions, conferences, and seminars, and the publication of journals like the *Howzeh va Daneshgah* (Seminary and University).[17] Whether or not such initiatives will succeed in the long run in bridging some of the intellectual gap between the secular and religious institutions of higher learning remains to be seen. So far, however, they appear not to have had a precipitous effect on the nature and direction of the *ijtihad* coming out of the conservative camp.

Sandwiched in-between learned analyses of jurisprudential and theological matters on the one hand and the populist sermons of local preachers on the other, there is a second, intermediate level in which the conservative Shi'a discourse is articulated. This discourse is made up of the theoretical contributions to Shi'a jurisprudence by the current Leader in office, Ayatollah Khamenei, and to a lesser extent by Ayatollah Rafsanjani.[18] Neither man is considered to be an original thinker or is necessarily distinguished for his mastery of jurisprudence. In fact, both are known for their primary preoccupation with politics as opposed to *fiqh*. Nevertheless, even if only out of necessity due to the high offices they occupy, both have to engage in discussing issues related to *fiqh* and *ijtihad*. This is particularly the case with Ayatollah Khamenei, the *Rahbar*, for whom certain jurisprudential pronouncements are unavoidable. In addition to publishing books, Khamenei expounds on many of the salient themes within the conservative religious discourse in many of the speeches he gives, most of them delivered before like-minded audiences.[19] Although these speeches are not always theoretically rich and rigorously constructed, they do serve as an important indication of the areas and issues that the Leader considers as important. Thus setting the tone and signaling the importance of specific issues, Khamenei influences the larger direction and focus of the conservative religious discourse. The

[17] One of the recent issues of the journal, for example, included the following article: Moslem Khalqi, "Pazhouhesh-e Hoquqi dar Internet" (Judicial Research on the Internet), *Howzeh va Daneshgah*, Vol. 9, No. 36 (2003), pp. 123–37.

[18] In addition to the considerable unofficial powers he wields throughout the system, Rafsanjani officially occupies the position of Head of the Expediency Council.

[19] See, for example, Ali Khamenei, "Bayanat-e Rahbar-e Mo'azzam-e Enqelab-e Eslami dar Didar-e A'za-ye Majles-e Khobregan'e Rahbari" (The Speech of the Esteemed Leader of the Islamic Revolution in the Meeting of the Leadership Assembly of Experts), *Hokumat-e Eslami*, Vol. 8, No. 2 (2003), pp. 3–11.

cues sent are in turn picked up by researchers and by other clerics belonging to the traditionalist camp, who then write more detailed articles or books in which they elaborate on the themes touched on by the Leader.

There is a third level at which the conservative discourse is articulated. At this lowest level, the traditionalist religious discourse is more accessible to the larger masses and tends to be more populist in tone and emphasis. This "populist conservatism" often focuses on issues of more immediate concern to the urban classes, especially morality and ethics, and is often articulated by the Friday Prayer Imams, who also act as the Leader's official representatives to the various provincial cities.[20] Also important in articulating and disseminating this brand of religious conservative thought are many of the mass circulation newspapers on the right of the ideological spectrum – notably *Keyhan*, *Resalat*, and *Jomhuri Eslami*, to name a few – and many of the ordinary, low-ranking clerics commonly referred to as *akhunds*.

All of this, of course, begs the question of exactly who is and who is not a conservative theologian. More specifically, what qualifies some *fiqh* scholars and jurists as "conservative" and qualifies others as "reformist" or, for that matter, "radical"? A thinker's political stance only partially explains his or her ideological dispositions. There are, inevitably, deeper philosophical convictions that account for ideological and political orientations. For the jurists and scholars of *fiqh* in Iran, these deeper philosophical convictions are rooted in how they interpret and internalize the tenets of the faith. In other words, for them it is a question of *ijtihad*.

A question of *ijtihad*

It would be simplistic at best to reduce the genesis and evolution of the conservative religious discourse to on-going political dynamics and political considerations only. Undeniably, most of the prominent theorists and thinkers within the conservative religious fold are personally and professionally close to the prevailing centers of political power in

---

[20] One of the more colorful Friday Prayer Imams currently in office is Gholamreza Hasani, the FPI of Orumiyeh. In one of his sermons, for example, referring to reformist politicians and President Khatami, he said: "in the last four years you have tried to rob people of their beliefs and values, but you have not succeeded...Oh Messenger of God, these [reformists] have done their best to turn the people and the children of the revolution away from the Revolution. Instead, they have promoted dog ownership under the banner of democracy!" Gholamreza Hasani, *Khotbeh-haye Namaz-e Jom'eh Orumiyeh Hojjatoleslam Hasani* (Sermons of the Friday Prayer Leader of Orumiyeh Hojjatoleslam Hasani) (Tehran: Jamehdaran, 1382/2003), pp. 92–93.

today's Islamic Republic. But to assume that political alliances – which are by nature fluid and all too frequently impermanent – account for the sole or even overwhelming cause of the continued resilience of the conservative religious discourse is to ignore deeper, and historically more resilient, currents of thought in Islamic and Shi'a jurisprudence. At its core, what makes the conservative religious discourse *conservative* is its *ijtihad*, or, more specifically, the sources and inspiration for, the analytical and philosophical depth and extent of, and the conclusions reached by its *ijtihad*. Put simply, at the broadest level, *ijtihad* separates and clumps together different currents of jurisprudential analysis. In contemporary Iran, it has led to the emergence of two, loosely categorized, religious discourses, one that may be considered as comparatively conservative and another as reformist.

Ijtihad has long been one of the central pillars of Islamic and especially Shi'a *fiqh*. It means "independent reasoning" or, more specifically, "personal, independent judgment of a jurist to infer precepts from authoritative sources like the Qur'an and the *Sunna*."[21] At least in Sunni jurisprudence, *ijtihad* has often been used as a contrast to *taqlid*, or imitation. In cases where the Qur'an and the *Sunna* are silent, *ijtihad* "is considered a required religious duty for those qualified to perform it. It should be practiced by means of analogical and syllogistic reasoning (*qiyas*). Its results may not contradict the Qur'an, and it may not be used in cases where consensus (*ijma*) has been reached, according to many scholars."[22]

As Iran's state religion, Shi'ism has become increasingly more institutionalized since the time of the Safavids and has developed a highly differentiated hierarchal structure, headed, according to most interpretations, by the institution that is today commonly referred to as the *Marja'-e Taqlid* (Source of Emulation).[23] As we shall see below, some contemporary thinkers, including Ayatollah Khomeini, have combined the two institutions of *Marja'-e Taqlid* and *Velayat-e Faqih* while others have separated the two. At any rate, key to the notion of *Marja'-e Taqlid*, and for some also the *Velayat-e Faqih*, is the practices of *taqlid*. *Taqlid*

[21] Abdulaziz Abdulhussein Sachedina, *The Just Ruler in Shi'ite Islam: The Comprehensive Authority of the Jurist in Imamate Jurisprudence* (Oxford: Oxford University Press, 1988), p. 135.

[22] John L. Esposito, *The Oxford Dictionary of Islam* (Oxford: Oxford University Press, 2003), p. 134.

[23] For a concise treatment of this topic see Abbas Amanat, "In Between the Madrasa and the Marketplace: The Designation of Clerical Leadership in Modern Shi'ism", in Said Amir Arjomand, ed., *Authority and Political Culture in Shi'ism* (Albany, NY: SUNY Press, 1988), pp. 98–132.

means not so much "blind imitation" but rather "'confidence' or 'trust' (*istinad*) in the rulings of another, someone authoritative, so as to base one's practice on them."[24]

A number of Shi'a scholars have resolved the ensuing tension between *ijtihad* and *Marja'iyyat* by regarding *ijtihad* and *taqlid* as "optionally incumbent." According to Professor Abdulaziz Sachedina,

This means that if *ijtihad* is undertaken by a sufficient number of believers, then others are relieved of undertaking this responsibility; instead, they can follow the course of *taqlid* individually and personally to fulfill their obligations. On the basis of both rational and revelational proofs, these jurists have contended, it is important for believers to feel confident in their religious observances, and that confidence can be obtained through *ijtihad*, *ihtiyat* (precaution; taking the most prudent line), or *taqlid*.[25]

The position of the *Marj'a-e Taqlid* "is the corollary of the rational necessity to consult those who are specialists in matter of the shari'a."[26] While this by no means implies that proponents of *Marja'-e Taqlid* oppose or ignore *ijtihad*, one of the pronounced practical consequences of institutionalizing the position has been a tightening of the scope and methodology of *ijtihad*. It is precisely over this scope and methodology of *ijtihad*, and somewhat tangentially over exactly who is rightfully qualified to engage in *ijtihad*, that the fault-lines separating today's conservative and reformist Shi'a thinkers lie.

The central question dividing the two camps is over the extent to which *ijtihad* can be used to reinterpret the *shari'a* according to changing circumstances and contexts. Shi'a scholars of all doctrinal persuasions have long prided themselves on the openness of "the gates of *ijtihad*" in Shi'a as compared to Sunni *fiqhs*.[27] In fact, both today and in the past, few if any Shi'a jurists would openly advocate closing the door to *ijtihad*. The question then becomes one of degree and scope. Put simply, how open are the gates of *ijtihad*, and exactly what aspects of the *shari'a*, and how much of it, are allowed through?

A broad survey of *ijtihad*s, at least as currently manifest in Iran, yields two general types. One type may be called "narrative-centered" *ijtihad* (*naql-mehvar*), whereby reason (*'aql*) is secondary to the narratives of the Qur'an and the *Sunna*. Reason and rationality are not at the center of the human endeavor, and man does not need them to understand his world.

---

[24] Sachedina, *The Just Ruler in Shi'ite Islam*, p. 213.   [25] Ibid.   [26] Ibid.

[27] Abolfazl Shakuri, *Fiqh-e Siyasi-e Eslam* (Islamic Political Theology) (Qom: Howzeh Elmiyeh, 1377/1998), pp. 35–36. For a brief discussion of Shi'ism's greater attention to philosophical issues as compared with Sunnism see the work of the eminent Shi'a scholar Ayatollah Mohammad Hosein Tabataba'i (1902–1981): *Shi'a dar Eslam* (Shi'ism in Islam) (Qom: Daroltafsir, 1379/2000), pp. 139–42.

Rather, what is important is the message and essence of Islam, its *narrative*, and reason must be used to discover the true meaning and essence of this narrative.[28] In this *ijtihad*, the assumption is that the Sacred Text and the prophetic tradition are of utmost importance.

The Almighty has not be given the jurists the key [of reason] so that they could open any secrets on their own. "Reason" is only a key to discovering the secrets of the "narrative," and it is in the narrative that the solutions to personal and collective problems can be found. God and His anointed have told man all that he needs to know. There is no need anymore for human thinking and reason in this regard. Man must learn the *shari'a*, analyze it, and in this endeavor he can employ reason.[29]

Through reliance on traditional sources and methodologies, as historically employed at the *howzeh*s, the narrative-center *ijtihad* tries to make minor modifications to *fiqh* in order to make it applicable to today's circumstances.[30] "Not all changes," cautions Ahmad Va'ezi (b. 1962), an instructor at the Qom *Howzeh*, "lead to changes in the nature of [Qur'anic] commandments." "Therefore, we cannot ignore the injunctions of the *shari'a* based on external and contextual changes, and instead replace the unshakable commands of the *shari'a* with conjectures and guesses."[31]

In contrast to narrative-centered *ijtihad* stands the "reason-centered" *ijtihad* (*'aql-mehvar*). Also called "*ijtihad* in fundamentals," reason-centered *ijtihad* starts out with the assumption that the world is ever-changing and ever-evolving, not only materially and instrumentally but, much more fundamentally, in its presuppositions, its goals and imaginations, and in the very people whose values and cultures comprise it.[32] Resort to an *ijtihad* that centers on the narratives of *fiqh*, the *shari'a*, or even the Qur'an is no longer sufficient and cannot address all contemporary issues and concerns. The gates of this *ijtihad* have been slammed shut and a new *ijtihad*, one based on reason, is now needed. "'Reason-centered' *ijtihad* does not mean neglect or abandonment of the texts and the various [traditional] sources of religion. But it means accepting reason as one of the sources of religion, and giving it primacy

---

[28] Saeed 'Edalatnezhad, "Moqaddameh: Kodam *Ijtihad?*" (Introduction: Which *Ijtihad?*), in Saeed 'Edalatnezhad, ed., *Andarbab-e Ejtehad: Darbar-ye Kar-amadiye Fiqh-e Eslami dar Donya-ye Emrouz* (On Ijtihad: On the Effectiveness of Islamic Jurisprudence in Today's World) (Tehran: Tarh-e No, 1382/2003), p. 10.

[29] Ibid.   [30] Ibid., p. 12.

[31] Ahmad Va'ezi, *Hokumat-e Dini: Ta'moli dar Andisheh-ye Siyasi-e Eslam* (Religious Government: A Look at Islamic Political Thought) (Tehran: Mersad, 1378/1999), pp. 90–91.

[32] 'Edalatnezhad, "Moqaddameh: Kodam *Ijtihad?*" (Introduction: Which *Ijtihad?*), p. 11.

when it comes into conflict with religion's narrative."[33] The assumption here is that *ijtihad* needs to be more in-depth and more fundamental rather than superficial and textual. "The correct way to guard and protect the cultural heritage of Islam," this *ijtihad* assumes, "is to reinterpret its products and its offerings according to changing times and contexts. Presenting the cultural heritage of Islam in old, traditional forms only brings about a loss of their appeal and their inapplicability [for the faithful]."[34]

It bears repeating that the assertion that the "gates of *ijtihad*" are slammed shut in the narrative-centered variety is, in many ways, an *accusation* levied against it by proponents of reason-centered *ijtihad*. In fact, as will be shown more fully in chapter 6, it is the reformists who vigorously criticize the conservatives for the inertness and the shallowness of their *ijtihad*. As far as the conservatives themselves are concerned, however, their *ijtihad* is in-depth and often extensive.

A case in point are the arguments of Ayatollah Montazeri, who is emphatic in his insistence that the gates of *ijtihad* in Shi'a *fiqh* remain wide open. In fact, he maintains, given the contemporary world, *ijtihad* is indeed a necessary duty of the Shi'a jurist.[35] But, he argues, not every old thought is irrelevant and ought to be discarded, and neither is every new idea worthy of embrace. More importantly, reason, while important, cannot always be trusted as it remains susceptible to such human frailties as lust, fear, and temperament.[36] "The commands of Islam are not based on reason alone and are more closely linked to belief and the essence of being, and the foundations for jurisprudential dictums can be found in the Book and the *Sunna*. Nevertheless, reason can help us better understand the Book and the *Sunna*."[37] *Taqlid*, particularly of a trusted *faqih*, is far more prudent than placing trust in reason.[38] As we shall see shortly, Ayatollah Montazeri is, not surprisingly, one of the main proponents of the concept of *Marja'iyyat*. Ayatollah Montazeri and other like-minded conservative theologians see the "perpetuation of *ijtihad*" as one of the key responsibilities of the *Marja'-e Taqlid*.[39] When *ijtihad* does take place, it should be done by a trusted "specialist of the *shari'a*", who can in turn be a guide and a "source of emulation" for others.[40]

---

[33] Ibid.   [34] Ibid., p. 12.
[35] Hoseinali Montazeri, "Bab-e Maftooh-e Ijtihad" (The Open Gates of Ijtihad), in 'Edalatnezhad, ed., *Andarbab-e Ejtehad*, pp. 36–37.
[36] Ibid., pp. 43–44.   [37] Ibid., p. 45.   [38] Ibid., p. 46.
[39] 'Abdollah Javadi Amoli, *Velayat-e Faqih* (The Supreme Jurisconsult) (Qom: Esra, 1379/2000), p. 240.
[40] Mohammad Soroush, *Din va Dowlat dar Andisheh-ye Eslami* (Religion and Politics in Islamic Thought) (Qom: Howzeh Elmiyeh, 1378/1999), p. 83; Shakuri, *Fiqh-e Siyasi-e Eslam* (Islamic Political Theology), p. 221.

To sum up, Iran's conservative theologians tend to take a comparatively cautious approach to *ijtihad*. Ayatollah Mesbah Yazdi's take on the issue is representative of most others belonging to the current. "We are among those," he writes, as if to deliberately distinguish himself from "others,"

who consider as valid the interpretations [of the Qur'an] of the past 1,400 years by both Sunni and Shi'a ulama. The Islam that we believe in is what has been interpreted by the Twelve Imams and, alongside them, by fourteen centuries of juridical work by the ulama. That is the interpretation that informs our understanding of Islam. If there are new interpretations that call for alterations to the teachings of Islam and the creation of a new Islam, we want nothing to do with it. And I do not think the average Muslim wants anything to do with this new Islam either, or with Muslim "Babs" or "Martin Luthers."[41]

Not surprisingly, conservative theologians often tend to have a more textual and literal interpretation of the Qur'an and the *Sunna* as compared to reformists, for many of whom the context, time, and place of Qur'anic injunctions are just as important as what the Qur'an actually says. In elaborating on the ideal order as they see it, conservative theologians tend to stay as close to either the literal text of the Qur'an and the accepted *Sunna* or, at best, to their traditional interpretations as enunciated and historically accepted by the clerical mainstream.[42] Both the ideal order thence articulated and, more importantly, its jurisprudential underpinnings, are therefore innately conservative. They are, more accurately, circumspect in their embracing of new *ijtihad*s and interpretations of *fiqh*.

Before examining the details of the social and political orders that are articulated and advocated by the conservative theologians, a cautionary note is in order. The label "conservative theologian" is, apart from other imperfections, very broad. As argued earlier, the "conservative" current in Iran is varied and multi-faceted. As is the case in the two chapters that follow, my focus here is not on the *political* differences – or shifting alliances and animosities – that characterize many of the thinkers discussed here. Rather, my focus is on their contributions to and

---

[41] Mohammad Taqi Mesbah Yazdi, *Nazariyyeh-e Siyasi-e Eslam: Qanoongozari* (Political Theory of Islam: Legislation) (Qom: Mo'asseseh-e Amozeshi va Pazhoheshi-e Emam Khomeini, 1380/2001), p. 205. The reference to Bab here is to Seyyed 'Ali Mohammad Shirazi who in 1844 declared himself to be "Bab" ("door" in Arabic) and started the Babi movement that later gave rise to Baha'ism.

[42] Two relevant examples include Ayatollah Mesbah Yazdi's analysis of the afterlife and hell, and Ayatollah Javadi Amoli's discussion of the need to have balanced material and spiritual lives. See, respectively, Mohammad Taqi Mesbah Yazdi, *Amouzesh-e 'Aqayed* (Teaching Beliefs) (Tehran: Beinolmelal, 1382/2003), pp. 411–19; and Javadi Amoli, *Falsafeh-ye Hoquq-e Bashar* (The Philosophy of Human Rights), pp. 175–81.

interpretations of *fiqh*, or their *ijtihad*, and on the larger theological discourse to which they have given rise. In this respect, figures otherwise as different as Ayatollahs Montazeri and Mesbah Yazdi are discussed in the same vein, though their significant political differences, and at times their theological disagreements, cannot and should not be overlooked.

The just order

What, then, does the proper Islamic order look like according to Iran's conservative theologians? What is man's role in it? And what roles if any do leaders and governments play in enabling man (*ensan*) to reach his destiny?

The Iranian religious conservatives' conception of the universe is comprised of man as being divinely empowered by free agency in order to make his own choices on his way toward heavenly ascent (*kamal*). These choices are made within a framework prescribed by the Almighty and handed down to man through His prophets. Religion and politics, inseparable and intimately entwined as they are, have "guidance" as a central phenomenon, leading the individual, and the larger society of which he is a part, along a path of moral and spiritual richness until the Imam Mehdi's return. Until such time, when perfection is achieved and when Mehdi defeats the forces of darkness and spreads peace and justice on Earth, it is critical that Islamic societies have the proper forms of leadership and government. It is no accident that Islam pays special attention to issues of leadership and government. An Islamic government must perform several significant functions, chief among which are encouraging social and economic development, fostering proximity to the Almighty, and defending the tenets of Islam against overt military threats or more subtle, creeping cultural invasions. In Shi'ism, during the period of Occultation of the Hidden Imam, the ideal form of government is one headed by the *Vali-ye Faqih*, who, having ascended to his esteemed position of leadership, derives his legitimacy from the Twelve Imams and, ultimately, from God. Long an important part of Shi'a theology, the system of *Velayat-e Faqih* was last fully articulated by Imam Khomeini, the founder of the Islamic Republic. Today, Ayatollah Khomeini's religio-political legacy, and the theocratic system which he so meticulously crafted, must be carefully safeguarded against threats from within and from the outside.

For most conservative theologians, the starting point is man (*ensan*) or the person (*shahks*). Man is God's vicegerent and successor on Earth.[43]

---

[43] Shakuri, *Fiqh-e Siyasi-e Eslam* (Islamic Political Theology), p. 110.

As such, he was created with free will and has the ability to make and reach his own decisions.[44] But along with the "right" (*haq*) to be free comes certain "responsibilities" (*takleef*), and these responsibilities are in relation to the individual himself, in relation to others, and in relation to the Almighty.[45] A key responsibility is to exercise free will and to make decisions in ways that facilitate man's evolutionary ascent toward God. Life on Earth is but an introduction to the far more supreme life that awaits us after death, and the steps we take now take us either closer to the glories of heaven or the agonies of hell.[46] The individual must constantly ask questions and search for answers: Who is responsible for life and for being? What is the ultimate goal of human life? What is the correct path to righteous living that ensures true bliss and ascent?[47]

Man, therefore, plays an important role in shaping his history and his own destiny. Islam, according to Ayatollah Mesbah Yazdi, categorically denies that there are no rules in the unfolding of history. All phenomena, including changes to history, are purposive, not merely accidental.[48] But neither is man's path toward good or evil predetermined. He is free to make his own choices.

The freedom that exists is based on divine will. God has willed that man be free so that he can shoulder the responsibility of his own ascent and discover the secrets of his own evolution. In the process, man must realize his need for and dependence on the Almighty, embarking on his evolutionary path in humbleness and mindful of his need for divine guidance.[49]

To make the right decisions, man is given the gift of religions, which serve as divinely ordained frameworks for decision-making and conduct. Religions make man's divine ascent possible and guide and nurture the human soul. This possibility to reach for ever-greater levels of ascent and betterment is man's right. He, in turn, is responsible to search for the just religion by deepening his spirituality and his understanding of the "straight path." This mission of enlightenment, in fact, is one of the

---

[44] Mesbah Yazdi, *Amouzesh-e 'Aqayed* (Teaching Beliefs), p. 177.

[45] Mohammad Taqi Mesbah Yazdi, *Nazariyyeh-e Hoquqi-e Eslam* (Legal Theory of Islam) (Qom: Mo'asseseh-e Amozeshi va Pazhoheshi-e Emam Khomeini, 1380/2001), p. 172.

[46] Mesbah Yazdi, *Nazariyyeh-e Siyasi-e Eslam* (Political Theory of Islam), p. 133.

[47] Mesbah Yazdi, *Amouzesh-e 'Aqayed* (Teaching Beliefs), p. 171.

[48] Mohammad Taqi Mesbah Yazdi, *Jame'eh va Tarikh az Didgah-e Qur'an* (Society and History from the Perspective of the Qur'an) (Tehran: Sazman-e Tablighat-e Eslami, 1380/2001), p. 137.

[49] Morteza Hoseini Esfahani, *Eslam va Azadi* (Islam and Freedom) (Qom: Farhang-e Quran, 1379/2000), p. 102.

central tasks of the Qur'an.[50] "Enlightening the inner soul of individuals and societies is one of the primary missions of the Qur'an," writes Ayatollah Javadi Amoli, "and if this were to occur, the inner constitution and essence of societies and individuals, as well as their deeds and conduct, become exalted and praiseworthy."[51]

As the most supreme blueprint for perfection, Islam cautions the individual against carnal desires and selfishness, for giving into the self ensures only ruin and stalls progress.[52] "There is no aspect to the life of man that is outside the purview of the laws of Islam. This does not mean that man has no freedom; it means that Islam shows man the correct way to use the freedom he has been granted."[53] Islam calls on the individual to "submit" himself to God, "and through this submission man frees himself of internal obligations and outside powers and begins to excel toward the worship of justice."[54] "Man is a multi-dimensional being," and the evolution of all these different dimensions – "not just material, industrial, and social evolution and economic comfort, but his spiritual evolution as well" – are all made possible through Islam.[55]

But Islam is more than a mere set of moral and ethical principles. It is, conservative theologians emphasize again and again, also innately political. "Islam's position concerning politics is that all things political, and all issues related to government, must be traced to Revelation and the commands of the Almighty," writes Ayatollah Mesbah Yazdi.[56] The extent to which this point is emphasized instead of simply being assumed – as one might expect – is instructive. The articulators of the conservative religious discourse are not being theoretically redundant; instead, they are being politically savvy. To insist on the inseparability of Islam and politics goes beyond constructing an Islamic cosmology within which the role of man and his surroundings can be situated. It is also to confront head-on the central assumption by the secular-modernist discourse of the need to divorce politics from religion. In fact, as we shall see in the next chapter, there are even some religious

---

[50] 'Abdollah Javadi Amoli, *Resalat-e Qor'an* (The Mission of the Qur'an) (Tehran: Raja', 1375/1996), p. 29.

[51] Javadi Amoli, *Resalat-e Qur'an* (The Mission of the Qur'an), p. 49.

[52] Hoseini Esfahani, *Eslam va Azadi* (Islam and Freedom). p. 153.

[53] Mohammad Javad Norouzi, *Nezam-e Siyasi-e Eslam* (Islam's Political System) (Qom: Mo'asseseh-e Amozeshi va Pazhoheshi-e Emam Khomeini, 1381/2002), p. 68.

[54] Soroush, *Din va Dowlat dar Andisheh-ye Eslami* (Religion and Politics in Islamic Thought), p. 177.

[55] Mesbah Yazdi, *Nazariyyeh-e Siyasi-e Eslam: Qanoongozari* (Political Theory of Islam: Legislation), p. 265.

[56] Ibid., p. 100.

reformists who call for the separation of religion and politics. This, to the conservative theologians, is unacceptable.

Islam, they emphatically maintain, is inherently political. Politics is part of the very essence and fabric of Islam.[57] A purposive religion, Islam is revealed for the guidance of mankind, a blueprint for social and political relations. As such, it is impossible for Islam to be apolitical, or, for that matter, for the political system not to be based on Islam.[58] This intimate connection between Islam and politics, as well as between Islam and social and economic relations, is enunciated in detail in the two central sources of Islam, namely the Qur'an and the *Sunna* (traditions of the Prophet).[59] "If there is a religion that can be separated from politics, it surely is not Islam."[60] In fact, to claim that Islam without politics is possible is to resort to trickery and deception of the masses.[61] Even worse, it can lead to a spreading of moral corruption and the steady degradation of religion.[62]

Islam, therefore, acts as an all-encompassing umbrella, an overall framework on which the theoretical and practical legitimacy of the political system is based.[63] It is no accident that the Prophet and the rightful Imams who succeeded him paid special attention to politics.[64] Central to their concern was ensuring the prevention of chaos and turmoil in society,[65] along with, of course, the proper guidance and leadership of the Muslim community. The centrality of Islamic government, and all that such a phenomenon would entail – the critical need for its existence, its overall format and structure, its leadership, and the basis of its legitimacy – quickly become apparent. Each of these areas have been greatly explored by the conservative theologians.

To begin with, according to the conservative theologians, there are a number of reasons why it is essential for all societies in general and for Islamic ones in particular to have governments. Governments are needed in order to evaluate, ratify, and enact laws and social regulations; resolve social tensions and conflicts; make political decisions and implement

---

[57] Shakuri, *Fiqh-e Siyasi-e Eslam* (Islamic Political Theology), p. 104.

[58] Esma'il Darabkala'i, *Negareshi bar Falsafeh-ye Siyasi-e Eslam* (A Look at Islamic Political Philosophy) (Qom: Bustan-e Ketab, 1380/2001), p. 37.

[59] Mesbah Yazdi, *Nazariyyeh-e Siyasi-e Eslam: Qanoongozari* (Political Theory of Islam: Legislation), p. 40.

[60] Ibid., p. 33.   [61] Shakuri, *Fiqh-e Siyasi-e Eslam* (Islamic Political Theology), p. 79.

[62] Javadi Amoli, *Resalat-e Qur'an* (The Mission of the Qur'an), p. 55.

[63] Va'ezi, *Hokumat-e Dini* (Religious Government), p. 37.

[64] Mohammad Javad Norouzi, *Daramadi bar Nezam-e Siyasi-e Eslam* (A Study of the Islamic Political System) (Qom: Mo'asseseh-e Amozeshi va Pazhoheshi-e Emam Khomeini, 1380/2001), p. 35.

[65] Soroush, *Din va Dowlat dar Andisheh-ye Eslami* (Religion and Politics in Islamic Thought), p. 151.

policies; and preside over and guarantee the voracity and validity of various social norms.[66] This last responsibility is what distinguishes the Islamic government from others. Governments, all governments, perform a menu of functions and have a host of responsibilities: ensuring the safety and security of society; providing for the needs of society; etc. What sets the Islamic government aside is its responsibility to provide for the emotional and spiritual needs of the Muslim community.[67] With man's evolution and divine ascendance (*kamal*) as the cornerstones of Islam, "guidance" becomes a prime responsibility of the Islamic government.[68] According to Ayatollah Mesbah Yazdi,

> the key difference between an Islamic government and secular governments is the former's obligation to give primacy to the execution of divine laws and to ensure that social relations are based on the guidelines presented by Islam. In Islamic government, if there are instances in which material priorities come into conflict with spiritual and moral priorities, the latter take precedence.

> Among the chief responsibilities of the Islamic government, therefore, is the need to preserve and to spread the message of Islam, to encourage the growth of Islamic culture, and to combat those behaviors and values that erode Islamic teachings.[69]

It is essential for the government to enjoin the good and forbid the evil, says another conservative theologian.[70] It must facilitate and encourage the spread of the principles and practices of Islam – prayer, fasting, the *hajj*, almsgiving, the performance of Islamic rites, etc. – and, as a way to help the religion's growth, it must build mosques.[71] The government is responsible for implementing the laws of Islam, and it must establish organs and institutions that carry out the religion's commands.[72]

Along similar lines, the Islamic government must make laws in ways that please God.[73] For the state's laws to be valid, they must take into account the spiritual needs and religious predicaments of the people alongside their material wellbeing.[74] Ultimately, laws must help man

---

[66] Darabkala'i, *Negareshi bar Falsafeh-ye Siyasi-e Eslam* (A Look at Islamic Political Philosophy), p. 94.

[67] Norouzi, *Nezam-e Siyasi-e Eslam* (Islam's Political System), p. 105.

[68] Shakuri, *Fiqh-e Siyasi-e Eslam* (Islamic Political Theology), p. 74.

[69] Mohammad Taqi Mesbah Yazdi, *Nazariyyeh-e Siyasi-e Eslam: Keshvardari* (Political Theory of Islam: Statecraft) (Qom: Mo'asseseh-e Amozeshi va Pazhoheshi-e Emam Khomeini, 1380/2001), p. 63.

[70] Shakuri, *Fiqh-e Siyasi-e Eslam* (Islamic Political Theology), p. 161.

[71] Ibid., p. 117.

[72] Norouzi, *Daramadi bar Nezam-e Siyasi-e Eslam* (A Study of the Islamic Political System), p. 63.

[73] Mesbah Yazdi, *Nazariyyeh-e Siyasi-e Eslam: Qanoongozari* (Political Theory of Islam: Legislation), p. 182.

[74] Ibid., p. 192.

draw himself closer to God.[75] In fact, it is not the individual but Revelation and ultimately God Himself that are the true sources of law, and any laws contradicting divine will, no matter how popular they may be among the masses, have no legitimacy whatsoever.[76] Man, it is important to remember, does not have the competence necessary to make laws. Only God does.[77]

Islamic laws need Islamic government.[78] And, more importantly, man's evolutionary ascent, along with his deepening spirituality, will not become possible in the absence of mechanisms of power and politics that are not based on the teaching and the precepts of Islam. Put differently, without an appropriate political system and the necessary political structures, the goals of Islam cannot be accomplished. Thus the kind of political system that Islam prescribes, and the type of polity which arises from and is based on it, is more than a product of the institutional preferences of the architects of the state. It is, essentially, a way-station and a facilitator for man's spiritual and religious ascent toward ever greater heights.

What, then, is the kind of political system that Islam prescribes? Despite the considerable volume of writings on the inseparability of Islam and politics, most conservative theologians remain vague on the details of the ideal political system in Islam. This is partly a product of the assumption by most that Islam does not prescribe a specific type of political system and does not detail the form that an Islamic system's institutions and structures should take. As Ayatollah Mesbah Yazdi maintains, "no one claims that Islam has mandated a specific set of institutional features for government."[79] The Islamic basis of a political system, he argues, is located not in its structural make-up but rather in its mission and its source of legitimacy, a topic we will explore shortly. But insofar as the specific institutions of power are concerned, they "are in constant processes of change and revision based on the conditions of the times and different places. It is impossible to determine only one kind of political system that would be appropriate for all times and all social circumstances."[80] What Islam does, instead, is to present an overall framework for government.[81]

[75] Ibid., p. 225.

[76] Norouzi, *Nezam-e Siyasi-e Eslam* (Islam's Political System), pp. 77–81.

[77] Ibid., pp. 81–82.

[78] Soroush, *Din va Dowlat dar Andisheh-ye Eslami* (Religion and Politics in Islamic Thought), pp. 160–61.

[79] Mesbah Yazdi, *Nazariyyeh-e Siyasi-e Eslam: Keshvardari* (Political Theory of Islam: Statecraft), p. 146.

[80] Ibid., pp. 147–48.

[81] Ibid., p. 148. See also Norouzi, *Nezam-e Siyasi-e Eslam* (Islam's Political System), pp. 116–17.

It is to this overall framework of Islamic government that the conservative theologians have paid considerable attention. Given the enormity of its responsibilities and obligations to society, for example, one conservative theologian argues that for an Islamic government to perform its manifold functions effectively, it must have a wide range of powers and facilities at its disposal.[82] Just as Iran's Islamic revolution was a product of a "revolution in thought," claims another, its longevity and continued success hinges on the health of Iran's Islamic and revolutionary culture.[83] Ahmad Va'ezi offers perhaps the most detailed picture of what an Islamic system ought to look like: it needs to have leaders with expertise in religion; must involve consultation in decision-making; allow for the supervision of the people over the political process; ensure the equality of all before the law; and refrain from making laws and policies that contravene Islam.[84] But he does not elaborate on any of the mechanisms necessary to ensure these provisions.

These are but three of the examples of the sweeping, general proclamations that often characterize the conservative theologian's writings on Islamic politics. There are, nevertheless, four areas of analyses that have been particularly prominent in the conservative theologians' writings on Islamic government. They include the role and nature of leadership that an Islamic system needs; the sources of legitimacy of an Islamic system; the specific institution of *Velayat-e Faqih*, the scope of its powers, and its political necessity in today's conditions; and the appropriateness of the institutional arrangements that the Islamic Republic has come to assume.

One of the most important aspects of Islamic society is its need to have the proper kind of leadership. According to Ayatollah Javadi Amoli, in fact, "for the Qur'an, the protection and perfection of Islam and its blessings rest on determining the leader and guardian of the Muslim community."[85] Broadly, the leadership of the Muslim community in general and the Shi'a in particular can be divided into three eras: the time of the Prophet; the period of the Twelve Imams; and the period of Occultation, which continues to exist up to the present.[86] During the first two eras, through divine will and according first to the commandments of the Qur'an and then the Prophetic tradition, the right of

---

[82] Norouzi, *Daramadi bar Nezam-e Siyasi-e Eslam* (A Study of the Islamic Political System), p. 121.

[83] Javadi Amoli, *Resalat-e Qur'an* (The Mission of the Qur'an), p. 65.

[84] Va'ezi, *Hokumat-e Dini* (Religious Government), pp. 151–53.

[85] Javadi Amoli, *Resalat-e Qur'an* (The Mission of the Qur'an), p. 53.

[86] Soroush, *Din va Dowlat dar Andisheh-ye Eslami* (Religion and Politics in Islamic Thought), p. 405.

leadership was bestowed upon the most perfect, and thus the most deserving, member of the community.[87] Today, in the absence of divinely ordained Imams, the right of leadership belongs to the person who comes closest to the purity of the Imams' hearts and their ethics, the depth of their knowledge, and their devotion to Islam.[88] In Shi'a *fiqh*, such a person is the *Vali-ye Faqih*.

Before discussing the specifics of the *Velayat-e Faqih* as the ideal system of leadership advocated by Iran's conservative theologians, some general observations on the role, nature, and significance of Islamic leadership in the era of Occultation are in order. In broad terms, the conservative theologians argue that the most perfect system of leadership is that of the Imamate. Some authors, like Abolfazl Shakuri (b. 1955), a political science professor at Tarbiat Modarres University, have used the two terms "Imamate" and "*Velayat*" interchangeably.[89] "In the culture and language of the Qur'an," he argues, "*Velayat* means the right to guardianship, the right to political leadership, and the right to social and ethical leadership, as practiced by the prophets over the people."

Velayat means the right to leadership and rule, the right to confiscate the person's belongings for the benefit of religion or the majority or the poor and destitute, the right to appoint military and civilian leaders, the right to appoint guardians for orphans and to decide their affairs, the right to determine the fate of properties with unknown owners, and, in general, the right to determine the affairs of society as deemed appropriate by God.[90]

Imamate has a similarly all-encompassing meaning. It means "complete and comprehensive leadership and supervision over all of the material and spiritual affairs of the Islamic community."[91]

In a polity based on the notion of *Velayat*, the Leader occupies the head of a pyramid-like political system. The Leader, or the *Vali* (literally, guardian), is the central fount of all power. He serves as the epitome of the political system and as the source within whom all power and authority are concentrated. The precise scope of these powers will be discussed below. Just beneath the *Vali*, however, power is diffuse and decentralized, divided and spread among the different branches of the government.[92] Necessitated by a need for specialized knowledge and the subsequent division of labor, the government must be divided into

---

⁸⁷ Norouzi, *Nezam-e Siyasi-e Eslam* (Islam's Political System), p. 169.
⁸⁸ Ibid., p. 202.
⁸⁹ Shakuri, *Fiqh-e Siyasi-e Eslam* (Islamic Political Theology), p. 218.
⁹⁰ Ibid., p. 219. ⁹¹ Mesbah Yazdi, *Amouzesh-e 'Aqayed* (Teaching Beliefs), p. 298.
⁹² Darabkala'i, *Negareshi bar Falsafeh-ye Siyasi-e Eslam* (A Look at Islamic Political Philosophy), p. 119.

the legislative, the executive, and the judiciary branches, a division which, according to Mesbah Yazdi, has been accepted since the time of Montesquieu.[93] Except for the *Vali*, none of these branches may devise and enact laws on their own without consulting higher authority, and members of the parliament essentially serve as advisors to the *Vali*. The legislation they pass can be enacted only when and if it meets with the *Vali*'s approval.[94]

Where does the legitimacy of the *Vali* come from? There is only one source of legitimacy, say the conservative theologians. In Islam, God is the ultimate source of legitimacy. All sources of power and authority ultimately lead to Him. And only God has the ability to bestow legitimacy on to political institutions and practices through His chosen Messenger and the select few who succeed him: "In Islamic political theory, the essence of the law is made by the Almighty. Moreover, in a system based on the notion of *Velayat-e Faqih*, only those laws ratified by God, His prophet, the Twelve Imams, or their especially chosen successors are valid. God must also choose the person who executes the law."[95] Legitimacy, therefore, comes not from some social contract or certain cultural norms. It does not come from a constitution or some man-made convention such as elections.[96] Legitimacy comes only from God. And God gave legitimacy to the Prophet Muhammad to embark on his mission, who then passed it on to his rightful successors, the Twelve Imams, to carry on his mantle after his death, who in turn passed it on to their successors, the *Vali-ye Faqih*s, who are today the only legitimate holders of power.[97] No one has the right to rule over others unless given the legitimacy to do so by God.[98]

Conservative theologians make an important distinction between "legitimacy" (*mashru'iyyat*) and "acceptability" (*maqbuliyyat*). Broadly, whereas legitimacy is the divinely sanctioned right to rule, *maqbuliyyat* refers to the functionality of the political system as it relates to the people's willingness to work with it. Legitimacy is the right to rule;

---

[93] Mesbah Yazdi, *Nazariyyeh-e Siyasi-e Eslam: Keshvardari* (Political Theory of Islam: Statecraft), p. 115.

[94] Mohammad Taqi Mesbah Yazdi, *Bahs-i Kotah va Sadeh Piramoun-e Hokumat-e Eslami va Velayat-e Faqih* (A Brief and Simple Discussion concerning Islamic Government and the Supreme Jurisconsult) (Tehran: Beinolmelal, 1382/2003), p. 113.

[95] Mesbah Yazdi, *Nazariyyeh-e Siyasi-e Eslam: Qanoongozari* (Political Theory of Islam: Legislation), p. 109.

[96] Mohammad Taqi Mesbah Yazdi, *Porsesh-ha va Pasokh-ha* (Questions and Answers) (Qom: Mo'asseseh-e Amozeshi va Pazhoheshi-e Emam Khomeini, 1380/2001), pp. 1:13–14.

[97] Ibid., p. 1:21.   [98] Ibid., p. 1:17.

maqbuliyyat is the power to actually do so.[99] Legitimacy concerns the divine nature of the political system and its rulers; *maqbuliyyat* revolves around its functionality. The former comes from the Almighty, the latter from the people. As such, they have no relationship to each other.[100] A political system based on the tenets of Islam and a leader who has ascended to his position because of his Islamic qualifications do not need *maqbuliyyat* in order to have legitimacy. Imam Ali's rule is a prime example. Although he was the rightful and legitimate successor to the Prophet, Ali's rule did not find *maqbuliyyat* for some twenty-five years. Out of concern for the welfare of the Muslim community, he did not resort to force to give *maqbuliyyat* to his legitimate right to govern.[101]

Among the conservative theologians, Ayatollah Mesbah Yazdi is the most adamant that elections play no role whatsoever in the bestowing of legitimacy on a leader, especially the *Vali-ye Faqih*.[102] For him the distinction between legitimacy and *maqbuliyyat* is absolute and unbridgeable. This seems to translate to a general disdain for popular elections. While acknowledging that there might be some benefits to the holding of elections, such as mollifying potential opponents, he states emphatically that "In our opinion the people's vote can never generate legitimacy. That would mean that with the nullification of an election, the basis of legitimacy would also be nullified, and that with a positive election legitimacy would also be realized."[103] This, he maintains, is a false assumption. Some other thinkers, however, have offered a more nuanced definition of the relationship between legitimacy and *maqbuliyyat*. For example, Mohammad Javad Norouzi (1964), a researcher based in Qom, maintains that popular acceptability and the electorate's vote is a necessary but insufficient precondition for legitimacy.[104] "There is no doubt that Islam pays attention to the importance of the consent and acceptance of the populace," he writes.[105] Nevertheless, he acknowledges that in the final analysis what is important is the right to rule by divine grace, i.e. legitimacy, rather than *maqbuliyyat* per se. As will be shown below, the subtle tension between these two positions – contempt for elections and disregard for the input of the people versus paying some heed to their views – has been institutionalized, if not

---

[99] Abbas Yazdani, *Gofteman-e Hokumat-e Dini* (The Discourse of Religious Government) (Qom: Farhang-e Teh, 1378/1999), p. 14.

[100] Norouzi, *Daramadi bar Nezam-e Siyasi-e Eslam* (A Study of the Islamic Political System), p. 69.

[101] Ibid., p. 69.

[102] Mesbah Yazdi, *Porsesh-ha va Pasokh-ha* (Questions and Answers), pp. 1:21–22.

[103] Ibid., p. 1:32.

[104] Norouzi, *Nezam-e Siyasi-e Eslam* (Islam's Political System), p. 150.

[105] Ibid., p. 149.

necessarily resolved, through the constitutional arrangements of the Islamic Republic.

All of this leads to what has emerged as the centerpiece of the conservative religious discourse in recent decades – indeed, its central preoccupation – namely the notion of *Velayat-e Faqih*. Literally every conservative theologian has devoted considerable time and intellectual energy to explaining the need and necessity for the position *Velayat-e Faqih*, its historic roots and depth within Shi'a and indeed Islamic jurisprudence, and the scope and extent of its powers both theoretically and in relation to the (Iranian) political system. According to the conservative theologians' reading of the history, there has been a long-standing consensus among Shi'a theologians and *fiqh* specialists that the *Velayat-e Faqih* is needed during the period of Occultation. This consensus, they claim, has gained strength and become more widespread with the passage of time.[106] Even if not all major Shi'a theologians have theorized about the *Velayat-e Faqih* (and its *Mutlaq* variant), none has specifically opposed it either.[107] In an attempt to emphasize the historic acceptance and resilience of the notion, conservative theologians remind their audiences that the position of *Velayat-e Faqih* is not an invention of Ayatollah Khomeini and has long been an accepted part of Shi'a theory and, to a lesser extent, even practice.[108] Khomeini's genius lies in reinvigorating and updating the notion and applying it to today's circumstances. More importantly, he gave practical applicability to what had been largely only a theoretical idea in Shi'ism's recent history.[109] As the doctrinal heirs and protectors of Ayatollah Khomeini's legacy, therefore, almost all conservative theologians refer to his writings extensively – or at least present their own interpretations of his writings – in forwarding their own arguments on the *Velayat-e Faqih*.[110]

One of the theoretical devices with which Ayatollah Khomeini is credited is the notion of *Velayat-e Mutlaq-e Faqih*, or the Absolute Jurisconsult.[111] According to Ayatollah Mesbah Yazdi, who at one point was a student of Ayatollah Khomeini, the Imam viewed the existence of

---

[106] Va'ezi, *Hokumat-e Dini* (Religious Government), pp. 172–73, 175.

[107] Mesbah Yazdi, *Porsesh-ha va Pasokh-ha* (Questions and Answers), p. 1:62.

[108] Javadi Amoli, *Resalat-e Qur'an* (The Mission of the Qur'an), p. 68.

[109] Ibid., p. 69.

[110] See, for example, Norouzi, *Daramadi bar Nezam-e Siyasi-e Eslam* (A Study of the Islamic Political System), pp. 232–33, 242.

[111] Saeed Hajjarian, *Jomhuriyyat; Afsonzedai az Qodrat* (Republicanism; Demystification of Power) (Tehran: Tarh-e No, 1379/2000), p. 259. According to Mohammad Soroush, *Velayat-e Mutlaq-e Faqih* may also be called *Velayat-e 'Ammeh-e Faqih*. In the context used here, "*'ammeh*" can be translated as "comprehensive". Soroush, *Din va Dowlat dar Andisheh-ye Eslami* (Religion and Politics in Islamic Thought), p. 600.

Velayat-e Mutlaq-e Faqih as both possible and necessary.[112] Significantly, in his seminal study by the same name, Ayatollah Khomeini never used the designation "*mutlaq*" to describe the nature and the scope of powers enjoyed by the *Vali-ye Faqih*.[113] Nevertheless, in this and in his other writings he is said to describe precisely such a system of rule.[114] Therefore, unless they specifically qualify the *Velayat-e Faqih* as "conditional" (*moqayyed*) as compared to "absolute" (*mutlaq*) (more of which below), the common assumption by conservative theologians is that the proper and necessary form of *velayat* is *mutlaq*. Ayatollah Javadi Amoli goes so far as to explicitly maintain that *Velayat-e Faqih* cannot be anything other than *mutlaq*, a *Velayat* that is occasionally *moqayyed* and occasionally *mutlaq* being meaningless.[115]

Once again, Ayatollah Mesbah Yazdi is at the forefront of defining, and more importantly advocating, the notion of *Velayat-e Mutlaq-e Faqih*. It is an Islamic system, he maintains, in which

the right to decide on all the affairs of the community goes to the person most resembling the Innocent Imams [of Shi'ism] in knowledge, piety, and managerial skills. When the *Veli-ye Faqih* has such extensive rights and responsibilities, all the laws, rules, and regulations of the Islamic government will have legitimacy (*mashruiyyat*) only when and if he ratifies them. No one else has the direct or indirect right to enact laws or to implement them without his consent. All affairs of the government become official only after his agreement and permission. In this system of government, officials of the state can rightfully occupy positions of power only if their appointments, or the procedures through which they acquire their offices, meet with the approval of the *Veli-ye Faqih*. In sum, neither the laws nor the officials of the state have any legitimacy unless and until they meet with the *Veli-ye Faqih*'s approval.[116]

In this sense, in the thoroughness of his rights and responsibilities, and in the all-encompassing nature and purview of his powers, the system of *Velayat* being called for here is absolute, *mutlaq*. It is the system of *Velayat-e Mutlaq-e Faqih*.

---

[112] Mesbah Yazdi, *Nazariyyeh-e Siyasi-e Eslam: Keshvardari* (Political Theory of Islam: Statecraft), p. 110.

[113] Khomeini, *Velayat-e Faqih, Jihad-e Akbar* (Jurisconsult, Greater Jihad).

[114] Mohammad Ja'fari-Harandi, *Foqaha va Hokumat* (Religious Scholars and Government) (Tehran: Rowzaneh, 1379/2000), pp. 288–91; Soroush, *Din va Dowlat dar Andisheh-ye Eslami* (Religion and Politics in Islamic Thought), pp. 615–16. It is important to note that Ayatollah Khomeini did start using the term "*mutlaqeh*" in some of his proclamations after the revolution's success.

[115] Javadi Amoli, *Velayat-e Faqih* (The Supreme Jurisconsult), p. 473.

[116] Mesbah Yazdi, *Nazariyyeh-e Siyasi-e Eslam: Keshvardari* (Political Theory of Islam: Statecraft), p. 111. For a very similar definition see also, Javadi Amoli, *Velayat-e Faqih* (The Supreme Jurisconsult), p. 249.

This does not mean that the *Vali-ye Faqih* can do anything and everything he likes. He may not, for example, meddle in the fundamental (*osoul*) principles of Islam; his job is to protect Islam, not distort it. Nor, as some of its detractors have claimed, is the *Velayat-e Mutlaq-e Faqih* an autocracy under the guise of religion.[117] The reason that the *Vali-ye Faqih*'s powers are said to be *mutlaq* as opposed to *moqayyed* is that they are not limited to superficial matters. The *Vali-ye Faqih* can interfere in all affairs of the polity, be they essential and emergency or non-essential and non-emergency.[118] In this respect, if and when it serves the higher interests of Islam, in a system based on the *Velayat-e Mutlaq-e Faqih*, the *Vali-ye Faqih* can temporarily suspend some of the religion's commands.[119] A typical example cited is Ayatollah Khomeini's explicit injunction that the annual pilgrimage to the Hajj can be cancelled if the interests of Islam are better served.[120]

How does one ascend to this esteemed and highly responsible position? According to the conservative theologians, the only proper and acceptable way for an eminent theologian to become a *Vali-ye Faqih* is to be designated as one by other scholars of *fiqh* and by the populace at large. This is called *entesab*, the closest English translation of which is "appointment" or "designation." There are two kinds of *nasb* (vb), a "general" and a "specific" one, the former being open to all who meet the requirements for becoming a *Vali-ye Faqih* and the latter limited to only one individual.[121] In contemporary societies, the *Vali-ye Faqih* is determined through general *nasb*. According to one conservative theologian,

based on the perspective of *entesab*, in the era of Occultation, those *foqaha* who meet the requirements for *Velayat* will be proclaimed as *Vali-ye Faqih* by the general public, and of those whichever *faqih* meets the requirements, he can take control of the Islamic government. It is then incumbent upon the people to obey him. Based on this perspective, just as the Prophet and the Imams were called to their missions by the Almighty, the *foqaha* have also been called upon and appointed to their guardianship (*velayat*) by the people. All guardianships ultimately lead to God, and if someone claims to have ascended to this guardianship through means other than divine sanction, such as popular elections, his guardianship is null and void.[122]

---

[117] Jaber Amiri, *Mabani-ye Andisheh-haye Eslami: Din va Siyasat* (Principles of Islamic Thought: Religion and Politics) (Qom: Gorgani, 1380/2001), p. 159.

[118] Mesbah Yazdi, *Porsesh-ha va Pasokh-ha* (Questions and Answers), p. 1:60.

[119] Norouzi, *Daramadi bar Nezam-e Siyasi-e Eslam* (A Study of the Islamic Political System), p. 241.

[120] Ibid., p. 242.

[121] Javadi Amoli, *Velayat-e Faqih* (The Supreme Jurisconsult), p. 391. "General" and of "specific" *nasb*s are "'am" and "*khas*" respectively.

[122] Darabkala'i, *Negareshi bar Falsafeh-ye Siyasi-e Eslam* (A Look at Islamic Political Philosophy), p. 250.

Elections, therefore, have absolutely no validity whatsoever in choosing a *Vali-ye Faqih*.[123] In a system based on *Velayat-e Faqih*, the Islamic ruler draws his legitimacy based on the fact that he is the deputy to the Twelve Imams. His continued *Velayat* depends solely on him remaining the Imams' deputy. If he were to be elected to his position, he would cease to be the Imams' deputy and would instead become the people's deputy, and his guardianship would end when and if the people change their minds. This is unacceptable.[124] In fact, *entesab*, which has the collective wisdom of both the public and the *foqaha*, is the only logical and justifiable way for determining the *Vali-ye Faqih*.[125] It so happens that in the Islamic Republic, through the genius of its founders, provisions for both *entekhab* (elections) and *entesab* were made: the electorate elects members of the Assembly of Experts, a body comprised of eminent clerics, who in turn decide on the *Vali-ye Faqih*. Nevertheless, even if there were no elections, "the legitimacy of the *Vali-ye Faqih* is such that for the benefit of Islam and out of good will, he can assume control of the affairs of the Muslim community even if the people do not vote for him. His rule will still have legitimacy without the vote of the people."[126] In cases where elections may indeed determine the *Vali-ye Faqih*, the people's input does not extend beyond the initial vote. They may have no say on how the *Vali* chooses to exercise his power, and cannot heed their popular demands at the expense of doing what is right. Elections are for the purposes of acceptability and functionality, or *maqbuliyyat*, not determining righteousness and legitimacy, or *mashru'iyyat*.[127]

Despite his incredibly wide range of responsibilities and the manner of his selection, most conservative theologians have outlined no more than a handful of general qualifications for a *Vali-ye Faqih* to have. According to Ayatollah Mesbah Yazdi, these qualifications include "sufficient knowledge of Islam"; integrity and piety; and knowledge and administrative skills.[128] "Sufficient knowledge of Islam" means the ability to engage in *ijtihad*.[129] "Among Muslims," he states, "the *foqaha* have the most in-depth knowledge of religion and the laws of *shari'a*."[130] This

---

[123] Ibid., pp. 247–48.

[124] Javadi Amoli, *Velayat-e Faqih* (The Supreme Jurisconsult), p. 211.

[125] Soroush, *Din va Dowlat dar Andisheh-ye Eslami* (Religion and Politics in Islamic Thought), p. 475.

[126] Ibid., p. 484.   [127] Ibid., p. 485.

[128] Mesbah Yazdi, *Bahs-i Kotah va Sadeh Piramoun-e Hokumat-e Eslami va Velayat-e Faqih* (A Brief and Simple Discussion concerning Islamic Government and the Supreme Jurisconsult), pp. 151–53.

[129] Mesbah Yazdi, *Porsesh-ha va Pasokh-ha* (Questions and Answers), p. 1:51.

[130] Ibid.

means that only clerics have the right to become *Vali-ye Faqih* and that lay scholars of Islam, no matter how devout and knowledgeable, may not engage in *Velayat* or even in *ijtihad*. Other conservative theologians do not necessarily disagree with Mesbah Yazdi, although they are somewhat less direct and blunt in their assertions. Esma'il Darabkala'i, for example, who is a researcher in Qom, outlines five, largely similar qualifications: knowledge of the law; knowledge of what is for the good of society; moral integrity; administrative and managerial skills; and "divine permission."[131] Although Darabkala'i does not quite define what this "divine permission" is or exactly how one acquires it, the clear implication is that non-clerics and non-*mujtaheds* (*mujtahed* being one who engages in *ijtihad*) are excluded from it. Ayatollah Javadi Amoli's list of qualifications is not too different: "absolute *ijtihad*" and thorough and in-depth familiarity with Islam and the Holy Qur'an; "absolute justice" and integrity, as well as intimate knowledge of laws and rules; and leadership skills and management abilities.[132]

A few conservative theologians have presented more detailed and stringent qualifications for *Vali-ye Faqih*. This is the case, for example, with Ayatollah Montazeri, who has outlined a number of qualifications for the person assuming the *Velayat*, including mental health, belief in Islam, a deep conviction to justice, knowledge of *fiqh*, leadership skills, having integrity, being male, and being of legitimate birth.[133] These are closely echoed by Abolfazl Shakuri, whose prescribed list of qualifications for the *Vali-ye Faqih* is similarly detailed: "maturity, having a sound mind, having unshakable faith, being just, being a man, having the ability to engage in *ijtihad*, being alive, being of legitimate birth, being a man of science, not being preoccupied with wealth and material belongings, and being humble."[134]

For both Ayatollah Montazeri and Professor Shakuri, these requirements apply to those who ascend to the dual positions of *Velayat* and *Marja'iyyat* simultaneously, hence the provisions that the person be alive and be a man.[135] This brings us to the contentious question of whether

---

[131] Darabkala'i, *Negareshi bar Falsafeh-ye Siyasi-e Eslam* (A Look at Islamic Political Philosophy), pp. 242–44.

[132] Javadi Amoli, *Velayat-e Faqih* (The Supreme Jurisconsult), pp. 137–40.

[133] Hoseinali Montazeri, *Mabani-ye Feqhi-ye Hokumat-e Eslami*, Volume II (The Jurisprudential Foundations of Islamic Government) (Qom: Saraee, n.d.), p. 141. Ayatollah Montazeri's discussion of *Velayat-e Faqih* deserves separate treatment and is examined more fully below.

[134] Shakuri, *Fiqh-e Siyasi-e Eslam* (Islamic Political Theology), p. 225.

[135] Shakuri admits that the requirement of manhood has been a subject of some debate among the *foqaha* and that there is no solid proof for it, except that "the tender temperament of women contradicts the requirements for *marja'iyyat* and *Velayat*."

or not the largely political position of *Velayat* and the overwhelmingly religious position of *Marja'iyyat* ought to be combined or not. More specifically, should the person occupying the position of *Velayat-e Faqih* also be a *Marja' Taqlid* as originally stipulated in the 1979 constitution and in Ayatollah Khomeini's writings, or, as is now the case, does the *Vali-ye Faqih* not need to be a *Marja'-e Taqlid* anymore?[136] Not surprisingly, the current answer by the country's conservative theologians is that while it would be beneficial if the same individual qualified for the positions both of *Velayat* and *Marja'iyyat*, it is not necessary for the *Vali-ye Faqih* to also be a *Marja'-e Taqlid*.

Before examining the theoretical justifications offered in support of this line of reasoning, brief mention must be made of the political background to the constitutional changes of 1989. Long before he burst into the scene of Iranian politics as the architect and leader of the 1978–79 revolution, Grand Ayatollah Khomeini was widely considered to be one of the main *Marja'-e Taqlid*s in Shi'ism. As such, he was considered a "source of emulation" and a respected judge and arbitrator in personal and *shari'a*-related issues for a significant number of devout followers in Iran and around the world.[137] But the man picked by regime insiders to succeed Ayatollah Khomeini after his death, Ali Khamenei, was not even considered to be an Ayatollah during his presidency of the Republic. In fact, both Khamenei's swift promotion to the rank of Ayatollah – having previously been a Hojjatoleslam – and his subsequent selection to the office of the *Velayat-e Faqih* (or *Rahbari*, literally "Leadership") were products of political considerations rather than his esteem as a religious scholar. To mollify some of the opposition to Khamenei's ascension – especially from the followers of Grand

Also, the *Marja'-e Taqlid* (Source of Emulation) ought to be alive. Ibid., pp. 229, 230–31.

[136] Article 109 of the 1979 constitution stipulated only two qualifications for the Leader: "1. The necessary scientific and religious competence for leadership and religious emulation (*marja'iyyat*); 2. Political and social competence and sufficient bravery, power, and management skills for leadership." In the 1989 revisions to the same article, the requirement that the leader must be a *Marja'* was dropped. The new article stipulates the following qualification for ascension to the *Velayat-e Faqih*: "1. The necessary scientific competence in the various areas of *fiqh*; 2. A sense of justice and piety necessary for leadership of the Islamic community; 3. The correct social and political perspective, prudence, bravery, management skills, and sufficient power for leadership." In addition to these changes, provisions for a Council of Leadership made up of three or five *Marja'*s in case no one *Marja'* emerged as *Vali-ye Faqih* was dropped. For a concise examination of the revised role and responsibilities of the *Velayat-e Faqih* in the 1989 constitution see Ehteshami, *After Khomeini*, pp. 48–50.

[137] For more on the *Marja'-e Taqlid* see Abdulaziz Abdulhussein Sachedina, *The Just Ruler in Shi'ite Islam*, pp. 213–14.

Ayatollah Montazeri and other contenders – the requirement that the *Vali-ye Faqih* must also be a *Marja'-e Taqlid* was dropped from the revised constitution.

Ayatollah Mesbah Yazdi offers the following justification for this issue:

In the past, when the assumption of power seemed remote, esteemed theologians called for rule by someone who as a *Marja'-e Taqlid* could best serve Muslim society. Today, thanks be to God, the groundwork has been prepared for someone to assume power that is more qualified than others, and this blessing deserves much gratitude.[138]

In a footnote he continues,

When Imam Khomeini was alive, we were fortunate (to have both the *Vali-ye Faqih* and the *Marja'-e Taqlid* in the same person). Today, most unfortunately, we do not enjoy the same blessing. The Almighty has continued to bless us with *Velayat-e Faqih* ... in the person of Ayatollah Khamenei.[139]

The separation of *Marja'iyyat* from *Velayat*, he insists, does not create any difficulties for *fiqh* or for the Islamic order in general as the two positions have separate domains of concern.[140] The *Vali-ye Faqih* is in overall charge of the political system, ensures the harmony and stability of society, and is the final authority on issues of social and political concern. To avoid confusion and chaos, therefore, there must be only one *Vali-ye Faqih*.[141] Insofar as *Marja'iyyat* is concerned, however, a plurality may in fact be preferable since the *Marja's'* main areas of concern – i.e. personal and ethical matters – often change based on varying circumstances and conditions.[142]

It is important to point out that not all conservative theologians are eager to draw clear distinctions between the *Velayat-e Faqih* and *Marja'iyyat* and to clear the *Vali-ye Faqih* from the earlier requirement that he must also be a *Marj'a*. As we shall see below, this is one of the main points of contention between Ayatollah Montazeri – who is, incidentally, considered a *Marja'-e Taqlid* by many and who was originally meant to succeed Ayatollah Khomeini – and the current holders of power in Iran. But even some of the conservative theologians who have remained

---

[138] Mesbah Yazdi, *Bahs-i Kotah va Sadeh Piramoun-e Hokumat-e Eslami va Velayat-e Faqih* (A Brief and Simple Discussion concerning Islamic Government and the *Velayat-e Faqih*), p. 155.

[139] Ibid., pp. 155–6.

[140] Mesbah Yazdi, *Porsesh-ha va Pasokh-ha* (Questions and Answers), p. 2:33.

[141] Yazdani, *Gofteman-e Hokumat-e Dini* (The Discourse of Religious Government), pp. 27–28.

[142] Javadi Amoli, *Velayat-e Faqih* (The Supreme Jurisconsult), p. 443.

generally supportive of the political establishment over the years prefer to either remain silent on the issue or to allude to it only in vague and broad terms. Shakuri's arguments in this regard are a case in point. Although he ultimately comes to the conclusion that the *Vali-ye Faqih* does not indeed have to be a *Marja'-e Taqlid* also, he does so only after avoiding a direct examination of the issue.[143]

One of the differences separating the *Vali-ye Faqih* from a *Marja'-e Taqlid* is that the former issues edicts and commands (*hukm*) while the latter issues opinions (*fatwa*).[144] In the case of the *Vali-ye Faqih*, obedience is mandatory, and all people are commanded to obey him.[145] Individuals voluntarily seek out the advice of a *Marja'-e Taqlid*, and the advice and opinions expressed as a result, and other similar *fatwa*s issued by the *Marja'*, are non-binding. But the responsibilities and functions of the *Vali-ye Faqih* are national in scope and are different from those of the *Marja'*. For the sake of social harmony and in order to avoid chaos and turmoil, the *Vali-ye Faqih* must necessarily be obeyed. Just as Muslims were obligated to follow and obey the commands of the Prophet during his lifetime, they must now obey those *foqaha* whose eminence and right to leadership has been recognized by the wider community and by his peers.[146]

The implicit – and at times very explicit – assumption in all of this is that the current political system of the Islamic Republic is as perfect as possible given today's circumstances, or, at least, has the fewest imperfections possible. According to Ayatollah Mesbah Yazdi, for example, the current political system in Iran offers a perfect mixture of democracy and religiosity and gives full meaning to the much sought-after notion of "religious democracy."[147]

The 1989 constitution, he maintains, is "one of the most progressive in the world,"[148] and the enemies of the system, be they counter-revolutionaries or reformists, must be dealt with and punished in the severest way.[149] Other lesser-known figures within the conservative theological fold often repeat similar assertions, claiming that secularist thinkers and even reformist clerics are nothing but puppets of the United

---

[143] Shakuri, *Fiqh-e Siyasi-e Eslam* (Islamic Political Theology), pp. 233–38.
[144] Yazdani, *Gofteman-e Hokumat-e Dini* (The Discourse of Religious Government), p. 28.
[145] Hoseini Esfahani, *Eslam va Azadi* (Islam and Freedom), p. 107.
[146] Norouzi, *Daramadi bar Nezam-e Siyasi-e Eslam* (A Study of the Islamic Political System), p. 69.
[147] Mohammad Taqi Mesbah Yazdi, "Tafsir-e Mardomsalari-ye Dini" (Commentary on Religious Democracy), *Hokumat-e Eslami*, Vol. 8, No. 3 (1382/2003), pp. 88–89.
[148] Mesbah Yazdi, *Nazariyyeh-e Siyasi-e Eslam: Keshvardari* (Political Theory of Islam: Statecraft), p. 13.
[149] Mesbah Yazdi, *Nazariyyeh-e Hoquqi-e Eslam* (Legal Theory of Islam), pp. 60–63.

States and need to be dealt with accordingly.[150] At any rate, as Ayatollah Javadi Amoli maintains, Western-style democracy and other similar, secular systems are based on *shirk* (assuming associates for God, polytheism).[151] God is the only rightful maker of laws, and, in the absence of the Twelfth Imam, the system of Islamic Republic as currently in existence comes as close to perfection as possible.

There is, it is important to keep in mind, one notable exception to this overwhelmingly supportive posture of the regime by Iran's conservative theologians, namely Ayatollah Hoseinali Montazeri. Ayatollah Montazeri's qualm with his old mentor Khomeini and with the current holders of office is more than merely political. At a much deeper level, it is theoretical and philosophical. In an in-depth, six-volume study entitled *The Jurisprudential Foundations of Islamic Government* (*Mabani-ye Feqhi-ye Hokumat-e Eslami*), Ayatollah Montazeri engages in a painstakingly detailed examination of the reasons for and the mechanisms through which limits should be imposed on the powers of the *Vali-ye Faqih*. In another study, comprised of a collection of his statements and shorter essays, he continues his critique of the current formulations of power in Iran. Finally, in a shorter work under the title of *A Thesis of Rights* (*Rasaleh-ye Hoquq*), he outlines a whole series of rights and liberties to which those living under an Islamic government are entitled.

Ayatollah Montazeri starts his treatise on Islamic government by a brief critique of various types of political systems, all of which he finds unsatisfactory for one reason or another. This includes democracies, which he maintains are based on the false assumption that people always have the maturity to make informed decisions on their own. In fact, he maintains, in those Western countries where the political system is supposedly democratic, "corporately-owned media, large corporations, and wealthy investors often control elections and their results. Elected officials, therefore, do not serve the people but instead serve the wealthy, and the political system becomes a tool for class domination."[152] Muslim societies need Islamic government, and an Islamic government is best served by a *Vali-ye Faqih*.[153] There are two main reasons for this,

---

[150] See, for example, Fatemeh Rajabi, *Rouhaniyyat Setizi dar tarish-e Mo'aser-e Iran* (Anti-Clericalism in Contemporary Iranian History) (Tehran: Amir Kabir, 1383/2004), pp. 168–70; and Hasan Va'ezi, *Eslahat va Foroupashi: Tashrih-e Tarh-e Bazsazi-shodeh-ye Foroupashi-e Shoravi dar Iran* (Reforms and Collapse: Surveys of a Reenactment of the Soviet-Style Collapse in Iran) (Tehran: Soroush, 1379/2000), pp. 13, 73, 76, 83.

[151] Javadi Amoli, *Falsafeh-ye Hoquq-e Bashar* (The Philosophy of Human Rights), p. 116.

[152] Montazeri, *Mabani-ye Feqhi-ye Hokumat-e Eslami. Volume 1* (The Jurisprudential Foundations of Islamic Government), p. 95.

[153] These themes are explored in volume 1 of *The Jurisprudential Foundations of Islamic Government*, which is generally devoted to explaining the superiorities of Islamic

Montazeri claims. First, "the basis and foundations of Islamic government are based on the just commands of the Almighty." Second, "the Islamic ruler must be a just *Faqih* who is knowledgeable and whose only political goal is to serve the commandments of God and His messenger."[154]

But the position of *Velayat-e Faqih* that Ayatollah Montazeri has in mind is very different from the one advocated – and politically supported – by figures such as Ayatollahs Mesbah Yazdi and Javadi Amoli and by other conservative theologians whose thinking is closely aligned with that of the political establishment. Ayatollah Montazeri's formulation of the notion of *Velayat-e Faqih* differs from the one that currently dominates Iran politically in three key respects. First, he maintains that the *Vali-ye Faqih* must also necessarily be a *Marja'-e Taqlid*. Second, he strongly refutes the notion of *Velayat-e Mutlaq-e Faqih*, arguing that the concentration of power embodied within this position easily lends itself to various corrupting influences. Third, he calls for the position of the *Velayat-e Faqih* to be an elected one, maintaining that *entesab* might have suited a time and a place when elections were not possible, but that is no longer the case.

Ayatollah Montazeri reminds his readers that in the months following the revolution's success, he was one of less than a handful of clerics who insisted that the notion of *Velayat-e Faqih* become codified in the new system's conclusion.[155] From the very beginning, as advocated by Ayatollah Khomeini, the constitutional and, more importantly, jurisprudential requirement for the *Vali-ye Faqih* was to also be a *Marja'*. The removal of this important provision in the 1989 rewrite of the constitution was, according to Ayatollah Montazeri, done in haste and was an absolute mistake.[156] Throughout Islamic history, and especially during the rule of Imam Ali and the other rightful Imams, the person of the *Vali-ye Faqih* was not only a political leader but was also one of the pre-eminent living authorities on jurisprudential matter, an esteemed scholar who served also as a moral and religious guide and a source of emulation for devout followers. Separating *Marja'iyyat* from *Velayat* for the sake of political expedience has endangered the legitimacy of the Islamic Republic system and the institution of the *Velayat-e Faqih*, and it has led to a growing chasm between the people and the political establishment.[157]

<hr>

government, the need for clerical involvement in politics, the need for a *Vali-ye Faqih*, and his general responsibilities. See, especially, pp. 96–100 and 114–17.

[154] Montazeri, *Mabani-ye Feqhi-ye Hokumat-e Eslami. Volume 3* (The Jurisprudential Foundations of Islamic Government), p. 30.

[155] Hoseinali Montazeri, *Didgah-ha* (Perspectives) (Qom: n.p., 1382/2003), p. 154.

[156] Ibid., pp. 46–47.   [157] Ibid., p. 52.

An even bigger corruption of the institution of the *Velayat-e Faqih*, according to Ayatollah Montazeri, has been its designation as "*Mutlaq*." Absolute guardianship is only that of the Almighty, claims the Ayatollah, and not even the Prophet Muhammad or the Twelve Imams could be considered to have had such vast and overarching powers as those accorded to the *Velayat-e Mutlaq-e Faqih*.[158] Given the complexities of the modern world today, and the importance of specialized skills in running the affairs of the state, the *Velayat-e Faqih* should concentrate on ensuring the Islamic character of the overall political system instead of interfering in all its operations and in areas with which he may have little or no familiarity.[159] *Velayat-e Mutlaq-e Faqih* smacks of autocracy, and the assumption that the person occupying such a position is above the law and the constitution is nothing but a justification for dictatorship.[160]

There must be constitutional and other legal mechanisms in place to limit the powers of the *Velayat-e Faqih*.[161] The original framers of the Islamic Republic's constitution, according to Ayatollah Montazeri, sought to strike a balance between the system's commitment to Islam, the people, and the principles of republicanism. With the introduction of the authoritarian institution of the *Velayat-e Mutlaq-e Faqih*, this delicate balance has been thrown into confusion. That original balance must once again be restored.[162] One way to do so is to impose limits on the *Vali-ye Faqih*'s term in office, to six or ten years for example, and to ensure that the Assembly of Experts, which is constitutionally empowered with selecting a *Vali-ye Faqih*, has actual oversight and supervisory powers over him.[163]

This call for the position of the *Vali-ye Faqih* to be elected runs directly counter to the argument in favor of *entesab* by figures such as Ayatollahs Mesbah Yazdi and Javadi Amoli. According to Ayatollah Montazeri, *entekhab*, or election, has the functionality of a contract, an understanding, between the *Vali* and the people.[164] Under current circumstances, the logic of *entesab* no longer makes sense.[165] Elections for the *Vali-ye Faqih* today are logical and are deeply rooted in the traditions of the Prophet Muhammad and the manner in which Imams Ali and Hassan conducted politics.[166] During the period of Occultation, when

---

[158] Ibid., 37–38.   [159] Ibid., p. 45.   [160] Ibid., pp. 186–87.   [161] Ibid., p. 45.
[162] Ibid., p. 54.   [163] Ibid., pp. 56–57.
[164] Montazeri, *Mabani-ye Feqhi-ye Hokumat-e Eslami. Volume 2* (The Jurisprudential Foundations of Islamic Government), pp. 286–287.
[165] Montazeri, *Didgah-ha* (Perspectives), p. 181.
[166] Montazeri, *Mabani-ye Feqhi-ye Hokumat-e Eslami. Volume 2* (The Jurisprudential Foundations of Islamic Government), pp. 283–99.

no one has been directly chosen by one of the Twelve Imams to lead the Muslim community, it is incumbent upon the people to actively get to know those who have the necessary qualifications to become a *Vali-ye Faqih* and to nominate them for the position. The eligible *foqaha* are also required to declare their candidacy.[167] Once the eligible candidates are known, they should then be elected through direct or indirect elections. To assure that the most qualified candidate is elected, indirect elections for the *Vali* are preferred, with people first voting for the esteemed clerics who make up the Assembly of Experts, who will in turn elect the *Vali-ye Faqih* from among a pool of qualified nominees.[168]

What the current holders of power in Iran have done, Montazeri claims, is to methodically change and subvert the constitutional arrangements that were initially devised in the aftermath of the revolution. The Leadership Council that was meant to combine the wisdom of three living *Marja*'s was disbanded. The Guardian Council was given the authority to vet and disqualify candidates for all elected offices. The Assembly of Experts lost much of its meaningful powers. Many of the powers of the presidency were transferred over to the *Velayat-e Faqih*. And the "illegal and highly harmful" Special Court for the Clergy was constitutionally enshrined as one of the central organs of the state.[169] As a result of all this, the current constitution abounds with contradictions, and, even more detrimentally, the chasm between the people and the state is now wide and growing.[170]

Contrary to its current political manifestations in Iran, Islam guarantees a whole series of rights and liberties, Ayatollah Montazeri claims. "Unfortunately, some groups in society are trying to portray Islam, which in reality is a religion of compassion and mercy, as harsh and opposed to the rights of the individual," he wrote in *A Thesis of Rights*, which was published in 2004.[171] The book is therefore devoted to outlining all the rights and liberties accorded to the individual by Islam. These include, among others, the right to freedom of thought and speech, the right to change one's mind, the right to political participation, the right to select and supervise the ruler, and the right to have one's privacy protected.[172] Political opponents cannot be persecuted simply because of their views, and the ruler must refrain from the abuse of power.[173]

Ayatollah Montazeri's emphasis on the importance of elections is informed by an assumption that is markedly different from those of most other conservative theologians discussed here. For Montazeri, legitimacy

---

[167] Ibid., pp. 327–28.   [168] Ibid., p. 346.
[169] Montazeri, *Didgah-ha* (Perspectives), pp. 52–59.   [170] Ibid., pp. 42–43.
[171] Hoseinali Montazeri, *Rasaleh-ye Hoquq* (A Thesis of Rights) (Qom: Saraee, 1383/ 2004), p. 10.
[172] Ibid., pp. 50–52, 62–63, 66–67, 72–74.   [173] Ibid., pp. 71, 94.

lies with the people.[174] This completely changes the locus of power, nullifying the claim that the divinely anointed *Vali-ye Faqih* is above man-made laws and the will of the people, making him instead beholden to an empowered electorate, a citizenry that is no longer assumed not to know what is in its best interests. Although he explicitly criticizes Western-style democracy, Ayatollah Montazeri's endorsement of the right of the people to elect and to supervise their rulers brings him exceedingly close to the arguments of those thinkers often identified with the religious reformist current. If, however, we accept the earlier argument that the sources for and the subjects open to *ijtihad* are key in differentiating "conservatives" and "reformists" from one another, then Ayatollah Montazeri fits squarely within the conservative camp. Nevertheless, what this demonstrates is the fluid boundaries between each of the three groupings of conservative theologians, religious reformists, and secular-modernists, and the subsequent discourses to which they have given rise.

As we will see in the next chapter, many of the diehard, ultra-dogmatic revolutionaries of yesteryears are today some of the most ardent advocates of religious moderation and reform. Some, like Akbar Ganji, whose ideas are explored in chapter 6, have no room for religion anymore in their new, evolving cosmologies. Ayatollah Montazeri, who still prides himself in his role in founding many of the institutions of the Islamic Republic, has also grown disenchanted with the excesses of the revolution and with what he perceives as the corruption of its goals and hopes. But, as "critical" as his *ijtihad* may be, it is still not "foundational," and he still continues to be deeply steeped in the tradition of jurisprudential conservatism. Politics in general and revolutions in particular often make for strange bedfellows. Just because the arguments of Ayatollah Montazeri and many of the religious reformists mirror each other does not mean that they get inspiration and guidance from the same jurisprudential source or follow the same jurisprudential blueprint. When and if the need arises, each side is only too eager to highlight its fundamental, and in many ways unbridgeable, differences with the other.

The modern world

As we have seen so far, both the language and, more importantly, the logic of the conservative religious discourse is firmly grounded in traditional interpretations of Islam and Shi'ism. For Iran's conservative theologians, the gates of *ijtihad* remain open, and *ijtihad* is in fact encouraged, but only so long as the new interpretation conforms with

---

[174] Ibid., p. 64.

established and already accepted tenets of Shi'a *fiqh*, or, alternatively, can be used to legitimate evolving political circumstances. The removal of *Marja'iyyat* as a precondition for *Velayat* is a case in point. A drastic step was taken toward reinterpreting Shi'a *fiqh*, led by none other than the archconservative Ayatollah Mesbah Yazdi, when political necessity and prudence mandated it.

But politically driven *ijtihad* is not always enough to align the conservative religious discourse with some of the realities of the modern world. More significantly, the discourse cannot afford to ignore many of the notions and ideals that are being advocated by the two other currents of thought with which it competes. As we shall see in the next two chapters, both the religious reformist and the secular-modernist discourses devote considerable attention to issues that they consider to be crucially relevant in today's world. Some of these issues include civil society, democracy, human rights, and modernity. As has been demonstrated, none of these topics form the central preoccupation of the conservative religious discourse. Neither have any of the main thinkers identified with the current studies of these and other related issues in a systematic and methodical manner.[175] Nevertheless, the topics have not gone completely unnoticed either, if only to be argued against.

As we will see in chapters 5 and 6, the notion of civil society as a critical component of any modern polity is at the center of both the reformist religious and the secular-modernist discourses. For the conservative theologians, civil society is also important and is, in fact, a key ingredient of any ideal Islamic polity. But the conservative theologians' conception of civil society is radically different from that articulated by their reformist coreligionists or by the secular-modernists. According to Ayatollah Mesbah Yazdi, the phenomenon of civil society is deeply rooted in Islam and those attributing it to the West only betray their own blind infatuation with all things Western. "An ideal civil society has roots in Islam and Islamic civilization," he writes, "and it will come to fruition with a return to Islam."

But there is another definition of civil society that is unacceptable to us. Today in the West, civil society is considered to be the opposite of religious society and is considered to be a society in which there is no religion and religion has no roles to play in social formations and activities. In such a non-religious civil society – which many people advocate today – all members of society have equal access to government employment. This means that if the Iranian society becomes a civil society, a Jewish person can become the country's president, since all people are

---

[175] A possible exception is Ayatollah Javadi Amoli's book, *Falsafeh-ye Hoquq-e Bashar* (The Philosophy of Human Rights), published in 1996.

equal and we do not have first- and second-rate individuals. Under the guise of civil society, those advocating it are trying to give official status to a deviant, anti-God religion that is linked with Zionism. Under the pretext that all people are equal, they are trying to install into high positions, such as the presidency, individuals who are puppets of the United States and Zionism.[176]

According to the Islamic conception of civil society, people are at the center of the life of the polity. They are in charge of their own affairs;[177] their rights are observed; they are involved in economic, social, and cultural endeavors; intellectual energies are maximized and focused on improving decision-making and social planning; social and political corruption is eradicated; people fulfill their various social and religious obligations; people receive guidance and direction; and government responsibilities are reduced.[178]

The flaws inherent in Western notions of civil society are rooted in the larger logic of liberalism that underlies it, which mistakenly places man at the center of the universe in place of God. In the words of Ayatollah Mesbah Yazdi, "one must be either an Allahist or a humanist."[179] It is impossible to be both. This is precisely why that bastion of Western liberalism that has been forced upon the rest of the world, namely the Universal Declaration of Human Rights, has been such a dismal failure. Four primary reasons, according to Ayatollah Javadi Amoli, account for this. The Declaration is not rooted in divine injunctions and is instead man-made; it fails to take into account man's spiritual needs and quests; it is routinely ignored by the very Westerners who seek to force it on others; and, it is often used as an excuse for domination and discrimination against the oppressed.[180]

It is unfortunate, laments Mesbah Yazdi, that the false allure of modernity has given rise to a new *jaheliyyat* reminiscent of the ignorance that prevailed before the rise of Islam.[181] The blame for much of this "post-modernist *jaheliyyat*," at least in Iran, goes both to those whose infatuation with the West has led them into the trap of secularism, as well as those who claim that Islam needs to be revised and reformed. The former are godless atheists whose sole mission is to ape the West, while the latter are proponents of some concocted "American Islam."

---

[176] Mesbah Yazdi, *Nazariyyeh-e Siyasi-e Eslam: Keshvardari* (Political Theory of Islam: Statecraft), p. 53.

[177] Ibid., p. 56.

[178] Mesbah Yazdi, *Porsesh-ha va Pasokh-ha* (Questions and Answers), p. 3:26.

[179] Mesbah Yazdi, *Nazariyyeh-e Siyasi-e Eslam: Qanoongozari* (Political Theory of Islam: Legislation), pp. 178–79.

[180] Javadi Amoli, *Falsafeh-ye Hoquq-e Bashar* (The Philosophy of Human Rights), pp. 257–71.

[181] Mesbah Yazdi, *Nazariyyeh-e Hoquqi-e Eslam* (Legal Theory of Islam), p. 370.

These so-called Muslim reformists learned about Islam in the West and from Western sources instead of in the historic centers of Islamic learning. Worse yet, they engage in *ijtihad* without the proper knowledge of Islam or the right to do so, leading the Muslims astray and ruining the country in the process. Not surprisingly, for most conservative theologians, religious reformists are as harmful to Islam and Iran as are the secular-modernists. It is to these two groups of intellectuals and the discourses they have initiated that we turn next.

5   The reformist religious discourse

Efforts aimed at "reforming" Islam go back to the earliest days of the religion relatively soon after the passing of Prophet Muhammad, and especially after Islam's political institutionalization by the Ummayids. Islamic history is replete with examples of reformist movements of one sort or another, the pace and intensity of which increased beginning in the eighteenth and nineteenth centuries as Muslims came into increasing, unequal, and often acrimonious contact with the West.[1] In Iran, efforts aimed at religious renewal and the articulation of more modernist *fiqh*s picked up pace at around the same time also, especially near the end of the nineteenth century, when jurists such as Ayatollahs Mohammad Hosein Na'ini and Mohammad Kazem Khorasani endorsed such political novelties as democratic government, elections, and parliaments during the Constitutional Revolution of 1905–11.[2] Twentieth-century Iran saw no shortage of such efforts, pioneered by the likes of Mehdi Bazargan, Ali Shariati, and Ayatollahs Morteza Mottahari and Mahmood Taleqani, culminating in the *Islamic* revolution of 1978–79.

By the time the late 1980s and the 1990s came around, therefore, what had come to be commonly known as "Islamic reformism" had had a long and influential history in both Iranian religious tradition and the popular imagination. This time, however, religious reformism was being articulated within the contexts of, and often in opposition to, a theocratic political system, one in which Islam informed the official ideology of the state. Just as importantly, as the last chapter showed, under the Islamic Republic, many religious actors within the state and their

---

[1] See Albert Hourani, *Arabic Thought in the Liberal Age, 1789–1939* (Oxford: Oxford University Press, 1962); and Charles Kurzman, ed., *Modernist Islam, 1840–1940: A Sourcebook* (Oxford: Oxford University Press, 2002).

[2] For more on the roles and arguments of these two jurists (and others) in the Constitutional Revolution see Adbul-Hadi Hairi, "Akund Korasani", in Ehsan Yarshater, ed., *Encyclopedia Iranica*, Volume I (London: Routledge & Kegan Paul, 1985), pp. 732–34; and Adbul-Hadi Hairi, *Shi'ism and Constitutionalism in Iran: A Study of the Persian Residents of Iraq in Iranian Politics* (Leiden: E. J. Brill, 1977), p. 165.

societal allies have articulated and politically supported traditionalist interpretations of *fiqh* that now form the basis of a conservative religious discourse. Its intellectual pedigree notwithstanding, therefore, the current discourse of religious reformism finds itself in a radically new predicament, defining itself in opposition to the discourse of religious conservatism on the one hand and an uncomfortable, often conflicted, relationship with the state on the other.

In some respects, the religious reformist discourse is being articulated at two *organically linked* levels, one more popular and more readily available to the urban middle classes, and another more academic and scholarly, with greater theoretical depth and complexity, and therefore less fit for popular consumption. The two levels are, of course, organically linked in the sense that many of the academics and intellectuals belonging to the latter category often give newspaper and journal interviews (or gave interviews to the press before the mass closure of "reformist" papers), many of which are subsequently reprinted in books and are widely available for purchase. Nevertheless, the arguments made and elaborated on in books are qualitatively different, in depth and complexity if in nothing else, from those made in response to questions posed in newspaper interviews. In this chapter, I will examine each of the levels of argumentation, both the more popular and the more academic. Naturally, the reader should not infer that one group of arguments, or the thinkers who articulate them, carry more or less weight than the other one. This is not the case at all. The distinction offered here is purely for analytical convenience. The religious reformist discourse is being put forward by a group of religious intellectuals, many of whom are considered "religious-nationalists." Of these, a small group of perhaps four or five have developed their arguments in greater depth. I will start this chapter with a discussion of who the religious intellectuals are and what they are advocating, and end with more detailed examinations of those whose arguments are more rigorously constructed. Together, the intellectual output that has thus been generated has given rise to a vibrant, and still evolving, discourse of religious reformism.

To better understand this discourse, first we need to have a firmer grasp of the so-called "religious intellectual" phenomenon that has brought it about, and, more specifically, the background and make-up of that group of individuals whose writings and arguments have aided in the discourse's formation. Not unlike its conservative counterpart, the reformist religious discourse is a direct product of *ijtihad*. The reformists, however, as we shall see shortly, complement their *ijtihad* and their broader understanding of religion with other, additional sciences, including especially hermeneutics. The study of the hermeneutics of

Islam is given particular prominence in the writings of some of the main architects of the reformist religious discourse, namely Mohammad Khatami, Mohammad Mojtahed Shabestari, Abdolkarim Soroush, and Mohsen Kadivar, four intellectuals whose works are highlighted here. Before doing so, however, it is important to paint a better picture of the larger group from which they hail, namely the "religious intellectuals" (*roshanfekran-e dini*).

The religious intellectual phenomenon

At the broadest level, there are two categories of religious intellectuals, or, as they are commonly and more accurately referred to, *no-andishan-e dini*, "religious new-thinkers." The individuals in one group tend to be more philosophical and academic, focusing overwhelmingly on intellectual endeavors such as teaching and writing. Soroush, Kadivar, and Mojtahed Shabestari are perhaps the most notable, as well as the most profound, among this category of thinkers. A second group of religious intellectuals is still commonly considered to be *intellectual* in the classics sense, but at the same time it has devoted some or even a majority of its efforts and energies toward political activism. Some of the better-known of these intellectual-activists include former President Khatami, Saeed Hajjarian, the former Intelligence Ministry official who went on to become a prominent member of the reform movement, and 'Emadeddin Baqi, the journalist and author who has spent long stints in prison. The boundaries separating the two groups are, of course, often blurred, sometimes because of prolonged bouts of quietism imposed on activists and thinkers alike by the whims of the state, and sometimes because of a slight political opening that allows for more direct forms of expression. Nevertheless, by and large, there are those who devote themselves overwhelmingly to academic endeavors as compared to others who complement their publishing efforts with political activism.

The intellectual-activists are often generically referred to as "religious-nationalists" (*melli-mazhabi*), a moniker widely used to refer to the individuals and groups that became especially active with Khatami's election and formed much of the President's base of support. For them, the arrival of the "reform era" was the opening they had long hoped for in order to put many of their ideas into action.[3] Most religious-nationalists

---

[3] Abbas Kazemi, *Jame'hshenasi-ye Roshanfekri-ye Dini dar Iran* (Sociology of the Religious Intellectual Movement in Iran) (Tehran: Tarh-e No, 1383/2004), pp. 100–01. See also above, chapter 2.

trace their intellectual and political genealogy back to the early days of the National Front party, and more specifically to the figure of Mehdi Bazargan and his Liberation Movement (*Nehzat-e Azadi*).[4] Bazargan, the first Prime Minister of the post-revolutionary Provisional Cabinet in 1979, was a highly regarded academic and long an important intellectual figure in Iran's religious reform movement throughout the 1970s.[5] Other inspirations include figures such as the nationalist hero Mohammad Mussadiq, the ideologue Ali Shariati, and the revolutionary Ayatollah Taleqani (1911–79).[6] As such, although they have frequently seen eye to eye with the reformist currents and individuals within the Islamic Republic's state apparatus, except for a brief period in the earliest days of the revolution, in many cases lasting no more than only a few months, they have been outside of the political establishment for the better part of the last two and a half decades. This has not prevented them from seeking elected office within the regime, especially as MPs and Municipal Council members,[7] an endeavor from which they have, nonetheless, been repeatedly barred.

Soon after Khatami's election, the religious-nationalists found allies from among a new crop of activists and reformers, this time of individuals who were once situated deep within the post-revolutionary state apparatus but were either purged or pulled away voluntarily and started advocating for the system's reform. These revolutionaries-turned-reformers never did quite identify with the "liberal" National Front. Instead, they ardently believed in Khomeini's revolutionary vision and leadership, and theologically often found themselves closer to Ayatollah Montazeri. The 1997 presidential elections ended their political marginalization, and, somewhat quite unexpectedly, they suddenly found themselves at the center of national politics. Also rejuvenated in the process were the religious-nationalists, and the two groups entered into a loose ideological and political coalition. Despite their past differences, for the two groups their newly found synergy proved quite beneficial, at least before Khatami's reforms started petering out. As 'Ezzatollah Sahhabi, one of the main figures with the religious-nationalist current and a long-time member of the Liberation Movement, once maintained,

---

[4] Ebrahim Yazdi, "Roshanfekri-ye Dini va Chalesh-haye Jadid" (Religious Intellectuals and New Crises), *Nameh*, No. 20 (1381/2002), p. 63.

[5] For a detailed treatment of the life and thoughts and career of Bazargan see Dabashi, *Theology of Discontent*, pp. 324–66.

[6] Ahmad Zeidabadi, "Naqd-e Melli-Mazhabi-ha" (Critique of Religious-Nationalists), *Aban*, No. 150 (1382/2003), p. 4.

[7] Mahmood 'Omrani, "Ahkam-e Melli-Mazhabi-ha" (The Religious-Nationlists' Sentence), *Nameh*, No. 22 (1382/2003), p. 7.

Mr. Khatami's electoral programs in the social and economic arenas were very similar to ours. These included balanced development, internal reforms, inclusiveness, curing the disease of addiction to oil, and others. I found these goals very similar to my own. After the passage of four years, however, some of these slogans proved to be empty promises.[8]

It goes without saying, of course, that the group broadly referred to in Iran as the religious intellectuals – or, alternatively, religious-nationalists or religious new-thinkers – feature a fair amount of internal diversity in thought and outlook (table 2). Some of these points of difference revolve around the degree to which continued conciliation with the hard-liners is feasible; the extent to which old outlooks and organizational structures need to be updated; and the precise nature of the new world of diplomacy and economics in which Iran finds itself.[9] Nevertheless, all of the religious-nationalists agree on three basic principles. First, they maintain, Iran's national interests are inseparable from its Islamic identity and heritage. Iran's progress, therefore, must be grounded in and consistent with its Islamic character. Second, the only proper route to progress is through reforms. In practice, this emphasis on incrementalism means resort to and participation within the legal and established mechanisms of the state. Third, whereas reforms are the only viable *method*, democracy is the only desirable *goal*. As the discussion below will illustrate, these are the general guiding principles of the religious intellectuals.

Much has been written on the "mission" (*resalat*) of the religious intellectuals, most of it by figures generally considered to be part of the group. The emerging consensus seems to be that what religious intellectuals seek to do is to break the monopoly of the clerical state over religious interpretation and *ijtihad*.[10] This point will be discussed more fully below. For now, it is important to keep in mind that one of their central preoccupations is to present an alternative interpretation of religion as compared to the official interpretation presented by the state. According to Abbas Kazemi (b. 1973), this alternative interpretation seeks to remove barriers to independent, civic organizations. In contrast, the official interpretation is a mixture of ideology and jurisprudence

---

8 'Ezzatollah Sahhabi, "Arzyabi-ye Noirouha-ye Melli-Mazhabi dar Bastar-e Tahavvolat-e Ejtema'i" (Evaluating Religious-Nationalist Forces in Light of Social Changes), *Cheshmandaz-e Iran*, No. 16 (1381/2002), p. 18.

9 Hada Saber, "Melli-Mazhabi; Douran-e Vahdat dar Ein-e Tazad" (Religious-Nationalist; Time for Unity against Tension), *Cheshmandaz-e Iran*, No. 18 (1381/ 2002), pp. 35–36.

10 Kazemi, *Jame'hshenasi-ye Roshanfekri-ye Dini dar Iran* (Sociology of the Religious Intellectual Movement in Iran), p. 154.

Table 2 *Notable religious reformists*

Name	Year of birth	Primary profession	Major publications
'Alavitabar, 'Alireza	1960	Author and independent researcher	*Intellectualism, Religiosity, Democracy*
Aqajari, Hashem	1957	Professor of history, Tarbiat Modarres University	various articles and speeches
Baqi, 'Emadeddin	1961	Author and independent researcher	*Contemporary Religious Discourses; The Clergy and Power; The Democratic Reform Movement in Iran*
Bastehnegar, Mohammad	1941	Author and independent researcher	*Clash of Tradition and Modernity in Iran; People's Rule from the Perspectives of the Qur'an and Islam*
Govaraee, Fatemeh	1962	Author and independent researcher	*Our Philosophical Heritage*
Hajjarian, Saeed	1954	Author and university lecturer	*Republicanism*
Kadivar, Mohsen	1959	Professor of philosophy, Tarbiat Modarres University	*Government of the Jurisconsult; Crises of Religious Government; Perspectives on Government in Shi'a Jurisprudence*
Khatami, Mohammad	1943	President of Iran, 1997–2005	*Fear of Wave; The Reviver Truth of Religion; Religion and Intellect Trapped in Tyranny*
Mohajerani, 'Ataollah	1954	Author and independent researcher	*The Story Still Remains; Grey Paradise*
Mohammadi, Narges	1973	Author and independent researcher	*Reforms, Both Strategy and Tactic*
Mojtahed Shabestari, Mohammad	1936	Cleric, author, and university lecturer	*Hermeneutics, the Scripture, and Tradition; A Critique of the Official Reading of Religion; Faith and Freedom*
Nouri, 'Abdollah	1949	Cleric, Interior Minister, 1997–98	*A Critique for All Seasons*
Omrani, Mahmood	1939	Private sector employment, author	various articles in *Iran Farda* magazine
Pedram, Mas'oud	1956	Author and university lecturer	*Religious Intellectuals and Modernity in Iran after the Revolution*
Peyman, Habibollah	1935	Journalist and publisher	*Man and Religion; Fundamentals of Tohidi Society*

Table 2 (*cont.*)

Name	Year of birth	Primary profession	Major publications
Rahmani, Taqi	1959	Author and independent researcher	*Critique of Power*
Sahhabi, 'Ezzatollah	1930	Publisher, author, and political activist	*An Introduction to the Nationalist Movement in Iran*
Soroush, Abdolkarim	1945	Author, former professor at the University of Tehran	*Healthier than Ideology; The Expansion and Contraction of Theory of Shari'a*
Yazdi, Ebrahim	1931	Author and political activist	*Three Republics*
Yusefi Eshkevari, Hasan	1949	Former cleric (disrobed), author, and political activist	*Religious Reformism; Thoughts in Solitude: An Introduction to Iranian Hermeneutics; Letters from Prison to My Daughter*

designed to present a mass-based (as opposed to democratic), max-imalist, and politically doctored version of Islam.[11] The articulation of an alternative worldview, one that is at once grounded in Islam and in the tenets of democracy and modernity, is the central project that religious intellectuals have set up for themselves.

Mas'oud Pedram (b. 1956), a prolific author and a religious intel-lectual of renown, defines the class of individuals to which he belongs in terms of their relationship with the discourses of traditional religion and modernity. First, he maintains, the religious intellectual "enters into the discourse of modernity, and, using its facilities of critical reasoning, takes into question the assumptions of religious tradition."[12] He thus seeks to highlight the contradictions of modernity and religious trad-ition. "In the next phase, he distances himself from modernity and its underlying rationality, and critiques them. This critique of modernity and critique of tradition open up space for religious intellectualism," a product of the "grey area" that results from a mixture of both.[13]

Ebrahim Yazdi (b. 1931), who assumed the leadership of the Liber-ation Front after Bazargan's passing and who today is considered to be an important figure within the religious-nationalists, agrees with both Pedram and Kazemi on the religious intellectuals' self-ascribed mission. As Yazdi sees it, religious intellectuals seek to resolve the "contradiction and conflict between the inevitable necessities of modern society and the religious aspects of the dominant culture."

They know that denial of modern society is neither possible nor beneficial. They also know that traditional outlooks can no longer answer the complexities of society. Therefore, they have assumed for themselves the mission of indigenizing – in Iran, Iranianizing and Islamizing – the elements of modern society. Without indigenization, the modernization of society will never last.[14]

After the Islamic revolution, Yazdi claims, the competition between the two forces of tradition and modernity was accentuated, with the traditionalists winning the upper hand, but only temporarily. Khatami's election signaled the political victory (at least temporarily) and the social stature of religious intellectuals. Today, regardless of what happens to the reform movement, it is all the more important for religious intel-lectuals to articulate their message and to go about their mission of

---

[11] Ibid., p. 151.
[12] Mas'oud Pedram, *Roshanfekran-e Dini va Moderniteh dar Iran Pas az Enqelab* (Religious Intellectuals and Modernity in Iran after the Revolution), p. 23.
[13] Ibid.
[14] Ebrahim Yazdi, *Se Jomhuri* (Three Republics) (Tehran: Jame'h Iranian, 1379/2000), p. 206.

constructing bridges between tradition and modernity.[15] Doing so means "reconstructing and renewing religious notions and beliefs"; "reforming, reconstructing, and renewing political, economic, and social, structure"; and encouraging belief in "relativism" and relativity between the two extremes of tradition and modernity.[16]

'Alireza 'Alavi-Tabar (b. 1960), another influential and prolific religious intellectual, is somewhat more specific about the characteristics and the mission of the category of thinkers to which he belongs. From the beginning, he maintains, religious intellectuals saw "critical reason," which is a key ingredient to solving the riddles of modern life, as necessary but insufficient. "Religion is the only source that can protect man against the crises and storms caused by modernity. Religious intellectuals endorse the need for a complete re-thinking [of religion], and also believe in the power and utility of critical reason. But they do also reject the notion of critical reason's absoluteness."[17] As such, according to 'Alavi-Tabar, religious intellectuals have four key goals:

1 Presenting a rational analysis of religion and religious precepts;
2 Critiquing prevailing social relations, institutions, and patterns of behavior;
3 Striving to regularize rational bases for collective social life and its different aspects; and,
4 Central attention to the three key values of freedom, equality, and progress, emphasizing each according to the needs and requirements of the times.[18]

Clearly, one of the central tasks of the religious intellectual is to "make religion contemporary" and "contemporary times religious."[19] The resulting "reconstruction of society" does not mean seeking to lead another revolution. It does mean, however, at least insofar as the religious intellectuals are concerned, internalizing a perspective of "critical realism" that is nurtured by science, philosophy, and religion, and which presents an alternative of "non-liberal democracy" consistent with the tenets of Islamic government.[20] Precisely how this is to happen, 'Alavi-Tabar does not discuss.

'Alavi-Tabar's vagueness on the means and methods for the reconstruction of society may be somewhat deliberate, perhaps a product of

---

[15] Ibid., pp. 271–73.
[16] Yazdi, "Roshanfekri-ye Dini va Chalesh-haye Jadid" (Religious Intellectuals and New Crises), p. 64.
[17] 'Alireza 'Alavi-Tabar, "Roshanfekri va Roshanfekri-ye Dini dar Iran" (Intellectualism and Religious Intellectualism in Iran", *Kiyan*, Vol. 6, No. 34 (1375/1997), p. 40.
[18] Ibid.
[19] 'Alireza 'Alavi-Tabar, "Roshanfekri-e Dini, Yek Barnameh-e Pishro" (Religious Intellectualism, a Progressive Program), *Aftab*, No. 10 (1380/2001), p. 5.
[20] 'Alavi-Tabar, *Roshanfekri, Dindari, Mardomsalari* (Intellectualism, Religiosity, Democracy), pp. 33–34.

the political atmosphere at the time of his writing. Hashem Aqajari (b. 1957), an outspoken history professor at Tarbiat Modarres University who was once given a death sentence after one of his lectures on the need for an Islamic reformation, is somewhat less circumscribed in describing the nature of the religious intellectuals' mission, but only slightly less so. Religious intellectuals, he maintains, need to assume the leadership of the social classes through a mixture of elitism and democracy. They would then guide the people in a "long-term, gradual, historic, and evolutionary process" through which the complementary phenomena of meritocracy and democracy become ultimately institutionalized throughout society.[21] "In our estimation," he goes on to assert, "in the theory of Shi'a imamate, nothing other than this evolutionary phenomenon can be found."[22]

None of the religious intellectuals cited here, nor any others, of course, advocate the violent overthrow of the existing political system or, for that matter, even breaking the law. In fact, working with the system and reforming it *from within* is one of the notable hallmarks of the religious intellectuals' strategies for change. In almost all of their essays and printed lectures, the religious intellectuals emphasize legalism and gradualism as their preferred *modus operandi*. According to 'Emadeddin Baqi, one of the country's most prominent religious intellectuals, the dominant strategy of activists and intellectuals like him could be described alternatively as either "quiet activism" or "active resistance," depending on the level of violent reaction they elicited from their rightist opponents.[23] At any rate, we must "refine and revise" rather than "eliminate" those aspects of traditional culture, and those proponents of tradition, who act as obstacles to progress.[24] Even "active resistance" does not necessarily mean breaking the law. "The primary goals and key characteristics of religious intellectuals are summed up in 'knowledge' and 'law', and the only knowledgeable and legal method of operation is 'reformism,'" states Ahmad Qabel (b. 1958), another figure commonly identified as a religious intellectual.[25]

This emphasis on reforms and gradualism as the only viable method of ensuring change is largely based on a reading of prevailing social and

---

[21] Hashem Aqajari, *Hokumat-e Dini va Hokumat-e Democratic* (Religious Government and Democratic Government) (Tehran: Zekr, 1381/2002), pp. 129–30.

[22] Ibid., p. 130.

[23] 'Emadeddin Baqi, *Jonbesh-e Eslahat-e Demokratik dar Iran* (The Democratic Reform Movement in Iran) (Tehran: Saraee, 1382/2003), p. 346.

[24] Baqi, *Gofteman-haye Dini-ye Mo'aser* (Contemporary Religious Discourses), p. 332.

[25] Ahmad Qabel, *Naqd-e Farhang-e Khoshunat: Khoshunat-e Siyasi va Taffakor-e Sonnati* (Critique of Culture of Violence: Political Violence and Traditional Thought) (Tehran: Saraee, 1381/2002), p. 230.

political conditions in Iran. According to Yazdi, for example, unlike what transpired in the 1970s, today none of the objective conditions for massive, radical change exist in Iran. Despite their profound dissatisfaction with the Islamic Republic's rulers, he maintains, today's Iranians, especially the youth, are far less willing to blindly follow those promising the regime's violent overthrow.[26] Instead of street protests and demonstrations, the best way to initiate the desired changes – deepening civil society, fostering political development, and reforming the system – is through the ballot box.[27] The opponent, Yazdi emphasizes, must be made to understand that he is only an *electoral* opponent, and that Iran has a new set of political "rules of the game" based on elections, not violence.[28] This, he claims, is precisely what the people would want Iranian intellectuals to do. Referring to Khatami's elections in 1997 and 2001 and the messages they entailed, he makes the following observation:

From within the depths of society, people sent us intellectuals a message. They told us that we like the revolution and are loyal to the system. But we cannot tolerate our present predicament. They showed us intellectuals the path we need to choose. Through democracy and the ballot box, they said, we will cast a negative vote [for the existing political environment]. This is a vote of no confidence, a protest vote.[29]

Along similar lines, 'Alavi-Tabar maintains that focus on and participation in the few remaining democratic vestiges of the state – such as the right to vote – itself helps to deepen democratic norms and values. The religious reformists, he maintains, have a democratic perspective about the Islamic Republican system.[30] Their ultimate goal is to bring about a religious democracy in Iran. But religious democracy can only thrive through the ballot box, not through any ideological impositions on society. "Religious democracy can be realized only when a majority of the people have freely accepted religion as the arbitrator of issues in the public domain, and when decisions are based on the vote of the majority."[31] Perhaps anticipating the criticism that a "religious democracy" is an oxymoron, he goes on to state: "In such conditions, even though laws and the rulers' basis of action are based on religion, the rights of the minority are protected, and the competition between the supporters of religious government and others becomes

---

[26] Yazdi, *Se Jomhuri* (Three Republics), pp. 52–53.   [27] Ibid., p. 194.
[28] Ibid., p. 280.   [29] Ibid., p. 450.
[30] 'Alavi-Tabar, *Roshanfekri, Dindari, Mardomsalari* (Intellectualism, Religiosity, Democracy), p. 187.
[31] Ibid., p. 193.

institutionalized."[32] "Our responsibility," speaking of religious intellectuals, "is to protect the liberties that the law allows and to guard against their violation. [These include] rights such as freedom of expression, the freedom to publish, and form political parties ... [Additionally,] there should be a dialogue between the different currents of thought and strategic perspectives."[33] The hope, according to Mostafa Tajzadeh (b. 1956), another prominent religious intellectual, is to give rise to a carefully designed and systematic "new perspective" that would usher in a "discourse of reformism."[34]

It seems befitting to end this discussion of reformism by religious intellectuals with a quotation by Hojjatoleslam 'Abdollah Nouri, the outspoken cleric who served as President Khatami's first Interior Minister in 1997–98 but who was subsequently impeached by the Majles within a few months of his appointment, taken before the Special Court for the Clergy in 1999, and sentenced to five years in prison. In the introduction to a wildly popular book that included his defense before the Special Court for the Clergy, Nouri wrote the following:

Based on my analysis, I have reached the conclusion that for the supporters of this [political] system, there is no endeavor more essential than the peaceful and fearless critique of the political order. Through reforms, and the granting of the right to criticize to the real holders of power, namely the people, the system will only enhance its own legitimacy and popularity ...

The substance of my argument in this defense is reformism. My goal in reforming the Islamic Republic is to bestow power to its rightful heirs and to deepen the system's political legitimacy. Presenting a compassionate and logical picture of Islam, and the attraction of large segments of the population, only become possible when we reform the levers of political power.[35]

Nouri's imprisonment, it must be mentioned, is not unique. Few of the more notable religious intellectuals have not at some point or another been imprisoned or not been harassed by government officials. Arrests, prolonged imprisonment, solitary confinement, purges and being barred from employment, and other, more subtle forms of harassment have been common types of treatment meted out to religious intellectuals by the conservative-dominated judiciary. Despite the heavy-handed reaction of the state, however, literally all religious intellectuals continue to call for conciliatory, reformist measures. Observing democratic norms and means on their own part, they insist, is necessary to bring about a democratic political system. The most they are willing to

---

[32] Ibid., pp. 193–94.   [33] Ibid., p. 194.
[34] Tajzadeh, *Siyasat, Kakh va Zendan* (Politics, Palace, and Prison), p. 155.
[35] Nouri, *Shoukaran-e Eslah* (Hemlock for Advocate of Reform), p. 12.

advocate, and seldom very openly, is a constitutional referendum aimed at revising some of the political system's less democratic features.[36] I shall have more to say on the reformists' tactics later on in the chapter. For now, it is worth emphasizing the reformist, religious intellectuals' abiding adherence to democratic norms and practices. What they articulate and advocate is an Islamic Republic that is wholly and truly democratic, a system that is at once Islamic and democratic. Key, therefore, is an Islamic democracy, or, alternatively, a democratic Islam.

Articulating an Islamic democracy

In outlining the principles of an Islamic democracy, a number of religious intellectuals begin by clarifying their conception of religion in general and Islam in particular. In simple terms, most argue, "religion is made up of a series of rules and regulations, comprising a divine worldview, that the Almighty has sent to humans through His prophets."[37] More specifically, according to Hojjatoleslam Hasan Yusofi Eshkevari, religion has three interrelated components: it has a worldview; it contains ethical (or ideological) commands; and it also features practical commands.[38] Each of these components is driven by the two internal logics of "guidance" and "justice" – guidance for man's spiritual growth and refinement, and justice as the driving principle in social relations, economy, ethics, legal rights, and freedom.[39]

The arguments of the religious intellectuals are guided by two important assumptions, one having to do with the larger nature and functions of religion, and another with religion's relationship with politics. First, all agree that religion does, and should continue to, play a pivotal role in the overall life of society. Aqajari, for example, maintains that secularism features internal logical contradictions that it cannot easily solve.[40] Most of these contradictions revolve around the spiritual needs of societies and individuals. One of the best-known religious intellectuals who has articulated the need to address this spiritual hunger

---

[36] See, for example, Qabel, *Naqd-e Farhang-e Khoshunat* (Critique of Culture of Violence), p. 33.

[37] Mostafa Katir'i, "Hokumat az Didgah-e Din" (Government from the Perspective of Religion), in Ali Mohammad Izadi *et al.*, *Din va Hokumat* (Religion and Government) (Tehran: Rasa, 1377/1998), p. 25.

[38] Hasan Yusofi Eshkevari, "Hokumat-e Demokratik-e Eslami" (Democratic Islamic Government), in Izadi *et al.*, *Din va Hokumat* (Religion and Government), p. 291.

[39] Yusofi Eshkevari, "Hokumat-e Demokratik-e Eslami" (Democratic Islamic Government), pp. 291–92.

[40] Aqajari, *Hokumat-e Dini va Hokumat-e Democratic* (Religious Government and Democratic Government), p. 243.

is Mostafa Malekian. According to Malekian, religion, and more specifically Islam, provides answers and solutions to a whole host of questions that, if unanswered, would bring misery and ruin to a person's life. "The mind and soul of the contemporary person has problems and difficulties that are existential in nature," he argues.

It is essential that we explore the Qur'an's perspective on these issues fully and thoroughly; problems and difficulties such as truth, good, compassion, beauty, justices, doubt, belief, calm, disquiet, anxiety, fear, happiness, depression, hopelessness, loneliness, death, meaning of life, self-discovery, self-alienation, selfishness, self-construction, pain and suffering, the changeable facets of life, the unchangeable facets of life, the differences between people and the secret of these differences.[41]

Apart from nourishing the soul, religion has important political functions. Yusofi Eshkevari's arguments in this regard are typical of many others. Without religion, he argues – and therefore without justice, religion's centerpiece – a balanced and spiritually fulfilling life is not possible.[42] This is where the second assumption in the religious intellectuals' arguments about religion comes in. While religion is an integral and important part of society's overall operations, including its politics, an overwhelming majority of religious reformists maintain that Islam does not mandate a specific form of government. Yusofi Eshkevari's emphatic arguments in this regard are typical of those made by other religious intellectuals. "Never in Islam has the act of governing been mandated as a function of religion."[43] Government, instead, is a purely human endeavor, cannot possibly have one form and type at all times, and is contextually dependent on the times and the conditions in which it finds itself.[44] These and other similar arguments, typical of the reformist religious discourse as they are, put it directly at odds with proponents of the conservative religious discourse.

Let us explore the theoretical propositions of the religious intellectuals regarding "religious government" in some depth. According to 'Ezzatollah Sahhabi, the Almighty has given man complete free will to choose and decide his own fate and destiny, including the type of political system under which he chooses to live.[45] While God is all-knowing and omnipotent, nowhere in the Holy Book or in the traditions has He

---

[41] Mostafa Malekian, *Rahi be Raha-ee* (A Path to Liberation) (Tehran: Negah-e Mo'aser, 1381/2002), p. 493.

[42] Yusofi Eshkevari, "Hokumat-e Demokratik-e Eslami" (Democratic Islamic Government), p. 306.

[43] Ibid., p. 299.   [44] Ibid., p. 300.

[45] 'Ezzatollah Sahhabi, "Emkan-e Hokumat-e Dini" (The Possibility of Religious Government), in Izadi *et al.*, *Din va Hokumat* (Religion and Government), p. 207.

mandated a specific form and type of government. In fact, claims 'Abdolali Bazargan, another religious intellectual, the Qur'an explicitly mentions – meaning endorses – a diverse variety of political systems, including those headed by women.[46] The Qur'an, in other words, does not mandate a specific type of political system. Also, the ideal political system does not necessarily have to be ruled by a prophet or a learned religious cleric. "We have had prophets who have governed, and we have had prophets who have only fulfilled spiritual roles and who have delegated military and political matters to qualified leaders."[47] There is a significant conclusion to be drawn here: "In sum, the ideal type of political system differs according to the conditions of the times and the people's knowledge and understanding, and insisting on a uniform structure of government [for all times] and giving it divine sanction is contrary to the logic and the contents of the Qur'an."[48] The construction of a religious system is man's prerogative, and this is precisely why Shi'a *fiqh* features such a diversity of opinions about the ideal political system.[49]

This subject has been extensively studied by Abdolkarim Soroush. Soroush divides the phenomenon of political rule into two distinct aspects, one administrative and managerial, that is thoroughly *a*religious, and another ethical and normative, in which religion can play a determining role.[50] Ideally, governments must attend to the material needs of the people so that people themselves can attend to their own spiritual needs. "Religious government is one that addresses the worldly needs of the people and enables them to nurture and sustain their own spirits."[51] Soroush makes an important distinction between a "religious government" (*hokumat-e dini*) and a "jurisprudential government" (*hokumat-e fiqhi*). A jurisprudential government is a theocracy that seeks to impose religious dictates on the population. Compliance is different from belief, and the pretence of being religious is fundamentally different from the internalization and voluntary, knowing acceptance of norms and values. "If the people of a society are not truly free to choose

---

[46] 'Abdolali Bazargan, "Marz-haye Miyan-e Din va Hokumat" (Boundaries between Religion and Government), in Ali Izadi *et al.*, *Din va Hokumat* (Religion and Government), p. 114.

[47] Ibid.   [48] Ibid.

[49] Sadeq Haqiqat, *Touzi'-e Qodrat dar Andisheh-ye Siyasi-e Shi'a* (Division of Power in Shi'a Political Thought) (Tehran: Hasti Nama, 1381/2002), p. 254.

[50] Abdolkarim Soroush, "Tahlil-e Mafhoum-e Hokumat-e Dini" (Analyzing the Meaning of Religious Government), in Ali Izadi *et al. Din va Hokumat* (Religion and Government) (Tehran: Rasa, 1377/1998), p. 173.

[51] Ibid., p. 186.

their beliefs, that society cannot be called truly 'religious'" even if it is ruled over by a government that claims the mantle of religion.[52] From this we can surmise what religious government is and is not:

A religious government is not one whose method of management is religious, since method can never be religious.

A religious government is not one that spreads and executes jurisprudential commands, since compulsion is not a yardstick for religiosity.

A religious government is not one that is based on the religious credentials and rights of the rulers, since government must also rely on the non-religious rights of the people.

A religious government is not one that imposes belief on to the hearts of the people, since religion cannot be imposed.

A religious government is one that is based on the non-religious rights of the people and the non-political responsibility of religious individuals toward management and critique of power. Its first responsibility is to provide for the needs of the people (based on rational methods and precedence) in order to rid them of material needs, so they can attend to matters that are more delicate and spiritual. The people can thus freely choose their beliefs, and also transform society into a stage for the open and free choice of religion.[53]

Insofar as the religious intellectuals' discussion of the relationship between religion – i.e. Islam – and government is concerned, democracy figures very prominently. In fact, as mentioned earlier, for these architects of the reformist religious discourse, reformism is the means through which democracy as the end can be achieved. For them, Islam and democracy are intimately and fundamentally compatible. The argument is simple: Islam has not mandated any specific forms of government except those that attend to the material and spiritual needs of the people. The ideal form of government, therefore, is changeable according to the needs and circumstances of the times, which, in the contemporary era, happens to be democracies. Islam, in fact, contains several built-in features and mechanisms that are consistent with and are supportive of democracy. What Muslim societies need, therefore, are Islamic democracies.

Among the crop of religious intellectuals, Yusofi Eshkevari has been at the forefront of articulating the relationship between Islam and democracy. He argues that "the democratic method is the most religious and the most appropriate manner to administer Muslim societies."[54] If the

[52] Ibid., p. 165.   [53] Ibid., p. 187.
[54] Yusofi Eshkevari, "Hokumat-e Demokratik-e Eslami" (Democratic Islamic Government), p. 296.

essence of religion is the spread of peace and justice, and if the guiding logic of democracy is checks and limits on political power and the right of all to participate in the political process, "undoubtedly then religious justice is not possible without resort to democratic methods. At the very least, democracy is the most appropriate method for ensuring justice."[55] In the Qur'an, Yusofi Eshkevari goes on to argue, man is created as a free and thinking being, and any form of compulsion and imposition is contrary to the spirit and essence of Islam. There is an important conclusion to be reached here: "In the fields of government and politics, not only are Islam and democracy not incompatible, in fact, to the contrary, no Muslim government can be undemocratic."[56] A truly Islamic government is a democratic one.

Elsewhere, Yusofi Eshkevari makes an important distinction between religious democracy as a political construct and religious pluralism as a theological notion. He rejects arguments by Friedrich Hayek and Soroush that all religions are equally just and righteous. Islam is, indeed, the only right and just religion, as enunciated in the Qur'an and demonstrated by the deeds of the Prophet.[57] If religious pluralism is taken to mean the equal merits of all religions, then it is wrong and misguided. However, if it is conceptualized differently, in the sense of the right to choose religions through free choice and dialogue, then religious pluralism makes sense:

As a Muslim, I know that my religion is more just and more complete. But I do not have a monopoly over the truth and I do not seek to monopolize others. In this sense I am pluralist. I also believe in dialogue, discourse, and mutual understanding among religions, and reject religious violence and force and compulsion, and in this sense I am pluralist as well. But I also defend the righteousness of my religion.[58]

Other religious intellectuals have been equally emphatic in their defense of democracy as one of the key aspects of Islam. Hashem Aqajari, for example, maintains that far from being contradictory, religion and democracy are mutually necessary and complement one another.[59] The ideal form of government is a "religious democracy," one that is based on two key assumptions: an acceptance of religious pluralism and diversity of beliefs; and an acknowledgment of democracy as

---

[55] Ibid.   [56] Ibid., p. 298.

[57] Hasan Yusofi Eshkevari, *Ta'amollat-e Tanha-ee: Dibacheh-ee bar Hermeneutic-e Irani* (Thoughts in Solitude: An Introduction to Iranian Hermeneutics) (Tehran: Saraee 1382/2003), pp. 147–48.

[58] Ibid., p. 149.

[59] Aqajari, *Hokumat-e Dini va Hokumat-e Democratic* (Religious Government and Democratic Government), p. 146.

the best method to run society and to handle social and political issues.[60] Religious government is one in which individuals govern based on their understanding of religious norms and precepts. For a religious government to be democratic, it must be open to a plurality of religious understandings. There cannot be a single, dominant reading of religion. Religious government is not the government of God but the government of man, and man is not infallible. Only when a government is guided by the spirit of religion and the logic of democracy will the chances for mistakes and embarking on the wrong path be reduced.[61] "Democratism in power, pluralism in religion" – for Aqajari, these are the core principles of religious government.[62]

Hojjatoleslam Mohammad Mojtahed Shabestari, another prominent figure in the religious reformist discourse, advocates an unconditional adoption of democracy even if it means the risk of a popular vote to set religion aside. Democracy, he argues, is neither a philosophy of rights nor a philosophy of ethics. It is, instead, a method of government in which people participate in their own destiny and in the running of their own affairs.[63] Democracy is not just an attractive form of government; it is a necessity. "In today's societies," he maintains, "it is only through democracy that the full potential of individuals in the reconstruction of society can be realized. It is only through democracy that collective, creative solutions can be formulated to address complex problems."[64] As a method of government, democracy has no contradictions whatsoever with people's beliefs and values, and today millions of religious individuals around the world live and practice their beliefs peacefully under democratic governments. Muslims can do so as well, and, if they so choose, they can use God's commandments as guides for making laws in a democratic framework.[65] Nevertheless, Mojtahed Shabestari goes on to argue, it is also theoretically possible for Iranians to democratically legislate religion out of public life, although such a possibility is remote and cannot used as a basis for denying the desirability of democratic rule.[66]

To be certain, as indicated by the careful attention to Islam by literally religious reformists in their discussions of democracy, religion and democracy are often viewed as intimately linked with one another. In certain instances, in fact, as Aqajari's discussion of "religious democracy" demonstrates, there are some important theoretical

---

[60] Ibid., p. 155.   [61] Ibid., p. 171.   [62] Ibid.

[63] Mas'oud Razavi, *Motefakeran-e Mo'aser va Endisheh-ye Siyasi-e Eslam* (Contemporary Thinkers and Islamic Political Thought) (Tehran: Farzan-e Ruz, 1378/1999), pp. 138–39.

[64] Quoted in ibid., p. 140.   [65] Quoted in ibid., p. 142.   [66] Quoted in ibid., p. 143.

differences between the conception of democracy as articulated by most Iranian religious intellectuals and the notion of liberal democracy as conventionally understood in the West. The sociologist 'Alireza Shoja'izand (b. 1959), for example, makes a distinction between *freedom of thought* in Islam, which he claims is unconditional, versus *freedom of opinion*, on which Islam imposes certain limitations.[67] Unlike Western liberalism, he claims, Islam is not indifferent to various opinions and considers its own teachings and values to be superior. But Islam does respect the rights of individuals to hold opinions that differ from its teachings and does not seek to impose itself on others by force.[68]

For the most part, nevertheless, the democracy that is articulated by the proponents of the religious reformist discourse is not significantly different from the democracies commonly found in the West. For Mostafa Tajzadeh, for example, religious democracy has the same underlying foundations as liberal democracy in the West – political liberties, respect for human rights, self-determination, etc. – but it is more thorough and complete. In Islam, political participation is not just a right, as it is in liberal democracies, but is indeed a religious obligation.[69] Similarly, according to the reformist political activist and one-time Intelligence Ministry official Mohsen Armin (b. 1954), Islam recognizes all basic freedoms, including the freedom of thought and expression, the right to vote on political and social issues, the right to live freely, and the right to equality.[70] Islamic *fiqh* recognizes the freedom of thought and religion, and it grants all individuals, regardless of their creed and religion, equal rights and protection before the law.[71] A proper reading of the Qur'an clearly demonstrates that "freedom can be a basis for religion."[72] Religion in general and Islam in particular have important roles to play in the lives of societies, but this role should be limited and is not absolute. Ultimately, Armin argues, this role should be played within a democratic framework.[73]

Democracies derive their legitimacy from the people, feature political participation and limitations on the powers of rulers, and are buttressed by civil society. In these important respects, Islamic democracies are no exception. As outlined in the Qur'an and in the *Nahjolbalagheh*, which is comprised of Imam Ali's sermons and letters, Muslim rulers have

---

[67] 'Alireza Shoja'izand, *Takapoo-haye Din-e Siyasi* (Efforts of Political Religion) (Tehran: Baz, 1383/2004), p. 206.

[68] Ibid., pp. 206–07.

[69] Tajzadeh, *Siyasat, Kakh va Zendan* (Politics, Palace, and Prison), p. 106.

[70] Mohsen Armin, *Eslam, Ejtema', Siyasat* (Islam, Society, Politics) (Tehran: Zekr, 1380/ 2001), pp. 10, 26.

[71] Ibid., p. 12.   [72] Ibid., p. 20.   [73] Ibid., p. 220.

important obligations to the people, chief among which is respect for the popular will. Equally importantly, no one can claim the right to rule based solely on religious rank and qualification.[74] A successful religious government, according to Soroush, is one in which people have the right to supervise and if necessary remove their leaders from power.[75] Also key is political participation. Maximum power and state capacity can be achieved when greater numbers of people participate in the political process, and by doing so deepen the Islamic system's legitimacy.[76] According to Ayatollah 'Abbasali 'Ameed Zanjani, the Qur'an (13:11) – "Verily God does not change the state of a people till they change themselves" – gives a clear command to individuals to actively partake in the social and political management of their societies.[77] This participation needs to be organized and orderly, structured in a way that would have maximum effect in limiting the potential abuse of power by the state.[78]

There are, of course, a wide variety of forms of political participation, voting being the most common one. One of the cornerstones of the Prophet's rule was the *Bey'at*, a ceremony in which an oath of allegiance was taken and the Prophet's leadership was reaffirmed. In fact, the Prophet personally engaged in *Bey'at* on eight different occasions, and the practice is mentioned in the Qur'an three separate times.[79] Today, voting and elections perform the same functions that the *Bey'at* did during the Prophet's time, albeit in a more thorough and complete fashion, and, therefore, must be integral parts of any Muslim political system.[80] This centrality of elections to the running of Muslim societies, modeled after the centrality of the *Bey'at* to the running of the original *ummah*, is a recurrent and significant theme in much of the religious

---

[74] Mohammad Ali Ayazi, "Din, Azadi, va Mas'ouliyyat" (Religion, Freedom, and Responsibility), in Mohsen Armin *et al.*, *Rabeteh-ye Din va Azadi* (The Relationship between Religion and Freedom) (Tehran: Zekr, 1379/2000), p. 66. This important point, which stands in direct opposition to the conservative religious discourse's formulation of *Velayat-e Faqih*, will be explored more fully below.

[75] Soroush, "Tahlil-e Mafhoum-e Hokumat-e Dini" (Analyzing the Meaning of Religious Government), pp. 170–71.

[76] Nouri, *Shoukaran-e Eslah* (Hemlock for Advocate of Reform), p. 11.

[77] 'Abbasali 'Ameed Zanjani, "Ab'ad-e Fiqhi-ye Mosharekat-e Siyasi" (The Jurisprudential Aspects of Political Participation), in 'Ali Akbar 'Alikhani, ed., *Mosharekat-e Siyasi* (Political Participation) (Tehran: Safir, 1377/1998), p. 32.

[78] Hajjarian, *Jomhuriyyat; Afsonzedai az Qodrat* (Republicanism; Demystification of Power), p. 361.

[79] Abolfazl Musavian, *Mabani-e Mashro'iyyat-e Hokumat* (Basis of Government Legitimacy) (Tehran: Zekr, 1381/2002), p. 26.

[80] Ibid., pp. 46, 126.

reformist literature in Iran today.[81] Applied to today's context, elections and voting are seen as one of the most essential aspects of politics in Islam.

With electoral politics and popular political participation comes legitimacy. It will be recalled that in the conservative religious discourse, political legitimacy is often attributed to divine sources that are beyond man's reach and control. At most, man may be able to play a role in the "acceptability" (*maqbuliyyat*) of a political system but not its legitimacy (*mashru'iyyat*). Proponents of the reformist religious discourse explicitly reject this subtle and important distinction between acceptability and legitimacy, along with its accompanying assumption of legitimacy's exclusivity to divinely ordained personages and institutions. Ayatollah Mohammad Musavi Bojnourdi, for example, addresses this question directly and reaches the conclusion that Islam's insistence on the right to vote makes people central to a regime's acquisition of popular legitimacy.[82] Islam, he maintains, pays careful attention to the wishes of the people and sees them as the central locus of power. Although those running the affairs of the *ummah* may have to meet certain pre-qualifications, the vote of the people is essential in giving them the right to rule.[83] Yusofi Eshkevari is equally emphatic on the worldly basis of political power. "[Both] the legitimacy and acceptance of the government and its leaders come from the results of popular elections, not from somewhere else. And the responsibility for elections rests on the shoulders of the people, not with God, or His prophet, or religion."[84]

Conversely, if for whatever reason people cease to engage in political participation, from the perspective of Islam, the system loses its legitimacy and will have to resort to force to stay in power.[85] Without legitimacy, a political system becomes dictatorial even if it continues to

---

[81] See, for example, 'Ameed Zanjani, "Ab'ad-e Fiqhi-ye Mosharekat-e Siyasi" (The Jurisprudential Aspects of Political Participation), pp. 40–41; Mohammad Qoochani, *Dowlat-e Dini va Din-e Dowlati* (Religious Government and Government's Religion) (Tehran: Saraee 1379/2000), pp. 28–29; and Asadollah Bayat, "Payambaran, Nokhostin Tarrahan-e Jame'h Madani" (The Prophets, The First Architects of Civil Society), in Mohsen Armin *et al.*, *Nesbat-e Din va Jame'h Madani* (The Relationship between Religion and Civil Society) (Tehran: Zekr, 1379/2000), p. 153.

[82] Mohammad Musavi Bojnourdi, "Naqsh-e Mosharekat-e Siyasi dar Mashru'iyyat-e Hokumat-e Eslami" (The Role of Political Participation in the Legitimacy of Islamic Government), in 'Alikhani, ed., *Mosharekat-e Siyasi* (Political Participation), pp. 24–25.

[83] Quoted in Razavi, *Motefakeran-e Mo'aser va Endisheh-ye Siyasi-e Eslam* (Contemporary Thinkers and Islamic Political Thought), p. 68.

[84] Yusofi Eshkevari, "Hokumat-e Demokratik-e Eslami" (Democratic Islamic Government), p. 301.

[85] Musavi Bojnourdi, "Naqsh-e Mosharekat-e Siyasi dar Mashru'iyyat-e Hokumat-e Eslami" (The Role of Political Participation in the Legitimacy of Islamic Government), pp. 26–28.

be "accepted" by the people. Not surprisingly, Aqajari maintains, legitimacy crises have been recurrent features of Iranian political history as traditional political forces have sought to locate their legitimacy not in the people but in aristocracy, patrimonialism, or charisma.[86] Today, a false distinction has been created between "legitimacy" and "acceptability" in order to remedy the existing regime's legitimacy crisis. But this is only a temporary solution, an attempt to justify a twenty-first-century version of the theory of divinely ordained kingship.[87] Substituting or mixing legitimacy with righteousness (*haqqaniyyat*) is only a recipe for dictatorship.[88] This, of course, is a not-too-subtle reference to the Right's formulation of the concept of *Velayat-e Faqih*.

Saeed Hajjarian agrees. Those conservative religious thinkers who see *maqbuliyyat* as a sufficient substitute for legitimacy, he maintains, are simply trying to justify dictatorial rule.[89] "The misleading distinction between *maqbuliyyat* and *mashru'iyyat* is a desperate theoretical device concocted by the Right" in order to rescue itself from the political dead-end it has reached.[90]

Equally important in solidifying the legitimacy of political systems is consultation (*shura*), which was used extensively by the Prophet, even in instances when the prevailing opinion was against his.[91] According to Hojjatoleslam Ayazi, the command to consult has been spelled out in the Qur'an (3:159 and 42:38). Consultation must, therefore, become the standard practice through which today's Islamic leaders are elected and political decisions are made.[92] Applied to contemporary circumstances, the best method of ensuring the consultative process is through parliamentary means, whereby legislatures become forums through which expert advice and opinion are formulated and taken into account.

Limitations on the powers of rulers, the people's right to vote, and the centrality of consultation all become easier to attain when civil society is realized. Civil society is one of the key ingredients of modern polities as it allows for a more balanced relationship between the rulers and the ruled.[93] Religious intellectuals have spent considerable energy defining

---

[86] Aqajari, *Hokumat-e Dini va Hokumat-e Democratic* (Religious Government and Democratic Government), p. 34.

[87] Ibid., p. 42.   [88] Ibid., p 156.   [89] Hajjarian, *Jomhuriyyat* (Republicanism), p. 475.

[90] Ibid., p. 476.

[91] Aqajari, *Hokumat-e Dini va Hokumat-e Democratic* (Religious Government and Democratic Government), p 23.

[92] Mohammad Ali Ayazi, "Jame'h Madani va Nesbat-e An ba Din" (Civil Society and its Relationship with Religion), in Armin *et al. Nesbat-e Din va Jame'h Madani* (The Relationship between Religion and Civil Society), p. 104; Bazargan, "Marz-haye Miyan-e Din va Hokumat" (Boundaries between Religion and Government), p. 117.

[93] Nouri, *Shoukaran-e Eslah* (Hemlock for Advocate of Reform), p. 9.

and emphasizing the need for civil society, and elaborating on its consistency with and support for religion.[94] Here I will mention the writings of only a few religious reformists on the topic, beginning with Hajjarian's. Hajjarian argues that civil society has a number of defining characteristics, some of the most important of which include the following: roots in society and independence from the state; voluntary, autonomous, and self-directed nature, as in clubs and associations, syndicates, and independent media; conciliatory spirit and civic-mindedness; and motivated by furthering the greater good and increasing societal limitations on the state's scope of power.[95] For the modern individual, civil society is key to learning from the experiences, scientific knowledge, and the cultural dispositions of others.

It is through civil society that individuals, each with their own unique personalities, learn how to live together and defend their mutual interests.

It is through civil society that sociability and the cultivation of future generations take place.

It is through civil society that individual and collective talents are nurtured and creativity thrives.

It is through civil society that division of labor and functional differentiation occur, therefore giving individuals sufficient time to pursue creative endeavors and the finer aspects of life.

It is through civil society that communication spreads and collective wisdom is deepened.

It is through civil society that mutually beneficial exchanges take place and rational decision-making grows.

It is through civil society that political pursuits become possible and the foundations for government are laid.[96]

Civil society, Hajjarian goes on to conclude, features no contradictions whatsoever with religion. In fact, he argues, the various institutions of civil society are necessary for the successful implementation of many of Islam's directives in society.[97]

This mutually reinforcing and beneficial connection between Islam and civil society is explored by a number of other religious intellectuals as well. Baqi, for example, maintains that religious institutions such as mosques, Friday Prayer ceremonies, seminaries, *Marja'iyyat*, and

---

[94] See, for example, the collection of essays in Armin *et al.*, *Nesbat-e Din va Jame'h Madani* (The Relationship between Religion and Civil Society).

[95] Hajjarian, *Jomhuriyyat* (Republicanism), pp. 356–57.   [96] Ibid., pp. 355–56.

[97] Ibid., p. 360.

religious taxes are in themselves organs of civil society.[98] Similarly, Aqajari argues that since civil society is "a methodology for organizing social relations," it has few or no differences with the *ummah*.[99] More specifically, he says, "if we accept a pluralist interpretation of religion and do not equate religion with only one, exclusivist reading of it, then we can have a religious society that is also a civil society."[100] This, of course, requires the construction of a new hermeneutics of religion that is consistent with the norms of civil society and democracy. "If our ideology and our conception of religion is pre-democratic and pre-civic, serious obstacles will appear on the path of the civil society project."[101] Aqajari's prognosis for the future is not very positive. "Unfortunately," he argues, "we face worrying deficiencies in this regard," especially the angry reaction of traditionalists, or, alternatively, the trap of Western-style secularism.[102] In his opinion, neither of these two extreme options would serve Iran well.

A discussion of civil society's conceptualization by the religious reformists would be somewhat incomplete without mention of some of former President Khatami's thoughts on the subject. As discussed in chapter 2, Khatami made the realization of civil society one of his main campaign slogans in the 1997 elections, and, once elected, he discussed and talked about the topic whenever he got the chance to do so. For Khatami, the connection between Islam and civil society is organic and deep-seated. "In the civil society that we have in mind," he writes, "the culture and norms of Islam form the primary orbit and standards of activity. But there is no room in it for personal despotism, group dictatorship, or even the dictatorship of the majority."

In this society, because man is who he is, he is respected and honorable, and his rights are observed. In an Islamic civil society, citizens can determine their own destiny, supervise their own affairs, and choose their own leaders. These political leaders are servants of the people and not their masters. They are answerable to the people, whom the Almighty has put in charge of their own future.[103]

---

[98] Baqi, *Jonbesh-e Eslahat-e Demokratik dar Iran* (The Democratic Reform Movement in Iran), p. 135.

[99] Hashem Aqajari, "Jame'h Madani va 'Avemel va Maven'eh-e Sheklgiri-ye An" (Civil Society and the Causes and Obstacles to its Formation), in Armin *et al.*, *Nesbat-e Din va Jame'h Madani* (The Relationship between Religion and Civil Society), pp. 31, 43.

[100] Aqajari, "Jame'h Madani va 'Avemel va Maven'eh-e Sheklgiri-ye An" (Civil Society and the Causes and Obstacles to its Formation), p. 50.

[101] Ibid., p. 70.   [102] Ibid., pp. 70–71.

[103] Mohammad Khatami, "Jame'h Madani az Negah-e Eslam" (Civil Society from the Perspective of Islam), in Armin *et al.*, *Nesbat-e Din va Jame'h Madani* (The Relationship between Religion and Civil Society), p. 181.

Khatami goes on to argue that Islamic civil society is an inclusive society in which all citizens enjoy equal rights and protection before the law regardless of their religious beliefs. Civil society ensures freedom and liberty within the framework of the law, and, over time, helps legal freedoms become routine and institutionalized.[104] As an integral part of Islamic government, "consultation (*shura*) is the most important basis of civil society, as are political development, popular participation, respect for the rights of the people, and reducing the role of the government."[105] Similar to Aqajari, Khatami offers a sobering assessment of the prospects for civil society's future. "The task ahead is indeed difficult," he goes on to conclude. "I appeal to all distinguished thinkers, all seminaries, all universities, and all university students to help us realize this important opportunity so that we can [place the realization of Islamic civil society] as one of our highest priorities."[106]

A question of hermeneutics

Viewing civil society, popular legitimacy, the right to vote, and democracy in general as deeply and innately consistent with Islam is the product of a specific line of *ijtihad*, a conscious effort to articulate a dynamic *fiqh* in which *context* – what is best for the community in a specific time and place – plays a central role. What we are currently witnessing in Iran is the articulation of a discourse of religious dynamism, one in which Islam is taken to be inherently adaptable to modern times and conditions. Even more, Islam is seen by the proponents of the discourse as an agent of change and progress, an invaluable blueprint for such contemporary necessities as democracy, equality, justice, peace, civility, and advancement.

At the heart of such an endeavor is the construction of a hermeneutics of jurisprudence that would make it changeable and fluid, ushering in a dynamic *fiqh* (*fiqh-e pouya*). Abbas Kazemi maintains that the architects of the reformist religious discourse have set a number of important tasks before themselves.[107] First, for them the articulation of a new hermeneutics of Islam has assumed the form of a "research project", a task about which they go in a reasoned, methodical, and academic manner. In the process, they seek to reform and update the application of Islamic dictums and teachings, separate religion as it really is from religion as it is popularly understood, and try to present a nuanced, historically and

---

[104] Ibid., p. 188.   [105] Ibid., p. 189.   [106] Ibid., p. 194.
[107] Kazemi, *Jame'hshenasi-ye Roshanfekri-ye Dini dar Iran* (Sociology of the Religious Intellectual Movement in Iran), pp. 137–42.

situationally contextualized understanding of Islam. Another goal of the religious reformists is to relocate the place of religion in society by reframing the central question in the popular imagination: people should not be asking themselves "what does religion expect from us?" Instead, they should ask: "what do we expect of religion?" This would "lessen the burden on religion," Kazemi quotes Soroush as having said, and challenges the notion that *fiqh* is sacrosanct and untouchable.[108] As it presently stands, the religious reformists maintain, *fiqh* needs to be complemented by the modern sciences and by reason (*'aql*) as well as by more contemporary inventions such as democracy and human rights.[109]

Of these self-ascribed tasks in relation to *fiqh*, two merit more detailed attention. First and foremost, the proponents of the reformist religious discourse maintain, the principles of *fiqh* are woefully outdated and need major revisions in order to regain their relevance to the lives of Muslims. Secondly, at present *fiqh* preoccupies itself with mostly personal matters and often neglects larger social issues. According to the religious reformists, over time this misplaced focus has reinforced the archaic nature of *fiqh* since solutions to personal issues tend to be less complicated than those demanded by the problems of complex, changing societies. *Fiqh*, therefore, needs to become at once both updated and social in scope.

Historically, as Mostafa Malekian points out, the science of hermeneutics has not made much of an inroad in Islam.[110] Today, therefore, there is particular need for hermeneutical studies that offer new and relevant interpretations of Islam and Shi'ism. These interpretative endeavors are made possible through *ijtihad*. As the scholar 'Alireza Feiz (b. 1925) has put it,

Because of accumulated historical dust, coupled with the residual effects of the travails of times and eras long gone by, the marginalization and indictment of Shi'ism, and the resulting personalism of *fiqh* and its distance from prevailing social and political realities, have all combined to distort the real essence of *fiqh* and *ijtihad*, make them devoid of vitality and dynamism, and make them irrelevant with respect to political, social, and even economic issues.[111]

Ossified *fiqh* – or outdated methods of *ijtihad*, for that matter – cannot deal with the complex issues of contemporary society and, therefore,

---

[108] Ibid., p. 140.   [109] Ibid., p. 142.
[110] Malekian, *Rahi be Raha-ee* (A Path to Liberation), pp. 35–36.
[111] 'Alireza Feiz, *Vizhegi-haye Ijtihad va Fiqhi-e Pouya* (The Characteristics of Ijtihad and Dynamic Jurisprudence) (Tehran: Pazhoheshkadeh-e 'Olum-e Ensani va Motale'at-e Farhangi, 1381/2002), p. 91.

must be constantly revised and updated.[112] Baqi concurs. "The reality is that our *fiqh* and our religious sciences belong to the pre-industrial age," he writes. "They show no traces of the complexities of [contemporary] capital, labor, economics, civil and political liberties, and medical and biological discoveries, or the needs of the computer age and satellite technology."[113] As a body of legal rights, Baqi maintains, *fiqh* is man-made and is not sacred, and, as such, it must be adapted to changing times and circumstances.[114] Neglecting this need for dynamism could have dire consequences, Feiz warns:

A changing society needs a changing *fiqh*, and since *fiqh* is the governing law of society at all times and places, it must necessarily be changeable and dynamic as well. If anyone or any forces stand in resistance to this dynamism, they ultimately endanger themselves and their society. Eventually, if they continue resisting the natural changes that are necessary in *fiqh*, they will disappear themselves.[115]

Aqajari goes so far as to maintain that some of Islam's most central injunctions, such as "doing good and prohibiting evil," must be fundamentally rethought and reformulated if they are to retain any measure of relevance to today's circumstances.[116] Similarly, Soroush calls the articulation of a new hermeneutics of Islam to be a matter of "greatest necessity" as demanded by the times.[117] As Feiz puts it, "we must work on *fiqh* extensively so that it can once again regain the position of esteem and relevance to society that it once had."[118]

How does *fiqh* become dynamic? Reason (*'aql*), the architects of the reformist religious discourse overwhelmingly maintain, plays a central role; in fact, it plays *the* central role. "Research *within fiqh* is not enough" to make it consistent with the logic and tenor of the times, Soroush warns. "Changes within the basic sciences can result in fundamental changes to *fiqh* as well."[119] *Fiqh* becomes dynamic when reason becomes the guiding principle according to which it is constructed, namely

[112] Ibid., p. 245.   [113] Baqi, *Gofteman-haye Dini-ye Mo'aser*, p. 138.

[114] 'Emadeddin Baqi, *E'dam va Qasas* (Execution and Qasas) (Tehran: Saraee 1381/ 2002), p. 39.

[115] Feiz, *Vizhegi-haye Ijtihad va Fiqhi-e Pouya* (The Characterstics of Ijtihad and Dynamic Jurisprudence), p. 93.

[116] Aqajari, *Hokumat-e Dini va Hokumat-e Democratic* (Religious Government and Democratic Government), pp. 110–11.

[117] Abdolkarim Soroush, "Fiqh dar Tarazoo" (Fiqh in the Balance) in 'Edalatnezhad, ed., *Andarbab-e Ejtehad: Darbar-ye Kar-amadiye Fiqh-e Eslami dar Donya-ye Emrouz* (On Ijtihad: On the Effectiveness of Islamic Jurisprudence in Today's World), p. 23.

[118] Feiz, *Vizhegi-haye Ijtihad va Fiqhi-e Pouya* (The Characteristics of Ijtihad and Dynamic Jurisprudence), p. 245.

[119] Soroush, "Fiqh dar Tarazoo" (Fiqh in the Balance), p. 33. Emphasis added.

through *ijtihad*. When *ijtihad* is based on reason – when it conforms to and pioneers the logic of the times – then through it a contextualized, dynamic *fiqh* is formulated.[120] "If reason is allowed to finds its way into *fiqh*," Feiz writes, "undoubtedly dynamism will become an integral part of *fiqh* and cannot be denied [or prevented] by any one individual."[121]

Concurrent with the rationalization of *fiqh*, a parallel effort is needed to expand the scope of its purview to the society at large and to put a stop to its preoccupation with personal matters only. According to Hajjarian, *fiqh* is nothing more than a collection of opinions issued by *mujtahid*s in relation to various aspects of life. These opinions, derived mostly from interpretations (*tafsir*) of the Qur'an and the *Sunna*, may address specific problems and issues a person faces in life, but seldom do they take into account the complexities of modern economy, politics, and society.[122] Without much elaboration, Hajjarian calls for the codification of *fiqh* as the basis of a social contract, one that, presumably, would be pivotal in leading society toward progress and "a better world."[123]

This preoccupation with minutia, says another religious reformist, is because most of today's jurists, even enlightened ones like Ayatollah Montazeri, are scientifically ill-equipped to conceptualize and tackle the complexities of the modern world. Instead, they spend their time addressing issues such as the undesirability of defecating under a fruit tree, whether or not a man should shave off his beard, how to pay the *khoms* tax, the age of maturity for girls, and whether or not a couple can have sexual intimacy without regard to the geographic direction in which they are lying down.[124] According to Feiz, having devoted much time to these and other similar personal matters, Shi'a *mujtahid*s have developed somewhat of a consensus over most of them. Such a consensus is lacking over larger social issues, however, precisely because of a lack of consistent attention to them by the ulama.[125]

The key to articulating a socially meaningful and dynamic *fiqh*, of course, lies in *ijtihad*, and, more specifically, in *ijtihad* that takes into account context, place, and time. According to Baqi, Imam Ali

---

[120] Feiz, *Vizhegi-haye Ijtihad va Fiqhi-e Pouya* (The Characterstics of Ijtihad and Dynamic Jurisprudence), p. 136.

[121] Ibid., p. 100.   [122] Hajjarian, *Jomhuriyyat* (Republicanism), pp. 461–62.

[123] Ibid., p. 462.

[124] Saeed 'Edalatnezhad, "Bab-e Masdood-e Ijtihad" (The Closed Gates of Ijtihad), in 'Edalatnezhad, ed., *Andarbab-e Ejtehad: Darbar-ye Kar-amadiye Fiqh-e Eslami dar Donya-ye Emrouz* (On Ijtihad: On the Effectiveness of Islamic Jurisprudence in Today's World), pp. 54, 58.

[125] Feiz, *Vizhegi-haye Ijtihad va Fiqhi-e Pouya* (The Characterstics of Ijtihad and Dynamic Jurisprudence), pp. 70, 76.

counseled his son Hasan on the necessity of *ijtihad* in accordance with the times: "In religious affairs, if you do not agree with the precedent set by your ancestors, do your own thinking and research, and seek help and advice from the Almighty, so that you do not sink into doubt and mistake."[126] More specifically, he claims, insofar as today's clergy are concerned, they need to stop pursuing a myopic "survival strategy," as they are currently doing, and instead embrace new sciences and teachings that would better equip them in solving today's complex problems.[127] Along similar lines, Yusofi Eshkevari criticizes those who seek piety in modeling their own behavior after the supposed deeds and sayings of the Prophet Muhammad. They forget, Yusofi Eshkevari claims, that what the Prophet did and what he commanded were specific to the Mecca and Medina of 1,400 years ago and may not apply to today's life.[128] Therefore, taking into account contemporary needs and circumstances should be the cornerstone of *ijtihad*. Qabel similarly maintains that we cannot rely on existing, old interpretations of the Qur'an alone. Doing so would close the "gates of *ijtihad*" and would keep the resulting *fiqh* stale and disconnected from reality.[129] Over time, there are changes to science, logic, norms, and values, 'Alavi-Tabar claims, and all of these innovations need to be taken into account when engaging in *ijtihad*.[130]

The religious reformist Hojjatoleslam Saeed 'Edalatnezhad has divided *ijtihad* into two basic kinds: reason-centered (*'aql mehvar*) and narrative-centered (*naql mehvar*).[131] In both the Sunni and the Shi'a traditions, he maintains, narrative-centered *ijtihad* has been historically dominant, therefore impeding the growth and spread of new and innovative jurisprudential interpretations.[132] Reason, in other words, is helpful only in better understanding revealed knowledge, not that which is so far unknown. In this respect, if tradition has any role in *ijtihad* at all, that role is only secondary.

By contrast, reason-centered *ijtihad* places reason at the center of intellectual activity.

---

[126] Baqi, *Gofteman-haye Dini-ye Mo'aser* (Contemporary Religious Discourses), p. 298.

[127] Baqi, *Rouhaniyyat va Qodrat: Jame'hshenasi-e Nahad-haye Dini* (The Clergy and Power: Sociology of Religious Institutions), pp. 176–77.

[128] Quoted in Qoochani, *Dowlat-e Dini va Din-e Dowlati* (Religious Government and Government's Religion), p. 32.

[129] Qabel, *Naqd-e Farhang-e Khoshunat* (Critique of Culture of Violence), pp. 143–44.

[130] 'Alavi-Tabar, *Roshanfekri, Dindari, Mardomsalari* (Intellectualism, Religiosity, Democracy), pp. 70–71.

[131] Saeed 'Edalatnezhad, "Kodam Ijtihad?" (Which Ijtihad?), in 'Edalatnezhad, ed. *Andarbab-e Ejtehad: Darbar-ye Kar-amadiye Fiqh-e Eslami dar Donya-ye Emrouz* (On Ijtihad: On the Effectiveness of Islamic Jurisprudence in Today's World), p. 8.

[132] 'Edalatnezhad, "Kodam Ijtihad?" (Which Ijtihad?), p. 10. See also above, chapter 4.

Reason-centered *ijtihad* does not mean abandoning or ignoring [existing] religious texts. It means using reason as one of the sources used [in interpretation] and, when there is a contradiction, giving primacy to reason over existing texts. Just as reason dictates that the interpreter not dwell on some Qur'anic precepts that contradict the laws of nature – such as the characteristics of God – reason also dictates that where there is a contradiction between existing texts and collective knowledge, primacy be given to the latter.[133]

Given its far-reaching nature, 'Edalatnezhad argues that this *ijtihad* may also be called "*ijtihad* in fundamentals," some of the primary characteristics of which include careful and detailed attention to the influence of time and place; concern with justice; drawing connections between individual thought and reasoning to collective knowledge and wisdom; and situating the rich products of Islamic heritage in their proper historical and geographic contexts.[134]

For 'Edalatnezhad and other like-minded religious reformists, conservative religious forces have kept the "gates of *ijtihad*" historically shut. In fact, 'Edalatnezhad claims, all too often, the reaction against new *ijtihad* has been quite severe:

Not only have the gates of *ijtihad* been closed for some time, if there is a new *ijtihad*, the prevalent interpretation that rules over the *howzeh* considers it deviant. This governing interpretation has turned the *howzeh* into a factory in which every *ijtihad* produced has to look like the last one and must have the same size, color, and functionality as the one before.[135]

Needless to say, as we saw in chapter 4, the proponents of the conservative religious discourse deny this accusation. Ayatollah Montazeri, for example, directly addresses this issue, maintaining that the continued openness of the gates of *ijtihad* is one of Shi'ism's strengths, and that not every interpretation ought to be discarded simply because it is old.[136] Nevertheless, he claims, reason cannot always be trusted, nor is it always deep and sufficiently evolved to guide the individual in understanding God's commands and His design. Reason must, therefore, necessarily be complemented by the *shari'a*.[137] And doing so requires trust in and *taqlid* (imitation) of learned *mujtahid*s. Just as individuals must seek advice on medical matters from specialists and physicians, they also need

---

[133] Ibid., p. 11.   [134] Ibid., pp. 11–12.
[135] 'Edalatnezhad, "Bab-e Masdood-e Ijtihad" (The Closed Gates of Ijtihad), p. 48.
[136] Hoseinali Montazeri, "Bab-e Maftooh-e Ijtihad" (The Open Gates of Ijtihad), in 'Edalatnezhad, ed., *Andarbab-e Ejtehad: Darbar-ye Kar-amadiye Fiqh-e Eslami dar Donya-ye Emrouz* (On Ijtihad: On the Effectiveness of Islamic Jurisprudence in Today's World), pp. 36–37.
[137] Ibid., pp. 44–45.

to seek the advice of religious specialists in regards to the *shari'a* and religion in general.[138]

This point goes to the heart of another argument by the religious reformists: if reason is to be trusted and employed in *ijtihad*, then why have a clerical class at all? This is the logical extension of the argument by the religious reformists that reason – individual reason – can be a proper, and supposedly sufficient, guide to *ijtihad*. Every individual, therefore, is a *mujtahed* and can engage in his or her own *ijtihad*. Surprisingly, this argument has not received as much attention as one would suspect, largely, I believe, because of the political costs associated with advocating the clergy's irrelevance. Nevertheless, a few religious reformists have alluded to this point in some of their arguments. Yusofi Eshkevari, for example, himself a clergyman, mentions in one of his interviews that initially Islam did not have a clerical class to begin with. Today, he further asserts, no one group, not even the clergy, can have a sole monopoly over the specialization of any one field.[139] Ahmad Qabel, another religious reformist, similarly rejects what he labels as a feudal mindset based on the presupposition that people need keepers.[140] Mojtahed Shabestari is far more explicit. "Understanding the Qur'an and the Islamic tradition is not the sole preserve of any particular group or class," he argues, "and whoever possesses the scientific and methodological tools necessary for interpreting them can do so, and may not be criticized by others."[141] As we shall see shortly, Mojtahed Shabestari develops this argument further in his more academic writings. Insofar as the more commonly available press and books are concerned, however, his questioning of the continued need for the clergy is by far the most forceful framing of the issue.

Reforming religion

As mentioned earlier in the chapter, from among the proponents of the reformist religious discourse, a handful of intellectuals stand out for the greater depth and complexity of their arguments. They include Mohsen Kadivar, Mohammad Mojtahed Shabestari, Abdolkarim Soroush, and former President Mohammad Khatami.

---

[138] Ibid., pp. 46–47.

[139] Quoted in Qoochani, *Dowlat-e Dini va Din-e Dowlati* (Religious Government and Government's Religion), p. 36.

[140] Qabel, *Naqd-e Farhang-e Khoshunat* (Critique of Culture of Violence), p. 161.

[141] Quoted in Razavi, *Motefakeran-e Mo'aser va Endisheh-ye Siyasi-e Eslam* (Contemporary Thinkers and Islamic Political Thought), p. 145.

Khatami's inclusion here may need some justification. There is no doubt that Khatami is a religious reformist and, by almost any standard, he is also considered an intellectual. Nevertheless, perhaps because of his many years of political activism and administrative responsibilities as opposed to opportunities for quiet contemplation, there may be a perception that the depth and complexity of his thoughts and arguments are not nearly of the same magnitude as those of the others mentioned here. Two important points need to be considered here. First, Khatami *is* indeed a deep and serious thinker, as evidenced by his books – mostly comprised of his university lectures – on such topics as Islamic thought,[142] Western philosophy,[143] and contemporary *fiqh*.[144] Second, and perhaps more important, is the prominent position he occupied in the Iranian polity for nearly a decade. By virtue of being the President of the Republic, Khatami's thoughts and arguments were given great prominence and exposure, and in many ways he emerged, at least in the early years of his presidency, as the symbolic figurehead of the religious reformist movement. A better understanding of some of his arguments, therefore, or at least of some of the themes that he kept repeating in his speeches and interviews, gives us better insight into both his arguments and the larger discourse of which they are a part.[145] Needless to say, the themes of the former President's speeches and the degree to which he elaborated on these themes were invariably influenced by prevailing political circumstances, by tactical and strategic considerations at the time, and by his political office. Still, politics notwithstanding, one can clearly discern a deliberate effort on Khatami's part to outline the contours of a broad discourse of religious reformism.

Similar to other religious reformists, Khatami is critical of the absence of serious self-study and scholarship in Islamic philosophy and thought. Ibn Khaldun was the last of the great Muslim thinkers, he maintains, and, over the last few centuries, political repression and authoritarianism have effectively ended what was once a vibrant tradition of critical thought and analysis among Muslims.[146] Instead, both Sunni and Shi'a

---

[142] Mohammad Khatami, *Aeen va Andisheh dar Dam-e Khodkamegi* (Religion and Intellect Trapped in Tyranny) (Tehran: Tarh-e No, 1378/1999).

[143] Khatami, *Az Donya-ye Shahr ta Shahr-e Donya* (From the World of the "City" to the City of the "World").

[144] Khatami, *Beem-e Mowj* (Fear of Wave), especially chapters 2 and 3.

[145] During the second term of his presidency, many of Khatami's speeches were collected, categorized based on subject matter, and published as books, many of which have been referenced in the following paragraphs below.

[146] Khatami, *Aeen va Andisheh dar Dam-e Khodkamegi* (Religion and Intellect Trapped in Tyranny), pp. 423–24.

rulers have historically manipulated Islam for their own political purposes, in the process often turning the religion into a tool for repression.[147] One of the most adverse consequences of this has been the
clergy's relative inattention to issues that really matter in people's lives,
issues such as political development and progress, justice and equality,
and freedom and democracy. Insofar as Islamic scholarship is concerned, Khatami argues, "we are facing a vacuum when it comes to
social order and life in the public domain, and the establishment of a
system that would regulate the lives and the interactions of members of
society."[148] Capitalizing on the respect and influence it has among the
population, the clergy must "equip itself with the newest and most
functionally relevant ideas."[149] The clergy needs to devote itself to
exploring new questions to ask to and coming up with new answers and
solutions to offer to the people. Khatami laments the fact that most
clergy appeared to have closed themselves to the modern world,
reminding them that today it is essential to have an understanding of the
modern world in general and of the West in particular.[150]

The West represents a worldview and a set of principles that were crystallized
during the Renaissance and have since shaped contemporary conditions. In
order to analyze the West we must first figure out how Westerners look at the
world around them, and to also see how we, based on our religious, cultural, and
civic values, look at the world.[151]

Khatami also decries "the pathology of despotism" (*estebdad-zadegi*)
that has historically plagued Iranian intellectual history and the popular
mindset. "We are all plagued by despotism," Khatami exclaims, "and
this manifests itself in our individual and group behaviors as well as in
our family and social lives."[152] This causes deep suspicion of state
institutions and their initiatives on the one hand, and intolerance toward
other views and opinions on the other.[153] What the Muslim world sorely
needs is intellectual diversity, something that should be a natural and
innate part of any society.[154] In specific relation to Iran, "the danger is

---

[147] Mohammad Khatami, *Eslam, Rouhaniyyat, va Enqelab-e Eslami* (Islam, the Clergy, and
the Islamic Revolution) (Tehran: Tarh-e No, 1379/2000), p. 95.

[148] Khatami, *Beem-e Mowj* (Fear of Wave), p. 139.

[149] Khatami, *Eslam, Rouhaniyyat, va Enqelab-e Eslami* (Islam, the Clergy, and the Islamic
Revolution), p. 109.

[150] Khatami. *Az Donya-ye Shahr ta Shahr-e Donya* (From the World of the "City" to the
City of the "World"), p. 14.

[151] Mohammad Khatami. *Mardomsalari* (Democracy) (Tehran: Tarh-e No, 1380/2001),
p. 61.

[152] Ibid., p. 53.   [153] Ibid., pp. 136–37.   [154] Ibid., p. 43.

that we treat as religious truth any one, single understanding of Islam, or *fiqh*, the *Velayat-e Faqih*, the Revolution, or the Imam's Path."[155]

In addition to the issues mentioned above, there are four interrelated themes and issues to which Khatami pays particular attention in his published speeches and his writings. They include attention to reason and logic as integral and complementary components of religious belief and devotion; advocacy of *ijtihad* and dynamic *fiqh*; calls for the deepening of civil society and democracy; and, perhaps what he is best known for outside of Iran, dialogue among civilizations.

Khatami argues that along with religion, reason must also play a determining role in the government of society. In fact, not only is there no contradiction between the dictates of logic and the directives of religion, he maintains, it would actually be a violation of religious duty not to resort to reason and logic in the conduct of one's daily life.[156] There is no contradiction whatsoever between reason and religion; "an irreligious scientist consults only one book, the book of nature, whereas a religious scientist consults two books, a book of nature and a book of divine revelations. Those who think the two are opposed only betray their own incomplete understanding of religion."[157] Rational reasoning and critical thought are the only proper ways to understand religion.[158] In Islam, and especially in Shi'ism, the goal is to bring about synchronicity between spirituality and logic.[159] This is, in fact, the central mission of the religious intellectual, the desired product of which is progressive *ijtihad* and dynamic *fiqh*.[160]

It is essential for all Muslims, and especially for the clergy, to demonstrate intellectual creativity. For those engaging in *ijtihad*, this means being aware of contemporary times and circumstances in order to avoid "the twin plagues of inflexibility and ossification" that have marked Islamic thought for so long.[161] Considerations of context – time and place – must therefore become essential to any contemporary *ijtihad* and to the proper understanding of Islam.[162] More specifically, just as the slogans and premises of the Islamic revolution had promised, *fiqh* must undergo constant changes in order to stay relevant at all times.[163] Islam

---

[155] Khatami, *Eslam, Rouhaniyyat, va Enqelab-e Eslami* (Islam, the Clergy, and the Islamic Revolution), p. 132.

[156] Khatami, *Beem-e Mowj* (Fear of Wave), p. 41.

[157] Mohammad Khatami, *Goftego-ye Tammadon-ha* (Dialogue of Civilizations) (Tehran: Tarh-e No, 1380/2001), p. 69.

[158] Khatami, *Eslam, Rouhaniyyat, va Enqelab-e Eslami* (Islam, the Clergy, and the Islamic Revolution), p. 40.

[159] Ibid., p. 49   [160] Ibid., p. 192.

[161] Khatami, *Beem-e Mowj* (Fear of Wave), pp. 71–72.   [162] Ibid., p. 77.

[163] Ibid., p. 142.

must once again exhibit the internal dynamism that was inherent to its original essence. "It is true that our identity is rooted in the past," argues Khatami, "but this does not mean that we should return to the past."

God's revelation did take place in the past, but revelation does not belong to a specific time. We must not remain in the past, for this is to be reactionary. We must move forward toward the future in order to better understand the contemporary world and to benefit from its positive offerings. Doing so would enable us to revive the glory and greatness of the past without living in it, and to construct a life for ourselves in which both God's revelation and human logic and civil rights are respected.[164]

Progress will not be possible without freedom and democracy, and the key to freedom and democracy is civil society. "The way to save Islam and to bring about progress to our society is to combine Islam and democracy," Khatami argues.[165] Civil society organizations ensure the participation of the people in their own affairs and lead to greater social transparency. They prevent individuals with specific goals from imposing their will on others under the pretext of defending freedom or even Islam and the Revolution.[166] "Civil society means government accountability before the people; it means recognizing their rights."[167]

For Khatami, the most perfect type of civil society was established by the Prophet in Medina. "In our conception of civil society," he said in one of his speeches, "the ideas and culture of Islam are central. But there is no room in it for personal autocracy or even the dictatorship of the majority at the expense of the minority."

In this society, because man is who he is, he is treated with respect and dignity and his rights are observed. The citizens of Islamic civil society determine their own destiny and are in charge of their own affairs. In such a society the government is the people's servant and is answerable to them; it is not their superior.

In our civil society, Muslims alone do not have the rights and privileges of citizenship, and, within the framework of the law, the rights and liberties of each person are protected and respected. I am not speaking of respect for human rights and civil liberties out of political considerations. Respect for human rights is an integral part of our religion and what Islam dictates.[168]

According to Khatami, the correct, democratic interpretation of Islam that is reflected in the constitution of the Islamic Republic is fundamentally supportive of civil society and its function as a forum for

---

[164] Khatami, *Goftego-ye Tammadon-ha* (Dialogue of Civilizations), pp. 69–70.
[165] Khatami, *Mardomsalari* (Democracy), p. 29.   [166] Ibid., p. 36.
[167] Khatami, *Eslam, Rouhaniyyat, va Enqelab-e Eslami* (Islam, the Clergy, and the Islamic Revolution), p. 178.
[168] Ibid., p. 25.

popular participation and empowerment. Although civil society organizations have not yet taken deep roots in Iran, ideally they should be established and become active in institutions such as the press and the universities in order to guarantee greater freedom and transparency.[169]

Perhaps what Khatami is best known for, especially outside Iran, is his introduction and championing of the concept of "dialogue among civilizations" (*goftogo-ye tamaddon-ha*). In response to Samuel Huntington's thesis of "clash of civilizations," Khatami maintains that it is essential for the East and the West to have a dialogue together and to actively seek to learn about and from each other. In this two-way process of give-and-take, the East can offer the West lessons on "balance, tranquility, and contemplation, all eventually leading to peace, security, and justice."[170] The West, for its part, can offer the East lessons on social and economic progress.[171] Khatami is careful to suggest that this "dialogue" must be free of coercion and must take place on equal footing in order to be meaningful. The West in particular must seek out the true representatives of Islamic and other Eastern civilizations and engage them in a dialogue. It should not simply talk to, or more commonly talk at, those Muslims and other Easterners who are already enamored with the West.[172]

Dialogue of civilizations is a novel movement for preventing the domination of cultural monologues and the development of conditions for the realization of a truly global civilization. Regional cooperation and integration, the growing criticism of globalization trends, the increased self-confidence of developing societies, increasing changes in theoretical perspectives, the growth of collaborative efforts among states, growing international cooperation and the global thirst for justice – all of these developments point to the serious need for dialogue among civilizations and its critical role in reducing international and political tensions.[173]

None of this, of course, means abandoning one's own culture, identity, or religion. It simply means a willingness to exchange ideas and to see how cultures and values can complement one another.[174]

Khatami in many ways symbolizes the *politics* of the religious reformist discourse. But perhaps no other intellectual is identified with the discourse more readily than Abdolkarim Soroush. Soroush, in fact, could easily be considered as the preeminent Iranian intellectual figure of the post-revolutionary era, if not indeed of the late twentieth and early

---

[169] Khatami, *Mardomsalari* (Democracy), pp. 64–81.
[170] Khatami, *Goftego-ye Tammadon-ha* (Dialogue of Civilizations), p. 44.
[171] Ibid., p. 45.   [172] Ibid., p. 47.   [173] Ibid., p. 64.
[174] Khatami, *Eslam, Rouhaniyyat, va Enqelab-e Eslami* (Islam, the Clergy, and the Islamic Revolution), p. 193.

twenty-first centuries. Born in Tehran in 1945, Soroush initially studied theology and religious sciences in Qom, but soon moved on to the natural sciences and earned a doctorate in pharmacy from the University of Tehran. He also pursued postgraduate education in history and the philosophy of science in London, but he returned to Iran during the revolution and became one of the members of the Council on Cultural Revolution (*Setad-e Enqelab-e Farhangi*). Many of Soroush's detractors today point to his membership in this committee as a sign of his early, suspect loyalties and his disservice to intellectual life in the immediate aftermath of the revolution. Soroush maintains, however, that the Council's primary mission was to restructure and revamp the curriculum taught in Iranian universities. In specific, he claims that his efforts were pivotal in "rescuing the social sciences and humanities from extremists" and also for establishing the disciplines of history and philosophy of science in Iranian universities.[175] He soon resigned from his post, however, due to the alleged "cultural fascism" he witnessed among some of the Council's members, and, in the years that followed, refused to accept any further positions in the government, including attractive offers such as the chancellorship of universities or the Ministry of Education portfolio.[176]

Since the mid-1980s, Soroush has emerged as one of Iran's most visible and most significant intellectual figures. In the 1990s he was forced out of his position at the University of Tehran, and since 1996 he has spent prolonged periods outside of the country. A prolific writer and a frequent speaker in university campuses and elsewhere, Soroush's theories on epistemology and Islamic hermeneutics are today widely discussed and debated by university students, by many of the educated middle classes, and among reform-minded clerics. His writings cover a wide variety of topics ranging from philosophy of science[177] to the nature of prophetic mission,[178] ethics[179] and prayer,[180] and the poetry and mysticism of Rumi.[181] These topics cannot all possibly be properly covered here, and, out of necessity, I will concentrate on some of

---

[175] Abdolkarim Soroush, *Raz-dani va Roshanfekri va Din-dari* (Knowing Secrets and Intellectualism and Religiosity) (Tehran: Sarat, 1377/1998), pp. 38–39.

[176] Ibid., p. 39.

[177] Abdolkarim Soroush, *'Elm Chist, Falsafeh Chist?* (What is Science, What is Philosophy?) (Tehran: Sarat, 1368/1989).

[178] Abdolkarim Soroush, *Bast-e Tajrobe-ye Nabavi* (Expansion of the Prophetic Experience) (Tehran: Sarat, 1378/1999).

[179] Abdolkarim Soroush, *Taffaroj-e San'* (The Pleasure of Creation) (Tehran: Sarat, 1379/2000).

[180] Abdolkarim Soroush, *Hadis-e bandegi va Delbordegi* (The Story of Slavery and Love) (Tehran: Sarat, 1375/1996).

[181] Abdolkarim Soroush, *Qomar-e 'Asheqaneh* (A Loving Gamble) (Tehran: Sarat, 1379/2000).

Soroush's most important and most widely discussed theoretical contributions to the study of Islam.[182]

Perhaps the most significant of Soroush's theoretical contributions is his thesis on "the contraction and expansion of the *shari'a*." The central premise of this thesis revolves around making two key distinctions: one between religion as revealed by the Almighty and religion as understood by man; the other between personal knowledge of religion and religious knowledge in general.[183] Soroush's central goal is to explore how religious knowledge is formed and how it evolves over time. The key to such an understanding, he maintains, lies in the realization that while religion itself is static and unchanging, its conception and knowledge (*ma'refat*) change and evolve over time.[184] There is a direct correlation, "a dialogue," between religious knowledge on the one hand and our general knowledge in areas and sciences that are unrelated to religion per se. There are three broad sources of knowledge – science, reason, and spirituality – each one of which can have a direct bearing on how our knowledge of religion is constructed and accumulated over time.[185] The science of theology (*kalam*, or "disputation") is therefore no longer sufficient in itself in order to properly understand religious knowledge. It needs to be complemented with careful attention to the dynamic and highly nuanced relationship that exists between changing scientific knowledge in general and religious knowledge in particular.[186] More importantly, as with any other scientific endeavor, theology and religious science in general must be open to critical analysis and scrutiny. In their present state, at any rate, they are far from perfection.[187]

Soroush sums up his thesis as follows:

Religious knowledge – meaning our knowledge of the Qur'an and the *Sunna* – is human knowledge, and, similar to other sciences, is in constant flux, evolution, and contraction and expansion. This contraction and expansion is directly produced by contractions and expansions in other areas of human knowledge, and understanding the *shari'a* is not independent of our understanding of nature and science, and changes to it. Therefore, just as philosophy and the

---

[182] One of Soroush's theoretical arguments that is not discussed here is his thesis that the universe and everything in it, including inanimate objects, are in constant, gradual motion while maintaining their essence at the same time. These argument are outlined in a small book entitled *Nahad-e Naaran-e Jahan* (The World's Tumultuous Nature) (Tehran: Sarat, 1378/1999).

[183] Abdolkarim Soroush, *Qabz va Bast-e Te'orik-e Shari'at: Nazariyyeh Takamol Ma'refat-e Dini* (The Expansion and Contraction of Theory of *Shari'a*: Analyzing the Evolution of Religious Knowledge) (Tehran: Sarat, 1374/1995), p. 56.

[184] Ibid., p. 86.   [185] Ibid., p. 160.   [186] Ibid., p. 173.

[187] Abdolkarim Soroush, *Modara va Modiriyyat* (Moderation and Administration) (Tehran: Sarat, 1376/1997), p. 308.

natural sciences are imperfect and continue to evolve, the sciences of jurisprudence [*fiqh*] and interpretation [*tafsir*] and ethics [*akhlaq*] and disputation [*kalam*] are also imperfect and also continue to evolve ... Consistent with the growth of science and philosophy, the ability of scholars to expand and deepen their understanding of the *shari'a* will also be enhanced.[188]

Although Soroush explicitly disavows any intent to articulate a dynamic *fiqh* or to "modernize religion,"[189] he does maintain that much of the *ijtihad* that is currently widely practiced itself needs *ijtihad*.[190] His repeated and forceful advocacy of this point in numerous speeches and writings has done little to endear him to the conservative religious establishment. But what has turned him into a real and potent threat to the conservatives, and ultimately his more important theoretical contribution to Islamic epistemology, concerns his call for "extra-religious" (*boron-dini*) approaches to understanding religion.[191] "We cannot see the inside accurately unless we stand on the outside," he writes, warning of the dangers of theological tunnel vision.[192] "Any new episteme of religion is based on two pillars," he maintains, one internal and the other external.[193] The external foundations of religious knowledge are those insights and bodies of information derived from contemporary science. Combined theological advances to religious knowledge (*daron-dini*) result in a new, evolving episteme of religion. Since human life and knowledge in general are in a state of constant flux and change, the evolution and renewal of religious knowledge is also inevitable.[194] New science leads to new questions, and new questions engender new research and new answers, and thus the depth of religious knowledge is increasingly enhanced.[195]

Another important theoretical notion advocated by Soroush is the de-ideologization of religion and society. Soroush readily acknowledges his deep personal fondness for and his intellectual affinity with the late

---

[188] Soroush, *Qabz va Bast-e Te'orik-e Shari'at* (The Expansion and Contraction of Theory of *Shari'ah*), p. 245.

[189] Ibid., pp. 56–57.   [190] Ibid., pp. 49–50.

[191] Soroush himself acknowledges the difficult challenges faced by scholars and researchers of religion who operate in profoundly religious societies (Soroush, *Modara va Modiriyyat* [Moderation and Administration], p. 84). Yet he perseveres, and there are no indications that when he is allowed to express himself, he sensors his lectures or his writings.

[192] Abdolkarim Soroush, *A'in-e Shahriyari va Dindari* (Rules of Sovereignty and Religiosity) (Tehran: Sarat, 1379/2000), p. 46.

[193] Soroush, *Qabz va Bast-e Te'orik-e Shari'at* (The Expansion and Contraction of Theory of *Shari'a*), p. 199.

[194] Ibid., pp. 199–200.

[195] Soroush, *Modara va Modiriyyat* (Moderation and Administration). p. 104.

Ali Shariati.[196] But he strongly disagrees with Shariati's project of turning Islam into an ideology, even if that ideology was progressive and revolutionary. Ideological Islam is superficial and, at best, perhaps attractive to the impatient youth.[197] More importantly, making religion ideological erodes its timeless and eternal message and nature, making it applicable only to specific circumstances and times.[198] Even if the project of making religion ideological succeeds, the resulting ideological religion is by nature impermanent and will eventually give way to non-ideological religion. This is bound to happen for several reasons. To begin with, whereas ideologies are context and time specific, revealed religions are timeless and formless and can apply to all mankind at all times. Moreover, religions are deliberately mysterious and mystical, esoteric and heavenly. None of these are goals toward which ideologies strive. Similarly, religion is inherently adaptable depending on the changing needs of the times and the circumstances, taking one form in the initial period of establishment and another when settled. This is another facet of the contraction and expansion of religion. Ideology, on the other hand, is innately inflexible and unchangeable.[199]

Soroush is even more disdainful of societies in which ideology reigns supreme. An "ideological society" is highly susceptible to dictatorships and demagogical movements, he maintains, and does not welcome diversity of views and approaches. Instead, it gives rise to an official and exclusive class of interpreters and opinion-makers who then shut "the gates of thought" and treat the ruling ideology as if it represented the perfection of reason.[200] With rationality thus subdued, scientific endeavors and objective research suffer, the search for truth instead replaced by imitation and sycophancy.[201] The law also becomes dependent on individual personalities rather than the other way around.[202]

The Qur'an, Soroush argues, is deeply and profoundly respectful of the independence of human thought and reason. Otherwise, it would not invite the believers to use the power of their rationality to combat disbelievers and to show them the right path.[203] "Guidance," he writes, "does not mean that a person becomes falsely self-confident and conceited. It means battling temptations, and, following in the footsteps of

---

[196] Abdolkarim Soroush, *Farbeh-tar az Ideolozhi* (Healthier than Ideology) (Tehran: Sarat, 1372/1993), p. 97.
[197] Ibid., p. 119.   [198] Ibid., p. 122.   [199] Ibid., pp. 125–30.
[200] Ibid., pp. 135–141.   [201] Ibid., p. 143.   [202] Ibid., p. 143.
[203] Abdolkarim Soroush, *Ideolozhi-ye Sheytani* (Satanic Ideology) (Tehran: Sarat, 1373/ 1994), p. 88.

the Prophet Abraham, smashing the idol that is the desire to become eternally victorious."[204]

Let us let reason reign supreme, is Soroush's recommendation. More specifically, he calls for the replacement of inherently undemocratic and combative "ideological discourses" with a discourse that is post-ideological, epistemological, and democratic.[205] Only then would we have paved the way for "religious pluralism, political pluralism, and democratic religious government."

Epistemology, hermeneutics, historicism, religious experience, pluralism, spirituality, being in awe, reform, establishment, civil society, democracy, justice, citizenship, rationality, abandonment of ideology, and even replacing God as the protector of the dispossessed with God as compassionate and merciful all produce a new discourse that is serene and appropriate for the era of (post-revolutionary) establishment as compared to the combative and ideological discourse that was needed in the early phases of the revolution. The revolutionary discourse was needed then. Today calls for its own discourse.[206]

Not surprisingly, Soroush reserves some of his sharpest criticisms for the clergy. On this point Soroush mostly agrees with Shariati, although the two thinkers approach the subject from very different perspectives. Whereas Shariati saw the clergy as a reactionary and counter-revolutionary force, Soroush sees them as mostly hostile to rational thought and new science. The clergy have historically confined themselves to seminaries and have mostly studied only theology at the expense of other equally important sciences taught in universities.[207] As a social class, the clergy is in dire need of familiarizing itself with the modern sciences and must complement its understanding of theology with other, extra-religious bodies of knowledge.[208] This is not an easy task, Soroush claims, as the clergy is a syndicate group whose economic interests and livelihood depend on presenting and perpetuating specific, often petrified, interpretations of religion.[209] Religious knowledge cannot progress and reach additional heights so long as it remains tied to the clergy's syndical interests.[210] It is no accident that the clergy by and large remains deeply steeped in tradition and that reformists among it represent no more than mere voices in the wilderness.[211]

The best environment within which the will of the majority, and more importantly the spirit of scientific inquiry, can thrive and grow is

---

[204] Ibid., p. 89.
[205] Soroush. *A'in-e Shahriyari va Dindari* (Rules of Sovereignty and Religiosity), p. 49.
[206] Ibid., p. 53.
[207] Soroush, *Raz-dani va Roshanfekri va Dindari* (Knowing Secrets and Intellectualism and Religiosity), p. 109.
[208] Soroush, *A'in-e Shahriyari va Dindari* (Rules of Sovereignty and Religiosity), p. 155.
[209] Soroush, *Modara va Modiriyyat* (Moderation and Administration), pp. 26, 32.
[210] Ibid., p. 47.   [211] Ibid., pp. 94–95.

democracy. The cultural pillars of democracy rest on phenomena such as wealth, power, justice, science, humanity, and God.[212] True democracy needs a moral compass, an ethical blueprint that would point to the dangers of corruption and decay, and such guidelines can best be found through religion. Thus the ideal political system, according to Soroush, is a religious democracy, where both the rights of man and the rights and dictates of the Almighty are observed and respected.[213] Soroush outlines his vision of an ideal, pluralist society as follows:

A pluralist society is a non-ideological one in which there is no one official interpretation and class of interpreters. It is based on a diversity of rationalities rather than unifying impulses. It features moderation and equity, and benefits from the free flow of information ... Its genesis is based on the realization by its rulers that the essence of science and society rest on diverse and plural pillars rather than uniformity and conformism, and that attempts to enforce a single model of life and religion and ethics and culture are doomed to failure.[214]

Social and political pluralism are natural corollaries of religious pluralism. According to Soroush, the first and most important advocate of religious pluralism was none other than the Almighty himself, who encouraged the diversity of religious views and beliefs by revealing His message to different prophets and at different times and places.[215] But the roots and benefits of religious pluralism cannot only be found within religion itself; extra-religious science and rationality calls for and supports it as well.[216] Rights and justice are two key entitlements for all human beings. "You must insist on your rights and resist those who want to impose their will on you," he once wrote to an audience of university students. "And you must defend plural interpretations from official (and forcibly imposed) ones. It is the right of all of us to have access to diverse sources of information, diverse political parties, diverse interpretations of religion, and diverse lifestyles."[217] Pluralism is only natural, whether in religion or in any other arena of human endeavor.

Pluralism, and more broadly democracy, forms one of the primary preoccupations of one of the other prominent religious intellectual figures in contemporary Iran, namely Mohsen Kadivar. Born in the south-central city of Safa in 1959, Kadivar received a traditional education in Qom, where he studied *fiqh*, philosophy, theology, mysticism, and *tafsir*. He completed his seminary studies in 1997, when he received a degree

---

[212] Soroush, *Farbeh-tar az Ideolozhi* (Healthier than Ideology), p. 270.

[213] Ibid., p. 274.

[214] Abdolkarim Soroush, *Sert-haye Mostaqim* (Straight Paths) (Tehran: Sarat, 1378/ 1999), p. 49.

[215] Ibid., p. 18.   [216] Ibid., p. 139.

[217] Soroush, *A'in-e Shahriyari va Dindari* (Rules of Sovereignty and Religiosity), p. 197.

in *ijtihad*, and two years later he also earned a doctorate degree in philosophy from Tehran's Tarbiat Modarres University, where he currently teaches Islamic philosophy and political science. Especially since the late 1990s, Hojjatoleslam Kadivar has emerged as one of the most influential, as well as most visible, opponents of what he calls "traditionalist" interpretations of Islam. More specifically, through his writings, he has repeatedly questioned the jurisprudential validity of the concept of the *Velayat*, maintaining that there is no viable basis or precedent for it in the Holy Qur'an or the *Sunna* of the Prophet. Islam needs to rid itself of this and other similar historical barnacles that have turned it into a source of inequality and political repression. Instead, it must embrace its original, democratic essence. Not surprisingly, his arguments have often landed him in political trouble, and in February 1998 he was sentenced to eighteen months in prison by the Special Court for the Clergy. He has been a prolific author ever since. However, because of the politically sensitive nature of many of the topics he tackles and the closure of numerous reformist periodicals by the authorities over the last few years, most of his essays are now available through his website on the Internet (www.kadivar.com) rather than in newspapers and magazines published inside the country.

Similar to Soroush and other religious intellectuals, so far in his intellectual career Kadivar has tackled a wide variety of issues related to religious and especially Islamic reformism. These have included such diverse topics as the vitality and importance of civil society[218] and the significance of contextualization and attention to time and place in *ijtihad*,[219] the underlying basis of Islamic philosophy, and the role and essence of spirituality in Islam.[220] Nevertheless, within the last decade or so, much of Kadivar's intellectual focus has been on the two topics of *Velayat-e Faqih* and democracy.

Kadivar argues that political theories within Shi'a jurisprudence have gone through four distinct yet interrelated phases. Initially, beginning in the fourth century AH, when Shi'a political theory began to form, it concentrated mostly on private and personal matters, a focus that was largely a product of the greater political environment within which it

---

[218] Mohsen Kadivar, *Daqdaqe-haye Hokumat-e Dini* (Crises of Religious Government) (Tehran: Ney, 1379/2000), pp. 257–58, 266–67, 282–84. This 880-page book contains eighty of the articles Kadivar has published over time and is an invaluable source of insight into his thoughts and his ideas.

[219] Ibid., pp. 14, 278.

[220] For more on Kadivar's thoughts on spirituality within Islam see Yasuyuki Matsunaga, "Mohsen Kadivar, A Clerical Advocate of Postrevivalist Islam in Iran," *British Journal of Middle Eastern Studies*, Vol. 34, No. 3 (December 2007), pp. 317–29.

found itself. Shi'ism then became the official state religion of Iran in the 1500s, when it entered a second phase and became closely allied with dynastic rule. Some four centuries later, however, in a third phase, Shi'ism become a force for change and political accountability, when in the early 1900s it became one of the major driving forces of the Constitutional Revolution. Eventually, in a fourth phase, with the Islamic Revolution of 1978–79, Shi'ism became the very basis of the state's *raison d'être*.[221] This last phase in the evolution of Shi'a political theory has been most fruitful and productive in reversing what has historically been a pattern of inattention and neglect to theories of politics by Shi'a jurists and *foqaha*.[222] The problem, as Kadivar sees it, is that in this last and still evolving phase in Shi'a jurisprudence, the theory of *Velayat-e Faqih* has been upheld by many jurists as an ideal political form. In reality, Kadivar claims, the notion of *Velayat-e Faqih* in Islam has neither theoretical validity nor is there any precedent for it in the traditions of the Prophet or in the Holy Book.

As a theoretical construct, *Velayat-e Faqih* was meant to replicate, and depending on the times and circumstances either compete with or complement, the dynastic functions of the Safavid monarchs in the realms of religious and social life.[223] Over time, through processes of historical change and maturation, two theoretical propositions concerning the role and overall nature of the *Velayat-e Faqih* have emerged, one that is appointive and unlimited in scope of power and authority – *Velayat-e Entesabi-e Mutlaqeh*, or Appointed, Absolutist *Velayat* – and another that is elective and has comparatively limited authority – *Velayat-e Entekhabi-e Moqayyadeh*, or Elected, Conditional *Velayat*. The theoretical works of Ayatollah Khomeini, especially after the revolution's success and toward the end of his life, brought him closer to the notion of *Velayat-e Entesabi-e Mutlaqeh*. In contrast, Ayatollah Montazeri explicitly articulates the concept of *Velayat-e Entekhabi-e Moqayyadeh*. Today, the constitution of the Islamic Republic represents a combination of both notions, though it comes closer to the appointive, absolutist position.[224] The *Veli-e Faqih* is elected for life by the Assembly of Experts and is given absolute (*mutlaq*) powers over the entire system.

The two theoretical propositions concerning the *Velayat-e Faqih* differ from one another in several important respects, as outlined in Table 3.

---

[221] Mohsen Kadivar, *Nazariye-haye Dowlat dar Fiqh-e Shi'a* (Perspectives on Government in Shi'a Jurisprudence) (Tehran: Ney, 1376/1997), pp. 13–21.
[222] Ibid., p. 28.
[223] Mohsen Kadivar, *Hokumat-e Velayi* (Government of the Jurisconsult) (Tehran: Ney, 1377/1998), pp. 103–06.
[224] Kadivar, *Daqdaqe-haye Hokumat-e Dini* (Crises of Religious Government), p. 64.

Table 3 *Kadivar's typology of the two main conceptions of* Velayat-e Faqih

	Velayat-e Entesabi-e Mutlaqeh	Velayat-e Entekhabi-e Moqayyadeh
Legitimacy	Derived from God	Based on the will of the people
Islamism	Guaranteed through rule of the leader	Depends on the ruler's conduct in office based on Islamic teachings
People's role	Irrelevant to ruler's legitimacy	Popular vote key to ruler's legitimacy
Republicanism (Jomhuriyyat)	Any Islamic political system governing the masses	Guaranteed through the electoral input of the citizenry
Allegiance (Bey'at)	A one-way oath obliging people to follow the ruler	An oath between the ruler and the people pledging mutual obligation and respect
Leadership	Just ruler installed by God	Just ruler elected by the people, and unjust ruler removed through constitutional means
Liberties	Must be limited in order to minimize the potential for the corruption of society	Must be allowed within Islamic framework to allow talent and creativity to thrive

Source: Kadivar, *Daqdaqe-haye Hokumat-e Dini* (Crises of Religious Government), pp. 65–73.

Basically, the *Velayat-e Entekhabi-e Moqayyadeh* is an elected position that is closely supervised by the people's elected representatives, is open to criticism, and the person occupying the position may be impeached and removed from office. Moreover, the limits of the office's powers and its term of office are stipulated in a constitution.[225] *Velayat-e Entesabi-e Mutlaqeh*, on the other hand, at least as articulated by Ayatollah Khomeini, faces few restrictions. Its powers extend from the public and political arenas to all aspects of society; the person occupying the office rules based on what he determines to be in society's best interests; his decisions are guided by his knowledge of the divine religion and are not limited by man-made laws; and, as was the case with the Prophet Muhammad and the Shi'a Imams, his powers are absolute and his term of office is unlimited.[226]

Throughout his writings, Kadivar is careful not to directly criticize Ayatollah Khomeini. In fact, literally all of his writings are characterized

[225] Ibid., p. 141.   [226] Ibid., p. 112.

by a remarkable degree of humility and civility toward those whose ideas he challenges. But his criticism remains sharp nonetheless. In specific relation to the *Velayat-e Faqih*, he argues that the whole institution, whether conditional or absolute, whether elected or appointed, is wholly and entirely without merit.[227] "While Islam is not consistent with all types of political systems, it does not prescribe a specific system either," he writes.

Since *Velayat-e Faqih* is an autocratic system that is based on the divine privilege of the clergy, it is inconsistent with democracy. Democracy is based on principles and foundations such as equality, popular sovereignty, political participation, the rule of law, and human rights ... There is no fundamental contradiction between a society whose members are predominantly Muslim and a political system that is democratic. In fact, Islam as a religion and democracy as a modern method of politics can be easily combined.[228]

Islam, Kadivar maintains, "explicitly rejects specific political models." Moreover, similar to the notion of the *Velayat-e Faqih*, "tens of other, competing political models can be presented that do not contradict the tenets of the *shari'a*." Since jurisprudence alone cannot possibly serve as the basis of politics, economy, management, sociology, and other related disciplines, the notion of the "*Velayat-e Faqih* is based on an incorrect understanding of *fiqh* and jurisprudence." The fact that Islamic dictates reach into the realm of politics does not necessarily mean that Islam recognizes a specific type of political system. In reality, in fact, "*Velayat-e Faqih* is more a reflection and a product of Iran's dynastic tradition and the legacy of the religious autocracy that has characterized the thinking of the country's Shi'a jurists."[229] It is based more on Plato's formulation of the philosopher-king rather than on Islamic *fiqh*.[230] Such a political system, and more specifically the notion of *entesab* (appointment), "are products of jurisprudential thought that historically has not been part of the mainstream of Shi'a *fiqh*, never mind being considered as central pillars of Shi'ism or the Imamate school."[231] In particular, those traditions (*Sunnas*) that are used to justify rule based on *entesab* lack valid historical proof.[232] Ultimately, according to Kadivar, "there is

---

[227] Mohsen Kadivar, "Velayat-e Faqih va Mardomsalari" (The Supreme Jurisconsult and Democracy), www.kadivar.com., accessed on January 29, 2007.

[228] Ibid.

[229] This and all the previous quotes in this paragraph are drawn from ibid.

[230] Mohsen Kadivar, "Foqahat va Siyasat" (Clericalism and Politics), www.kadivar.com., accessed on January 29, 2007.

[231] Mohsen Kadivar, "Barresi-ye Mostanadat-e Ravaee" (Analysis of Commonly Accepted Documents), *Aftab*, No. 11, (1380/2001), p. 60.

[232] Ibid., p. 61.

no logical necessity for the *Velayat-e Faqih*," and all Shi'a jurists and scholars agree that it is nothing more than a theoretical proposition rather than a mainstay of Shi'ism or Islam.[233]

While Kadivar rejects the *Velayat-e Faqih* as the basis of government, he does endorse a type of political system that he labels as "theo-democracy," or, more specifically, Islamic democracy.[234] "The ideal government is one that can prove its compatibility with the citizenry during three phases," he writes: during the initial phase of attaining power; while governing; and during the phase when it is asked to give up power by popular demand. Whenever the will of the people is not observed in any of these phases, the government has slipped into autocracy.[235] The best way for Muslims to govern their lives in the modern era is through an Islamic democracy. Such a political system is logical and does not contradict the tenets of Islam, brings stability and order to the lives of the believers, and allows Muslims to use their religion as the philosophical basis of their democratic system. Within an Islamic democracy all individuals – regardless of their race, gender, skin color, religion, and political belief – enjoy equal rights and privileges; people become the central source of the state's legitimacy and authority; popular political participation becomes the norm; laws are created with the consent and approval of the people; those in power are obligated to obey the law; the religious soul of society serves as a guiding light for the social and political will of the people; and a consistency will prevail between the will of the Almighty and the will of the people.[236] If any of these principles are abrogated, then the political system ceases to be a religious democracy.

For Kadivar, then, Islam is a larger blueprint for life, a general guide for righteous living and spiritual elevation rather than a detailed and specific set of directives governing the minutia of life. As a religion, Islam features no contradiction with democracy as a method. So far, according to Kadivar, most of Iran's religious intellectuals have failed to adequately indigenize notions of freedom and democracy in a way that would not be contradictory to the tenets of Islam.[237] This is one of the central tasks he sets for himself:

We can be religious in a way that allows us to obey all divine rules and dictates while observing those legal and natural rights of man that have been guaranteed

[233] Kadivar, *Hokumat-e Velayi* (Government of the Jurisconsult), p. 226.

[234] Mohsen Kadivar, "Mardomsalari-e Dini" (Religious Democracy), www.kadivar.com, accessed on January 29, 2007.

[235] Mohsen Kadivar, "Hokumat-e Qesri" (Autocratic Government), www.kadivar.com, accessed on January 29, 2007.

[236] Kadivar, "Mardomsalari-e Dini" (Religious Democracy).

[237] Kadivar, *Daqdaqe-haye Hokumat-e Dini* (Crises of Religious Government), p. 427.

by Islam. In areas where there are no religious dictates or prohibitions – and in my opinion most social, political, economic, and cultural areas fall under this category – we can refer to the "legal conditions" of mankind. Many of the tenets of human rights that are being observed outside of Islam and Iran can be adopted in areas where religion is silent ... We accept this rationality because it does not contradict our religion and is [in fact] necessary for our religiosity and Muslim identity.[238]

Given the thrust of Kadivar's thoughts and writings in recent years, it seems befitting to conclude this discussion of him by emphasizing his repeated endorsement of civil and religious rights. He emphatically endorses freedom of belief and religion, rejecting the use of force and compulsion to enforce religious belief, and maintaining that apostasy should not be considered a punishable crime.[239] Islam is a religion that encourages the believer to use the faculties of reason and logic to search for the truth and to ask questions, not one based on forced compliance and repression.[240] The Holy Qur'an explicitly mandates against practices such as capital punishment for apostates, or the forced conversion of non-believers, or other practices that have been commonplace in Islamic history.[241] The problem is with "historical Islam," an Islam corrupted by centuries of political machinations and manipulations, one in which gender and religious discrimination became prevalent, human rights became non-existent, and the free flow and exchange of ideas were suppressed.[242] Real Islam, the Islam that we once again need to redis-cover anew, is different. Real Islam is democratic in both the public and the private spheres. It guarantees equality between the sexes[243] and members of different religions, within the family and among members of the larger polity.

Kadivar's passionate advocacy of civil and political liberties as inher-ent features of Islam is echoed by another notable contemporary reli-gious intellectual, namely Hojjatoleslam Mohammad Mojtahed Shabestari. Born in 1936, Mojtahed Shabestari received a traditional religious education in Qom and attained the rank of Hojjatoleslam. In the 1960s and the 1970s, he became heavily influenced by the ideas of Ali Shariati and Ayatollah Morteza Mottahari. In 1970, he assumed the directorship of the Shi'a Islamic Center in the Imam Ali Mosque in

---

[238] Ibid., p. 314.

[239] Mohsen Kadivar, "Azadi-ye 'Aqideh va Mazhab dar Eslam" (Freedom of Opinion and Belief in Islam), *Aftab*, No. 23 (1381/2002), p. 54.

[240] Ibid., p. 56.   [241] Ibid., p. 58.

[242] Mohsen Kadivar, "Hoquq-e Bashar va Roshanfekri-ye Dini" (Human Rights and Religious Intellectualism), *Aftab*, No. 28 (1382/2003), pp. 106–15.

[243] Mohsen Kadivar, "Roshanfekri-e Dini va Hoquq-e Zanan" (Religious Intellectuals and Women's Rights), www.kadivar.com, accessed on January 29, 2007.

Hamburg, where he studied German and became familiar with the writings of theologians such as Paul Tillich, Karl Barth, and Karl Rahner, as well as the philosophies of Immanuel Kant, Hans-Georg Gadamer, and others. During this time he became a strong advocate of Muslim–Christian dialogue, a theme that still remains prominent in many of his writings.[244] Returning to Iran in 1978, he was elected to the first Majles after the Islamic revolution, and, beginning in 1985, assumed a teaching position at the University of Tehran's Faculty of Theological and Islamic Sciences, where he still teaches. Over the last two decades or so, Mojtahed Shabestari has emerged one of the country's most influential religious intellectuals, with his ideas on Islamic hermeneutics and *ijtihad* closely followed by interested members of the middle classes, and especially by the university student population.

Similar to Soroush and Kadivar, Mojtahed Shabestari pays particular attention to hermeneutics, *ijtihad*, and democracy. "Islamic sciences must embrace the discipline of hermeneutics," he writes, "since it is the discipline that clarifies the critical details and proper interpretations of Islam, especially insofar as *ijtihad* is concerned. [Hermeneutics] can help us attain meaningful interpretation of Islam in the contemporary era."[245] Like Soroush, Mojtahed Shabestari points to the imperfection of religion as it is popularly represented and practiced. In reality, what passes for religion is only man's knowledge of it, and that knowledge is imperfect and in need of critical analysis.[246] In today's Iran, this need for critical analysis has become all the more pressing at a time when the state has taken over and seeks to monopolize religious discourse. But this "official Islam" stands in direct contradiction to the true essence and spirit of the religion, one in which rationality reigns supreme and critical thought is encouraged, and, more importantly, in which there are no provisions whatsoever for an official class of guardians and interpreters.[247]

In his highly popular *A Critique of the Official Reading of Religion*, Mojtahed Shabestari paints a devastating portrait of the official doctrinal underpinnings of the Islamic Republic. "The official reading of religion has thrown our society into crisis," he writes.[248] At its core, this crisis

---

[244] See, for example, Mohammad Mojtahed Shabestari, *Iman va Azadi* (Faith and Freedom) (Tehran: Tarh-e No, 1379/2000), pp. 145–47.

[245] Mohammad Mojtahed Shabestari, *Hermeneutic, Ketab va Sonnat* (Hermeneutics, the Scripture and the Tradition) (Tehran: Tarh-e No, 1379/2000), p. 33.

[246] Ibid., pp. 205–06.

[247] Mohammad Mojtahed Shabestari, *Naqdi bar Qara't-e Rasmi az Din* (A Critique of the Official Reading of Religion) (Tehran: Tarh-e No, 1379/2000), p. 97.

[248] Ibid., p. 11.

arises out of two central misconceptions on which the official doctrine is based: first, the mistaken assumption that *fiqh* can indeed serve as the basis for modern politics, economics, and law; and second, the equally incorrect belief that the state is responsible for executing Islamic laws and dictates in society.[249] The roots of this "official religious doctrine" can be traced back to the earliest days of the revolution, when the clericalization of religion gave birth to what Mojtahed Shabestari calls "jurisprudential Islam" (*Islam-e foqahati*). Today, with the revolution nearing its third decade, official Islam has become so plagued with crises and problems that it can no longer properly govern. Specifically, official Islam cannot sustain itself because of its innate opposition to democracy, its frequent resort to violence in order to force itself on society, and its philosophical dearth and poverty.[250]

Renewal of Islamic discourse, and of Islamic culture more broadly, is key, as is the need to make it transparent and clear. "The starting point in our society is revision of religious culture." "If we do indeed decide to revise religious culture, we must revise religious discourse by highlighting its true essence and figuring out which aspects of it address religious belief, which aspects address politics, which ones address philosophy, and so on."[251]

In this endeavor, we must utilize the analytical tools available to us both within and outside of religion in order to reconstruct our knowledge and understanding of Islam. Only then will we be able to get to Islam's "central meaning" ("*ma'na-ye markazi*").[252]

This is where *ijtihad* plays a most central role in the reconstruction of Islamic knowledge. The essence of the Qur'an and the *Sunna* are unchangeable. But our understanding of them must necessarily be dynamic. And this dynamism in the understanding and conception of Islam is reached through "continuous *ijtihad*" (*ijtihad-e mostamar*).[253] We cannot continue imitating past *faqih*s, and, especially given the rapidly changing world around us, there is pressing need for new *ijtihad* on all fronts of Islamic knowledge.[254] We must refine our *a priori* knowledge and assumptions about the Text and the *Sunna* according to the needs of the time, Mojtahed Shabestari argues unequivocally, adding that Muslims cannot afford to neglect complementing their *fiqh* with knowledge and insights from other sciences and disciplines.[255] *Fiqh*

---

[249] Ibid.   [250] Ibid., p. 31.   [251] Ibid., p. 341.

[252] Mohammad Mojtahed Shabestari, *Ta'amilati dar Qara't-e Ensani az Din* (Reflections on a Humane Reading of Religion) (Tehran: Tarh-e No, 1383/2004), p. 341.

[253] Mojtahed Shabestari, *Hermeneutic, Ketab va Sonnat* (Hermeneutics, the Scripture and the Tradition), pp. 92–93.

[254] Ibid., p. 50.   [255] Ibid., p. 51.

must evolve, and this evolution cannot be made possible without contribution from the modern sciences. "*Ijtihad* is realized when the *faqih* begins to ask new questions" and searches for new answers, not when he keeps giving old answers to old questions.[256] And some of the most pressing questions that need to be asked and answered revolve around the essential details of contemporary social and political life: what is the proper basis of government in today's world? How permissible is it to limit popular economic freedoms through centralized planning? Is capitalism a desirable system? How much direct and indirect influence should the government be allowed to exert in people's daily lives? Is it permissible to violate national sovereignty? Is it permissible to abide by the rules of the global economy that may contradict man's spiritual life and ethical norms?[257] To remain relevant to the lives of Muslims and Iranians, Islam and especially *fiqh* must address these and other similar questions.

These answers, according to Mojtahed Shabestari, cannot be searched for in the original sources of Islam. Many of the moral, political, and philosophical issues and concerns that confront contemporary societies did not exist during the time of the Prophet Muhammad, and, as a result, are not addressed or even mentioned in the original Islamic sources. There are fundamental differences between the conditions and the context of the Prophet's rule and the predicaments in which modern societies and democratic political systems find themselves.[258]

This is not to imply that Islam is antithetical to the tenets of modernity, among the most important of which are liberty and democracy. Mojtahed Shabestari in fact maintains that there are two critical links between Islam and democracy. To begin with, "we can transpose the values of democracy on Islamic culture" and easily create an amalgam of the two.[259] The spirit of Islam and the values of democracy are highly compatible, and combining them is, in fact, a matter of urgent necessity:

I endorse democracy because it is the only system in contemporary times that allows mankind to reach the twin ideals of freedom and justice, without which humanity cannot fulfill its full potential and adequately perform its responsibilities before the Almighty. Only through free choice can mankind meet the full range of his responsibilities before God.[260]

---

[256] Ibid., pp. 63–64.   [257] Ibid., p. 66.

[258] Mojtahed Shabestari, *Naqdi bar Qara't-e Rasmi az Din* (A Critique of the Official Reading of Religion), pp. 276–77.

[259] Mojtahed Shabestari, *Ta'amilati dar Qara't-e Ensani az Din* (Reflections on a Humane Reading of Religion), p. 139.

[260] Ibid., p. 147.

Secondly, and more importantly, Mojtahed Shabestari maintains, belief is meaningless without free choice.[261] God created man free and responsible, he claims, and it is his choices that affirm man's belief or disbelief in Islam. Insofar as political systems are concerned, democracy is most conducive to the meaningful attainment of religious beliefs. "The logic of belief dictates that believers be aware of social and political realities, and themselves be responsible in political matters, so that they can consciously and freely search for their beliefs."[262] Beliefs are especially strengthened in religious democracies, where there tends to be a preponderance of interpretations and discourses of religion, thus giving believers the opportunity to freely explore, critically analyze, and then internalize their religious beliefs.[263] Of course, such a religious democracy will not become possible in Iran unless and until there is reform of religion as it has come to be known. "There must be fundamental reforms in those religious opinions, *fatwa*s, beliefs, values, and rules that govern our society," writes Mojtahed Shabestari.

Many of the *fatwa*s need to change. Those values that are male-centered, opinion-centered, and leader-centered need to change and to make room for democracy. What has become known as historical religion and has assumed the shape of ossified beliefs, commands, and slogans, and in the process has subsumed the "central meaning" of Islam, needs to change in order to once again facilitate man's spiritual ascension toward the Almighty.[264]

Democracy is a necessity for Islam, and an Islamic democracy is a necessity for Iran.

Conclusion

The efforts of Mojtahed Shabestari, Khatami, Soroush, and Kadivar, along with those of the many other religious reformists mentioned here, have collectively given rise to a vibrant, intellectually sophisticated, and expansive discourse of Islamic reformism. Although similar discourses in the past have been a part of the mainstream of Islamic thought in Iran for some time, this latest incarnation stands out for several reasons. To begin with, the current discourse is being articulated in a radically new context that, unlike any other time in Iranian history, features a heritage of Islamic revolutionism, a theocratic political system, a politically backed discourse of religious conservatism, and unprecedented levels of

---

[261] Mojtahed Shabestari, *Iman va Azadi* (Faith and Freedom), p. 15.   [262] Ibid., p. 79.
[263] Mojtahed Shabestari, *Ta'amilati dar Qara't-e Ensani az Din* (Reflections on a Humane Reading of Religion), pp. 149–50.
[264] Ibid., p. 177.

and speeds in the flow of information and knowledge. Equally significant is the relatively new focus of the current discourse as compared to its previous incarnations, with themes relevant to, and often a product of, Iran of the late twentieth and the early twenty-first centuries – civil society, democracy, civil liberties, hermeneutics, and the like. Today's architects of the discourse of Islamic reformism are indeed the heirs of a rich and historically resonant strand of Muslim thought. But the larger context within which they find themselves, and the themes and topics they tackle, bear little or no resemblance to previous epochs of Iranian history. In tremendously important ways, therefore, they are blazing new trails.

Alone, however, they are not. Just as these religious intellectuals are articulating a reformist religious discourse, their conservative counterparts, as we saw earlier, continue to produce intellectual blueprints and signposts of their own and are seeking to advance, or rather hold on to, traditionalist religious propositions about the ideal polity. But the ensuing competition among discourses is not only two-way. While the conservative and the reformist religious discourses fiercely compete with one another on multiple levels – doctrinally, for more popular appeal, greater political power, etc. – they also face competition from a third discourse, this one avowedly non-religious and secular, one that prides in presenting itself as "the modern" alternative to existing, often religious, worldviews. It is to the examination of this secular-modernist discourse that the book turns next.

Of all the dilemmas and challenges facing contemporary Iran, one of the most pressing is the force and momentum of modernity. Modernity is a phenomenon that cannot be stopped. It is a phase in the evolution of humanity that started in earnest in eighteenth-century Europe and has now come to engulf all aspects of human life and thought. Those societies and governments that somehow try to resist or negate this inevitable process only marginalize themselves and the communities they govern. At best, they selectively pick and choose those aspects of modernity that they find politically and culturally least objectionable. At worst, in an attempt to safeguard some supposed social, cultural, and political authenticity, they erect ostensibly insurmountable barriers to what they perceive to be the intrusion of modern norms, practices, and institutions. The central task facing those hitherto robbed of the fruits of modernity is to articulate and implement their own conceptions of modernity. What needs to occur is first to understand the nature and gravity of the problem of being unmodern, and then to devise feasible and meaningful strategies of reaching and accommodating modernity.

This, in a nutshell, is the essence of the arguments made by a growing number of contemporary Iranian intellectuals. Central to their scholarly outputs – which is almost exclusively through books – is the notion of *modernity* and a host of attendant questions – what is it, what social and political consequences does it have for those affected by it, and what explains the extent to which it has gained resonance or has been absent from Iranian society? Collectively, through an expansive body of literature, they have given rise to what may best be classified as the "secular-modernist" discourse.

Let us, at the outset, look more closely at the two defining features of this discourse, namely *modernity* and *secularism*. For many of these secular, modernist intellectuals, modernity and secularism are intertwined and naturally complementary, one being impossible without the other. For the past four or five centuries, and especially in the last 150 years, they argue, a coalescence of historical and political forces have either prevented the introduction of modernity into the country altogether or have greatly undermined its meaningful resonance throughout Iranian society. Given where we are and what has become of us, they ask, where do we go from here? How do we come to terms with modernity and yet not lose ourselves by aping others? How do we articulate our own conception of what it means to be modern and calibrate our identity accordingly? Central to their answers is the notion and phenomenon of modernity, a modernity in which, at least for this group of intellectuals, religion plays no public role whatsoever. They do not simply ignore religion; they call for its privatization. Religion for them has no role in the public domain. It is best left to be worshipped at home and in other especially designated places. Public life in general, and politics in particular, must be secularized.

Before examining the main premises of the secular-modernist discourse, it is important to see who are some of its main articulators. Primarily, the thinkers who fall into this category are made up of academics with high levels of familiarity with Western approaches to the study of the social sciences. Many have received postgraduate training and degrees in the social sciences and the humanities from French, British, or American universities – in fields such as economics, sociology, political science, and philosophy – or, if graduates of one of Iran's growing number of universities, they have had instructors well versed in Western-language literature and theories. Academically and intellectually, most of the intellectuals and thinkers under study here mostly came of age either immediately around the time of the revolution's success in 1978–79 or in its wake in the mid- to the late 1980s. By and large, many supported the revolution's larger ideals. In fact, similar to the proponents of the reformist religious discourse, some even actively identified with the revolutionary establishment in its early years. Steadily, however, the ideological chasm between the direction of the political establishment on the one hand, and its accompanying conservative religious discourse, and the secular-modernists' own predispositions on the other could not be ignored. With the unprecedented flowering of publications following Khatami's election to the presidency in 1997, the secular-modernist discourse began carving out a distinct identity for itself. Today, more than a decade later, it can no longer be ignored.

Some of the more prominent figures readily identified with the secular-modernist discourse include Babak Ahmadi (b. 1948), Daryush Ashouri (b. 1938), Hosein Bashiriyeh (1953), Jamshid Behnam (b. 1928), Musa Ghaninezhad (b. 1951), and Ramin Jahanbegloo (1956).[1] There are a

---

[1] On April 30, 2006, Ramin Jahanbegloo was arrested and spent four months in prison, then released just as suddenly and unexpectedly on August 30, 2006. While still in prison, government officials claimed that Jahanbegloo had sought to start a "velvet revolution" in Iran of the kind that took place across Eastern Europe. Immediately prior to his arrest, Jahanbegloo had given an interview with a foreign journalist in which he had allegedly criticized comments made by President Ahmadinejad about the

whole host of other writers and academics, with varying degrees of renown and most of them generally younger in age, whose writings and arguments have also come to collectively form the corpus of the secular-modernist discourse. Some, but by no means all, of these academics and commentators include Hosein Kaji (b. 1971), Hamid 'Azadanlou (b. 1948), Ahmad Golmohammadi (b. 1968), Hooshang Mahrouyan (b. 1946), Majid Mohammadi (b. 1960), and Mahmood Sariolghalam (b. 1959). Table 4 provides a summary of their main professions and their publications. It goes without saying that this is by no means an exhaustive list and is not meant to reflect the scholarly depth of the named individuals' arguments or their wider social and political significance. Neither do these individuals represent a single school of thought or would necessarily welcome the designation "intellectual," however defined. By the same token, given their different scholarly backgrounds and often their diametrically opposed political persuasions and experiences, many of the thinkers themselves would no doubt object to being clustered together as representing members of the same intellectual current. Nevertheless, the cumulative effect of their thoughts and their arguments are not all that dissimilar and, in fact, often reinforce one another. What does bring them together – at least in the context of the discussion here – is the collective influence of their writings as they coalesce into a general discourse whose prominent features are emphasis on modernity and secularism.

There are, as we shall see presently, a number of perceived threads attached to the phenomenon of modernity, and many of the intellectuals named above have often focused on one or two of these specific threads. Predictably, most of the Iranian scholars reflecting on modernity have approached the study of the phenomenon from the perspective of the discipline in which they received academic training. The larger philosophical underpinnings of modernity, for example, along with the historical obstacles it has faced in Iran, constitute the primary focus of the writings of intellectuals such as Babak Ahmadi, Daryush Ashouri, and Ramin Jahanbegloo. The political scientist Hosein Bashiriyeh examines the historical and contemporary impediments to political development

"mythical" nature of the Holocaust. According to those who know him personally, Jahanbegloo has assiduously avoided politics and political activism throughout his academic career, preferring to dwell only on the plane of ideas. Upon his release, on his way home from Tehran's Evin prison, Jahanbegloo stopped by the offices of the Iranian Student News Agency, ISNA, where in an "interview" he said that some of the audiences in his talks might have misunderstood his arguments as a call to start a velvet revolution in Iran. How the aftermath of this imprisonment influences Jahanbegloo's scholarly activities, if in any way at all, remains to be seen.

Table 4 *Notable secular-modernists*

Name	Year of birth	Primary profession	Major book(s)
Ahmadi, Babak	1948	Independent researcher	*Modernity and Critical Thought*
Ashouri, Daryush	1938	Independent researcher	*Us and Modernity*
ʻAzadanlou, Hamid	1948	Professor of political science, Azad University, Tehran	*Discourse and Society*
Bashiriyeh, Hosein	1953	Professor of political science, University of Tehran	*Obstacles to Political Development in Iran; Political Sociology*
Behnam, Jamshid	1928	Independent researcher	*Iranians and the Idea of Modernity*
Ganji, Akbar	1959	Political activist	*Republican Manifesto; A Fascist Interpretation of Religion and Government; Darkroom of Ghosts; Constructive Reformation: Pathology of Transformation to the Developmental Democratic State*
Ghaninezhad, Musa	1951	Professor of economics, University of Tehran	*Modernism and Development in Contemporary Iran; Civil Society, Liberty, Economics, and Politics*
Golmohammadi, Ahmad	1968	Professor of political science, ʻAllameh Tabatabai University	*Globalization, Culture, Identity*
Hoodashtian, ʻAta	1951	Instructor of philosophy, various universities in Paris	*Modernity, Globalization and Iran*
Jahanbegloo, Ramin	1956	author, researcher	*Modernity, Democracy and Intellectuals; The Moderns; Iran and Modernity; The Fourth Wave*
Kaji, Hosein	1971	Electrical engineer (MA degree in Western Philosophy)	*Our Existence from the Perspective of Iranian Intellectuals*
Kar, Mehrangiz	1944	Attorney	*Legal Obstacles to Development in Iran*
Mahrouyan, Hooshang	1946	Independent researcher, author	*Modernity and Our Crisis*
Mardiha, Seyyed Morteza	1960	Professor of political science, ʻAllameh Tabatabai University	*In Defense of Rationality*

Milani, Abbas	1949	Professor of Political Science, Stanford University	*Modernity and Modernity-Fighting in Iran*
Mohammadi, Majid	1960	Lecturer in sociology, Binghamton University	*Iranian Liberalism, Unfinished Agenda; Civil Society as a Method; Reform's Difficult Road; Moral Systems in Islam and Iran*
Rajaee, Farhang	1952	Professor of political science, Carlton University (Canada)	*The Problematic of Contemporary Iranian Identity*
Sariolghalam, Mahmood	1959	Professor of international relations, Shahid Beheshti University	*Rationality and the Future of Iran's Development*
Tabataba'i, Seyyed Javad	1945	Independent researcher (former professor at the University of Tehran)	*A Philosophical Look at Political Thought in Iran; Paucity of Political Thought in Iran; The Meaning of Absolute Velayat in the Political Thought of the Middle Ages*

in Iran, which, as with a number of other academics, he sees as one of the primary pillars of modernity. Some of the other political scientists have turned their attention to the other features of the phenomenon they deem as crucial, such as rationality (e.g. Sariolghalam) or secularism (e.g. Vasiq). Meanwhile, some of the sociologists who have figured prominently in the discourse have turned their attention to the impediments to and the necessities of the development of civil society in Iran (e.g. Majid Mohammadi).

The significance of these writings, it is important to repeat, rests not necessarily in their individual contributions, whose depth and import in themselves should not be minimized or ignored nonetheless. Their even greater significance lies in their convergence to form a larger intellectual discourse, one that places modernity and secularism as its central themes and, more importantly, as its central goals. Within the academic and learned community in Iran, not every single author writing on these topics is recognized as a major and deliberate architect of the secular-modernist discourse. Some are far more readily recognized by the larger public than others, and, through their writings or frequent interviews with printed media, some have attained general recognition as *public intellectuals*. Others, in the meanwhile, continue to pursue relatively more quiet lives as obscure academics. Some of these authors are even openly dismissive or outright hostile and antagonistic toward one another. But intellectually they all agree on a number of core principles, and these points of convergence have culminated into the secular-reformist discourse.

Grasping modernity

Regardless of the precise focus of their arguments, literally all thinkers and intellectuals falling into the secular-modernist current agree on the reasons for its absence so far from Iranian society and political history, on the overall definition of modernity, and on why it is imperative for the country as a whole to embrace it in a meaningful and resonant manner. The general consensus over the three key questions of *why*, *what*, and *how* has given rise to a rich literature in which Iran's past and present predicaments, as well as the roles of the country's political and intellectual elites in the construction of an Iranian identity, are all critically examined.

There is considerable unanimity among Iran's contemporary secular-modernist thinkers over the general definition of modernity. Not surprisingly, literally all of the definitions of modernity that are forwarded are firmly and consciously grounded in the Western philosophical tradition. Ramin Jahanbegloo, for example, who is by all accounts a most prolific scholar,[2] maintains that an adequate conception of modernity is impossible without a proper understanding of Western political philosophy.[3] In his book *Sovereignty and Freedom*, he begins his exploration of the roots of modern Western political philosophy with Machiavelli and Jean Bodin and then presents in-depth analyses of the thoughts of Hobbes, Locke, Espinoza, Rousseau, Voltaire, Montesquieu, Burke, Kant, Hegel, Marx, de Tocqueville, Benjamin Constant, and John Stuart Mill.[4] Other Iranian secular-modernists are equally mindful of the centrality of Western thought to the project of modernity. In addition to those studied and frequently referenced by Jahanbegloo, other renowned Western philosophers such as Descartes, Baudelaire, Weber, and Habermas figure prominently in the writings of Babak Ahmadi,[5] Daryush Ashouri,[6] Hamid 'Azadanlou,[7] Jamshid Behnam,[8] 'Ata Houdashtiyan,[9] Hooshang Mahrouyan,[10] and literally all others writing on the topic.[11]

With Western philosophy as the common background to the formulation of the concept of modernity, there is also general consensus among Iran's secular-modernists over what the phenomenon means and entails. To begin with, modernity means the permanence of change, rooted in a perspective within which critical reason plays a central role. In contemporary times, Jahanbegloo claims, modernity begins when

---

[2] Some of Jahanbegloo's publications include: *Moderniteh, Demokrasi va Roshanfekran* (Modernity, Democracy and Intellectuals); *Modern-ha* (The Moderns); *Iran va Moderniteh* (Iran and Modernity) (Tehran: Goftar, 1380/2001); "Tasahol va Khoshunat Parhizi" (Tolerance and Conflict Avoidance), *Aftab*, No. 8 (1380/2001), pp. 54–59; *Mowj-e Chaharom* (The Fourth Wave); "Roshanfekr-e Nasl-e Chaharom va Haqiqat-i Faratar az Ideolozhi" (Fourth Generation Intellectual and a Truth Bigger than Ideology); *Hakemiyyat va Azadi: Dars-hai dar Zanineh-ye Falsafeh-e Siyasi-e Modern* (Sovereignty and Freedom: Lessons in Modern Political Philosophy) (Tehran: Ney, 1383/2004); and, *Iran Dar Jostejo-ye Moderniteh* (Iran in Search of Modernity) (Tehran: Markaz, 1384/2005).

[3] Jahanbegloo, *Hakemiyyat va Azadi*, p. 9.

[4] As indicated by the book's subtitle, *Lessons in Modern Political Philosophy*, the book is based on lessons Jahanbegloo gave at the University of Toronto from 1999 to 2001.

[5] Babak Ahmadi, *Moderniteh va Andisheha-ye Enteqadi* (Modernity and Critical Thoughts) (Tehran: Markaz, 1373/1994), pp. 10–13.

[6] Ashouri, *Ma va Moderniteh* (Us and Modernity).

[7] 'Azadanlou, *Gofteman va Jame'h* (Discourse and Society).

[8] Jamshid Behnam, *Iranian va Andisheh-ye Tajaddod* (Iranians and the Idea of Modernity) (Tehran: Farzan Rouz, 1375/1996).

[9] 'Ata Hoodashtiyan, *Moderniteh, Jahani-shodan va Iran* (Modernity, Globalization and Iran) (Tehran: Chapakhsh, 1381/2002).

[10] Hooshang Mahrouyan, *Moderniteh va Bohran-e Ma* (Modernity and our Crisis) (Tehran: Akhtaran, 1383/2004).

[11] See, for example, compilations such as Ganji's *Sonnat, Moderniteh, Postmodern* (Tradition, Modernity, Post-Modern).

society no longer upholds tradition as a model to emulate and recognizes the need to move past it. "Modernity is the only movement in human society through which fundamental changes occur to our conception of time and history."[12] Modernity is "permanent reconstruction" and entails the constant restart of a new era.[13] It means reconstructing the past through critical lenses. In the words of Babak Ahmadi, "we need to relearn that which the West has taught us, and do so critically," always mindful that Western material dominance does not means its valuative superiority.[14] We need to learn from the West by embracing our heritage and critiquing it at the same time, revive our artistic and literary traditions not for the sake of cultural authenticity but in order to re-evaluate them, learn from their shortcomings, and to build on them in order to advance.[15]

Hamid 'Azadanlou similarly perceives of modernity as "an awareness of the dynamic nature of time, separation from tradition, a feeling of newness, and 'vertigo in the face of passing moment'."[16] "Modernity is more than simply accepting the permanence of change," he argues, and revolves around "accepting the self as a complex and complicated subject capable of growth and development."[17] The modern individual, and by extension to the larger modern society, both face the responsibility of "permanent production," which in turn facilitates the appearance of higher stages of intellectual evolution and enlightenment. "Enlightenment opens the door to modernity, and both enlightenment and modernity pave the way for intellectualism."[18]

Entry into modernity does not, of course, necessarily entail the abandoning of tradition. Perhaps the most articulate discussion of the relationship between tradition and modernity has been forwarded by Akbar Ganji (b. 1959), a serious thinker with keen insight into Iranian history and politics, though more recently known for his political activism and long periods of solitary confinement in prison.[19] There is

---

[12] Jahanbegloo, *Iran va Moderniteh* (Iran and Modernity), p. 9.

[13] Jahanbegloo, *Mowj-e Chaharom* (The Fourth Wave), p. 17.

[14] Ahmadi, *Moderniteh va Andisheha-ye Enteqadi* (Modernity and Critical Thoughts), p. 11.

[15] Ibid., pp. 9–11.   [16] 'Azadanlou, *Gofteman va Jame'h* (Discourse and Society), p. 113.

[17] Ibid., p. 114.   [18] Ibid.

[19] A prolific author and investigative journalist, Ganji was arrested in 2000, ostensibly on charges of taking part in an anti-government conference in Berlin. He had earlier published a book in which he implicated former President Rafsanjani in the murder of five prominent writers. Held in solitary confinement and alleging torture while in detention, Ganji was released in March 2006, although as of this writing he is still not fully free to go about his life. Some of his publications include: *Sonnat, Moderniteh, Post-modern* (Tradition, Modernity, Post-Modern); *Tarik-khaneh Ashab* (Darkroom of Ghosts) (Tehran: Tarh-e No, 1379/2000); *'Alijenab Sorkhpoush va 'Alijenaban-e Khakestari* (The Red Eminence and the Gray Eminences) (Tehran: Tarh-e No, 1379/

an intimate relationship between tradition and modernity, Ganji maintains, the latter arising out of the former. Modernity is a reconceptua-
lization of reality in a new light. Modernity does not necessarily revolve
around imitation; instead, it centers on adaptation and adoption – the
adaptation of existing values and perspectives to new and evolving
circumstances, and the adoption of those values and perspectives from
others that are consistent with and further facilitate the production of a
dynamic outlook.[20] Every tradition and every civilization, therefore, can
have its own modernity, taking its norms and values and reinterpreting
them according to new realities and new needs.[21]

This permanence of change is made possible by the central role that
critical reason plays in the project of modernity. The modern person is a
thinking individual, asserts Jahanbegloo, citing Descartes and Bacon.[22]
More specifically, modernity engages in the constant criticism of tradition and of itself, writes Ahmadi, and constitutes a complex cultural
phenomenon in which reason reigns supreme and freedom becomes
possible.[23] Hooshang Mahrouyan (b. 1946) similarly emphasizes the
importance of rationality and the intellect in turning the individual into a
subject, a subject of study as well as liberation. "The modern person
destroys all the mythical and metaphysical constructs that inundate his
world, and replaces metaphysics with knowledge."[24]

The emphasis on critical reasoning puts the individual, the "doer," at
the center of the modernity project. In modernity, the individual is no
longer an *object* but is a critical, thinking, doing *subject*. "Self-awareness,
self-discovery, and self-centeredness – these are the central premises of
modernity."[25] As Jahanbegloo maintains, modernity means "awareness"
of a new epoch, one in which the power of the intellect is supreme and
when reason places the individual – having emerged as the "subject" – at

---

2000); *Tallaqi-ye Fashisti az Din va Hokumat* (A Fascist Interpretation of Religion and
Government) (Tehran: Tarh-e No, 1379/2000); *Eslah-gari-ye Me'maraneh: Asib-shebasi-e
Gozar be Dowlat-e Demokratik-e Tose'h-gozar* (Constructive Reformation: Pathology of
Transformation to the Developmental Democratic State) (Tehran: Tarh-e No, 1379/
2000); *Kimiya-ye Azadi: Defa'iyat-e Akbar Ganji dar Dadgah-e Berlin* (Exile of Freedom:
Akbar Ganji's Defense at the Berlin Conference Trial) (Tehran: Tarh-e No, 1380/2001);
"Eslah-talabi, Enqelabi-gari va Mohafeze-kari" (Reformism, Revolutionisum and
Conservatism), *Aftab*, No. 7 (1380/2001), pp. 14–25; and "Ejra-ye Hodood dar
Zaman-e Ma" (Executing Limits in our Times), *Aftab*, No. 9 (1380/2001), pp. 26–31.
While in prison, Ganji wrote a "Republican Manifesto", more on which below.
20   Quoted in Changiz Pahlevan, *Panj Goftego* (Five Conversations) (Tehran: 'Atai, 1382/
2003), pp. 131–32.
21   Quoted in ibid., p. 131.
22   Jahanbegloo, *Iran va Moderniteh* (Iran and Modernity), pp. 25–26.
23   Ahmadi, *Moderniteh va Andisheha-ye Enteqadi* (Modernity and Critical Thoughts), p. 10.
24   Mahrouyan, *Moderniteh va Bohran-e Ma* (Modernity and our Crisis), p. 115.
25   Ahmadi, *Moderniteh va Andisheha-ye Enteqadi* (Modernity and Critical Thoughts), p. 37.

the apex and in command of nature, history, and self-actualization.[26] Modernity is a perspective, a worldview in which the individual has deliberately created the surrounding world and the realities of his society.[27] The individual's awareness of the supremacy of his critical faculties – of his individuality – is central to the conception of modernity. Self-awareness, and more specifically awareness of what is "historic" and significant, become key in modern life.[28] Perhaps more than anything else, the intellectuals maintain, modernity bestows the individual with the power to will, to be knowing, and to be deliberate.

Being modern means being critically aware of one's time and place in history. It means a deliberate search for scientific truth and knowledge, a deliberate distancing of the self from tradition, and a deliberate employment of rationality in the construction of ethics and gnosis (*shenakht*).[29] This means that there are no absolutes in modernity insofar as values are concerned. Grand normative frameworks, chief among which is religion, no longer hold the unattainable mysteries of life. Rationality fosters secularism, pushing religion into the private domain, and the secrets of the universe become revealed through scientific knowledge and reason.[30] The only constant in modernity is the principle of "criticism" and critical choice, leading to intellectual and philosophical pluralism and the deliberate choices of individuals, because of which history progresses.[31] This freedom of choice, enshrined in inescapable "social contracts," makes modernity synonymous with democracy, whereby the individual is recognized as a citizen who enjoys social and political liberties.[32]

'Ata Hoodashtiyan (b. 1951), who teaches philosophy at Paris VIII University, elaborates on this "modern subjectivity." Basing his analysis on Hegel's arguments, Hoodashtiyan posits that modernity offers a new conception of the individual, transforming the person for a passive object (*maf'ol*) to an active subject (*fa'el*), from a marginal bystander to a central actor. The person who once lived in fear of the unknown, the supernatural, and the mythical is now a knowing creator.[33] The essence of modernity is an "unrelenting search for rationality, political autonomy,

---

[26] Jahanbegloo, *Iran va Moderniteh* (Iran and Modernity), pp. 9–10.

[27] Behnam and Jahanbegloo, *Tamaddon va Tajaddod* (Civilization and Modernity), p. 5.

[28] Milani, *Tajaddod va Tajaddod-Setizi dar Iran* (Modernity and Modernity-Fighting in Iran), p. 129.

[29] Jahanbegloo, *Mowj-e Chaharom* (The Fourth Wave), pp. 114–15.

[30] Milani, *Tajaddod va Tajaddod-Setizi dar Iran* (Modernity and Modernity-Fighting in Iran), p. 129.

[31] Jahanbegloo, *Modern-ha* (The Moderns), p. 3.   [32] Ibid., pp. 13–14.

[33] Hoodashtiyan, *Moderniteh, Jahani-shodan va Iran* (Modernity, Globalization and Iran), pp. 18–19.

and individual freedom."[34] The centrality of individuality and rationality to modernity find their expression in all the fields of human activity that modernity has overcome, from economics and politics to culture, religion, ethics, aesthetics, and architecture.[35] In practical terms, what this translates to is "capitalist economics, the secularization of politics, the retreat of religion into the private sphere, the spread of critical rationality, public participation in politics, and the expansion of the private, non-governmental sector."[36]

Despite its overarching significance, modernity's introduction and its spread in Iran has been at best stunted and, at worst, often blocked altogether. This blockage, the secular-modernists argue, needs to be reversed. As Farhang Rajaee (b. 1952) maintains, devising strategies of accommodation with modernity is the panacea that Iran desperately needs. More specifically, Iran needs a native and distinctively Iranian interpretation of modernity, just as it offered the world a distinctively Iranian interpretation of Islam in the form of Shi'ism.[37] Echoing the sentiments of many like-minded colleagues, Rajaee claims that "the crisis of modernity is the biggest obstacle to the Iranians' self-discovery and also to their progress ... If we do not enter into it voluntarily and are dragged to it by force, we would have made ourselves too weak and marginal to shape it."[38] Akbar Ganji is equally blunt about the urgency of Iran's entry into, and active participation within, the world of modernity:

We cannot ignore the modern world. We must internalize those aspects of this world [of modernity] that are in sync with us. Many of the phenomena that exist in the Western world are suited to our realities. We have entered a period in world history in which there exist a series of global models, some of which fit all civilizations. We are in a period in history when there are certain common global models that can benefit all. This adoption (and internalization) of other models should not be confused as allowing one civilization to dominate others.[39]

We cannot have a culture that is closed to the outside world, Ganji goes on to maintain, for we then run the risk of running it into oblivion altogether.[40] Similar to the West, we must have an "absorbing" culture, one that is sufficiently secure in its own identity and its foundations but is also willing to open itself to positive influences from the outside.[41]

---

[34] Jahanbegloo, *Iran va Moderniteh* (Iran and Modernity), p. 11.
[35] Milani, *Tajaddod va Tajaddod-Setizi dar Iran* (Modernity and Modernity-Fighting in Iran), p. 9.
[36] Ibid., pp. 9–10.
[37] Farhang Rajaee, *Moshkeleh-e Hoviyyat-e Iranian-e Emrouz* (The Problematic of Contemporary Iranian Identity) (Tehran: Ney, 1382/2003), p. 163.
[38] Ibid., p. 163.   [39] Quoted in Pahlevan, *Panj Goftego* (Five Conversations), pp. 20–21.
[40] Quoted in ibid., pp. 26–27.   [41] Quoted in ibid., p. 28.

In addition to defining the phenomenon and concept of modernity, much of the secular-modernist discourse is devoted to exploring the manifold obstacles that have impeded modernity's growth and spread in Iran. Broadly, these impediments are said to fall into one or more of three categories. They include social and political dynamics at work in Iranian history over the last millennium; the manner and extent of Iran's encounter with European colonialism over the last century and a half; and a persistent confusion of the two phenomena of *modernity* and *modernization*.

One of the most penetrating analyses of modernity in Iran is presented by Abbas Milani in his *Modernity and Modernity-Fighting in Iran*, a carefully crafted study of Iran's cultural and political history.[42] Milani maintains that Iran's unceremonious relationship with modernity started not with the country's fall into the Western colonial orbit in the nineteenth century, as commonly believed, but rather it dates back to the seventeenth and the eighteenth centuries, and in many ways even earlier, when many of the tenets of Iranian political philosophy were shaped.[43] Nevertheless, despite the insurmountable odds rooted within Iran's history, culture, and politics, many of the key ingredients to modernity have been able to find expression in Iranian history – in its literature, in the layout of its cities, and in the efforts of its political and cultural elites. In each case, however, any gains made in the direction of modernity have been overwhelmed and then reversed by forces far more powerful and more entrenched.

In the thirteenth and fourteenth centuries, for example, Iranian Sufism reached its greatest cultural resonance, and, both as a method and a tradition, it continues to permeate many Iranians' thinking and worldview to this day. Sufism's continued emphasis on mysticism and the ascetic life, becoming increasingly salient at a time when Europe was beginning to embark on its steady journey to modernity, has continued to erode cultural dynamism and the spread of the critical rationality which modernity demands.[44] Similarly, Sufism's near-complete negation of individuality and individual self-assertion, its dogged denunciation of worldly possessions and material goods, and its conception of "knowledge" as an esoteric, untransferable personal closeness to God have all combined to seriously undermine the possibilities for the spread of critical and scientific reasoning and technological progress.[45]

---

[42] Prior to its publication, many chapters of Milani's book had previously appeared as articles in various Iranian journals, thus making its arguments available to a wider readership.

[43] Milani, *Tajaddod va Tajaddod-Setizi dar Iran* (Modernity and Modernity-Fighting in Iran), p. 104.

[44] Ibid., pp. 53–59.   [45] Ibid., pp. 61–69.

If there have been occasional efforts at forging a modern rationality, they have either been overwhelmed by larger antithetical forces or, worse yet, they have been misunderstood by their intended audiences. This, according to Milani, is precisely what has happened to the works of Sa'di (*c.* 1200–1292), one of Iran's greatest poets and thinkers. Milani points to a number of features in Sa'di's main book of prose, *Golestan* (The Rose Garden), which, in Milani's analysis, bespeak of the poet's pioneering modernity. Long before Luther sought to popularize the understanding of the Bible by translating it from Latin into German, an act for which he was persecuted, Sa'di translated some of the verses of the Qur'an into Persian. At the same time, he used simple prose in his writings during a time when obfuscation was the norm. More importantly, he may be considered as one of the first authors of the essay as a form of literary expression, all of which in the West are often associated with the advent of modernity.[46] Equally significant is Sa'di's attention to the self and his efforts to reconcile competing cultural and philosophical forces, what Milani sees as an indication of the poet's early attention to "interiority" and "interior monologue".[47] In subtle and indirect ways, Sa'di also found ways to criticize the despotism of the political establishment at the time, though remaining careful not to offend his powerful patrons.[48]

In the early years of the twentieth century, Iran's first generation of intellectuals condemned Sa'di and his literary contributions as archaic and mystical, antiquated and irredeemably traditionalist.[49] These same intellectuals, Milani reminds his readers, conceived of modernity as "parrot-like imitations of the West" and failed to see it as Sa'di had centuries earlier, namely critiquing and building up on a tradition that is pregnant with meaning and the potential for progress.[50]

Similarly piercing is the work of Seyyed Javad Tabataba'i (b. 1945), former professor at the University of Tehran who specializes in the history of philosophical thought in Iran. Tabataba'i argues that Iran had a rich tradition of political thought up until the Mongol invasion in the 1220s.[51] For much of the remainder of Iranian history, according to Tabataba'i, with the possible exception of the first century of Safavid rule, the country was plunged into chaos and lawlessness. In the process, three things suffered: the once-robust tradition of political thought; historiography; and, perhaps most importantly, Iranian notions of

---

[46] Ibid., pp. 81–87.   [47] Ibid., p. 86.   [48] Ibid., pp. 89–92.   [49] Ibid., pp. 83–84.
[50] Ibid., p. 84.
[51] Seyyed Javad Tabataba'i, *Zaval-e Andisheh-e Siyasi dar Iran* (Paucity of Political Thought in Iran) (Tehran: Kavir, 1838/2004), p. 353.

historical "progress" and evolution.[52] By the nineteenth and the twentieth centuries, "on the one hand our connection with the old tradition of political philosophy was cut off and, on the other hand, it became impossible for us to think about carving out a new identity in the modern era."[53] Iran forcibly entered the era of modernity at a time when it was philosophically ill-equipped to do so, and therefore for many "tradition" became something of an anchor, cherished by most rather than critiqued by the intelligentsia.[54] Today, Tabataba'i laments, "the prevalence of ideology, coupled with the fact that we cannot distinguish between thought and ideology", have had two tragic consequences: first, "we have been unable to grasp the essence of modern identity and Western thought"; secondly, we have not understood "the relationship between modern identity and Iranian thought."[55] We remain, ultimately, somewhere in-between, dangling between tradition and modernity, philosophically incapable of solving a way out of the quagmire.

While Milani focuses on home-bred philosophical and historical obstacles to modernity in Iran, and Tabataba'i on the effects of the Mongol invasion, neither necessarily denies that Iran's encounter with the West has been equally instrumental in preventing the emergence of an Iranian modernity. Significantly, most contemporary Iranian thinkers do not blame the West per se for deliberately blocking the introduction and spread of modernity in Iran. Instead, they point to the conceptions of modernity as understood by their own intellectual predecessors, especially Iran's so-called first- and second-generation intellectuals, as serious impediments to the development of a critical and dynamic mindset.

Jamshid Behnam is a case in point. He traces the stunted introduction of modernity to Iran to the irregular, uneven manner in which the country's learned elites have been exposed to the phenomenon and to the West in general. Historically, he maintains, Iranian elites learned about the West and its modern ways and philosophy only through second-hand sources, many of which were translated into Persian from Arabic or Turkish publications. In the process, "as we lost interest in other cultures also, we lost our own intellectual dynamism."[56] At the same time, perhaps the most important social strata, namely the clergy, staunchly opposed it.[57] When a number of Iranian intellectuals eventually did discover the importance of modernity, neither they nor the larger masses

---

[52] Ibid., p. 356.
[53] Seyyed Javad Tabataba'i, *Daramadi Falsafi bar Tarikh-e Andisheh-e Siyasi dar Iran* (A Philosophical Look at Political Thought in Iran) (Tehran: Kavir, 1374/1995), p. 26.
[54] Ibid., p. 27.   [55] Ibid.
[56] Behnam, *Iranian va Andisheh-ye Tajaddod* (Iranians and the Idea of Modernity), p. 171.
[57] Ibid., pp. 172–73.

grasped or experienced it uniformly. Since Iran never became an official colony of a Western power, Behnam continues to argue, it did not develop extensive economic and cultural links with a dominant European metropolis. Consequently, Iranian elites were exposed to different traditions of Western philosophy – Latin, Germanic, and Anglo-Saxon – which in turn undermined their efficacy as a uniform social group.[58]

Hoodashtiyan's analysis is somewhat similar. After a long period of dormancy and hibernation, he maintains, Iranian society was changed, but only by force and imposition. "Over the last century, the primary engine of change in Iran has been external rather than internal."[59] "In Iran we have had neither meaningful technology nor a balanced government, neither the rule of law nor a rational bureaucracy" to help facilitate the spread of rational thought and modernity.[60] Change, therefore, has been erratic and has often taken the form of crisis. More importantly, because this change was imposed from the outside – or, put differently, because the roots of the crisis is external – a "critical mindset" has not developed among Iranian intellectuals, "leaving us somewhere in-between abandoning tradition and embracing modernity."[61]

Hamid 'Azadanlou approaches the issue from a somewhat similar but slightly different perspective. Not having been through an intellectual renaissance or a scientific revolution of their own, he maintains, when the earliest generations of Iranian thinkers saw the military and economic might of the West – to which they were tragically exposed in two successive defeats by Russia – they became enamored with Western thought. They abandoned their own intellectual pursuits and started to blindly embrace all the thoughts and philosophies that the West had to offer. This unintentional "intellectual surrender" only paved the way for an "intellectual colonialism" of sorts, and reduced the depth and complexities of modernity to blind imitation and Westernization.[62] 'Azadanlou is careful not to affix blame or be accusatory. In fact, he praises the intellectuals of yesteryear for their courage and pioneering spirit. Nevertheless, he maintains, although their hearts might have been in the right place, their imitative, superficial scholarly efforts failed to usher in an era of modernity in Iran.[63] Political autocracy, meanwhile, turned the production of intellectual discourse into an inherently revolutionary – and therefore demagogic – act. As a result, in-depth critical thought was

---

[58] Ibid., p. 174.
[59] Hoodashtiyan, *Moderniteh, Jahani-shodan va Iran* (Modernity, Globalization and Iran), p. 82.
[60] Ibid., p. 83.   [61] Ibid., p. 89.
[62] 'Azadanlou, *Gofteman va Jame'h* (Discourse and Society), p. 121.
[63] Ibid., pp. 123–24.

unceremoniously morphed into sloganeering and heroism.[64] The ultimate outcome, claims 'Azadanlou, has not boded well for democracy.

Along similar lines, Daryush Ashouri also points to approaches to and perceptions of the West common among Iranian intellectuals as a key explanatory factor in Iran's checkered relationship with modernity. Iranian intellectuals, he claims, have either advocated the wholesale Europeanization of Iranian life and society, as many first generation intellectuals did, or, alternatively, they have pointed to the West as a source of all of the ills plaguing Iran's past and present.[65] Blind imitation or dogmatic rejection of the West has made the Iranian intellectuals' conception of modernity both superficial and ideological. So long as we do not have an objective and accurate understanding of Western modernity and its philosophical foundations, Ashouri warns, we cannot escape the ideological lenses through which we see the world or grasp the scientific basis of Western philosophy and technology. And so long as we do not equip ourselves with such essential tools, he maintains, we cannot understand our own predicament and will continue to remain "Third Worlders inebriated with the West."[66] This line of analysis, incidentally, is very similar to Jahanbegloo's, who, as discussed earlier, calls on "Fourth Generation" intellectuals to critically understand and analyze not only their own history and tradition but that of the West as well.[67]

Finally, particularly in the twentieth century, Iranian intellectuals and the masses at large often saw modernity only in terms of its material and technological manifestations and not as the more fundamental and complex change in worldview that it is. In other words, most Iranians have been confusing modernity with modernization, reducing it to economics and technology and viewing it devoid of its philosophical underpinnings. According to Hoodashtiyan, "the reduction of modernity to modernism is the biggest danger we face in Iran in our efforts to understand and analyze the West."[68] Modernism, or modernization, comprises "the *tools* and ingredients that are the outward manifestations of Western civilization"; modernity is "a set of *concepts* that go beyond outward manifestations and make them possible."[69] Jamshid Behnam agrees: "Modernity is an in-depth movement in worldview and thought process that requires a long time," he writes, whereas "modernization can appear in a short period of time and can have social, economic, and

[64] Ibid., pp. 141–42.   [65] Ashouri, *Ma va Moderniteh* (Us and Modernity), p. 280.
[66] Ibid.   [67] Jahanbegloo, *Mowj-e Chaharom* (The Fourth Wave), pp. 156–57.
[68] Hoodashtiyan, *Moderniteh, Jahani-shodan va Iran* (Modernity, Globalization and Iran), p. 71.
[69] Ibid. Original emphasis.

political consequences."[70] In Iran and elsewhere in the developing world, the two phenomena are frequently confused – often deliberately so by political leaders – when the material and scientific advances made possible by modernity are grossly and deliberately substituted for the worldview and approach to nature that made them possible.[71]

Conspicuously absent from this line of analysis has been finger pointing at the West. Indeed, quite unlike many of their immediate predecessors, and consistent with the spirit of modernity, almost all of the "Fourth Generation," secular-modernist intellectuals focus inwardly, on Iranian political history and culture and the internal dynamics driving them, as the primary culprits keeping modernity at bay. The West, of course, did not go out of its way to share its rich philosophical traditions with the non-Western world. And, inadvertently, many Western Orientalists glorified or at best glossed over some of the most entrenched and archaic features of Iranian philosophical tradition, such as Sufism and mysticism. At the same time, Western powers did prop up a political system for which modernity meant only economic development and implied political submission. Nevertheless, none of the main articulators of the secular-modernist discourse point accusatory fingers at the West or its individual members. Iran's wretched history of political autocracy may have found an anchor in the twentieth century in Western capitals. But, ultimately, the roots of both despotism and philosophical conservatism lie deep within, inside Iranian tradition and history.

Any discussion of modernity would be incomplete without mentioning its latest progeny and perhaps sharpest critic, namely post-modernity. Keenly aware of theoretical and philosophical developments in the West, Iran's secular-modernist intellectuals have had to address the question of post-modernity.[72] With the state and understanding of modernity in Iran being what it is, does it make sense to speak of post-modernity in the Iranian context? And, if so, what are the meaning and parameters of a supposedly Iranian post-modernity? In the West, post-modernity was born out of a "crisis of modernity," whereby the individual's soul was increasingly being replaced by machines and mechanical relationships. In the words of Daryush Ashouri, modernity led man to wage war on nature and also on other men. "This

---

[70] Quoted in Behnam and Jahanbegloo, *Tamaddon va Tajaddod* (Civilization and Modernity), p. 13.

[71] Jahanbegloo, *Iran va Moderniteh* (Iran and Modernity), p. 10.

[72] As an example, Akbar Ganji has devoted an entire book, made up of interviews with some of the country's most renowned intellectuals, to the question of modernity and post-modernity in Iran. In *Tradition, Modernity, Post-Modern*, Ganji starts nearly every interview by asking about the meaning of post-modernity and its relevance to Iran.

youthfully exuberant assault on nature, which was backed up by modern science and technology, ushered in a new plain of knowledge, one whose focus was to learn and discover the causes of the ruins brought on nature, the ensuing imbalance between man and nature, and man's own constant anxiety."[73] Iran, the secular-modernists claim, has not yet achieved modernity in a meaningful and substantive manner. Where does it then stand in relation to post-modernity?

Jahanbegloo concedes that post-modernists address some of the crises and difficulties caused by modernity and also acknowledge variations in national identities and cultures, which modernist philosophers often overlook.[74] Nonetheless, given that "we do not have a full understanding of modern philosophers," he wonders if discussions of post-modernist thinkers in Iran are more a matter of "fashion" rather than in-depth understanding and conviction.[75] Perhaps half-jokingly, Musa Ghaninezhad goes so far as to claim that "discussions of post-modernism are very dangerous for our society." "We know what modernity means because it stands in contradiction to tradition and signifies economic development. But discussions of post-modernity are convoluted and unclear. They only add to the confusions that transitional societies already experience as they find themselves torn between modernity and tradition."[76] Nevertheless, there appears to be a general consensus among most secular-modernist intellectuals that post-modernity as a supposedly evolutionary completion to modernity neither exists in Iran nor does it apply to the country's current predicament. Ghaninezhad and others draw sharp distinctions between the historical phase that post-modernity is supposed to designate versus a certain approach and mindset. As a broader philosophical framework, however, focusing on the self and on the larger context of one's life, post-modernity may have a few useful insights to offer. For example, "the post-modern perspective," or what Ashouri calls "the post-modern technology," can "help us preserve certain aspects of our tradition," such as family and history.[77] Hosein Bashiriyeh also sees positive and significant contributions by post-modernity in a number of "scientific" areas, including the contextualization of the social sciences, viewing science as part of culture, rejecting a single scientific paradigm

---

[73] Quoted in Ganji's *Sonnat, Moderniteh, Postmodern* (Tradition, Modernity, Post-Modern), p. 9.

[74] Jahanbegloo, *Iran Dar Jostejo-ye Moderniteh* (Iran in Search of Modernity), p. 30.

[75] Ibid., p. 32.

[76] Quoted in Ganji's *Sonnat, Moderniteh, Postmodern* (Tradition, Modernity, Post-Modern), pp. 175–76.

[77] Quoted in ibid., p. 12.

and general theorizing, and pointing to the intimate relationship between science and power, among many others.[78]

Modernity's pillars

One of the central questions the secular-modernists seek to answer is the nature of the challenges ahead. With general and broad consensus over the meanings of modernity and post-modernity in the context of Iran's modern political history, and having defined the obstacles that have impeded modernity's spread, where do we go and how do we get there? In more concrete terms, what does it mean for Iran to be modern? Note that the question is not "what does it mean to be modern in Iran?", for modernity is not a phenomenon that is limited to individuals or groups of them, but is, instead, national in scale. To assume that there are pockets of modernity in an otherwise unmodern society is to have the wrong conception of modernity and to confuse it with being fashionable. The burgeoning literature on modernity, produced and articulated by the secular-modernists, defines modernity in terms of national rather than communal or class identity. How, then, it is important to ask, does Iran become modern?

Here our task is slightly complicated by the fact that only one or two of the secular-modernists have clearly articulated the concrete steps that need to be taken for modernity to emerge and thrive in Iran. Throughout the literature, five themes are consistently highlighted as key indicators of modernity and as essential elements that Iran needs to embrace. Seldom, however, are they discussed in tandem.[79] Nor are they, it is important to note, necessarily viewed as mutually exclusive. In fact, in going through the literature, one gets the impression that these five phenomena, by virtue of their integral connection to modernity, are interconnected and complementary. Each scholar, it seems, deems some aspect of modernity to be more important than others, a product, often, of his or her disciplinary training, or intellectual preference, or both. These perceived pillars of modernity include secularism, rationalism, civil society, development, and globalization. For Iran to become modern, the arguments go, it needs to embrace each of these five phenomena, either individually or in connection with one another.

---

[78] Quoted in ibid., p. 89.

[79] One of the few scholars who outlines the multiple pillars of modernity that Iran needs to seek after is 'Ata Hoodashtiyan. See Hoodashtiyan, *Moderniteh, Jahani-shodan va Iran* (Modernity, Globalization and Iran), p. 3

Let us begin with a discussion of rationality and its critical importance to modernity, a topic about which two authors, Morteza Mardiha and Mahmood Sariolghalam, have had much to contribute. For Mardiha (b. 1960), who is Professor of Political Science at Tehran's 'Allameh Tabatabai University, rationality is central to all human endeavors, be it the production of culture, the adoption of and belief in religion, the conduct of politics, or the organization of society. "Reason is superior to culture," he states emphatically.[80] This supremacy extends to all other communal sources of identity as well – race, kinship, ethnicity, and religion – and draws humans closer to social formations such as national government and international society.[81] While never quite explicitly defining rationality, Mardiha seems to equate it with education. He argues that all cultures, regardless of their specificities and the core of their identity, move in a unilinear direction. The West, by virtue of its educational advances, has progressed further along a set of goals toward which all cultures strive. "The culture of the West, and all its central elements – democracy, liberalism, individualism, human rights, pan-sexualism, transcendence of familial and religious obligations, balanced conception of subject-citizen, etc. – is not really (an exclusively) Western culture. It is a culture that sooner or later all societies, closed or open, will reach."[82] This is not meant to be a normative endorsement of Western culture, Mardiha claims,[83] careful perhaps not to be accused of "Westoxication" or of endorsing facets of Western culture offensive to Iranian sensibilities (for example, "pan-sexualism," which he never defines). Education has allowed the West to pioneer a path that is the destiny of all cultures if and when they attain the same levels of education and rationality. "The principal core of any culture, and especially Western culture, is not necessarily the depth of its history and its geography; it is human nature."[84]

Rationality changes cultures by allowing them to evolve, search for new frontiers, and attain new heights.[85] By doing so, rationality opens a host of possibilities for all cultures. It allows for the establishment of liberal democracies with capitalist economies,[86] and reduces the potential frictions between national and individual interests.[87] It facilitates the spread of civil society,[88] and also fosters religious freedom.[89]

Professor Sariolghalam, who teaches international relations at Tehran's Shahid Beheshti University, argues along similar lines, though from a

---

[80] Seyyed Morteza Mardiha, *Defa'a az 'Aqlaniyat* (In Defense of Rationality) (Tehran: Naqsh-o Negar, 1379/2000), p. 6.
[81] Ibid., p. 8.   [82] Ibid., p. 16.   [83] Ibid., p. 41.   [84] Ibid., p. 16.   [85] Ibid., p. 38.
[86] Ibid., pp. 25–26.   [87] Ibid., pp. 76–77.   [88] Ibid., p. 179.   [89] Ibid., pp. 180–81.

slightly different angle. Sariolghalam's arguments are more pointedly critical of the characteristics found in "Iranian personality," which, he maintains, are shaped and influenced by the country's existing social, political, and economic structures. He frames his analysis not so much in terms of how to reach where the West has already arrived, as Mardiha does, but rather looks for ways of overcoming obstacles to "Iran's development." These obstacles, he maintains, reside in an "Iranian personality" that is victim to prevailing structures, and cannot be overcome unless rationality thrives and takes over.

If we do not create structures that will change our personality, and do not create cooperative relationships amongst one another, we will be unable to create structures that facilitate political, economic, and social development. The critical task confronting us, therefore, is to quickly adopt a rational mentality that will allow us to implement fundamental changes to our personality.[90]

Iran needs to be developed, and being developed means having seven key characteristics: a non-rentier economy; a strong sense of nationalism among political elites and their commitment to the idea of development; common and in-depth understanding by political elites of domestic and global conditions; technological, scientific, and managerial contacts with the West; a foreign policy welcoming of foreign investments; an economic, political, and social culture that facilitates development as understood internationally; and a stable and secure environment both domestically and internationally.[91] None of these features will come about, however, if there is not a fundamental change in Iranian culture and personality.[92] This requires changing those structures that directly bear on Iranian personality. "We have constantly changed our political and social structures, but those aspects of our personality that are tribal and anti-developmentalist have remained constant ... Our thoughts are modern, but our personality is non-modern."[93] "We need a new Iranian, an Iranian who is responsible, fair, hardworking, devout but not fanatical, self-assured, self-motivated, knows limits, takes pride in his land, is willing to take criticism, is not gullible, and is not boastful."[94] This is where rationalism comes in. Rationalism is rooted "in the foundations of personality and behavior, and no nation, regardless of its culture and history, can achieve development without it."[95] "The most basic definition of rationalism is the utilization of thought and science in the conduct of any task. Rationalism is the solution to being excitable,

---

[90] Mahmood Sariolghalam, *'Aqlaniyyat va Ayandeh-e Tose'eh-yaftegi-ye Iran* (Rationality and the Future of Iran's Development) (Tehran: Center for Scientific Research and Middle East Strategic Studies, 1382/2003), p. 3.
[91] Ibid., p. 12.   [92] Ibid., p. 17.   [93] Ibid., p. 18.   [94] Ibid., p. 21.   [95] Ibid., p. 22.

whimsical, sentimental, and unpredictable. Within this framework, our actions belong to the pre-modern era."[96] Sariolghalam's sweeping indictment is most directly pointed at Iran's political and intellectual elites, although he does not spare the average person. What sector or class holds the key to Iran's development, he asks rhetorically? "Is it the private sector, the state, the clergy, particular individuals, political groups, the armed forces, or the agricultural sector?" "It is not clear," he goes on to answer. "Our problem in Iran is that such a leading group [that would spearhead development] has not been formed."[97] No group has the rationality needed to foster and to take on this task, neither the elites nor the masses. "In the opinion of this writer," he writes, "even our nationalism is based on feelings and excitement rather than rationalism. If we truly and rationally loved our country, we would not throw litter into streets out of our cars."[98]

On whom does the responsibility fall for instilling rationality, or, more specifically, creating institutions conducive to the spread of rationality? Sariolghalam sees this as the duty of the state. "Given our current condition, the responsibility for design and implementation of the doctrine of rationality in Iran is that of the state."[99] Since the absence of political parties has resulted in the weakness of Iranian society, the primary responsibility for bringing about change – in both structures as well as political culture and personality – falls on the state. "It is my hope that in the next half century, Iranian society surpasses the strength currently enjoyed by the state, and that the state is no longer a rentier one, so that civil society can materialize in a more meaningful fashion."[100] At that point, hopefully rationality would have already spread throughout Iranian society. In the meanwhile, "a house cleaning of the institutions of the state is a necessary first step."[101] Not surprisingly, Sariolghalam does not elaborate on this point. He simply asserts that in the absence of viable abilities on the part of society, in present-day Iran at least, the state should take the lead in fostering rationalism, and this it must do through the creation of structures that change and reform the Iranian personality.

For Sariolghalam, rationalism is not an end in itself but rather only a means to achieving a higher goal, that of development. Development is an inherently political phenomenon, he maintains, which requires a mixture of appropriate state initiatives coupled with a supportive cultural framework.[102] There are several "cultural plagues" in the Third World, however, that obstruct developmentalism. They include superstition, lack of a

---

[96] Ibid.   [97] Ibid., p. 25.   [98] Ibid.   [99] Ibid., p. 24.   [100] Ibid., p. 27.
[101] Ibid., p. 13.   [102] Ibid., p. 46.

questioning and critical mentality, neglect of process (in reaching goals), one-dimensional outlooks, personalism in thought and taste (rather than rationalism), absolutism rather than relativism, and seeking to control phenomena instead of managing and administering them.[103] Once these cultural obstacles are removed, development's "crisis of legitimacy" is resolved and the cultural groundwork for it is prepared.

From a historical perspective, according to Sariolghalam, there are two paths to development. One path, which occurred in the West, involves the complex formation and evolution of social institutions that in turn influence the state and press for its accountability. A second path, which needs to be adopted by developing countries, involves the consensus of intellectual and political elites over developmental goals and objectives.[104] In specific relation to Iran, he argues, "development will not become possible so long as there is no intellectual and theoretical consensus and cooperation among elites."[105] But this is precisely where the problem lies. The chronic weaknesses of Iran's political elites have made them too paranoid to work with or to at least accommodate the country's intellectual elite. This has eroded the scientific basis and the usefulness of their policies and their initiatives. The country's intellectual elites, for their part, have failed to devise theoretical frameworks that adequately apply to and describe the nature and depth of Iran's predicament and conditions.[106] The necessary consensus between the two has so far not emerged, therefore, and the country, as a result, continues to remain underdeveloped.

In line with Sariolghalam's analysis of the characteristics of and impediments to development, to which the bulk of his writings are devoted, a number of other secular-modernist intellectuals have also conducted detailed studies of development and its organic relationship with modernity. Sariolghalam appears to have a holistic conception of "development" and does not differentiate between political and industrial or economic development. Most other secular-modernists, however, tend to concentrate on one or the other variety. More specifically, the political scientist Bashiriyeh focuses on the political aspects of development, while the economist Ghaninezhad tends to be more interested in economic and industrial development.

The subject of political development has been studied in depth by one of Iran's most renowned secular-modernist thinkers, Hosein Bashiriyeh.

---

[103] Ibid., pp. 43–45.

[104] Quoted in Mas'oud Razavi, *Roshanfekran, Ahzab, va Manaf'e Melli* (Intellectuals, Parties, and National Interests) (Tehran: Farzan-e Ruz, 1379/2000), p. 69.

[105] Quoted in ibid., p. 56.   [106] Quoted in ibid., pp. 60–61.

Educated in Britain and extremely well-versed in Western political science literature, Bashiriyeh is a professor of political science at the University of Tehran and has today emerged as one of the country's most influential and most serious thinkers and analysts. Bashiriyeh's works on political development are particularly influential among academic circles and are frequently quoted at length.[107] Moreover, his university teachings and mentoring since the 1980s have left indelible marks on successive generations of political science graduates, many of whom have gone on to become academics themselves or have secured policy-making positions in the state bureaucracy.[108] He is, in short, one of the country's most important, if low-key, intellectuals.

Bashiriyeh's most important work on political development is the book *Obstacles to Political Development in Iran*, although, like many of his other colleagues, he is also the author of a number of journal articles – many of which appear in the form of interviews conducted with him – as well as other books.[109] Bashiriyeh's conception of political development is firmly located within the tradition of "developmentalist" thought prevalent in the study of comparative politics in the United States in the 1960s and the 1970s.[110] For him political development ultimately means an expansion of the scope and depth of political participation and political competition among various social groups. More specifically, he argues, political development entails several essential features: increasing levels of organization among the different social groups and forces; the freedom of these groups to compete and participate in the political process; the existence within political structure of mechanisms for conflict resolution; an absence of violence from political endeavors; an absence of religious sources of political power; and the existence of institutional and legal safeguards for political competition as the primary source of political legitimacy.[111]

---

[107] See, for example, Hadi Khaniki, *Qodrat, Jame'h Madani va Matbo'at* (Power, Civil Society and the Press) (Tehran: Tarh-e No, 1381/2002), pp. 71–74.

[108] Amanian, *Kalbodshekafi-e Jaryan-haye Roshanfekri va Eslahtalabi dar Iran* (Autopsy of Intellectual and Reformist Trends in Iran) p. 109.

[109] Another significant work by Bashiriyeh is *Jame'hshenashi-e Siyasi: Naqsh-e Nirohaye Ejtema'i dar Zendegi-ye Siyasi* (Political Sociology: The Role of Social Forces in Political Life) (Tehran: Ney, 1377/1998). For an example of one of Bashiriyeh's articles see his, "Daneshgah-e Siyasi, Daneshgah-e Ideolozhik" (Political University, Ideological University), *Nameh*, No. 22 (1382/2003), pp. 51–52.

[110] For an in-depth discussion of the so-called "developmentalist" perspective in comparative politics see James A. Bill and Robert L. Hardgrave, Jr., *Comparative Politics: The Quest for Theory* (Washington, DC: University Press of America, 1981), pp. 66–83.

[111] Hosein Bashiriyeh, *Mavane' Tose'h Siyasi dar Iran* (Obstacles to Political Development in Iran) (Tehran: Gam-e Nou, 1380/2001), pp. 12–13.

At the broadest level, there are three main obstacles to political development, each of which has been ever-present in Iranian political history. They include a centralization of political power, an absence of social consensus, and political cultures and ideologies that lend themselves to absolutist, non-compromising interpretations of politics. Contrary to what some political scientists such as Samuel Huntington have claimed, Bashiriyeh argues, political centralism is not a requirement for political development.[112] In fact, in Iran, the political centralism that eventually occurred in the aftermath of the Constitutional Revolution quickly morphed into political absolutism beginning in the 1920s, resulting in the banning of most forms of political participation, crushing civil society, and ultimately undermining the possibilities for political development.[113]

Equally detrimental in Bashiriyeh's view has been a deep and persistent chasm in Iranian society that has impeded the emergence of a meaningful level of social and cultural consensus among urban Iranians. Societies may have internal cleavages along regional, cultural, class, or ethnic lines. The main chasm that internally divides urban Iranians from one another is cultural or civilizational, and, so far at least, it has proven unbridgeable.[114] Contemporary Iranian civilization and culture is a hodgepodge composite of three different civilizational layers:

the culture and civilization of ancient Iran, which on occasion presents itself in the political and cultural arenas: an Islamic culture and civilization whose purchase has risen and declined at different points in Iranian history; and a Western culture and civilization that over the last century or two has left indelible marks on various facets of Iranian society and has provoked sharp reactions from Islamic culture and civilization.[115]

These cultural layers have so far failed to meld together successfully, preventing the spread of meaningful consensus and cooperation among the urban classes, and therefore having devastating consequences for political development. In specific, Bashiriyeh claims, these seemingly irreconcilable civilizational and cultural differences have combined to make Iranian politics characterized by "cynicism, mistrust, fear, and violence," thus greatly eroding the possibility of mutual acceptance and the emergence of competitive rules of the game.[116]

Finally, Bashiriyeh points to the larger features of the political culture of Iran's ruling elites as obstacles to the country's political development. "For a variety of complex historical reasons," he writes, "the political

---

[112] Ibid., p. 23.   [113] Ibid., p. 22.   [114] Ibid., p. 27.   [115] Ibid.   [116] Ibid.

culture of the Iranian elite has always been patrimonial with deep roots in Oriental despotism and oligarchic rule."[117]

The assumption of a direct relationship between the Ruler and the Creator has given the political system a legitimacy that does not welcome political competition of any sort. Historically, in Iran power has been considered to be something sacred, and as soon as there has been a perceived distance between the source of power and its claim to sanctity, it has been overthrown. It is no accident that in Iran there has been a strong tendency toward ideological totalitarianism, and this has naturally influenced the orientations of those in power. In this type of a political culture, politics is often viewed as something rife with conflict, and it is thought to move forward only through conflict ... This conflict-ridden perception of politics is so deeply entrenched in Iran that the notion of "compromise" is often viewed negatively and is misperceived as submission.[118]

Combined with persistent authoritarianism and lack of cultural consensus over political objectives, the non-democratic political culture of Iranian elites has seriously eroded the possibilities for political development. This, needless to say, does not bode for the prospects of modernity in Iran in the future, a key ingredient of which is political development. To become modern Iran needs to be politically developed, and Bashiriyeh's prognosis for the country's political development in the near future is not that promising.

Insofar as *political* development is concerned, brief mention must also be made of the arguments of Mehrangiz Kar (b. 1944), one of Iran's most renowned human rights lawyers. Similar to Bashiriyeh, Kar focuses on obstacles to political development in Iran, but from a legal and judicial perspective rather than a strictly institutional one. According to Kar, the essence of political development revolves around the extent to which civil and political liberties are protected and observed, and in this respect, she maintains, Iran is woefully politically underdeveloped. "If we take political development to mean the free and unfettered participation in national affairs of independent groups of citizens from different political, cultural, or commercial backgrounds irrespective of their gender, race, beliefs, and religion, then political development has not occurred in Iran."[119] For that to happen, the legal and constitutional basis of the political system, and more specifically the legal foundations on which Iranians' civil and political rights are based, need to be changed. In concrete terms, this includes the provision of legal guarantees for social

---

[117] Ibid., p. 30.   [118] Ibid., p. 31.

[119] Mehrangiz Kar, *Mavane'-e Hoquqi-e Touse'h dar Iran* (Legal Obstacles to Development in Iran) (Tehran: Qatreh, 1381/2002), p. 14.

and individual liberties, as well as the removal of legal barriers to the establishment and operation of political parties, unions, various civic and cultural organizations, and professional associations.[120]

For both Bashiriyeh and Kar, their politically grounded conception of development is synonymous with democracy. Both, in other words, see a developed system as a democratic one, with all the political and constitutional guarantees for individual and social liberties that democracies feature. The economist Musa Ghaninezhad, however, sees development through the lenses of industrial advancement and modernization, viewing a developed system as one that has embraced capitalist economics. For Ghaninezhad, democracy and capitalism have a symbiotic relationship: "political freedom (democracy) cannot last without economic freedom (market economics), and, at the same time, only through democracy can market economics resolve its own internal contradictions."[121] Similar to most other secular-modernists, Ghaninezhad locates the primary obstacle to development in the people's mindset and in their mistaken perceptions of what development is supposed to entail.[122] In contemporary times, this has resulted in the convergence of a number of political, economic, and intellectual phenomena that have impeded the country's development.

From its earliest days, development in Iran has been controlled and directed by the state, often directly and at times indirectly. One of the most negative consequences of this pervasive statism has been the underdevelopment of individual property rights in Iran.[123] Economic competition, based on the operations of firms and supported by protected property rights, is the real engine of economic development. Despite occasional efforts at economic privatization in Iran, however, the state has remained, and is often popularly perceived as, the primary patron and protector of the economy. For development to occur, "the state bureaucracy needs to retreat from the economy and give way to legal protections and regulations governing economic relationships and activities. Only then will individual property rights become meaningful."[124]

Ghaninezhad ends his call for the adoption of capitalist economic relations by seeking to debunk what he perceives to be two commonly held misperceptions. First, he claims, developmental thinking often

[120] Ibid., p. 15.
[121] Musa Ghaninezhad, *Jame'h Madani, Azadi, Eqtesad va Siyasat* (Civil Society, Liberty, Economics, and Politics) (Tehran: Tarh-e No, 1377/1998), p. 8.
[122] Ghaninezhad, *Tajaddod Talabi va Touse'eh dar Iran-e Mo'aser* (Modernism and Development in Contemporary Iran), p. 29.
[123] Ibid., p. 139.   [124] Ibid., p. 141.

assumes that one of the biggest challenges facing developing countries, including Iran, is their high rate of population growth. This, according to Ghaninezhad, runs counter to the very logic of development, namely man's mastery of nature. Those who call for controlling population growth rates seem to have forgotten that increased life expectancy and declining mortality rates are some of development's crowning accomplishments.[125] "What prevents development is neither population growth rate nor insufficient capital. Instead, it is a combination of ways of thinking and the values and customs of society that do not allow a political and socioeconomic order to emerge that would support development."[126]

Second, multinational corporations should not be kept out of domestic markets on grounds of economic nationalism or their supposedly exploitative intentions. Here Ghaninezhad does not frame his arguments in terms of embracing globalization. Instead, he maintains that countries like Iran, and more specifically Iranian firms and entrepreneurs, can learn invaluable lessons from the successes of most multinational firms. Just as important is the transfer of technology that occurs while working with such firms.[127] While the state in places like Iran should ideally protect infant domestic industries through supportive tax and tariff policies, this support should not be indefinite and must be based on sound economic thinking rather than on political or other considerations.[128]

Whether development is defined in economic or in political terms – as capitalist economics or political democracy, or both – its core focus is social empowerment. Through development society becomes more powerful in relation to the state, capable of safeguarding its autonomy and its interests from state encroachment. Modernity, it should be remembered, is fiercely protective of individual rights and privacy both at a personal and a collective, societal level. Perhaps nowhere in the secular-modernist discourse has this defense of social autonomy and empowerment been more thoroughly and passionately articulated than in its discussion of the role and importance of civil society. Civil society is seen as the linchpin of social and political freedom. As such, its realization in Iran is of utmost importance not only insofar as the project of modernity is concerned, but, more broadly, for the country's larger process of democratization as a whole. In fact, as chapter 5 demonstrated, the secular-modernists are not the only ones articulating notions of and calling for the establishment of civil society in Iran. Many of the

---

[125] Ibid., p. 158.   [126] Ibid.   [127] Ibid., p. 193.   [128] Ibid., p. 196.

country's religious reformers also see it as a crucial feature of their own discourse as well.

This centrality ascribed to civil society arises out of its perceived intimate relationship with democracy. Most of the Iranian intellectuals writing in this area agree that civil society is a necessary precondition for the establishment of a vibrant and meaningful democracy. For example, according to Sadeq Zibakalam (b. 1948), who is a professor of political science at the University of Tehran, civil society is essential to the maintenance of law and order, both through society and, more importantly, against the arbitrary exercise of political power.[129] For many others the connection between civil society and democracy is more direct and explicit. As one scholar maintains, regardless of how democracy comes about, through the initiatives of political elites or a series of socially based dynamics, "all experiences demonstrate that there is a close relationship between democracy and civil society. In brief, this means that the growth and development of civil society is the most important element in the security, increasing depth, and strength of democracy and the safeguarding of citizens' human rights."[130]

As already mentioned, a number of Iranian scholars have written on the nature and importance of civil society, many of them secular but some also arguing from a religious perspective.[131] Here, I will highlight the arguments of three of the secular-modernists whose analyses, I believe, are the most thoroughly developed and articulated. They are Musa Ghaninezhad, Majid Mohammadi, and Mohsen Heydarian. Interestingly, despite coming from three separate disciplinary backgrounds – Ghaninezhad being an economist, Mohammadi a sociologist, and Heydarian a political scientist – the arguments of all three parallel and complement each other in significant ways. Nevertheless, it is again important to remember that these authors by no means represent an exhaustive list of the many Iranian thinkers theorizing on civil society. Just as was the case in Western, and especially American, academic circles throughout the 1990s, the study of civil society – and its organic links with democracy and, more broadly, with modernity – became very prevalent among many Iranian academics, especially those of the

---

[129] Sadeq Zibakalam, '*Aks-haye Yadegari be Jame'h Madani* (Memorial Photos with Civil Society) (Tehran: Rouzaneh, 1378/1999), p. 91.

[130] Mohsen Heydarian, *Mardomsalari, Chalesh-e Sarnevesht Saz-e Iran* (Democracy, the Crisis of Iran's Destiny) (Tehran: Saraee, 1381/2002), p. 117.

[131] For a discussion of civil society from a religious perspective see, for example, Naser Shafi'i, *Jame'h Madani, dar Kodamin Negah?* (Civil Society, From which Outlook?) (Tehran: Honarsara-ye Andisheh, 1378/1999).

secular-modernist persuasion.[132] The three scholars mentioned here, however, simply appear to have more in-depth analyses of the phenomenon.

For all three intellectuals, their conception of civil society is firmly grounded in the Western philosophical tradition, particularly in the writings of Locke, Hobbes, Hegel, Marx, Spencer, Rousseau, and others. Consequently, their definitions of civil society closely mirror one another. Mohammadi, for example, defines civil society as "a society in which there are a number of self-motivated, volunteer-driven, and politically autonomous groups whose members share similar preferences and objectives."[133] Such organizations may include various syndicates and trades unions, clubs, political parties, and independent media organizations belonging to publishers, radio and television broadcasters, and the press. These components of civil organization operate based on the consensus of their members and free of outside dictates. This creates a special, internal dynamic within each of these organizations that leads to the emergence of natural leaders within each. Social formations, therefore, develop their own, internal sources of legitimacy, based on and nourished by the individual and collective efforts of socially conscientious activists. No one, Mohammadi asserts, can claim special privileges based on supernatural qualities or a special relationship with a supernatural entity.[134] Needless to say, this is a direct challenge to the position of *Marja'-e Taqlid*, discussed in chapter 4, on which the theoretical and constitutional legitimacy of the Islamic Republic system is based.

Membership in the organizations comprising civil society is completely voluntary. Moreover, while neither the organizations nor the individuals within them are capable of extraordinary feats on their own, they do begin to control their destiny in specific ways that were not

---

[132] Apart from the works cited in this section, discussions of civil society may be found in Hamid Reza Mazaheri Seyf, *Tahaqqoq-e Jame'h Mdani dar Iran va Rah-haye Aan* (Manifesting Civil Society in Iran and its Means) (Tehran: Javanan-e Movvafaq, 1379/2000); Reza Akbari Nouri, "Mafhoum-e Jame'h Madani dar Iran" (The Meaning of Civil Society in Iran), *Jame'h No*. Vol. 1, No. 12 (1381/2002), pp. 8–9; Reza Akbari Nouri, "Jame'h Madani az Andisheh ta Raftar" (Civil Society from Thought to Conduct), *Jame'h No*. Vol. 2, No. 13 (1381/2002), pp. 14–15; Mas'oud Kamali, *Do Enqelab dar Iran: Moderniteh, Jame'h Madani, Mobarezeh Tabaqati* (Two Revolutions in Iran: Modernity, Civil Society, Class Struggle) (Tehran: Digar, 1381/2002); and Khaniki, *Qodrat, Jame'h Madani va Matbo'at* (Power, Civil Society and the Press). See also Mehran Kamrava, "The Civil Society Discourse in Iran," *British Journal of Middle Eastern Studies*, Vol. 28, No. 2 (2001), pp. 165–85.

[133] Majid Mohammadi, *Jame'h Madani Be Manzeleh Yek Ravesh* (Civil Society as a Method) (Tehran: Qatreh, 1376/1997), p. 8.

[134] Ibid., p. 9.

possible before. This empowerment will be an attractive incentive for individuals to willingly join civil society.[135] More importantly, civil society becomes a guarantor of civic and political liberties, since its constituent organizations can mobilize resources and efforts to guard against the arbitrary exercise of state power.[136] Once again, the contribution of civil society to democracy is undeniable.

For Ghaninezhad, the key to civil society is an individual's economically grounded civil rights. "Civil society," he writes, "is made up of that aspect of the social lives of individuals that is protected by law, in which individuals can make their own decisions and judgments based on their own free will and independent reasoning and without any fear [of the government]. More than anything else, this necessitates the protection of individual property rights."[137] More specifically, civil society only becomes possible through capitalism. "The critical and primary ingredient of civil society is a competitive market economy," Ghaninezhad writes, "and outside of this market economy civil society becomes baseless and hollow."[138] Market economics presents the individual with choices – free choices – and allows him to choose freely in the domains of politics, culture, commercial activities, artistic endeavors, and science.[139] This requires belief in and respect for the individual as the ultimate maker of decisions and chooser of his own destiny.[140]

For Ghaninezhad, civil society is part of a more complete circle, that of modernity.[141] In this respect, civil society fits in with, and is incomplete without, modernity's other constituent parts, namely rational thinking, free market economics, and political development. For his part, Heydarian zeros in on this last aspect of civil society, namely its relationship with political development. Based in Sweden, Heydarian heads a small association there named *Kulturforeningen Azad*, or the Azad [Free] Cultural Association. Despite his distance from Iran, nevertheless, his book, *Democracy, the Crisis of Iran's Destiny*, has been well received inside the country.

Heydarian maintains that the important contribution of civil society lies in its transformation of the individual into a citizen, one with political rights and liberties. "Civil society is a shield that protects citizens from the state, and organizes the relationship between the state and the citizenry based on public participation in the affairs of society."[142] This

---

[135] Ibid., pp. 21–22.   [136] Ibid., p. 39.
[137] Ghaninezhad, *Jame'h Madani, Azadi, Eqtesad va Siyasat* (Civil Society, Liberty, Economics, and Politics), pp. 29–30.
[138] Ibid., p. 32.   [139] Ibid., p. 33.   [140] Ibid., p. 35.   [141] Ibid., p. 14.
[142] Heydarian, *Mardomsalari, Chalesh-e Sarnevesht Saz-e Iran* (Democracy, The Crisis of Iran's Destiny), p. 118.

calls for two essential preconditions. First, for civil society to develop there must exist a secular state which derives its legitimacy from the law and from the active participation of the electorate in the political process. Second, the citizenry must not only enjoy equality before the law, but at the same time, they must actively partake in the articulation of social identity. Civil society, in other words, results in the spread of civic and national consciousness, encourages the emergence of a common (democratic) purpose on a national scale, and deepens the prevailing sense of national identity.[143]

The organic relationship between civil society and democracy is inescapable. "One of the most important consequences of civil society is the curtailment of the powers of the state and the creation of a political and legal balance between the powers of the state and society." "In this respect, civil society is the biggest and most logical obstacle to combating autocracy. Through discussing and forwarding those issues, needs, and opinions that are important to the public, civil society becomes an important channel for the circulation of information in society and a powerful lever in influencing the decisions of policymakers."[144] At the same time, by bestowing legal identity on various civic-oriented, self-organized groups, civil society reduces the possibilities for the emergence of groups with inflexible tribal, familial, or ideological loyalties that are prone to extremism and absolutist politics.[145]

Not surprisingly, most of the intellectuals writing on civil society have devoted significant attention to its obstacles in Iran. Of the three secular-modernists mentioned here, Mohammadi and Heydarian have elaborated on these obstacles extensively. Mohammadi divides these impediments into cultural, social, and political categories. Some of the most important cultural obstacles, he maintains, are the lack of clarity between jurisprudential obligations and civic rights, the inability of various civic organizations to bestow their members with non-primordial identities, widespread belief in the appearance of a savior that would right all of society's wrongs, the prevalence of patrimonialism, and the tendency by some to view the idea of civil society as something alien and fit only for Western cultures.[146] Of the social impediments to civil society, some of the most significant include the transience and fluidity of the population which prevents them from developing roots within stable organizations, the slow pace of social division of labor, minimal levels of social trust, the primacy of kinship ties over civic relations, the slowness of accumulating

---

[143] Ibid., p. 119.   [144] Ibid., p. 121.   [145] Ibid.
[146] Mohammadi, *Jame'h Madani Be Manzeleh Yek Ravesh* (Civil Society as a Method) p. 43.

wealth and power, and also the slow pace of accumulating scientific knowledge and professionalism.[147] Finally, the most important political obstacles include the misuse of political power toward personal ends, equating the strength of civic organizations with the weakness of the state, the prevalence of absolutist ideologies, and the preponderance of revolutionary change.[148]

In contrast to Mohammadi's largely sociological analysis, Heydarian's discussion of the obstacles to civil society tends to be more strictly political. He points to three overall obstacles: existing political circumstances; an absence of political development; and the nature of the prevailing political culture. Historically, Iranian politics has been characterized by political selfishness and monopolistic power structures that have undermined the rule of law. "In Iran," he writes, "the law has never ruled. Self-interest and absolutism have governed the law as well."[149] Instead, the state has sought to impose absolute rule over the nation and its destiny.

Compounding this has been the country's political underdevelopment, which Heydarian traces back to the Pahlavi era. Instead of turning Iranians into politically sophisticated citizens, the Pahlavis turned them into a shapeless, confused, and drifting mass whose anger and revulsion resulted in the 1978–79 revolution. Political development, in other words, did not occur during the Pahlavis' half-century rule, and it has yet to occur under the Islamic Republic.[150] Finally, the absence of political parties, and more broadly political stability, have had adverse consequences for Iran's political culture, which remains rife with conspiracy theories. Moreover, traditionally politics in Iran has been viewed as a zero-sum game in which the possibilities for compromise are at best minimal.[151] Combined with political underdevelopment and a number of harsh political realities, such a political culture has been decidedly antithetical to the rise and spread of civil society in Iran.

In addition to civil society and pluralism, another key pillar of modernity is secularism. Not surprisingly, secularism has been a running theme throughout the secular-modernist discourse. Somewhat surprisingly, however, few authors have tackled the subject of secularism head-on, at least through the open publication of books and articles in Iran, although there are a number of Internet-based articles on the subject. This is no doubt a function of the atmosphere that governs Iran's publishing industry. Secularism, which challenges the core legitimacy of what the Islamic Republic is all about, is not a red line that is open

147 Ibid., pp. 43–44.   148 Ibid., p. 44.   149 Ibid., p. 125.   150 Ibid., pp. 128–29.
151 Ibid., pp. 130–31.

to interpretation. It cannot be easily breached, and even then only at great risk.

Ironically, the notion of secularism is central to both the secular-modernist and the religious reformist discourses. And, interestingly, the conception of secularism that proponents of the two discourses operationalize is nearly identical. This can partly be explained by the fact that the construction and defense of a theocratic political system is what the conservative religious discourse is all about, against which both the secular-modernist and the religious reformist discourses define and identify themselves. Nevertheless, as the previous chapter demonstrated, at times secularism is more pointedly highlighted in the arguments of religious reformists than it is by secular-modernists, many of whom often take it as *a priori*. There are, nonetheless, a few secular-modernist intellectuals who have openly and explicitly discussed the merits of secularism, at least academically if not practically. Mahmood Sariolghalam, for example, maintains that secularism is an essential ingredient of liberal democracy, neither being possible without the other.[152] Secularism is not, as is often mistakenly perceived in Iran, a separation of religion from politics and government. It is, instead, religion's lack of interference with the specialized policies of the government.[153] Another such scholar is Sheydan Vasiq, whose detailed study of the two notions of *secularism* and *laicism* contains summaries and critiques of the arguments on secularism presented by Iranian intellectuals with different theoretical dispositions.[154]

Special mention must be made of Akbar Ganji, whose treatise on secularism, and on democratic republicanism more broadly, has emerged in recent years as one of the most thorough and poignant critiques of the Islamic Republican system's religious legitimacy. While still in prison, in 2002 Ganji wrote and clandestinely released his *Republican Manifesto* (*Manifest-e Jomhuri-khahi*). The *Manifesto* was soon made available through the Internet, and today its arguments have become important elements in the secular-modernist discourse.[155] Ganji

---

[152] Sariolghalam, *'Aqlaniyyat va Ayandeh-e Tose'eh-yaftegi-ye Iran* (Rationality and the Future of Iran's Development), p. 372.

[153] Ibid., p. 368.

[154] Sheydan Vasiq, *Laicism Cheest?* (What is Laicism?) (Tehran: Akhtaran, 1384/2005), especially pp. 155–203.

[155] Since it is available through the Internet, Ganji's *Republican Manifesto* can be found as both a Word Document or formatted in PDF, each with a different pagination. The version cited here comes from the electronic archives of "Dr. Baghai's Foundation for Culture and Enlightenment," available on www.fariborzbaghai.org/archives/individual/000281.php, accessed on June 2, 2006. I have added the page numbers to this PDF version of the document, with the first full page of its text as page 1. An

maintains that a political system cannot be truly democratic unless it is secular. In his *Manifesto*, he presents a detailed outline of the essential features of a "modern republic," a key characteristic of which is its unwavering attention to secularism. "The modern republic is ideologically neutral," he writes.

Due to its structural and methodological differentiations, in the modern republic the two institutions of religion and the state are separated from each other. From a theoretical perspective, we can say that neither is a "state religion" a true religion nor a "religious state" a true state. At the same time, "religious democracy" (or a "religious republic") is a paradoxical construct. What is important is for the state not to have the right to interfere in religion, although like any other institution in civil society, religion can express itself in relation to various public policies. Religion cannot, however, rule politically. Nor can it be a source of inspiration for politics. If religious institutions enter the political arena, as is the case with Christian Democratic parties for example, they have to abide by the general rules governing the modern republic. A country cannot function without a state. But a country without a religious state or an official religion is both conceivable and desirable.[156]

Justice dictates that states remain neutral in regards to religion, and "no political rights or responsibilities can be assigned on the basis of one's religious beliefs."[157] Modern republics, Ganji maintains, "recognize those rights that are not rooted in religion and are respectful of intellectual and philosophical pluralism."[158]

Ganji's *Manifesto* is not meant to be a critique of Iran's current political establishment only. On a deeper level, it also refutes the religious reformist perspective that seeks to point to the inherent compatibilities of Islam and democracy. Ganji, who in the earliest days of the revolution was himself an ardent follower of the notion of an *Islamic* Republic and was employed in the notorious Intelligence Ministry, today has little patience for even the reformist religious discourse, one for which a reformed Islam continues to be a guiding political blueprint. In so doing, in the *Republican Manifesto* he embarks on a detailed and frontal attack on the ideas of Abdolkarim Soroush, one of the most influential architects of the reformist religious discourse.

As comforting and valuable as religion might be in one's personal life, Ganji argues, ideally it should have no role in politics. "Through resort

amended and abridged English translation of the *Manifesto* can be found in Akbar Ganji, "The Struggle against Sultanism," *Journal of Democracy*. Vol. 16, No. 4 (October 2005), pp. 38–51.

[156] Ganji, *Manifest-e Jomhuri-khahi* (Republican Manifesto) (Tehran: n.p., 1381/2002), p. 5.

[157] Ibid.   [158] Ibid.

to hermeneutics," he writes, "some religious reformist thinkers have theorized about the compatibility between Islam and democracy, pluralism, human rights, civil society, and tolerance."

This is an incorrect perspective. Hermeneutics does not mean interpretive free-for-all. And neither does the "structure of text" lend itself to every interpretation and analysis. The Book and the Tradition are absolute, and stand in contradiction with "liberal democracy" or "social democracy". Such interpretations (synchronizing the two) are incorrect.[159]

According to Ganji, one can be a democrat and a faithful believer at the same time. However, a religious government cannot be democratic. Democracy is not attainable through "a religion whose jurisprudence calls for the establishment of a theocracy that would make worldly and divine salvation possible."[160] More specifically, "Islam cannot be democratic unless it becomes thoroughly secular."[161] Secularism, Ganji continues, does not mean abandoning faith and belief. It means "separating rationally-founded institutions, such as the state, from faith-based institutions. According to the perspective of secularism, religion is neither the basis of the state's public policy making or its laws, nor is it a source of legitimacy for state institutions and its central figures."[162]

These analyses bring Ganji to the conclusion that the Islamic Republican system is fundamentally unreformable. "Within the framework of the Islamic Republic's constitution," he writes, "there is no possibility for establishing a democratic political system. Democracy or republic as defined by the rest of the world is in contradiction with our constitution, and one cannot believe in this constitution and be a democrat at the same time."[163] In a radical departure from the reform movement of the Khatami years, Ganji calls for a popular referendum to decide whether or not the current political system, with its existing constitutional arrangement, should continue to exist. Note that Ganji's call is not for an overthrow of the system through mass mobilization or a popular uprising that would inevitably entail some measure of violence. Instead, he advocates civil disobedience, which in the Iranian context can take several forms. A boycott of elections, which the non-democratic system sponsors in order to enhance its legitimacy, is one form of non-violent resistance to the state. The use of satellite television stations, which is banned in the Islamic Republic, is another form of civil disobedience, presumably especially if used for the spread of democratic values. And yet another means of civil disobedience would be to ignore court summons for supposed political infractions, about which Ganji

---

[159] Ibid., p. 19.   [160] Ibid.   [161] Ibid.   [162] Ibid.   [163] Ibid., p. 23.

himself knows too well. How many people, Ganji asks rhetorically, can the government imprison for ignoring its court summons?[164]

There are, of course, certain costs involved in all of this. Ganji reminds his readers that democracy's cause will not be furthered without the sacrifice of those who believe in it.

One of the essential preconditions of democracy is the existence of courageous and committed individuals who are willing to pay the necessary price for its establishment. Mandela, Vaclav Havel, Dubcek, and others demonstrated their commitment to democracy through their deeds. In authoritarian societies, democracy does not appear through the efforts of those in ivory towers. There are Aung San Suu Kyis in the world who stand up to dictators and their unjust rules, but they also pay a price for their commitment.[165]

What is ultimately needed is a free and fair referendum that would give people real political choices. Only then can the people's will be truly represented. In the immediate aftermath of the revolution, in March 1979, Iranians assumed they were voting for a democratic system when they participated in a popular referendum that officially ended the Pahlavi monarchy. But the constitution that was drafted afterward, approved in yet another referendum in which 25 percent fewer Iranians voted, was hardly democratic. A new referendum needs to give Iranians real choices, and if they choose to maintain the political system in its current format or in some altered form, then so be it.[166] What is certain, Ganji concludes in his *Manifesto*, is that the people's voices need to be heard.

If our difficulties and our crises are real, if it is indeed true that our society is being robbed of freedom and liberty, then we must set aside those excuses that explain away silence and escape from responsibility. We cannot theoretically justify living in political fear. Instead, we must have "civic courage" rooted in an "enlightened outlook."[167]

A fifth and final pillar of modernity is considered to be globalization. There is general consensus among the secular-modernists that globalization may be economic in locus, or political, or cultural.[168] According to Ahmad Golmohammadi (b. 1968), a professor of political science at 'Allameh Tabatabai University, globalization may be defined as a phenomenon that leads to "the compression of time and space, because of which people throughout the globe become more or less cognizant, especially relative to the past, of the fact that they belong to a single,

---

[164] Ibid., p. 46.   [165] Ibid.   [166] Ibid., p. 50.   [167] Ibid.
[168] Sariolghalam, *'Aqlaniyyat va Ayandeh-e Tose'eh-yaftegi-ye Iran* (Rationality and the Future of Iran's Development), p. 394.

integrated world."[169] Because of globalization, the costs of communication and transportation are reduced while their pace is quickened; borders and other inhibiting social mores become eroded or collapse altogether; people throughout the world become increasingly more interdependent on one another; and the structures and institutions that comprise different societies around the world assume increasing uniformity.[170]

By its very nature, modernity cannot stop at national borders. It is a global and globalizing phenomenon. Its very constitutive elements are global in nature, for although they might have originated in the West, according to Hoodashtiyan, they now have universal reach and appeal.[171] Jahanbegloo agrees with the basic premise of this thesis, but approaches the question of the relationship between globalization and modernity from a slightly different angle. Modernity, and along with it the diffusion of certain norms and values throughout the globe, are inevitable processes whose speed and depth continue to grow with the spread of science and technology. "Today," he maintains, "distinctions such as East or West, or tradition or modernity no longer make sense. In a society that is undergoing globalization, past traditions must be made receptive to changing dynamics while maintaining their unique and positive characters."[172]

In specific relation to political institutions and practices, globalization, along with its concomitant communications revolution, help "erode the legitimacy of authoritarian systems and facilitate the spread of democratization and participatory political cultures."[173] It was precisely this increasing awareness of international norms and the yearning human rights, and greater demands for observing the rule of the law – all integral to globalization – that resulted in the limited democratic opening of Iran with the election of Khatami to the presidency.[174] As such, not only is globalization inevitable, but its careful and programatic accommodation is beneficial politically as well as culturally and

[169] Ahmad Golmohammadi, *Jahani-shodan, Farhang, Hoviyyat* (Globalization, Culture, Identity) (Tehran: Ney, 1383/2004), p. 11.

[170] Ibid., pp. 11–12.

[171] Hoodashtiyan, *Moderniteh, Jahani-shodan va Iran* (Modernity, Globalization and Iran), p. 170.

[172] Jahanbegloo, *Mowj-e Chaharom* (The Fourth Wave), p. 62.

[173] Khalilollah Sardarabadi, "Jahani-shodan dar Qalamro-ve Siyasat va Farhang-e Siyasi" (Globalization in relation to Politics and Political Culture), *Aftan*. No. 20 (1381/2002), p. 50.

[174] Hamid Reza Jalaeepour, "Jonbesh-haye Bonyadgara va Mardom-salar dar Jahan-e Jahani-shodeh" (Democratic and Fundamentalist Movements in the Globalized World), *Aftab*, No. 8 (1380/2001), p. 13.

economically. According to Baqer Asadi, one of the Islamic Republic's former diplomats, active and principled engagement in globalization is essential to Iran's political and economic development.[175] Iran suffers from a myriad of economic maladies, many of which have had devastating political consequences. The country's development, whether defined politically or economically, dictates that Iran take an active role in the globalization process. Doing so requires the careful provision of national strategies. Only then will Iran's economic future become secured and democracy a reality.[176]

Constructing a discourse

Whether it is through emphasis on globalization or on civil society, or on development, secularism, or rationality, a group of writers and thinkers in Iran have begun articulating what may be called collectively the secular-modernist discourse. Many of the key figures involved in this intellectual venture are university professors, but they also include journalists and attorneys, and, in Ganji's case at least, an unwitting political activist. Most live and work in Iran, but a few are also employed in Western academic institutions, although their publications and their arguments are carefully read and followed in Iran.

Together, at times consciously and at times unwittingly, these intellectuals have embarked on the construction of a worldview that professes to be democratic, secular, globally integrationist, and forward-looking. The world is moving in the direction of modernity, they all argue, and Iran cannot afford to be left behind any more than it already has. The task they have therefore set before themselves, both collectively and individually, is to explain to larger audiences, to whoever listens, that Iran needs to become modern, and in order to do so it needs rationalism, secularism, civil society, globalization, and development. As things currently stand, modernity faces deeply entrenched challenges in Iran. Mystical Sufism and other esoteric philosophical currents have eroded the possibilities for rational thought throughout the country's rich history. Superstition has found an ally in political despotism and autocracy in stunting the growth of critical thinking on an intellectual level and civil society's mobilization on a practical level. And autocracy has been fueled by a rentier economics that is rooted in oil resources, in turn

---

[175] Baqer Asadi, "Ta'sir-e Jahani-shodan bar Tose'eh Melli-ye Boland Moddat-e Iran" (The Effects of Globalization on Iran's Long-Term Development), *Aftab*, No. 22 (1381/2002), p. 43.
[176] Ibid.

undermining the possibilities for economic and political development. The outside world, in the meanwhile, keeps passing Iran by, combining and integrating its resources and expertise to further its advancement. What Iran needs first is a realization of its predicament in relation to the rest of the world, and then a blueprint on how to carve out its own modern identity and its place among the community of nations.

In articulating their discourse, Iran's secular-modernists come perilously close to running afoul of the political establishment. As proponents of many of the notions that stand in direct contradiction to the legitimacy of the Islamic Republic system, and more importantly in directly challenging the state-supported conservative religious discourse, Iran's secular-modernists often push the limits of the state's tolerance and remain just within its red lines. Often times, however, even if their endeavors remain purely intellectual, as the case of Ramin Jahanbegloo frighteningly demonstrates, the secular-modernists who remain in Iran run the ever-present risk of harassment by the authorities, dismissal from their university positions, or even imprisonment. How the Ahmadinejad presidency and the resulting changing environment at the country's universities affect this evolving discourse remains to be seen. In the summer of 2006, there were rumors of wholesale purges and dismissals in many universities, and anecdotal evidence suggests a huge slump in the publishing market. Similar to its reformist religious counterpart, the secular-modernist discourse no doubt suffered a setback with the outcome of the 2005 presidential elections. If nothing else, it has lost the mildly tolerant milieu of the Khatami years within which it could articulate and express itself. Nevertheless, despite the manifold obstacles it has faced in the past and will no doubt continue to face in the future, it would be a mistake to write its obituary just yet or to totally dismiss it out of hand as the fanciful musings of ivory tower intellectuals. Many of the notions they propose and advocate are deeply and profoundly attractive to a growing number of urban middle classes, and they frequently enjoy genuine popularity and respect among the country's university student population. For the foreseeable future, and quite possibly more so in the coming years than is the case now, the secular-modernist discourse remains a force to be reckoned with.

What remains uncertain is whether, and if so when, this intellectual trend will stop being a purely academic exercise and make its influence felt in policy making and political circles. For now, with tremendous help from the Americans, the Ahmadinejad administration has effectively shifted the focus of the national discourse away from the domestic arena – "civil society" having been Khatami's campaign slogan – and toward national security and pride, with Iran's right to nuclear

technology as its centerpiece. For the middle classes, there could be
nothing more disastrous than a confrontation with the United States.
But the Americans' outright bullying of Iran and their duplicitous
approach to the nuclear issue have done much to strengthen and legitimize Ahmadinejad's erratic presidency before the Iranian middle
classes. For Iranian academics and especially for the secular-modernist
intellectuals, however, Iran's troubled tussle with modernity is precisely
why someone like Ahmadinejad was elected to the presidency in the first
place. Only a full and principled embrace of modernity, and all that it
entails, will finally rid Iran of the plethora of plagues that have gripped
its history and continue to choke its present and its future.

7   Iran's silent revolution

The 1978–79 revolution ushered in a new era of thought and intellectual endeavor shaped by the realities of post-revolutionary zeal, war and international tensions, the institutionalization of supreme religious authority, and the reconstruction of the institutions of the state that the revolution had dismantled. After about a decade of revolutionary fervor and unprecedented levels of political repression, the end of the war with Iraq in 1988 and the death of Ayatollah Khomeini the following year resulted in a gradual opening of political space. Slowly but steadily, this allowed for the measured articulation of alternative, non-state sanctioned worldviews about idealized visions of the polity and the self. Before long, three different discourses were vying for greater acceptance and popularity by the urban middle classes. These are a discourse of religious conservatism, which largely underwrites the theoretical assumptions and institutional arrangements of the Islamic Republican state; a discourse of religious reformism, which seeks to fundamentally alter the interpretations on which most Islamic doctrines and notions are based; and a discourse of secular-modernism, which assumes that the acquisition of modernity and its many offerings will only be made possible through pushing religion out of the public arena. Previous chapters examined the emergence of each discourse and the main premises on which it is based. Here, by way of conclusion, I assess the relative strengths and weaknesses of each discourse and point to some of the factors likely for their success or failure in the coming years. As I shall argue shortly, just as the emergence of each discourse is largely a product of – and in many ways slave to – structural and institutional developments in the larger environment within which they are being articulated, their eventual success among urban Iranians also depends largely on the evolving direction of the country's political system.

Assessing the discourses

Discourses, it was earlier discussed, take shape and emerge in environments in which institutions and resources play important roles. These

214

institutions may be formal or informal, state-related or non-state. In relation to the three discourses that have appeared in Iran since the start of the second republic, their respective relationships with the state and with the urban middle classes are key to their articulation so far and their evolution in the future. Each discourse has a different relationship with the state and with the middle classes, and each enjoys a different level of internal cohesion and consistency. As of now, none are necessarily destined to become institutionalized as the dominant worldview through which most urban Iranians see their place in the world. If any were to have a chance, however, it would most likely to be either the discourses of religious reformism or the secular-modernist discourse, both of which seem to be far better positioned among the urban middle classes as compared to the conservative religious discourse.

It is my contention that of all three discourses in present-day Iran, the emerging discourse of religious reformism is of the most profound historical and theological significance, despite the fact that its immediate political impact may be mitigated by the vested interests of the Islamic Republic state as it currently exists. This is a discourse that is rooted in tradition but advocates modernity; it is religious but promotes secularism; it seeks neither to maintain the politico-ideological status quo nor its radical overthrow. This religious reformist discourse may not be politically or even intellectually dominant today, but it is one of great historical and doctrinal significance, particularly insofar as the longer-term relationship between Shi'ism and politics is concerned. In seeking to reform the body politic, it appears to be revolutionizing Shi'a jurisprudence, and that is precisely where its significance lies.

Conversely, the conservative religious discourse runs perhaps the biggest risk of relegating itself into oblivion and irrelevance. The discourse is faced with a number of fundamental disadvantages that substantially erode its popularity among the urban middle classes. These include close identification with the state, the discourse's lack of flexibility and its reluctance to address many issues of daily concern, its perceived extremism, and its internal squabbles, both now and in the future, over power. All things considered, the religious conservative discourse is unlikely to garner significant and sustained public support among the middle classes despite – or, because of – having the might of state behind it. Moreover, given its reluctance to be innovative and adaptable, in the long run it is also less likely to address issues of real concern to the middle classes.

To begin with, the discourse's very source of strength, namely its affiliation with the state and with state-related institutions, is also a liability for it insofar as the middle classes are concerned. Clearly, there are still those within the urban-based population in Tehran and elsewhere, and among seminary students and scholars in Qom, that remain supportive of the traditional religious right and its intellectual spokesmen, especially the likes of Ayatollahs Mesbah Yazdi and Javadi Amoli. Nevertheless, if the widespread enthusiasm with which Khatami's elections and his presidency were met are any indication, the system in its conservative garb and posture has very little popular support. Khatami's elections in 1997 and 2001 demonstrated the degree to which conservative Islamism has lost its purchase, and President Ahamadinejad, who was elected in 2005, has shown himself to be more of a populist radical than a religious conservative. But even if he is not from the same ideological and intellectual camp, for most middle-class Iranians Ahmadinejad is a creature of the system, and his populist antics, which are seldom popular among them anyway, further erode the legitimacy and popularity of the conservative religious discourse.

Also problematic for the discourse is its rigid inflexibility in relation to some core principles, not the least of which is the *Velayat-e Mutlaq-e Faqih*. Given the speed and the extent to which global values concerning democracy and "modernity" (however vague and ill-defined) travel across national boundaries, it seems doubtful that an unaccountable political system modeled after the Imamate of the caliph would find much popularity among the urban middle classes. This is not to imply that urban Iranians have internalized the norms and values of democracy and are therefore unwilling to buy into a worldview that has an undemocratic political order at its centerpiece. That may indeed be the case, although it is hard to prove in the absence of hard facts and data. But, given the discourse's lack of theoretical innovativeness, many of the propositions on which it is based are increasingly untenable in the twenty-first century. As chapter 4 demonstrated, the conservative religious discourse only begrudgingly and reluctantly acknowledges the importance of some of the phenomena that are becoming increasingly important to the lives and concerns of the urban middle classes – globalization, civil society, civil rights, pluralism, and the like. Instead, the discourse asks the people to put their trust in the person of the *Vali* simply because he has reached an esteemed religious position and to "accept" his rule since it already enjoys divine legitimacy. For many educated Iranians, even for those who are generally supportive of the regime, this is a difficult proposition to stomach. None other than Ayatollah Khomeini said that legitimacy rests with the people, many non-conservatives say, and any attempts to take it away from them is unacceptable.[1]

---

[1] Hajjarian, *Jomhuriyyat; Afsonzedai az Qodrat* (Republicanism; Demystification of Power) pp. 500–513.

Perhaps because some of its main propositions contradict positions held by Ayatollah Khomeini, whose rightful interpreter it often claims to be, the conservative religious discourse is frequently combative and defensive in tone. Religious reformists, in fact, often call the discourse radical, extremist, and outright dangerous.[2] Some ammunition is given to them by figures such as Ayatollah Mesbah Yazdi, who goes so far as to openly endorse the use of violence in defense of the system against its enemies.[3] Again, while this might resonate with a small minority of die-hard regime supporters, most urban Iranians, especially following the relative moderation and civility of the Khatami years, are unlikely to accept and internalize the use of violence against opponents as a routine aspect of the political system's ideology.

More importantly, as the bitter dispute between Ayatollah Montazeri and other conservative theologians demonstrates, given the discourse's proximity to the state and other semi-official institutions of power, like the *Howzeh*, the high political stakes at work can significantly undermine its apparent cohesion and internal unity. As we saw earlier, much of Ayataollah Montazeri's differences with other conservative theologians revolve around the rights and responsibilities of the *Velayat-e Faqih* and not over such other important principles as *ijtihad* and *tafsir*. It is difficult to imagine that Ayatollah Montazeri's removal from office as the designated successor to Ayatollah Khomeini back in 1989 does not influence his writings on the subject today. Similarly, the growing ideological chasms between Ayatollahs Rafsanjani and Mesbah Yazdi have become particularly acute since the start of Ahmadinejad's presidency in 2005, with an eye, no doubt, toward the future succession to Ayatollah Khamenei as the next *Rahbar*. The Islamic Republic has seldom been immune from political factionalism, and the intellectual discourse that supports it can be similarly affected.

At the opposite end of the spectrum stands the secular-modernist discourse. In some ways this is the easiest discourse for the middle classes to understand, if not necessarily agree with. The central premise of this discourse revolves around the omnipresent issue of modernity and what it means to be modern. The analysis of the secular-modernists is straightforward, and their remedy is simple. Modernity is sweeping across the globe, they claim, and, in order not to be left behind, one needs to become democratic, rational, developed, and secular. This

---

[2] See, for example, Mojtahed Shabestari, *Naqdi bar Qara't-e Rasmi az Din* (A Critique of the Official Reading of Religion), p. 31.

[3] Mesbah Yazdi, *Nazariyyeh-e Siyasi-e Eslam: Keshvardari* (Political Theory of Islam: Statecraft), p. 227.

much most middle-class Iranians can easily understand. The problem occurs when the secular-modernists engage in discussions of post-modernity, about which there is little agreement among themselves. Nevertheless, by and large, the discourse has been able to carve out for itself a respectable audience and following among a broad cross-section of Iranian academics, journalists, university students, and the professional classes. Through its emphasis on respect for and renewal of aspects of Iranian tradition, it has largely protected itself against potential accusations of "Westoxication," and, for the most part, it enjoys internal cohesion and consistency.

As things stand, the secular-modernist discourse has no institutional support whatsoever, and its architects often find themselves in the political wilderness. The religious conservatives have easy access to most levers of state power, and the religious reformists, despite their setbacks, still can use some of the resources of the state to protect some of their interests and to push a limited number of their intellectual agendas through. But the articulators of the secular-modernists have very few or no patrons in the state bureaucracy, and the venues open to them for expressing their views are especially vulnerable to shifting political winds. As such theirs remains a minority discourse – solid and cohesive, but facing great obstacles in the way of getting a wider hearing.

For its part, the religious reformist discourse is confronted with a whole different set of obstacles that have eroded – and continue to erode – some of its popularity among the middle classes. But popularity is not the same as long-term historical significance. Comparatively, the reformist religious discourse appears to enjoy far greater support among the educated urban middle classes as compared to its conservative counterpart. In the absence of hard data, we can only point to anecdotal evidence – such as the number of printings a reformist author's books go through – to get a sense for the general enthusiasm with which the reformist religious discourse is followed and received by its intended audiences. Still, the discourse leaves unanswered certain key questions that related to the lives of the middle classes, and it also glosses over, or leaves completely unresolved, a number of important tensions in its own underlying premises. I shall address these unresolved tensions shortly. Despite these lingering question marks, however, the reformist religious discourse appears to have sparked a fundamental process of rethinking about some core religious precepts and about the proper place of religion in politics and society. In this respect, today's unfolding discourse of religious reformism appears to have great historical significance.

Insofar as its popularity among the middle classes is concerned, the reformist religious discourse appears to suffer from three shortcomings.

First, the arguments of some of the discourse's main architects are too abstract and overly philosophical to be easily understood by most middle-class Iranians. This is especially the case with the writings of Soroush and Mojtahed Shabestari, whose understanding requires a fair amount of philosophical knowledge and sophistication. This problem is in many ways remedied by the discourse's own large spectrum of articulators that involves political activists as well as philosophers, academics, as well as journalists. In addition to a number of significant books and treatises, figures like Soroush and Mojtahed Shabestari also give newspaper interviews and write more accessible essays in print publications or on the Internet – when allowed by the authorities that is – thus expanding the potentially limited range of their audiences.

A second problem with the religious reformist discourse arises from its precarious relationship with the state. Because of their theories and their ideological dispositions, the architects of the discourse are often forced to walk an extremely fine line, seeking to critique the ideological underpinnings of today's Islamic Republic – i.e. the post-Khomeini republic – without crossing elusive and ever-shifting red lines. At other times, they deliberately set out to test the limits of free speech and try to determine how far they can stretch the regime's red lines. The outcome is a fair amount of ambiguity and dancing around some issues that would otherwise be addressed directly. Perhaps the most important of such issues is the theoretical basis and the validity of the concept of *Velayat-e Faqih*, which is often not open to discussion at all as far as the state is concerned. It is unclear, for example, how much of the attempt by religious reformers to democratize the institution of the *Velayat-e Faqih* is a product of conviction and belief as opposed to a strategic move to make the best out of an untenable situation. The outcome is all the same ambiguous: democracy is heralded as an end to strive toward and an ingrained feature of Islam, but an institution with an innately undemocratic basis of legitimacy and *modus operandi* remains mostly unchallenged.

Third and lastly, for all their discussions about equality and civil rights, the architects of the religious reformist discourse tend to be eerily silent on the question of women. Religious conservatives are unabashed in their declaration of the secondary position of women in society, law, and politics. Women are esteemed as mothers and as the pivot around which the sacred institution of the family revolves, but they cannot become leaders. For the secular-modernists, women are in every sense equal to men, and that, by implication, extends to their ability to appear in public as they like.[4] But the

---

[4] *Implied* is key here. To my knowledge, none of the male secular reformists has gone so far as to openly call for the abolition of the *hijab*, although such a position is implicit in

position of the reformist religious discourse on women is not even implicitly apparent. For most of the discourse's chief architects, it is as if there was no women's issue to consider, the topic being conspicuously absent from their otherwise copious writings.

As with the issue of the *Velayat-e Faqih*, it is possible that the religious reformists' silence on the issue of women is tactical and strategic. Given the centrality of the issue of *hijab* to the project of Islamizing Iranian society by the state, this could indeed be the case. I am somewhat reluctant, however, to come to this conclusion. *Hijab* is certainly the most symbolic and the most apparent manifestation of the Islamic Republic's treatment of women. But it is only one of the many areas in which the regime holds women to a different standard as compared to men. And, at least as far as appearances and a sense of fashion are concerned, Iranian women have for the most part incorporated the *hijab* into their sense of fashion.[5] In other words, as much of a "hassle" as observing the *hijab* might be for the long-haired Iranian woman, at least for the time being, its removal does not appear to be the central pre-occupation of most middle-class Iranians, who have learned to live with and around it. But *hijab* does go to the core of women's place and position in Islam, and it is in this respect that the religious reformists appear not to have resolved a basic tension in their thinking: if men and women are equal in every sense, then why should women observe the *hijab*? It appears that in order to avoid having to answer this vexing question, religious reformists have stayed away from discussing women's issues altogether.

This is more than a philosophical dilemma that is best avoided rather than tackled. It is one of the key questions asked about Iranian identity, an identity that is literally worn on the head. Unlike a man's suit, which can mask all sorts of identities, in the context of today's Iran a woman's choice of *hijab*, rightly or wrongly, tells much about where she stands in the universe of cultural values swirling around her. For the most part, the religious reformists have yet to figure out where they stand on this simple and yet central issue, one that touches on the very core of Iranian identity.

None of this, however, should detract from the longer-term historical significance of the reformist religious discourse. Its ambiguities and its shifting political fortunes notwithstanding, because of the reformist

---

their writings and their arguments. Again, it appears that political considerations appear to be instrumental here in influencing the contours of the discourse.

[5] For a fascinating account of the lives of Iranian women see Azadeh Moaveni, *Lipstick Jihad: A Memoir of Growing up Iranian in America and American in Iran* (New York: Public Affairs, 2005).

religious discourse, Shi'a jurisprudence in Iran today stands on the cusp of major doctrinal change. I would not go so far as to argue that the reformist religious discourse has sparked a religious "reformation" in Iran. But it has indeed started a process that, *if given the right type of institutional support*, could result in a fundamental reformation of Iranian Shi'ism. At a minimum, the discourse of religious reformism has raised important questions whose answers, while not necessarily within easy reach, cannot be ignored indefinitely. The relationship between Islam and civil society, pluralism, dynamic *ijtihad*, and dialogue among civilizations – these are important questions whose answers may be politically unpalatable to the stewards of the Islamic Republic. But now that the taboo of asking them has been broken, they cannot be unasked anymore. The curiosity and the intellectual impetus for searching for answers is there; now all that is needed is the right set of institutional support mechanisms that would facilitate the articulation and institutionalization of answers to these and other similar questions.

Up until recent years, there have been three primary underlying reasons for the obstruction of reformation in *fiqh* in modern Iran, particularly since the late 1800s. The first has to do with the role of the state, which initially suppressed and sought to marginalize Shi'a doctrine and then, after the 1978–79 revolution, used it as its own basis of legitimacy and institutional framework. This, in turn, led to a second impediment to the reformation of Shi'a jurisprudence, namely the emergence of a clerical class many of whose members positioned themselves as the primary protector of Iranian culture and society against an oppressive and intrusive state. Largely as a result of this, Shi'a doctrine became increasingly politicized throughout the twentieth century, its revolutionary posture undermining its attention to internal reform. A third impediment, and directly related to the latter two, has been the traditional role of Shi'a clerics as social mediators and as protectors of culturally salient rituals. This pervasive social influence marginalized the voices of those calling for reforming the *fiqh*. Partly as a result of their own actual or threatened marginalization and partly due to their conviction, those calling for the doctrinal reform of Shi'ism never quite went so far as to call for its jurisprudential "reformation," often tempering their call for reforms and balancing it with resort to some of Shi'ism's orthodox, and at times archaic, notions and value systems. Farzin Vahdat has labeled this phenomenon "mediated subjectivity."[6]

Today, however, nearly three decades after the success of the Islamic Revolution, only the first impediment to the reformation of the Shi'a

---

[6] Vahdat, *God and Juggernaut*, p. 60.

doctrine remains – i.e. the nature and role of the state in relation to Shi'ism – while the other two impediments are undergoing fundamental changes. Whether these changes are by themselves sufficient to foster a process of religious reformation, or will propel changes to the remaining impediments as well, remains to be seen. What is certain, however, is that today Iranian Shi'ism stands at the gates of historic doctrinal changes, changes which will most likely manifest themselves in the years to come.

The road ahead

Needless to say, the interplay of the three discourses in Iran and their evolving direction are of tremendous significance for Iran's political future, as well as in determining dominant cultural themes in the urban landscape. Also affected will be the future direction of state–religion relations in general and Shi'a jurisprudence in particular. There is a vibrant and profound debate in Iran's learned and scholarly circles over such critical questions as the proper role and place of religion in politics, the role of reason and the nature of interpretation in understanding Shi'a jurisprudence, and the place of the self and the country as a whole in the modern world. The collective effects of these intellectual activities amount to nothing less than a revolution in perceptions of the self, hermeneutics of Islam, and the emergence of new political ideas and values. All too frequently, the sounds and the significance of this revolution are drowned out by the dramatic gestures of politicians, both Iranian and non-Iranian, and the multiple international crises swirling around the country. Silent and silenced as it might appear, though, there is indeed a revolution brewing in Iran, this time over identity and the place of the collective and the individual selves in the modern world.

As momentous historical occasions, seldom are the outcomes of revolutions predetermined or even reasonably predictable, and Iran's silent, intellectual revolution is hardly an exception. For the foreseeable future, the Islamic Republic is here to stay, even as Washington drops occasional hints of wanting to bring about "regime change" in Tehran.[7] But the Islamic Republic itself continues to change from within, and with institutional and political change come changes to the larger polity and political culture. Today, one cannot overemphasize the role of ideology in the formulation and implementation of the Iranian state's policies, whether in the international or in the domestic arenas. While

---

[7] Ehsani, "High Stakes for Iran."

Islam forms the larger context and frame of reference within which Iranian policy-makers formulate and implement their policies, today's Iran may be most aptly described as "post-Islamist."[8] At the same time, the regime's legitimacy among the urban middle classes has steadily declined in the last decade or so, particularly after the initial enthusiasm with which Khamati's presidency was met in the late 1990s turned into widespread disappointment and disillusionment by the latter half of his second term in office. The dissonance and disconnect between urban Iranians' personal and public lives continue to grow in the meanwhile, with the country seeming to move increasingly in the direction of the "Chinese model,"[9] becoming as nominally Islamic as China is supposedly communist.

I started this book by pointing to the importance of "environmental factors" such as institutional and political developments in shaping the nature and direction of a discourse, and I will conclude here by reiterating their significance in influencing the intellectual life of Iran over the coming years and decades. I have offered here a small snapshot of the internal debates and arguments within each discourse. The picture remains far from complete, however. What happens to each discourse from this point on depends in large measure on what happens in the country's universities, mosques, and seminaries, to its journalists and professors, to its university and seminary students, its clergy, and to its learned elites inside and outside of the country and the links they forge together. The resources each group has, its relations with the state and with other sources of power, its links and connections with larger audiences, and, of course, the state's own institutional make up and policy priorities are all instrumental in influencing, and perhaps even determining, the fate of each discourse. For now, the intellectual revolution brewing in Iran remains relatively quiet.

But quiet does not mean ineffectual. In fact, the very deliberate, studied, and at times halted manner in which Iran's intellectual revolution is unfolding is perhaps its biggest source of strength. This is a revolution of ideas, a steady rethinking of some basic assumptions and premises. It is a revolution fought neither through guerrilla warfare nor mass mobilization, but rather through carefully constructed arguments, professorial theses, and books and journal articles. What it lacks in noise and inflamed passions it more than makes up for in depth and in

---

[8] Azadeh Kian-Thiebaut, "Political and Social Transformations in Post-Islamist Iran," *Middle East Report*, No. 212 (Fall 1999), p. 12–16.

[9] Afshin Molavi, "Buying Time in Tehran: Iran and the China Model," *Foreign Affairs*, Vol. 83, No. 6 (November–December 2004), pp. 9–16.

substance. And it speaks to, and is articulated by, academics and thinkers, opinion-makers and men of letters.

Reflecting on a life of intellectual exile, Abbas Milani, himself a gifted thinker affiliated with Stanford University in the United States, makes the following observation:

Something uncanny has happened in Iran. Relative freedom of the press came, and soon Iranian intellectuals at home began to write with such bold vigor and innovation that the creative texture, the immediacy, and the theoretical depth of their writings eclipsed nearly all that the exiled intellectuals had to offer. And so a change of historic dimension is taking place today. The main idea for new ideas about politics and democracy, civil society and reform, even modernity and tradition, is no longer located in Persian intellectual circles exiled in the West, but in Iran.[10]

Farzin Vahdat takes this one step further. The reformist Islamic discourse has numerous internal contradictions, he claims, and the Iranian clergy are bound to strive for the resolution of these contradictions. The quest to resolve internal theoretical and doctrinal contradictions, according to Vahdat, will help usher in modernity in Iran.[11] The assertion that modernity is the natural outcome of Iranian intellectuals' efforts is open to debate. But, as the ample evidence offered throughout this book attests, the process of rethinking some of the core, existing assumptions about political Islam – and of seeking to resolve their internal contradictions – has indeed ushered in a period of intense and sustained intellectual fervor. At the same time, an entire generation of undergraduate and graduate university students have been taught by many of the authors quoted throughout this book, or, at the very least, they are, in one way or another, familiar with these intellectuals' arguments. Iran's intellectual revolution is well underway, and its consequences are likely to unfold and to reverberate throughout Iranian society for some time to come.

Seldom are the outcomes of political revolutions predetermined or perfectly predictable, and, at least in this case, Iran's unfolding intellectual revolution is no exception. Looking ahead, nevertheless, one cannot help but to discern several likely possibilities based on current trends and developments. First and perhaps most important is the reality that there is indeed an intellectual revolution underway in Iran, one that is a product of the inter- and intra-play among the three discourses of religious conservatism, religious reformism, and secular-modernism.

---

[10] Abbas Milani, *Lost Wisdom: Rethinking Modernity in Iran* (Washington, DC: Mage, 2004), p. 168.
[11] Vahdat, *God and Juggernaut*, p. 216.

Second, there is a symbiotic relationship between each of the discourses and their collectivity on one side and institutional and political developments on the other. Political and other "environmental" factors are responsible for providing the initial circumstances and the space within which discourses form. Once a discourse has begun to take shape, it can then begin to exert a variety of influences on existing and emerging institutional arrangements and political developments. It was the relatively permissive posture of Iranian politics beginning with the death of Ayatollah Khomeini in 1989 that gave rise to open contestation among the previously dormant religious reformist and secular-modernist discourses, which in turn prompted the conservative religious discourse into defensive theorizing. Today, nearly a decade later, vested old guards within the state find themselves in a defensive mode, seeking actively to suppress and to derail the two discourses of religious reformism and secular-modernism and to instead prop up the conservative religious discourse as their own source of doctrinal support.

Therein lies a simple folly. The revolution's old guard is no longer perceived as heroic today by most Iranians but is instead seen as regressive, stale, and repressive. Not surprisingly, the old guard's endorsement of the religious conservative discourse does little to enhance the discourse's legitimacy among most educated middle-class Iranians. Compounding the discourse's problems are its own image problems, many of which, given the discourse's main tenets, are not without justification. By and large, at least among educated Iranians, the religious conservative discourse is seen as archaic, blind to the realities of contemporary life, and politically repressive. In particular, the discourse's doctrinal endorsement of violence and repression as legitimate means of instilling and ensuring religiously ordained political legitimacy do not attract but in fact repel and frighten many of those whose support it tries to court. In sum, were it not for the continued threat and the actual use of force to ensure its longevity, the religious conservative discourse, at least in its current garb, would have lost steam some time ago.

A third and final likely possibility is the continued growth and salience of the two discourses of religious reformism and secular-modernism. For all its internal inconsistencies and contradictions, the discourse of religious reformism continues to capture the imagination of successive generations of middle-class Iranians, for many of whom both religion and modernity are essential ingredients of daily life which must somehow be reconciled. For its part, the secular-modernist discourse sees the relationship between modernity and public religion as fundamentally antithetical, perceiving of modernity as an inescapable facet of contemporary life and of religion as a singularly private phenomenon.

Political setbacks notwithstanding, there is no indication that as doctrinal blueprints either of these two discourses have lost any of their luster among their respective adherents, both of whom generally are drawn from among university students, the professional classes, and other educated elites. Only time will tell which discourse eventually emerges as dominant, the outcome depending on far too many unknown variables to make it predictable. For now, what is certain is that Iran's intellectual revolution continues.

Bibliography

Abazari, Yosuf. "Forupashi-e Ejtema'i" (Social Disintegration), *Aftab*, No. 19 (1381/2002), pp. 32–41.

'Abbasi, Hosein. "Dar Band-e Naqsh-e Eyvan" (On the Plan of the Patio), *Aftab*, No. 14 (1381/2002), pp. 44–47.

"Roshanfekran Iran va Gharb-shenasi" (Iranian Intellectuals and Studying the West), *Aftab*, No. 27 (1382/2003), pp. 90–95.

'Abdi, Abbas. *Qodrat, Qanun, Farhang* (Power, Law, Culture). Tehran: Tarh-e No, 1377/1998.

Dar Masir-e Azadi (In Freedom's Path). Tehran: Negah-e Emruz, 1378/1999.

Enqelab 'Alayhe Tahqir (Revolution against Contempt). Tehran: Zekr, 1380/2001.

"Khorouj az Sakhtar-e Mowjoud" (Exit from the Existing Structure), *Aftab*, No. 10 (1380/2001), pp. 12–15.

"Tabar-shenasiye Eslahtalaban, Naqsh-ha va Karkardha" (Genealogy of Reformists, Roles, and Functions), *Nameh*, No. 16 (1381/2002), pp. 3–11.

'Abdi, 'Abbas, ed. *Mo'amma-ye Hakemiyyat-e Qanun dar Iran* (The Enigma of the Rule of Law in Iran). Tehran: Tarh-e No, 1381/2002.

'Abdi, 'Abbas, and Mohsen Godarzi. *Tahavvolat-e Farhangi dar Iran* (Cultural Transformations in Iran). Tehran: Ravesh, 1378/1999.

Abdo, Geneive. "Re-Thinking the Islamic Republic: A 'Conversation' with Ayatollah Hossein 'Ali Montazeri", *Middle East Journal*, Vol. 55, No. 1 (Winter 2001), pp. 9–24.

Abrahamian, Ervand. *Khomeinism: Essays on the Islamic Republic*. Berkeley, CA: University of California Press, 1993.

Tortured Confessions: Prisons and Public Recantations in Modern Iran. Berkeley, CA: University of California Press, 1999.

Abu Zeid, Nasr Hamed. *Ma'na-ye Matn: Pazhoheshi dar 'Oloom-e Qor'an* (The Meaning of Text: A Research in Quranic Sciences). Morteza Kariminia, trans. Tehran: Tarh-e No, 1380/2001.

Adib, Mohammad Hosein. *Jame'hshenasi-ye Iran* (Sociology of Iran). Tehran: Hash Behesht, 1374/1995.

"Estehale-ye Mohafezeh-karan dar Darya-ye Motalebat-e Mardomi" (The Analysis of the Conservatives in the Sea of Popular Studies), *Aftab*, No. 4 (1380/2001), pp. 14–15.

"Roshanfekran-e Ma" (Our Intellectuals), *Cheshmandaz-e Iran*, Vol. 2, No. 9 (1380/2001), pp. 72–80.

Afshari, Reza. *Human Rights in Iran: The Abuse of Cultural Relativism*. Philadelphia, PA: University of Pennsylvania Press, 2001.

Aghajari, Hashem. "Kalbod Shekafi-e Enqelab, Khosunat va Eslahat" (Autopsy of Revolution, Violence and Reforms), *Aftab*, No. 3 (1380/2001), pp. 10–22.

Hokumat-e Dini va Hokumat-e Demokratik (Religious Government and Democratic Government). Tehran: Zekr, 1381/2002.

Ahmadi, Babak. *Moderniteh va Andisheha-ye Enteqadi* (Modernity and Critical Thoughts). Tehran: Markaz, 1373/1994.

Ahmadi, Hamid. *Qomiyyat va Qomiyyat-garaee dar Iran* (Ethnicity and Ethnicism in Iran). Tehran: Ney, 1378/1999.

Ahmadi, Hamid, and Mohammad Hosein Fatehian. *Jaryan-e Roshanfekri va Roshanfekran dar Iran* (The Trend of Intellectuals and Intellectualism in Iran). Qom: Beh Bavaran, 1379/2000.

Ahmadi, Naser. "Entesab ya Entekhab" (Election or Appointment), *Aftab*, No. 28 (1382/2003), pp. 22–25.

Ahmadi, Reza. "Rohaniyyat-e Dirouz va Emrouz – 1" (The Clergy of Yesterday and Today – 1), *Jame'h No*, Vol. 1, No. 9 (1381/2002), p. 23.

"Howzeh 'Elmiyyeh Ba'd az Enqelab: Rohaniyyat-e Dirouz va Emrouz – 2" (Religious Seminary after the Revolution: The Clergy of Yesterday and Today – 2), *Jame'h No*, Vol. 1, No. 11 (1381/2002), pp. 18–19.

Ahrari, Hamid, *et al.* "Bayaniyeh-e Tahlili-e Jam'i az Fa'alan-e Melli-Mazhabi darbareh-ye Entekhabat-e Shoura" (The Analytical Communiqué of a Group of Religious-Nationalist Activists concerning Council Elections), *Nameh*, No. 21 (1381), pp. 32–34.

Ajodani, Mashallah. *Mashroteh-ye Irani* (Iranian Constitutionalism). Tehran: Akhtaran, 1382/2003.

Ya Marg Ya Tajaddod (Either Death or Modernity). Tehran: Akhtaran, 1382/2003.

Akbari, Hashem. "Eqtedar-garaee, Takassor-garaee va Farhang-e Siyasi" (Autocracy, Pluralism and Political Culture), *Iran Farda*, Vol. 5, No. 29 (1376/1997), pp. 25–27.

Akbari, Mehdi. "Gam-haye Mardomsalari dar Botteh-e Naqd" (Democratic Steps in a Critical Path), *Aftab*, No. 22 (1381/2002), pp. 108–09.

Akbari Nouri, Reza. "Mafhoum-e Jame'h Madani dar Iran" (The Meaning of Civil Society in Iran), *Jame'h No*, Vol. 1, No. 12 (1381/2002), pp. 8–9.

"Jame'h Madani az Andisheh ta Raftar" (Civil Society from Thought to Conduct), *Jame'h No*, Vol. 2, No. 13 (1381/2002), pp. 14–15.

Akhavan Kazemi, Bahram. *'Edalat dar Andisheh-haye Siyasi-e Eslam* (Justice in Islamic Political Thought). Qom, Bustan-e Ketab, 1382/2003.

Akhavi, Shahrough. *Religion and Politics in Contemporary Iran: Clergy–State Relations in the Pahlavi Era*. Albany, NY: SUNY Press, 1980.

Akrami, Amir. "Tabeen-e Nazariyeh-e Ma'refat-e Dini-e Doctor Soroush" (Analysis of Dr. Soroush's Religious Science), *Jame'h No*, Vol. 1, No. 12 (1381/2002), pp. 10–12.

Al-'Arawi, 'Abdollah. *Eslam va Moderniteh* (Islam and Modernity). Trans. Amir Rezai. Tehran: Qasideh Sara, 1381/2002.

'Alavi, Ebrahim. " 'Edalat Khahan-e Noandish-e Eslami" (New Islamic Thinkers who Seek Justice), *Aftab*, No. 7 (1380/2001), pp. 44–47.

'Alavi-Tabar, 'Alireza. "Roshanfekri va Roshanfekri-ye Dini dar Iran" (Intellectualism and Religious Intellectualism in Iran), *Kiyan*, Vol. 6, No. 34 (1375/1997), pp. 38–43.

Roshanfekri, Dindari, Mardomsalari (Intellectualism, Religiosity, Democracy). Tehran: Farhang-o Andisheh, 1379/2000.

"Molahezat-e Rahbordi dar barabar-e Jonbesh-e Daneshjo-i" (Methodological Considerations concerning the Student Movement), *Aftab*, No. 7 (1380/2001), pp. 10–13.

"Chand Porsesh Piramoun-e Mardomsalari-e Dini" (A Few Questions concerning Religious Democracy), *Aftab*, No. 9 (1380/2001), pp. 4–7.

"Roshanfekri-e Dini, Yek Barnameh-e Pishro" (Religious Intellectualism, a Progressive Program), *Aftab*, No. 10 (1380/2001), pp. 4–7.

"Taqlil Gara-ee Rah-e Hall Nist" (Minimalism is not the Solution), *Aftab*, No. 11 (1380/2001), pp. 42–45.

"Ayandeh-e Iran, Rahkar-haye Eslah-talaban" (Iran's Future, The Reformists' Methodology), *Aftab*, No. 12 (1380/2001), pp. 4–5.

"No-Andishane Rast" (The Right's New Thinkers), *Nameh*, No. 19 (1381/2002), pp. 4–5.

"Eslah-paziri va Azmoun-e Feysaleh Bakhsh" (Reformism and the Unfulfilling Experiment), *Aftab*, No. 16 (1381/2002), pp. 4–5.

"Gozar be Mardomsalari dar Se Gam" (A Look at Democracy in Three Steps), *Aftab*, No. 19 (1381/2002), pp. 4–5.

"Lavazem-e Nazari-ye Esteqrar-e Mardomsalari dar Javame' Dini" (Theoretical Tools for Establishing Democracy in Religious Societies), *Aftab*, No. 22 (1381/2002), pp. 20–21.

"Jebhe-ye Dovvom-e Khordad: Negahi az Daroon" (Second of Khordad Front: A Look from the Inside), *Nameh*, No. 24 (1382/2003), pp. 23–25.

"Sekularism va Demokrasi: Mored-e Jomhuri-e Eslami-e Iran" (Secularism and Democracy: Concerning the Islamic Republic of Iran), *Aftab*, No. 33 (1382/2003), pp. 80–83.

'Alavi-Tabar, 'Alireza, and Morad Saqafi. "Eslahat va Shiveh-haye Eslahtalabaneh" (Reforms and Reformists' Methods), *Aftab*, No. 17 (1381/2002), pp. 4–9.

Al-e Ahmad, Jalal. *Gharbzadegi* (Westoxication). Tehran: Ravvaq, 1344/1965.

Dar Khedmat va Khiyanat-e Roshanfekran, Volumes I–II (On the Service and Treason of Intellectuals). Tehran: Kharazmi, 1357/1978.

Aliabadi, Youssef. "The Idea of Civil Liberties and the Problem of Institutional Government in Iran," *Social Research*, Vol. 67, No. 2 (Summer 2000), pp. 345–76.

'Aliakbari, Ma'soumeh. "Rahi be Rahaee: Jastar-hayee dar 'Aqlaniyyat va Ma'naviyyat" (A Path to Liberation: Researching Rationality and Spirituality), *Aftab*, No. 23 (1381/2002), pp. 100–01.

'Alijani, Reza. "Arzyabi-ye Noirouha-ye Melli-Mazhabi dar Bastar-e Tahavvolat-e Ejtema'i" (Evaluating Religious-Nationalist Forces in Light of Social Changes), *Cheshmandaz-e Iran*, No. 15 (1381/2002), pp. 26–42.

'Alikhani, 'Ali Akbar, ed. *Mosharekat-e Siyasi* (Political Participation). Tehran: Safir, 1377/1998.

    Negahi beh Padideh-ye Gosast-e Nasl-ha (A Look at the Phenomenon of the Rupture of Generations). Tehran: Pazhoheshkadeh-e 'Oloom-e Ensani va 'Ejtema'i, 1382/2003.

Al-Taie, 'Ali. *Bohran-e Hoviyyat-e Qomi dar Iran* (The Crisis of Ethnic Identity in Iran). Tehran: Shadegan, 1382/2003.

Amanat, Abbas. "In between the Madrasa and the Marketplace: The Designation of Clerical Leadership in Modern Shi'ism," in Said Amir Arjomand, ed., *Authority and Political Culture in Shi'ism*. Albany, NY: SUNY Press, 1988, pp. 98–132.

Amanian, Hosein. *Kalbodshekafi-e Jaryan-haye Roshanfekri va Eslahtalabi dar Iran* (Autopsy of Intellectual and Reformist Trends in Iran). Tehran: Porseman, 1382/2003.

Amini, E., *et al. Hokumat-e Alavi*, Volume IX (Ali's Reign). Qom: Majles-e Khobregan, 1381/2002.

Amirahmadi, Hooshang. "Emerging Civil Society in Iran," *SAIS Review*, Vol. 16, No. 2 (Summer–Fall 1996), pp. 87–107.

Amiri, Jaber. *Mabani-ye Andisheh-haye Eslami: Din va Siyasat* (Principles of Islamic Thought: Religion and Politics). Qom: Gorgani, 1380/2001.

Amirpur, Katajun. "'Abdolkarim Soroush's Ray of Hope," *Cooperation and Development*, Vol. 31, No. 2 (2004), pp. 60–63.

Amirsadeqi, Nasireddin. "Eslahat dar Howzeh-haye 'Elmiye" (Reforms in Religious Seminaries), *Jame'h No*, Vol. 1, No. 3 (1380/2001), pp. 8–11.

Amnesty International, *Iran: Violations of Human Rights 1987–1990*. London: Amnesty International, 1990.

    Iran: Imprisonment, Torture and Execution of Political Opponents. London: Amnesty International, 1992.

Ansari, Hosein. "Roshanfekri-ye Irani va Eslah az Daroun" (Iranian Intellectualism and Reform from Within), *Aftab*, No. 27 (1382/2003), pp. 86–89.

Aqajari, Hashem. "Kalbodshekafi-e Enqelab, Khoshunat va Eslahat" (Autopsy of Revolution, Violence and Reforms), *Aftab*, No. 3 (1379/2000), pp. 10–23.

    Hokumat-e Dini va Hokumat-e Democratic (Religious Government and Democratic Government). Tehran: Zekr, 1381/2002.

'Arabi Zanjani, Behnam. *Shariati va Soroush: Barresi-ye Moqabeleh-ie Ara' va Nazariyyat* (Shariati and Soroush: Comparative Analysis of Beliefs and Opinions). Tehran: Aryaban, 1380/2001.

Arjomand, Said Amir. *The Shadow of God and the Hidden Imam: Religion, Political Order, and Societal Change in Shi'ite Iran from the Beginning to 1890*. Chicago, IL: University of Chicago Press, 1984.

    "Civil Society and the Rule of Law in the Constitutional Politics of Iran under Khatami," *Social Research*, Vol. 67, No. 2 (Summer 2000), pp. 283–301.

Arjomand, Said Amir, ed. *From Nationalism to Revolutionary Islam*. Albany, NY: SUNY Press, 1984.

    Authority and Political Culture in Shi'ism. Albany, NY: SUNY Press, 1988.

Armin, Mohsen. *Eslam, Ejtema', Siyasat* (Islam, Society, Politics). Tehran: Zekr, 1380/2001.

Armin, Mohsen, *et al. Nesbat-e Din va Jame'h Madani* (The Relationship between Religion and Civil Society). Tehran: Zekr, 1379/2000.

'Obour az Khatami: Majmo'eh Maqalat (To Leave behind Khatami: The Essays). Tehran: Zekr, 1379/2000.

Rabeteh-ye Din va Azadi (The Relationship between Religion and Freedom). Tehran: Zekr, 1379/2000.

Asadi, Baqer. "Ta'sir-e Jahani-shodan bar Tose'eh Melli-ye Boland Moddat-e Iran" (The Effects of Globalization on Iran's Long-Term Development), *Aftab*, No. 22 (1381/2002), pp. 38–43.

Ashouri, Daryush. *Ma va Moderniteh* (Us and Modernity). Tehran: Sarat, 1377/1998.

Azad, K. "Marz-banidye Rast-e Sonnati va Shabakeh-ye Vahshat" (The Position of the Traditional Right and the Network of Terror), *Cheshmandaz-e Iran*, Vol. 1, No. 4 (1379/2000), pp. 62–63.

Azad, Mahmood. "Kodam Demokrasi?" (Which Democracy?), *Andisheh-ye Jame'h*, No. 30 (1382/2003), pp. 65–69.

'Azadanlou, Hamid. *Gofteman va Jame'h* (Discourse and Society). Tehran: Ney, 1380/2001.

Azadaramaki, Taghi. *Moderniteh-e Irani* (Iranian Modernity). Tehran: Ejtema', 1380/2001.

Azmayesh, Mostafa, ed. *'Erfan-e Iran* (Iran's Gnosticism). Tehran: Haqiqat, 1379/2000.

Azqandi, 'Alireza. *Tarikh-e Tahavvolat-e Siyasi va Ejtema'i Iran.* Vol. I (History of Social and Political Development in Iran). Tehran: Semat, 1379/2000.

Babapour, Mohammad Mehdi. *Erteja'e Roshanfekri dar Iran* (Reaction of Enlightenment in Iran). Qom: Al-e Samad, 1381/2002.

Bahrampour, 'Ali. "Masayel va Moshkelat-e Matbo'at dar Iran" (Problems and Difficulties of Press in Iran), *Aftab*, No. 9 (1380/2001), pp. 40–47.

"Tahavvol-e Mohtavai-ye Matbo'at Pas az Dovvom-e Khordad" (Changes of the Contents of the Press after the Second of Khordad), *Aftab*, No. 10 (1380/2001), pp. 48–53.

Bakhash, Shaul. *The Reign of the Ayatollahs: Iran and the Islamic Revolution.* London: I. B. Tauris, 1985.

Bakhtiarinezhad, Parvin. "Roshanfekr Masraf Konandeh Nist" (The Intellectual is not a Consumer), *Jame'h No*, Vol. 1, No. 9 (1381/2002), pp. 18–19.

Bana, S. "Tarh-i Baraye Taharrok-e Eslahat ya Tarh-i az Tafakkor-e Eslahtalaban" (A Plan for Moving Reforms or a Plan Based on the Reformist's Thoughts), *Aftab*, No. 23 (1381/2002), pp. 118–19.

Baqi, 'Emadeddin. "Qasas, Hayat Bakhshi va Bazdarandegi" (Qasas, Life-giving and Resistance), *Cheshmandaz-e Iran*, Vol. 1, No. 5 (1379/2000), pp. 20–25.

"Dadfgah-e Vizheh-e Rouhaniyyat: Didgah-e Movafeqan va Mokhalefan" (The Special Court for the Clergy: The Perspective of Opponents and Supporters), *Aftab*, No. 10 (1380/2001), pp. 40–47.

"Do Pendar dar Tarazo" (Two Perspectives in Balance), *Aftab*, No. 13 (1380/ 2001), pp. 56–65.

"Na Enqelab, Na Reform, Eslahat-e Radikal" (Neither Revolution Nor Reform, Radical Reforms), *Jame'h No*, No. 2 (1380/2001), pp. 3–5.

E'dam va Qasas (Execution and Qasas). Tehran: Sarai 1381/2002.

Bahar-e Rokn-e Chaharom (Spring of the Fourth Column). Tehran: Sarai 1381/2002.

Hoquq-e Mokhalefan: Tamrin-e Demokrasi baraye Jame'h Irani (The Rights of Opponents: Practicing Democracy in Iranian Society). Tehran: Saraee 1381/2002.

Parasteshgah dar 'Ahd-e Sonnat va Tajaddod (Place of Worship in the Era or Tradition and Modernity). Tehran: Saraee 1381/2002.

Gofteman-haye Dini-ye Mo'aser (Contemporary Religious Discourses). Tehran: Sarai, 1382/2003.

Rouhaniyyat va Qodrat: Jame'hshenasi-e Nahad-haye Dini (The Clergy and Power: Sociology of Religious Institutions). Tehran: Sarai, 1382/2003.

Jonbesh-e Eslahat-e Demokratik dar Iran (The Democratic Reform Movement in Iran). Tehran: Sarai, 1382/2003.

Bashir, Hasan. "Gofteman-e Shariati, Gofteman-e Roshanfekri-ye Dini" (Shariati's Discourse, the Discourse of Religious Intellectuals), *Aftab*, Vol. 2, No. 17 (1381/2002), pp. 90–91.

Bashiriyeh, Hosein. *Jame'hshenashi-e Siyasi: Naqsh-e Nirohaye Ejtema'i dar Zendegi-ye Siyasi* (Political Sociology: The Role of Social Forces in Political Life). Tehran: Ney, 1377/1998.

Mavane' Tose'h Siyasi dar Iran (Obstacles to Political Development in Iran). Tehran: Gam-e Nou, 1380/2001.

"Daneshgah-e Siyasi, Daneshgah-e Ideolozhik" (Political University, Ideological University), *Nameh*, No. 22 (1382/2003), pp. 51–52.

Basir, Abbas. "Mardomsalrai-e Dini: Demokrasi-e Mahdoud be Arzesh-ha" (Religious Democracy: Democracy Limited to Values), *Aftab*, No. 24 (1380/2001), pp. 92–93.

Basir, Manochehr. "Bohran" (Crisis), *Nameh*, No. 23 (1382/2003), pp. 48–49.

Bastehnegar, Mohammad. "Arzyabi-ye Noirouha-ye Melli-Mazhabi dar Bastar-e Tahavvolat-e Ejtema'i" (Evaluating Religious-Nationalist Forces in Light of Social Changes), *Cheshmandaz-e Iran*, No. 15 (1381/2002), pp. 12–23.

"Rohaniyyat: Tabaqeh ya Qeshr" (The Clergy: Class or Sector), *Nameh*, No. 18 (1381/2002), pp. 42–45.

"Cheh Niyaz-i Ast be Shariati" (What Need is there for Shariati), *Jame'h No*, Vol. 2, No. 17 (1382/2003), pp. 12–13.

"Shariati va mardomsalari" (Shariati and Democracy), *Aftab*, No. 26 (1382/ 2003), pp. 46–49.

Bastehnegar, Mohammad, *et al.* "Vafaq-e Melli: Chand Porsesh, Chand Pasokh" (National Conciliation: Some Questions, Some Answers), *Nameh*, No. 17 (1381/2002), pp. 3–6.

Beheshti, 'Alireza. "Doshvari-haye Nazari-ye Tahaqqoq-e Mardomsalari-e Dini" (Theoretical Difficulties of Realizing Religious Democracy), *Aftab*, No. 16 (1381/2002), pp. 6–9.

Behnam, Jamshid. *Iranian va Andisheh-ye Tajaddod* (Iranians and the Idea of Modernity). Tehran: Farzan Rouz, 1375/1996.

Behnam, Jamshid, and Ramin Jahanbegloo. *Tamaddon va Tajaddod* (Civilization and Modernity). Tehran: Markaz, 1382/2003.

Behzadi, Mohammad. "Eslahtalabi dar Kocheh-ye Bonbast" (Reformism in a Dead-End Alley), *Nameh*, No. 23 (1382/2003), pp. 3–4.

Bill, James A., and Robert L. Hardgrave, Jr. *Comparative Politics: The Quest for Theory*. Washington, DC: University Press of America, 1981.

Bokharaee, Ahmad. *Demokrasi va Doshmananash dar Iran* (Democracy and its Enemies in Iran). Tehran: Gam-e No, 1381/2002.

Boroujerdi, Javad. "Eslah-e Dini dar 'Asr-e Hazer" (Religious Reformism in the Present Age), *Aftab*, No. 16 (1381/2002), pp. 72–73.

Boroujerdi, Mehrzad. *Iranian Intellectuals and the West: The Tormented Triumph of Nativism*. Syracuse, NY: Syracuse University Press, 1996.

Bozorgan, Amin. "Din, Ma'naviyyat va Ensan-e Modern" (Religion, Spirituality and the Modern Person), *Aftab*, No. 17 (1381/2002), pp. 74–81.

"Degargoni Jame'h va Pazhoheshgaran-e Ejtema'i" (Social Changes and Social Researchers), *Aftab*, No. 23 (1382/2003), pp. 44–45.

"Sarkoub-e Nasl-e Jadid: Bahs-i dar Bab-e Masa'leh Shekaf-e Nasl-ha" (Repressing the New Generation: A Look at the Problem of Generation Gap), *Aftab*, No. 27 (1382/2003), pp. 64–69.

Brumberg, Daniel. *Reinventing Khomeini: The Struggle for Reform in Iran*. Chicago, IL: Chicago University Press, 2001.

Buchta, Wilfried. *Who Rules Iran? The Structure of Power in the Islamic Republic*. Washington, DC: Washington Institute for Near East Policy, 2000.

Taking Stock of a Quarter Century of the Islamic Republic of Iran. Islamic Legal Studies Program, Harvard Law School, Occasional Publications 5, June 2005.

Chew, Sing C., and Robert A. Denmark, eds. *The Underdevelopment of Development: Essays in Honor of Andre Gunder Frank*. London: Sage, 1999.

Cole, Juan. *Sacred Space and Holy War: The Politics, Culture and History of Shi'ite Islam*. London: I. B. Tauris, 2002.

Daad, Babak. *Ra'y-e Mardom: Mohakemeh va Defa'iyat-e Seyyed Mostafa Taj-zadeh* (People's Vote: The Trial and Defense of Seyyed Mostafa Taj-zadeh). Tehran: Tarh-e No, 1380/2001.

Dabashi, Hamid. *Theology of Discontent: The Ideological Foundations of the Islamic Revolution in Iran*. New York: NYU Press, 1993.

Dadkhah, Kamran. "Andisheh-ye Eqtesadi va Roshanfekran-e Irani" (Economic Theories and Iranian Intellectuals), *Aftab*, No. 16 (1381/2002), pp. 22–27.

Dainezhad, Mohammadali. "Akhlaq-e Sekular-ha dar Royaroi be Fiqh va Foqaha" (The Seculars' Attitudes in Confronting Theology and Clerics), *Aftab*, No. 22 (1381/2002), p. 90.

Damad, Mohaqqeq. "Foqaha-ye Shi'a va Ejraye Hodood dar Zaman-e Gheybat" (Shi'a Clerics and the Performance of Islamic Precepts in the Period of Occultation), *Aftab*, No. 7 (1380/2001), pp. 48–51.

Darabkala'i, Esma'il. *Negareshi bar Falsafeh-ye Siyasi-e Eslam* (A Look at Islamic Political Philosophy). Qom: Bustan-e Ketab, 1380/2001.

Dargahi, Mahmood. "Hafez va Hokumat-e Dini" (Hafiz and Religious Government), *Aftab*, No. 29 (1382/2003), pp. 58–65.

Darvish, Mohammad Reza. "Mardomsalari-e Dini ya Mardomsalari-e Dindaran" (Religious Democracy or the Democracy of the Religious), *Aftab*, No. 23 (1381/2002), pp. 30–33.

Davari Ardekani, Reza. *Darbareh-ye 'Elm* (Concerning Science). Tehran: Hermes, 1379/2000.

Darbareh-ye Gharb (Concerning the West). Tehran: Hermes, 1379/2000.

Falsafeh-ye Tatbiqi (Comparative Philosophy). Tehran: Saqi, 1383/2004.

Deihimi, Khashayar. "Mardomsalari-ye Dini; Bed'at dar 'Elm-e Siyasat" (Religious Democracy; Innovation in Political Science), *Aftab*, No. 22 (1381/2002), p. 27.

Deihimi, Khashayar, and Hamidreza Jalaeepour. "Jame'hshenasi-ye Siyasi-e Eslahat" (Political Sociology of Reforms), *Aftab*, No. 18 (1381/2002), pp. 4–11.

Dinparast, Manochehr. *Seyyed Hosein Nasr: Delbakhteh-ye Ma'naviyyat* (Seyyed Hosein Nasr: Lover of Spirituality). Tehran: Kavir, 1383/2004.

Doroodi, Saeed. "Melli-Mazhabi-ha ve Elzamat-e 'Amal-e Siyasi" (Religious-Nationalists and the Necessity of Political Action), *Nameh*, No. 18 (1381/2002), pp. 36–37.

Ebrahimi-Dinani, Gholamhosein. *Majara-ye Fekr-e Falsafi dar Jahan-e Islam*, Volumes I–II (The Story of Philosophical Thought in the Muslim World). Tehran: Tarh-e No, 1376–79/1997–2000.

'Aqlaniyyat va Ma'naviyyat (Rationality and Spirituality). Tehran: Mo'asseseh-e Tahqiqat va Touse'h-e 'Oloom-e Ensani, 1383/2004.

'Edalatnezhad, Saeed, ed. *Andarbab-e Ejtehad: Darbar-ye Kar-amadiye Fiqh-e Eslami dar Donya-ye Emrouz* (On Ijtihad: On the Effectiveness of Islamic Jurisprudence in Today's World). Tehran: Tarh-e No, 1382/2003.

Eftekhari, Asghar. *Daramadi bar Khotoot-e Qermez dar Reqabat-haye Siyasi* (A Look at the Red Lines of Political Competition). Tehran: Center for Strategic Studies, 1381/2002.

Eftekharirad, Amir Hooshang. "Roshanfekri; Noqteh-e Sarr-e Khat" (Intellectualism: The Starting Point), *Aftab*, No. 27 (1382/2003), pp. 98–105.

Ehsani, Kaveh. "Estratezhi-haye Demokrasi" (Strategies of Democracy), *Aftab*, No. 16 (1381/2002), pp. 10–17.

"High Stakes for Iran". *Middle East Report* No. 227 (Summer 2003), pp. 38–41.

Ehteshami, Anoushiravan. *After Khomeini: The Iranian Second Republic*. London: Routledge, 1995.

Eisenstadt, S. N. and S. R. Grubard, eds. *Intellectuals and Tradition*. New York, NY: Humanities Press, 1973.

Entesharat-e Soroush. *Royaroi-ye Farhangi-ye Iran va Gharb dar Dowreh-ye Mo'aser* (The Cultural Confrontation between Iran and the West in Modern Times). Tehran: Soroush, 1375/1996.

Eslami Nadoushan, Mohammad Ali. *Iran Che Harfi Baraye Goftan Darad?* (What Does Iran Have to Say?). Tehran: Enteshar, 1379/2000.

Esposito, John L. *The Oxford Dictionary of Islam*. Oxford: Oxford University Press, 2003.

Eta'at, Javad. "Shekaf-haye Ejtema'i va Gorohbandi-e Siyasi dar Iran" (Social Cleavages and Political Groupings in Iran), *Aftab*, No. 19 (1381/2002), pp. 10–11.

E'temadi, Fariborz, ed. *Doctor Mohajerani, Az Ra'y-e E'temad ta Estizah* (Doctor Mohajerani. From Vote of Confidence to Impeachment). Tehran: Hezb-e Kargozaran-e Sazandegi, 1378/1999.

Fa'al, Ahmad. "Konesh-e Azadi va Vakonesh-e Qodrat" (Action of Freedom and Reaction of Power), *Aftab*, No. 33 (1382/2003), pp. 12–15.

Fairclough, Norman, *Discourse and Social Change*. Cambridge: Polity, 1993.

Farahani, Mohammad. *Kalbodshakafi-e Tose'h dar Iran* (Dissection of Development in Iran). Tehran: Porseman, 1376/1997.

Fathali, Mahmoud. *Daramadi bar Mabani-e Andisheh-ye Eslami* (A Look at the Principles of Islamic Thought). Qom: Mo'asseseh-e Amozeshi va Pazhoheshi-e Emam Khomeini, 1381/2002.

Fazel Mahmoodi Lankarani, Mohammad. *Ain-e Keshvardari az Didgah-e Emam 'Ali* (The Governing Tradition from Imam Ali's Perspective). Tehran: Farhang-e Eslami, 1379/1990.

Feiz, 'Alireza. *Vizhegi-haye Ijtihad va Fiqhi-e Pouya* (The Characteristics of Ijtihad and Dynamic Jurisprudence). Tehran: Pazhoheshkadeh-e 'Olum-e Ensani va Motale'at-e Farhangi, 1381/2002.

Feizi Tabrizi, Karim. *'Orfan-e Shi'ee* (Shi'a Mysticism). Qom: Yaas, 1380/2001.

Feuer, Lewis. "What Is an Intellectual?," in Alexander Gella, ed., *The Intelligentsia and the Intellectuals: Theory, Methods, and Case Study*. London: Sage, 1976, pp. 47–58.

Fischer, Michael M.J. *Iran: From Religious Dispute to Revolution*. Cambridge, MA: Harvard University Press, 1980.

Frank, Andre Gunder. *Development of Underdevelopment*. Indianapolis, IN: Bobbs-Merrill, 1969.

Ganji, Akbar. *Sonnat, Moderniteh, Post-Modern* (Tradition, Modernity, Postmodern). Tehran: Sarat, 1375/1996.

'Alijenab Sorkhpoush va 'Alijenaban-e Khakestari (The Red Eminence and the Gray Eminences). Tehran: Tarh-e No, 1379/2000.

Eslah-gari-ye Me'maraneh: Asib-shebasi-e Gozar be Dowlat-e Demokratik-e Tose'h-gozar (Constructive Reformation: Pathology of Transformation to the Developmental Democratic State). Tehran: Tarh-e No, 1379/2000.

Tallaqi-ye Fashisti az Din va Hokumat (A Fascist Interpretation of Religion and Government). Tehran: Tarh-e No, 1379/2000.

Tarik-khaneh Ashab (Darkroom of Ghosts). Tehran: Tarh-e No, 1379/2000.

"Eslah-talabi, Enqelabi-gari va Mohafeze-kari" (Reformism, Revolutionism and Conservatism), *Aftab*, No. 7 (1380/2001), pp. 14–25.

"Ejra-ye Hodood dar Zaman-e Ma" (Executing Limits in our Times), *Aftab*, No. 9 (1380/2001), pp. 26–31.

Kimiya-ye Azadi: Defa'iyat-e Akbar Ganji dar Dadgah-e Berlin (Exile of Freedom: Akbar Ganji's Defense at the Berlin Conference Trial). Tehran: Tarh-e No, 1380/2001.

Manifest-e Jomhuri-khahi (Republican Manifesto). Tehran: n.p., 1381/2002.

"The Struggle against Sultanism," *Journal of Democracy*, Vol. 16, No. 4 (October 2005), pp. 38–51.

Ghaffouri, Ali, and Ali Qasemi. "'Obour az Shariati" (Passage from Shariati), *Jame'h No*, Vol. 2, No. 17 (1382/2003), pp. 6–8.

Ghani, Mehdi. "Bazkhani-e Nazariyyeh-e Ma'refat-e Dini Abdolkarim Soroush" (Review of Abdolkarim Soroush's Theory of Religious Knowledge), *Jame'h No*, Vol. 1, No. 4 (1381/2002), p. 13.

Ghaninezhad, Musa. *Jame'h Madani, Azadi, Eqtesad va Siyasat* (Civil Society, Liberty, Economics, and Politics). Tehran: Tarh-e No, 1377/1998.

Tajaddod Talabi va Touse'h dar Iran-e Mo'aser (Modernism and Development in Contemporary Iran). Tehran: Markaz, 1377/1998.

Gheissari, Ali. *Iranian Intellectuals in the Twentieth Century*. Austin, TX: University of Texas Press, 1998.

Golbaf, Abolqasem. "Dar Khedmat va Khiyanat-e Roshanfekran-e Din-e Hokumat" (On the Service and Disservice of State Religious Intellectuals), *Gozaresh*, No. 134 (1381/2002), pp. 2–3.

Golmohammadi, Ahmad. *Jahani-shodan, Farhang, Hoviyyat* (Globalization, Culture, Identity). Tehran: Ney, 1383/2004.

Gorji, Abolqasem. *Tarikh-e Fiqh va Foqaha* (History of Jurisprudence and Jurisprudents). Tehran: Semat, 1381/2002.

Hadaee, Yashar. "Shatranj-e Siyasat dar Sali ke Gozasht" (Political Chess in the Year that Passed), *Nameh*, No. 22 (1382/2003), pp. 53–56.

Hair, Abdul-Hadi. *Shi'sm and Constitutionalism in Iran: A Study of the Persian Residents of Iraq in Iranian Politics*. Leiden: E. J. Brill, 1977.

Halabi, Ali Asghar. *Mabani-ye Andisheh-haye Siyasi dar Iran av Jahan-e Eslami* (Fundamentals of Political Thought in Iran and the Islamic World). Tehran: Behbahani, 1375/1996.

Tarikh-e Falsafeh-ye Irani az Aqhaz-e Eslam ta Emrouz (History of Iranian Philosophy from the Beginning of Islam until Today). Tehran: Zavvar, 1381/2002.

Hajiqasemi, 'Ali. "Bohran-e Jonbesh-e Eslahtalabi" (The Crisis of the Reform Movement), *Aftab*, No. 28 (1382/2003), pp. 14–19.

Hajizadeh, Mohammad. *Aya Ejra-ye Hodood-e Eslami bar Aqazade-ha ham Ravast?* (Are their Excellencies Exempt from Islamic Precepts?). Tehran: Jame Ravan, 1381/2003.

Hajizadeh, Pourya and Pardis Hajizadeh. *Aqajari* (Aqajari). Tehran: Jameh Daran, 1382/2003.

Hajjarian, Saeed. *Jomhuriyyat; Afsonzedai az Qodrat* (Republicanism; Demystification of Power). Tehran: Tarh-e No, 1379/2000.

Az Shahed-e Qodsi ta Shahed-e Bazari: 'Orfi Shodan-e Din dar Sepehr-e Siyasat (From the Sacred Witness to the Profane Witness: The Secularization of Religion in the Sphere of Politics). Tehran: Tarh-e No, 1380/2001.

"Estratezhi-haye Siyasi dar Iran-e Emrouz" (Political Strategies in Today's Iran), *Aftab*, No. 12 (1380/2001), pp. 12–15.

"Jomhuriyyat, Qalebi baraye Mazmon-e Azadi" (Republicanism. A Framework for Guaranteeing Freedom), *Aftab*, No. 13 (1380/2001), pp. 4–7.

"Takamol-e Gofteman-e Takamol dar Iran" (The Evolution of the Discourse of Evolution in Iran), *Aftab*, No. 15 (1381/2002), pp. 4–7.

"Farhang-e Siyasi: Enqelab ya Eslah" (Political Culture: Revolution or Reform), *Nameh*, No. 22 (1382/2003), pp. 31–34.

"Mashroteh-e Mashro'eh va Jomhuri-ye Islami" (Religious Constitutionalism and the Islamic Republic), *Aftab*, No. 25 (1382/2003), pp. 6–7.

Hajjarian, Saeed, *et al. Eslahat dar Barabar-e Eslahat* (Reforms against Reforms). Tehran: Tarh-e No, 1382/2003.

Haqdar, Ali Asghar. *Faraso-ye Postmoderniteh* (Beyond Post-Modernity). Tehran: Shafi'ee, 1380/2001.

Daryush Shayegan va Bohran-e Ma'naviyyat-e Sonnati (Daryush Shayegan and the Crisis of Traditional Spirituality). Tehran: Kavir, 1382/2003.

Qodrat-e Siyasi dar Andisheh-ye Irani: Az Farabi ta Na'ini (Political Power in Iranian Thought: From Farabi to Na'ini). Tehran: Kavir, 1382/2003.

Haqiqat, Sadeq. *Touzi'-e Qodrat dar Andisheh-ye Siyasi-e Shi'a* (Division of Power in Shi'a Political Thought). Tehran: Hasti Nama, 1381/2002.

Hasani, Gholamreza. *Khotbeh-haye Namaz-e Jom'eh Orumiyeh Hojjatoleslam Hasani* (Sermons of the Friday Prayer Leader of Orumiyeh Hojjatoleslam Hasani). Tehran: Jamehdaran, 1382/2003.

Hasvari, Ali. "Dar Vaz'iyati ke Qarar Darim" (The Condition We Are In), *Jame'h Salem*, Vol. 8, No. 40 (1377/1998), pp. 4–9.

Hedayati, Hashem. "Modeli baraye Tadvin-e Rahbord-haye Jonbesh-e Eslahat" (A Model for Synthesizing Strategies of the Reform Movement), *Aftab*, No. 25 (1382/2003), pp. 22–27.

Heidari, Mohammad. "Rastgarayan Iran-e Emrouz" (Rightists in Today's Iran), *Nameh*, No. 19 (1381/2002), pp. 15–19.

Heydarian, Mohsen. *Mardomsalari, Chalesh-e Sarnevesht Saz-e Iran* (Democracy, the Crisis of Iran's Destiny). Tehran: Saraee, 1381/2002.

Hojjati Kermani, Mohammad Javad. *Az Khodad ta Khordad* (From Khordad to Khordad). Tehran: Ettela'at, 1380/2001.

Hosein ibn Ali: Hamaseh-ye Tarikh (Hosein Ibn Ali: Legend of History). Tehran: Beinolmelal, 1381/2002.

Hoodashtiyan, 'Ata. *Moderniteh, Jahani-shodan va Iran* (Modernity, Globalization and Iran). Tehran: Chapakhsh, 1381/2002.

Hooshmand, Ehsan. "Nahanjari-haye Jame'h Emrouz-e Ma" (The Difficulties of our Contemporary Society), *Jame'h No*, Vol. 2, No. 17 (1382/2003), pp. 22–24.

Hoseini Esfahani, Morteza. *Eslam va Azadi* (Islam and Freedom). Qom: Farhang-e Quran, 1379/2000.

Hoseinian, Rohullah. *Bist Sal Takapo-ye Eslam-e Shi'i dar Iran, 1320–1340* (Twenty Years of Shi'ite Struggle in Iran, 1941–1961). Tehran: Center for Islam Revolution Documents, 1381/2001.

Chaharadah Qarn Talash-e Shi'a, baraye Mandab va Tose'h (Fourteen Centuries of Shi'a Struggle, for Survival and Growth). Tehran: Center for Islam Revolution Documents, 1382/2003.

Seh Sal Setiz-e Marja'iyyat-e Shia (Shi'a Leadership's Three Year Campaign). Tehran: Center for Islam Revolution Documents, 1382/2003.

Hoseinzadeh, Mohammad. *Din Shenasi* (Learning Religion). Qom: Mo'asseseh-e Amozeshi va Pazhoheshi-e Emam Khomeini, 1381/2002.

Hourani, Albert. *Arabic Thought in the Liberal Age, 1789–1939.* Oxford: Oxford University Press, 1962.

Izadi, Ali Mohammad, *et al. Din va Hokumat* (Religion and Government). Tehran: Rasa, 1377/1998.

Izadi, Mostafa. *Azadi dar Hesar* (Freedom under Control). Tehran: Saraee 1381/2002.

Jabraeeli, Ahmad Ali. *Zemamdari-ye Jame'h Eslami: Bonyad-ha va Negaresh-ha* (Governing Islamic Society: Organs and Outlooks). Mashhad: Bonyad-e Pazhohesh-haye Eslami, 1377/1998.

Ja'fari-Harandi, Mohammad. *Foqaha va Hokumat* (Religious Scholars and Government). Tehran: Rowzaneh, 1379/2000.

Ja'farian, Rasoul. *Tarikh-e Tashayy'o dar Iran: Az Aqaz ta Qarn-e Dahom-e Hejri,* Volumes I–II (History of Shi'ism in Iran: From the Beginning to the Tenth Century AH). Qom: Ansarian, 1380/2001.

Jahan Bozorgi, Ahmad. *Osol-e Siyasat va Hokoomat* (Principles of Politics and State). Tehran: 1378/1999.

Jahanbakhsh, Forough. *Islam, Democracy and Religious Modernity in Iran (1953–2000).* Leiden: Brill 2001.

 Eslam, Demokrasi va No-Garai-ye Dini dar Iran (Islam, Democracy and Religious Modernism in Iran). Trans. Jalil Tarvin. Tehran: Gam-e No, 1383/2004.

Jahanbegloo, Ramin. *Moderniteh, Demokrasi va Roshanfekran* (Modernity, Democracy and Intellectuals). Tehran: Markaz, 1374/1995.

 Modern-ha (The Moderns). Tehran: Markaz, 1376/1997.

 Iran va Moderniteh (Iran and Modernity). Tehran: Goftar, 1380/2001.

 "Tasahol va Khoshunat Parhizi" (Tolerance and Conflict Avoidance), *Aftab,* No. 8 (1380/2001), pp. 54–59.

 Mowj-e Chaharom (The Fourth Wave). Trans. Mansour Goodarzi. Tehran: Ney, 1381/2002.

 "Roshanfekr-e Nasl-e Chaharom va Haqiqat-i Faratar az Ideolozhi" (Fourth Generation Intellectual and a Truth Bigger than Ideology), *Jame'h No,* Vol. 2, No. 16 (1382/2003), pp. 6–10.

 Hakemiyyat va Azadi: Dars-hai dar Zanineh-ye Falsafeh-e Siyasi-e Modern (Sovereignty and Freedom: Lessons in Modern Political Philosophy). Tehran: Ney, 1383/2004.

 Iran Dar Jostejo-ye Moderniteh (Iran in Search of Modernity). Tehran: Markaz, 1384/2005.

Jahanbegloo, Ramin, ed. *Iran between Tradition and Modernity.* Lanham, MD: Lexington, 2004.

Jalaee, 'Alireza' and Akireza Siyasirad. "Daftar-e Tahkim-e Vahdat: Vizhegi-ha, Shekaf-ha va Tanaqoz-ha" (Office of Strengthening Unity: Characteristics, Fissures, and Contradictions), *Aftab,* No. 14 (1381/2002), pp. 36–39.

Jalaeepour, Hamid Reza. *Pas-az Dovvom-e Khordad: Negahi Jame'h-shenakhti be Jonbeshe Madani-e Iran, 1376–78* (After Second of Khordad: A Socially Aware Look at the Civil Movement in Iran, 1997–1999). Tehran: Kavir, 1378/1999.

Dowlat-e Penhan (Secret Government). Tehran: Tarh-e No, 1379/2000.

"Jonbesh-haye Bonyadgara va Mardom-salar dar Jahan-e Jahani-shodeh" (Democratic and Fundamentalist Movements in the Globalized World), *Aftab*, No. 8 (1380/2001), pp. 10–15.

Jame'hshenasi-e Jonbesh-haye Ejtema'i, ba Ta'kid bar Jonbesh-e Eslahi-ye Dovvom-e Khordad (Sociology of Social Movements, with Emphasis on the Reform Movement of the Second of Khordad). Tehran: Tarh-e No, 1831/2002.

Jala'ian, Naser. "Chap va Rast va Demokrasi-ye Boomi" (Left and Right and Native Democracy), *Cheshmandaz-e Iran*, No. 10 (1380/2001), pp. 36–43.

"Mabani-ye Demokrasi-ye Boomi-ye Iran" (Principles of Iran's Native Democracy), *Cheshmandaz-e Iran*, No. 12 (1380/2001), pp. 20–5.

Jalali-Moghaddam, Mas'oud. *Daramadi be Jame'hshenasi-e Din* (A Look at the Sociology of Religion). Tehran: Markaz, 1379/2000.

Jamalpour, Bahram, *et al. Falsafeh dar Iran* (Philosophy in Iran). Tehran: Hekmat, 1378/1999.

Javadi Amoli, 'Abdollah. *Resalat-e Qor'an* (The Mission of the Qur'an). Tehran: Raja', 1375/1996.

Falsafeh-ye Hoquq-e Bashar (The Philosophy of Human Rights). Qom: Isra, 1375/1996.

Shari'at dar Ayeneh-e Ma'refat (Shariat in the Light of Cognition). Qom: Isra, 1378/1999.

Velayat-e Faqih (The Supreme Jurisconsult). Qom: Esra, 1379/2000.

Javan Arasteh, Husayn. *Mabani-ye Hokumat-e Eslami* (Fundamentals of Islamic Government). Qom: Howzeh Elmiye, 1379/2000.

Kachooyan, Hosein. *Kandokavi dar Mahiyat-e Mo'amai-e Iran* (An Inquiry into the Puzzling Nature of Iran). Qom: Bustan-e Ketab, 1383/2004.

Kadivar, Jamileh. *Tahavvol-e Gofteman-e Siyasi-e Shi'a dar Iran* (The Development of Shi'a Political Discourse in Iran). Tehran: Tarh-e No, 1379/2000.

Tavvahom-e Towte'e az Cheshm-e Sharqi (Paranoia of Conspiracy in Eastern Eyes). Tehran: Ettela'at, 1379/2000.

Kadivar, Mohsen. *Nazariye-haye Dowlat dar Fiqh-e Shi'a* (Perspectives on Government in Shi'a Jurisprudence). Tehran: Ney, 1376/1997.

Hokumat-e Velayi (Government of the Jurisconsult). Tehran: Ney, 1377/1998.

Daqdaqe-haye Hokumat-e Dini (Crises of Religious Government). Tehran: Ney, 1379/2000.

"Hokumat Entesabi" (Appointed Government), *Aftab*, No. 1 (1379/2000), pp. 8–13.

Kadivar, Mohsen. "Hokumat Entesabi" (Appointed Government), *Aftab*, No. 2 (1379/2000), pp. 44–51.

"Entesab, Etesab va Entekhab" (Dependence, Appointment and Election), *Aftab*, No. 3 (1380/2001), pp. 66–71.

"Hoquq-e Mokhalef-e Siyasi dar Jame'h Dini" (The Rights of Political Opposition in Religious Society), *Aftab*, No. 4 (1380/2001), pp. 4–13.

"Nezarat bar 'Amalkard-e Vali-e Faqih" (Supervision of the Supreme Jurisconsult's Functions), *Aftab*, No. 7 (1380/2001), pp. 56–65.

"Barresi-ye Mostanadat-e Ravaee" (Analysis of Commonly Accepted Documents), *Aftab*, No. 11 (1380/2001), pp. 60–69.

"Hokumat-e Entesabi, Ebtekar-e Moteshar'h Na Rah-e Hall-e Share'" (Appointive Government, the Moteshar'h's Choice, Not a Religious Solution), *Aftab*, No. 12 (1380/2001), pp. 64–69.

"Rishehyabi-e Hokumat-e Entesabi dar Jomhuri-e Eslami" (Finding the Roots of Appointive Government in the Islamic Republic), *Aftab*, No. 14 (1381/2002), pp. 54–61.

"Azadi-ye 'Aqideh va Mazhab dar Eslam" (Freedom of Opinion and Belief in Islam), *Aftab*, No. 23 (1381/2002), pp. 54–63.

"Mo'azel-e Bardeh-dari dar Eslam-e Mo'aser" (The Slavery Dilemma in Contemporary Islam), *Aftab*, No. 25 (1382/2003), pp. 80–89.

"Hoquq-e Bashar va Roshanfekri-ye Dini" (Human Rights and Religious Intellectualism), *Aftab*, No. 27 (1382/2003), pp. 54–59.

"Hoquq-e Bashar va Roshanfekri-ye Dini" (Human Rights and Religious Intellectualism), *Aftab*, No. 28 (1382/2003), pp. 106–15.

"Shar'-e Shoura-ye Negahban dar Barabar-e Qanun-e Majles" (The Religious Law of the Guardian Council Compared to the Law of the Majles), *Aftab*, No. 29 (1382/2003), pp. 16–25.

"Az Mashroteh-e Saltanati ta Jomhuri-ye Valayati" (From Dynastic Monarchy to Guardian Republic). www.kadivar.com, accessed on January 29, 2007.

"Azadi-e Aqideh va Mazhab dar Eslam va Asnad-e Hoquq-e Bashar" (Freedom of Religion and Thought in Islam and Human Rights Documents). www.kadivar.com, accessed on January 29, 2007.

"Eslahat, Naqd-e Marhaleh-ye Avval, Doornama-ye Marhaleh-ye Dovvom" (Reforms, Critique of the First Phase, Outlook of the Second Phase". www.kadivar.com, accessed on January 29, 2007.

"Eslam va Farhang-e Demokrasi" (Islam and the Culture of Democracy). www.kadivar.com, accessed on January 29, 2007.

"Foqahat va Siyasat" (Clericalism and Politics). www.kadivar.com, accessed on January 29, 2007.

"Hokumat-e Qeseri" (Immune Government). www.kadivar.com, accessed on January 29, 2007.

"Hoquq-e Zanan dar Eslam-e Mo'aser az Zaviyeh-ee Digar" (Women's Rights in Contemporary Islam from a Different Angle). www.kadivar.com, accessed on January 29, 2007.

"Mardomsalari-e Dini" (Religious Democracy). www.kadivar.com, accessed on January 29, 2007.

"Pishdaramad-i bar Bahs-e 'Umoomi va Khosoosi' dar Fahnag-e Eslam" (A Preface to "Public and Private" in Islam). www.kadivar.com, accessed on January 29, 2007.

"Roshanfekri-ye Dini va Hoquq-e Zanan" (Religious Intellectualism and Women's Rights). www.kadivar.com, accessed on January 29, 2004.

"Velayat-e Faqih va Mardomsalari" (The Supreme Jurisconsult and Democracy). www.kadivar.com, accessed on January 29, 2007.

"Zendeginameh" (Biography). www.kadivar.com, accessed on January 29, 2007.

Kaji, Hosein. *Kisti-ye ma az Negah-e Roshanfekran-e Irani* (Our Existence from the Perspective of Iranian Intellectuals). Tehran: Rowzaneh, 1378/ 1999.

Kamali, Mohammad Hashem. *Azadi-e Bayan dar Eslam* (Freedom of Speech in Islam). Tehran: Qasideh Sara, 1381/2002.

Kamali, Mas'oud. *Do Enqelab dar Iran: Moderniteh, Jame'h Madani, Mobarezeh Tabaqati* (Two Revolutions in Iran: Modernity, Civil Society, Class Struggle). Tehran: Digar, 1381/2002.

Kamrava, Mehran. "The Civil Society Discourse in Iran," *British Journal of Middle Eastern Studies*, Vol. 28, No. 2 (2001), pp. 165–85.

"Iranian Shiism under Debate," *Middle East Policy*, Vol. 10, No. 2 (2003), pp. 102–12.

The Modern Middle East: A Political History since the First World War. Berkeley, CA: University of California Press, 2005.

Kamrava, Mehran, and Houchang Hassan-Yari. "Suspended Equilibrium in Iran's Political System," *The Muslim World*, Vol. 94, No. 4 (October 2004), pp. 495–524.

Kar, Mehrangiz. *Mavane'-e Hoquqi-e Touse'h dar Iran* (Legal Obstacles to Development in Iran). Tehran: Qatreh, 1381/2002.

Karami, Akbar. "Defa' az Din-e Tarikh-i" (Defending Historic Religion), *Aftab*, No. 21 (1381/2002), pp. 96–97.

Karbaschi, Gholamreza. *Tarikh-e Shafahi-ye Enqelab-e Eslami* (Oral History of the Islamic Revolution). Tehran: Markaz-e Asnad-e Enqelab-e Eslami, 1380/2001.

Karimi Jooni, Nader. "Iran: Abestan-e Bin Laden-e Shi'a?!" (Iran: Pregnant with a Shi 'a Bin Laden?!), *Gozaresh*, No. 140 (1381/2002), pp. 13–16.

Karimi Zanjani Asl, Mohammad. *Emamiyyeh va Siyasat dar Nokhostin Sadeh-haye Gheybat* (The Imamate and Politics in the Early Centuries after the Occultation). Tehran: Ney, 1380/2001.

Kashef, Ja'far. *Defa'a az Haqqaniyat-e Shi'a* (Defending Shi'ism's Truth). Trans. Gholamhosein Moharrami. Qom: Mo'menin, 1378/1999.

Kashi, Mohammad Javad Gholamreza. "Tabar-shenasi; Bi 'Etebari-ye Bonyadha-ye Rangbakhteh" (Genealogy; The Illegitimacy of Colorless Foundations), *Nameh*, No. 16 (1381/2002), pp. 12–17.

"Danesh-Qodrat va Prozhe-ye Roshanfekri dar Iran" (Knowledge-Power and the Intellectual Project in Iran), *Jame'h No*, Vol. 1, No. 7 (1381/2002), pp. 9–11.

Katir'i, Mostafa. "Hokumat az Didgah-e Din" (Government from the Perspective of Religion), in Ali Mohammad Izadi, *et al.*, *Din va Hokumat* (Religion and Government). Tehran: Rasa, 1377/1998, pp. 25–37.

Kavyani, Hamid. *Jarrahi dar Qodrat: Gam be Gam dar Masir-e Eslahat* (Surgery of Power: Step by Step on the Route of Reformation). Tehran: Zekr, 1379/ 2000.

Kazemi, Abbas. *Jame'hshenasi-ye Roshanfekri-ye Dini dar Iran* (Sociology of the Religious Intellectual Movement in Iran). Tehran: Tarh-e No, 1383/2004.

Kazemian, Morteza. "Melli-Mazhabi-ha va Tahavvolat-e Ayandeh-e Iran" (Religious-Nationalists and Changes in Iran's Future), *Aftab*, No. 25 (1382/2003), pp. 18–21.

"Shariati, Roshanfekr-e Mote'ahed va Mas'oul va Roshanfekran-e Emrouz" (Shariati, Committed and Responsible Intellectual and Today's Intellectuals), *Aftab*, No. 26 (1382/2003), pp. 14–19.

Kazemipour, 'Abdolmohammad. "Jeme'hshenasi-e Din dar Astaneh-e Yek Charkhesh-e Paradym-i" (Sociology of Religion in the Midst of a Paradigmatic Shift), *Aftab*, No. 11 (1380/2001), pp. 40–41.

"Rah-e Tey Shodeh, Rah-e Pishro: Tarh-i baraye Tajdid-e Sazman-e Ejtema'i-e Eslahat" (The Path Traversed, the Path Ahead: A Plan for Renewing the Social Organization of Reforms), *Aftab*, No. 23 (1381/2002), pp. 4–11.

Khalili, Esma'il. "Moderniteh, Jame'h Madani va Hey'at-haye Mazhabi" (Modernity, Civil Society and Religious Associations), *Andisheh-ye Jame'h*, No. 5 (1378/1999), pp. 5–7.

Khalji, Mohammad Taqi. *Tashayy'o va Entezar* (Shi'ism and Awaiting). Qom: Meysam Tammar, 1378/1999.

Khalkhali, Sadeq. *Ayyam-e Enzeva: Khaterat-e Ayatollah Khalkhali.* Vol. 2 (Days of Solace: Memoirs of Ayatollah Khalkhali). Tehran: Sayeh, 1380/2001.

Khalqi, Moslem. "Pazhouhesh-e Hogugi dar Internet" (Judicial Research on the Internet), *Howzeh va Daneshgah*, Vol. 9, No. 36 (2003), pp. 123–37.

Khamenei, Ali. "Bayanat-e Rahbar-e Mo'azzam-e Engelab-e Eslami dar Didar-e A'za-ye Majles-e Khobregan'e Rahbari" (The Speech of the Esteemed Leader of the Islamic Revolution in the Meeting of the Leadership Assembly of Experts), *Hokumat-e Eslami*, Vol. 8, No. 2 (2003), pp. 3–11.

Khaniki, Hadi. *Qodrat, Jame'h Madani va Matbo'at* (Power, Civil Society and the Press). Tehran: Tarh-e No, 1381/2002.

Khatami, Mohammad. *Beem-e Mowj* (Fear of Wave). Tehran: Seema-ye Javan, 1372/1993.

Az Donya-ye Shahr ta Shahr-e Donya (From the World of the "City" to the City of "Donya"). Tehran: Ney, 1376/1997.

Aeen va Andisheh dar Dam-e Khodkamegi (Religion and Intellect Trapped in Tyranny).Tehran: Tarh-e No, 1378/1999.

Ehya-gare Haqiqat-e Din (The Reviver Truth of Religion). Tehran: 1378/1999.

Eslam, Rouhaniyyat, va Enqelab-e Eslami (Islam, the Clergy, and the Islamic Revolution). Tehran: Tarh-e No, 1379/2000.

Tose'h Siyasi, Tose'h Eqtesadi va Amniyat. Tehran: Tarh-e No, 1379/2000.

Zanan va Javanan (Women and the Youth). Tehran: Tarh-e No, 1379/2000.

Ahzab va Shoura-ha (Parties and Councils). Tehran: Tarh-e No, 1380/2001.

Goftego-ye Tammadon-ha (Dialogue of Civilizations). Tehran: Tarh-e No, 1380/2001.

Mardomsalari (Democracy). Tehran: Tarh-e No, 1380/2001.

Nameh-ee baraye Farda (A Letter for Tomorrow). Tehran: Mo'asseseh-e Khaneh-e Farhang-e Khatami, 1388/2004.

Khatami, Mohammad Reza. "Gostaresh-e Jebhe-ye Mardomsalari" (Expanding the Democratic Front), *Aftab*, No. 21 (1381/2002), pp. 14–19.

Khomeini, Rohullah. *Sahife-ye Enqelab-e Eslami: Vasiyat Nameh-e Elahi-Siyasi-e Rahbar-e Mo'azzam-e Enqelab-e Eslami-e Iran* (The Book of Islamic Revolution: The Religion-Political Will and Testament of the Great Leader of the Islamic Revolution). Tehran: Aryaban, 1378/1999.

   Velayat-e Faqih, Jehad-e Akbar (Supreme Jurisconsult, the Great Struggle). Tehran: Seyyed Jamal, n.d.

Kian-Thiebaut, Azadeh. "Political and Social Transformations in Post-Islamist Iran," *Middle East Report*, No. 212 (Fall 1999), pp. 12–16.

Kohestani-Nezhad, Mas'oud. *Chalesh-e Mazhab va Modernism: Seyr-e Andisheh-ye Siyasi-e Mazhabi dar Iran* (The Struggle between Religion and Modernism: The Evolution of Religion-Political Thought in Iran). Tehran: Ney, 1381/2002.

Kordzadeh Kermani, Mohammad. *Eqtesad-e Siyasi-e Jomhuriye Eslami-ye Iran* (The Political Economy of the Islamic Republic of Iran). Tehran: Institute for Political and International Studies, 1380/2001.

Kurzman, Charles, ed. *Modernist Islam, 1840–1940: A Sourcebook*. Oxford: Oxford University Press, 2002.

La'ali, Mas'oud. *Khatami az cheh Migouyad?* (What Is Khatami Talking About?). Tehran: Azadi-ye Andisheh, 1378/1999.

Labbaf, Ali. *Setareh-ye 'Arsh* (Celestial Star). Tehran: Sa'eb, 1378/1999.

Ladjevardi, Habib, ed. *Khaterat-e Doctor Mehdi Hairi-Yazdi* (Memories of Dr. Hairi-Yazdi). Tehran: Ketab-e Nader, 1381/2003.

Lakzaee, Najaf. *Andisheh-ye Siyasi-e Ayatollah Mottahari* (The Political Thought of Ayatollah Mottahari). Qom: Bustan-e Ketab, 1382/2003.

Madani, Saeed. "Pishniyaz-haye Farayand-e Vafaq-e Melli" (Prerequisites of the Phenomenon of National Conciliation), *Nameh*, No. 17 (1381/2002), pp. 7–13.

   "Nasl-e Tajdid-e Nazar Talab" (The Questioning Generation), *Nameh*, No. 18 (1381/2002), pp. 20–22.

Mahdasi, Hasan. "Sonnat-haye 'Ashura'ee va Rouzmarreh Shodan-e 'Eteqad" ('Ashura-Like Traditions and the Reutilization of Belief), *Aftab*, No. 23 (1381/2002), pp. 92–99.

   "Roshanfekr Masraf-konandeh Nist" (Intellectual Is Not a Consumer), *Jame'h No*, No. 9 (1381/2002), pp. 18–19.

Mahdavi Alhoseini, Mohammad Ali. "Posht be Din, Ro be Sekolarism" (Turning the Back to Religion, Facing Secularism), *Aftab*, No. 33 (1382/2003), pp. 136–38.

Mahmoudi, Seyyed Ali. "Opozisiyon-e Madani Jonbesh-e Eslahtalabane-ye Mellat-e Iran" (Civic Opposition, the Reformist Movement of the Iranian People"), *Aftab*, No. 34 (1383/2004), pp. 4–7.

Mahmoudian, Mohammad Rafi'. "'Aqlaniyat-e Din, Poya'ie Noandishi-ye Dini" (Religious Rationalism, the Dynamic of Religious Modernism), *Aftab*, No. 12 (1380/2001), pp. 54–59.

Mahrouyan, Hooshang. *Moderniteh va Bohran-e Ma* (Modernity and our Crisis). Tehran: Akhtaran, 1383/2004.

Makiani, Hassan. *Payamad-haye A'mal-e Afrad-e Khodsar va Qatl-haye Zanjire-ee* (Consequences of the Deeds of Self-Righteous Individuals and the Chain Murders). Tehran: Mo'alef, 1381/2002.

Malekian, Mostafa. "Roshanfekri-e Dini va Eslahat-e Ejtema'i" (Religious Intellectualism and Social Reforms), *Aftab*, No. 10 (1380/2001), pp. 70–73.

"'Aqlaniyyat, Din, va 'No Andishi'" (Rationality, Religion, and "New Thinking"), *Nameh*, No. 16 (1381/2002), pp. 60–72.

"Mardomsalari va Ma'naviyyat" (Democracy and Spirituality), *Nameh*, No. 24 (1382/2003), pp. 42–45.

Rahi be Raha-ee (A Path to Liberation). Tehran: Negah-e Mo'aser, 1381/2002.

Malekzadeh, Mohammad. "Nazariyyeh-e Mardomsalari-e Dini dar Te'ori va 'Amal" (The Theory of Religious Democracy in Theory and Practice), *Aftab*, No. 24 (1382/2003), pp. 90–93.

"Rahbari-e Farahmand, Rahbari-e Qanuni" (Wise Leadership, Legal Leadership), *Aftab*, No. 28 (1382/2003), p. 144.

Mansournezhad, Mohammad. *Goftego-ye Tamaddon-ha* (Dialogue of Civilizations). Tehran: Pazhoheshkadeh-ye 'Oloom-e Ensani va 'Ejtema'i, 1381/2002.

Maqsoodi, Mojtaba. "Hoviyyat-e Melli Hoviyyat-e Qomi, Vafaq-e Melli" (National Identity, Tribal Identity, and National Conciliation), *Nameh*. No. 17 (1381/2002), pp. 25–27.

Mardiha, Seyyed Morteza. *Ba Mas'ouliyat-e Sardabir: Moqaddameh-i bar Prozheh-ye Eslahat* (With the Editor's Responsibility: An Introduction to the Reform Project). Tehran: Jame'eh Iranian, 1379/2000.

Defa'a az 'Aqlaniyat (In Defense of Rationality). Tehran: Naqsh-o Negar, 1379/2000.

Martin, Vanessa. *Creating an Islamic State: Khomeini and the Making of a New Iran*. London: I. B. Tauris, 2003.

Mashayekhi, Mehrdad. "Degardisi Mabani-ye Siyasat va Roshanfekri-ye Siaysi" (Changes in Political Principles and Political Intellectuals), *Aftab*, No. 28 (1382/2003), pp. 8–13.

"Iran va Drasha-ee az Enqelab-haye Oropa-ye Sharqi" (Iran and Lessons from East European Revolutions), *Aftab*, No. 33 (1382/2003), pp. 132–33.

"Ahang-e Shetaban-e Secularizision va Secularism dar Iran" (The Hurried Song of Secularisation and Secularism in Iran). www.nilgoon.org, accessed on June 3, 2006.

Mashkoor, Mohammad Javad. *Tarikh-e Shi'a va Ferqe-haye Eslam ta Qarn-e Chaharom* (History of Shi'ism and Islamic Sects until the Fourth Century). Tehran: Esraqi, 1368/1989.

Ma'somi, Seyyed Mas'oud. *Negahi No be Hokumat-e Dini* (A New Look at Religious Government). Qom: Howzeh Elmiyeh, 1379/2000.

Matsunaga, Yasuyuki. "Mohsen Kadivar, A Clerical Advocate of Postrevivalist Islam in Iran," *British Journal of Middle Eastern Studies*, Vol. 34, No. 3 (December 2007), pp. 317–29.

Mazaheri Seyf, Hamid Reza. *Tahaqqoq-e Jame'h Mdani dar Iran va Rah-haye Aan* (Manifesting Civil Society in Iran and its Means). Tehran: Javanan-e Movvafaq, 1379/2000.

Mesbah, Mojtaba. *Falsafeh-ye Akhlaq* (Moral Philosophy). Qom: Mo'asseseh-e Amozeshi va Pazhoheshi-e Emam Khomeini, 1378/1999.

Mesbah Yazdi, Mohammad Taqi. *Jame'eh va Tarikh az Didgah-e Qor'an* (Society and History from the Perspective of the Quran). Tehran: Sazman-e Tablighat-e Eslami, 1380/2001.

Nazariyyeh-e Hoquqi-e Eslam (Legal Theory of Islam). Qom: Mo'asseseh-e Amozeshi va Pazhoheshi-e Emam Khomeini, 1380/2001.

Nazariyyeh-e Siyasi-e Eslam: Qanoongozari (Political Theory of Islam: Legislation). Qom: Mo'asseseh-e Amozeshi va Pazhoheshi-e Emam Khomeini, 1380/2001.

Nazariyyeh-e Siyasi-e Eslam: Keshvardari (Political Theory of Islam: Statecraft). Qom: Mo'asseseh-e Amozeshi va Pazhoheshi-e Emam Khomeini, 1380/2001.

Porsesh-ha va Pasokh-ha (Questions and Answers). Qom: Mo'asseseh-e Amozeshi va Pazhoheshi-e Emam Khomeini, 1380/2001.

Khod-shenasi baraye Khod-sazi (Self-Awareness for Self-Improvement). Qom: Mo'asseseh-e Amozeshi va Pazhoheshi-e Emam Khomeini, 1381/2002.

Rahiyan-e Koy-e Doost: Sharh-e Hadis-e Me'raj (Travelers to Friend's Village: Explaining the Ascension Hadith). Qom: Mo'asseseh-e Amozeshi va Pazhoheshi-e Emam Khomeini, 1381/2002.

Amouzesh-e 'Aqayed (Teaching Beliefs). Tehran: Beinolmelal, 1382/2003.

Bahs-i Kotah va Sadeh Piramoun-e Hokumat-e Eslami va Velayat-e Faqih (A Brief and Simple Discussion concerning Islamic Government and the Supreme Jurisconsult). Tehran: Beinolmelal, 1382/2003.

Porsesh-ha va Pasokh-ha, Volume I (Questions and Answers). Qom: Mo'asseseh-e Amozeshi va Pazhoheshi-e Emam Khomeini, 1382/2003.

"Tafsir-e Mardomsalari-ye Dini" (Commentary on Religious Democracy). *Hokumat-e Eslami*, Vol. 8, No. 3 (1382/2003), pp. 73–89.

Meysami, Lotfollah. "Din-e Shaffaf" (Transparent Religion), *Cheshmandaz-e Iran*, Vol. 1, No. 6 (1379/2000), pp. 2–14.

"Ayandeh az an-e No-andishan-e Dini Ast" (The Future Belongs to Reformist Religious Thinkers), *Cheshmandaz-e Iran*, No. 11 (1380/2001), pp. 2–14.

"Jang-e Solteh va Demokrasi dar Iran" (The Battle between Dictatorship and Democracy in Iran), *Nameh*, No. 22 (1382/2003), pp. 8–17.

Milani, Abbas. *Tajaddod va Tajaddod-Setizi dar Iran* (Modernity and Modernity-Fighting in Iran). Tehran: Akhtaran, 1382/2003.

Lost Wisdom: Rethinking Modernity in Iran. Washington, DC: Mage, 2004.

Miraghai, Jalal. *Ejtehad va No Andishi*, Volumes I–II (Ijtihad and Reformist Thinking). Tehran: Majma'-e Jahani-e Taqrib-e Mazhab-e Eslami, 1382/2003.

Miri, Ahmad. *Dibache-ee bar Farhang-e Estebdad dar Iran* (An Introduction to the Culture of Despotism in Iran). Tehran: Negar-e Mo'aser, 1380/2001.

Mirmoosavi, Ali. 'Eslam, Sonnat, Dowlat-e Modern (Islam, Tradition, Modern State). Ph.D. Dissertation, University of Tehran, Faculty of Law and Political Science, 1381/2002.

Mirsepassi, Ali. *Intellectual Discourse and the Politics of Modernization: Negotiating Modernity in Iran.* Cambridge: Cambridge University Press, 2000.

Demokrasi ya Haqiqat: Rasale-ee Jame'h-shenakhti dar bab-e Roshanfekri-ye Irani (Democracy or Truth: A Sociological Study on Iranian Intellectuals). Tehran: Tarh-e No, 1381/2002.

Mo'asseseh-e Amozeshi va Pazhoheshi-e Emam Khomeini. *Tabeen-e Mardomsalari-e Dini,* Volume II (Explaining Religious Democracy). Qom: Mo'asseseh-e Amozeshi va Pazhoheshi-e Emam Khomeini, 1383/2004.

Moaveni, Azadeh. *Lipstick Jihad: A Memoir of Growing up Iranian in America and American in Iran.* New York: Public Affairs, 2005.

Moddaresi, Mohammad Taqi. *Emaman-e Shi'a va Jonbesh-haye Maktabi* (Shi'a Imams and Religious Movements). Trans. Hamid Reza Azhir. Mashhad: Islamic Research Foundation, 1378/1999.

Mohajerani, 'Ataollah. *Hekayat Hamchenan Baqi Ast...* (The Story Still Remains...). Tehran: Ettela'at, 1379/2000.

Naqd-e Tote'h-e Ayat-e Sheytani (Critique of *The Satanic Verses* Conspiracy). Tehran: Ettela'at, 1379/2000.

Behesht-e Khakestari (Grey Paradise). Tehran: Omid-e Iranian, 1382/2003.

Mohammadi, Majid. *Jame'h Madani Be Manzeleh Yek Ravesh* (Civil Society as a Method). Tehran: Qatreh, 1376/1997.

"Barnameh-haye Siyasi: Hokumat-e Motlaqeh, Mashrotiyyat va Jomhuriyyat" (Political Programs: Absolutist Regime, Constitutionalism and Republicanism), *Jame'h Salem,* Vol. 8, No. 40 (1377/1998), pp. 13–16.

Dar-amadi bar Raftarshenasi-e Siyasi-e Daneshjoyan dar Iran-e Emrouz (An Analysis of the Political Behavior of University Students in Today's Iran). Tehran: Kavir, 1378/1999.

Rah-e Doshvar-e Eslahat (Reform's Difficult Road). Tehran: Iran-e Emrouz, 1379/2000.

Liberalism-e Irani, Olgo-ye Natamam (Iranian Liberalism, Unfinished Agenda). Tehran: Iran-e Emrouz, 1379/2000.

Nezam-haye Akhlaqi dar Eslam va Iran (Moral Systems in Islam and Iran). Tehran: Kavir, 1379/2000.

Mohammadi, Meysam. "Takvin-e Ma'kous-e Mardomsalari dar Eslam" (The Emergence of Democracy's Antithesis in Islam), *Aftab,* No. 22 (1381/2002), pp. 76–83.

Mohammadi, Mohammad Ali. "Iran, Eslam va Post Moderniteh" (Iran, Islam and Post-Modernity). *Nameh.* No. 19 (1381/2002), pp. 32–37.

Mohammadi Asl, Abbas. "Bohran-e Mashro'iyat dar Jomhuri-ye Eslami Iran va Rah-e Hall-e An" (Legitimacy Crisis in the Islamic Republic of Iran and Way to Solve It), *Gozaresh,* No. 140 (1381/2002), p. 36.

Mohammadi-Eshtehardi, Mohammad. *Rabete-ye Iran ba Eslam va Tashayy'o* (Iran's Relations with Islam and Shi'ism). Tehran: Borhan, 1377/1998.

Mohammadi-Gorgani, Mohammad. "Ayandeh-e Eslahat: Tahavvol Yek Shabeh Emkan Pazir Nist" (The Future of Reforms: Overnight Change Is Not Possible), *Aftab,* No. 10 (1380/2001), pp. 26–33.

Mohammadian, Nayereh. "Mas'oliyat-e Roshanfekr be Ravayat-e Shariati" (The Intellectual's Responsibility according to Shariati), *Jame'h No*, Vol. 2, No. 14 (1382/2003), pp. 5, 25.

Mohammad-Pour, Ali, and Karim Jalil Nezhad Mamqani, eds. *Dovvom-e Khordad Hammaseh-e Beyad Mandani* (Second of Khordad, A Memorable Legend). Tehran, Resanesh, 1378/1999.

Mohtashemi-Pour, Ali Akbar. *Chand Seda'i dar Jame'h va Rouhaniyyat* (Multiple Voices in Society and the Clergy). Tehran: Khaneh-e Andisheh-ye Javan, 1379/2000.

Mojtahed Shabestri, Mohammad. *Hermeneutic, Ketab va Sonnat* (Hermeneutics, the Scripture and the Tradition). Tehran: Tarh-e No, 1379/2000.

Iman va Azadi (Faith and Freedom). Tehran: Tarh-e No, 1379/2000.

Naqdi bar Qara't-e Rasmi az Din (A Critique of the Official Reading of Religion). Tehran: Tarh-e No, 1379/2000.

"Mardomsalari-e Dini Chist?" (What Is Religious Democracy?), *Aftab*, No. 7 (1380/2001), pp. 4–9.

"Se Qara'at az Sonnat dar 'Asr-e Moderniteh" (Three Interpretations from the Tradition in the Age of Modernity), *Aftab*, No. 9 (1380/2001), pp. 52–57.

"Tahavvolat-e Tarikhi-e Din ta 'Asr-e Hazer" (Historic Changes to Religion to the Present Day), *Aftab*, No. 14 (1381/2002), pp. 50–53.

"Rah-e Doshvar-e Mardomsalari" (Democracy's Difficult Path), *Aftab*, No. 22 (1381/2002), pp. 30–37.

Ta'amilati dar Qara't-e Ensani az Din (Reflections on a Humane Reading of Religion). Tehran: Tarh-e No, 1383/2004.

Molavi Afshin. "Buying Time in Tehran: Iran and the China Model," *Foreign Affairs*, Vol. 83, No. 6 (November–December 2004), pp. 9–16.

Mo'meni, Ali Akbar. "Roshanfekran-e Emrouz va Gharat-e Andisheh-ye Shariati" (Today's Intellectuals and the Theft of Shariati's Thoughts), *Aftab*, No. 28 (1382/2003), p. 145.

Montazeri, Hoseinali. *Az Aghaz ta Anjam* (From Start to Implementation). Qom: Sarai, 1382/2003.

Didgah-ha (Perspectives). Qom. n.p., 1382/2003.

Rasaleh-ye Hoquq (A Thesis of Rights). Qom: Sarai, 1383/2004.

Mabani-ye Feqhi-ye Hokumat-e Eslami, Volumes I–VI (The Jurisprudential Foundations of Islamic Government). Qom: Sarai, n.d.

Moqimi, Saeed. "Doulat-Mellat: Qanun-madari va Mosharekat-e Siyasi" (Government-People: Legalism and Political Participation), *Aftab*, No. 22 (1381/2002), pp. 60–69.

"Mardomsalari, Chalesh-ha va Pasokh-ha" (Democracy, Efforts and Answers), *Aftab*, No. 29 (1382/2003), pp. 124–27.

Moridiha, Morteza. "Mordeh Rig-e Sonnat-e Roshanfekri" (The Dead Stone of Intellectual Tradition), *Aftab*, No. 27 (1382/2003), pp. 80–85.

Mosaffa, Nasrin. *Mosharekat-e Siyasi-e Zanan dar Iran* (Women's Political Participation in Iran). Tehran: Vezarat-e Omoor-e Kharejeh, 1375/1996.

Moshkaver, Mohammad Javad. *Tarikh-e Shi'a va Ferqe-haye Eslam ta Qarn-e Chaharom* (History of Shi'ism and Islamic Sects until the Fourth Century). Tehran: Eshraqi, 1379/2000.

Moslem, Mehdi. *Factional Politics in Post-Khomeini Iran*. Syracuse, NY: Syracuse University Press, 2002.

Mottahedeh, Roy. *The Mantle of the Prophet: Religion and Politics in Iran*. New York: Pantheon, 1985.

Mottaheri, Morteza. *Eslam va Niyaz-haye Zaman*, Volumes I–II (Islam and the Needs of Time). Tehran, Sadra, 1362–73/1983–94.

    Harkat va Zaman dar Falsafeh-ye Eslami, Volumes I–VI (Movement and Time in Islamic Philosophy). Tehran: Hekmat, 1366/1987.

    Barresi-ye Ejmali-ye Nehzatha-ye Eslami dar Sad Sal-e Akhir (A Brief Examination of Islamic Movements in the Last One Hundred Years). Tehran: Sadra, 1378/1999.

    Qiyam va Enqelab-e Mehdi (Mehdi's Uprising and Revolution). Tehran: Sadra, 1378/1999.

Mottaqi, Mohsen. "Karnameh-e Karyab-e Soroush" (Soroush's Employment-seeking Report Card), *Aftab*, No. 19 (1381/2002), pp. 44–51.

    "Tadavom-e Miras-e Shariati dar Roshanfekri-e Dini-e Emrouz" (Continuity of Shariati's Heritage in Today's Religious Intellectualism), *Aftab*, No, 26 (1382/2003), pp. 4–11.

Movahhed, Zia. "Falsafeh, Din va Siyasat" (Philosophy, Religion and Politics), *Aftab*, No. 16 (1381/2002), pp. 18–21.

Musavian, Abolfazl. *Mabani-e Mashro'iyyat-e Hokumat* (Basis of Government Legitimacy). Tehran: Zekr, 1381/2002.

Nabavi, Negin. *Intellectuals and the State in Iran: Politics, Discourse, and the Dilemmas of Authenticity*. Gainesville, FL: University Press of Florida, 2003.

Nabavi, Negin, ed. *Intellectual Trends in Twentieth Century Iran: A Critical Survey*. Gainesville, FL: University Press of Florida, 2003.

Nabavi, Seyyed Ebrahim. *Goftegohaye Sarih* (Frank Talk). Tehran: Rowzaneh, 1378/1999.

Najafi, Mousa. *Madkhali bar Tarikh-e Andisheh-ye Siyasi dar Eslam va Iran* (The Entry to the History of the Political Thoughts in Islam and Iran). Tehran: Farandish, 1381/2002.

    Falsafeh-ye Tajjadod dar Iran (The Philosophy of Modernity in Iran). Tehran: Amir Kabir, 1383/2004.

Naraqi, Hasan. "Az Koja Aghaz Konim" (Where Do We Begin From?), *Jame'h No*, Vol. 2, No. 18 (1382/2003), pp. 12–15.

Nargesi, Ramezan, *et al. Tabyeen-e Mardomsalari-ye Dini* (Analysis of Religious Democracy). Qom: Mo'asseseh-e Amozeshi va Pazhoheshi-e Emam Khomeini, 1383/2004.

Nasiri, Mehdi. *Eslam va Tajaddod* (Islam and Modernity). Tehran: Ketab-e Sobh, 1380/2001.

Nasri, Abdollah. *Gofteman-e Moderniteh: Negahi be Barkhi Jaryanha-ye Fekri-ye Mo'aser-e Iran* (Discourse of Modernity: A Survey of Iran's Contemporary Currents of Thoughts). Tehran: Nashr-e Farhang-e Eslami, 1382/2003.

Nikfar, Mohammadreza. "Akhlaq-e Eslah va Eslah-e Akhlaq" (The Morality of Reform and the Reform of Morality), *Aftab*, No. 8 (1380/2001), pp. 48–53.

"Tarh-e Yek Nazariyyeh-e Bioumi darbareh-ye Sekularizasion" (Proposing an Indigenous Theory of Secularization), *Aftab* No. 27 (1382/2003), pp. 128–39.

Norouzi, Mohammad Javad. *Daramadi bar Nezam-e Siyasi-e Eslam* (A Study of the Islamic Political System). Qom: Mo'asseseh-e Amozeshi va Pazhoheshi-e Emam Khomeini, 1380/2001.

Falsafeh-ye Siyasat (Philosophy of Politics). Qom: Mo'asseseh-e Amozeshi va Pazhoheshi-e Emam Khomeini, 1380/2001.

Nezam-e Siyasi-e Eslam (Islam's Political System). Qom: Mo'asseseh-e Amozeshi va Pazhoheshi-e Emam Khomeini, 1381/2002.

Nouri, 'Abdollah. *Naqdi baraye Tamam Fosoul* (A Critique for All Seasons). Tehran: Tarh-e No, 1378/1999.

Shoukaran-e Eslah (Hemlock for Advocate of Reform). Tehran: Tarh-e No, 1379/2000.

Nozari, Ezzatollah. *Tarikh-e Ahzab-e Siyasi dar Iran* (History of Political Parties in Iran). Shiraz: Navid-e Shiraz: 1380/2001.

Tarikhe Ejtema'i-ye Iran az Aghaz ta Mashrutiyyat (Social History of Iran from the Beginning to Constitutionalism). Tehran: Khojasteh, 1380/2001.

O'Donnell, Guillermo. "Delegative Democracies," *Journal of Democracy*, Vol. 5, No. 2 (January 1994), pp. 34–51.

'Omrani, Mahmood. "Ahkam-e Melli-Mazhabi-ha" (The Religious-Nationlists' Sentence), *Nameh*, No. 22 (1382/2003), pp. 7–8.

Pahlevan, Changiz. *Panj Goftego* (Five Conversations). Tehran: 'Atai, 1382/2003.

Panah, Khosrow. "Naqd-e Nazariyyeh-e Doktor Soroush" (Critique of Doctor Soroush's Theory), *Jame'h No*, Vol. 2, No. 13 (1381/2002), pp. 10–13.

Parishi, Mohammad Reza. "Bisavadi, Dard-e Tarikhi-ye Ma" (Illiteracy, Our Historic Pain), *Aftab*, No. 27 (1382/2003), pp. 176–77.

"Ma Iranian: Nesbat-e Melliyat va Mazhab dar Vaz'itat-e Modern" (We Iranians: The Relationship of Nationality and Religion in the Modern Era), *Aftab*, No. 8 (1380/2001), pp. 16–19.

Pedram, Mas'oud. "Demokrasi-e Asil, Gofego dar 'Arseh-ye 'Omoomi" (Authentic Democracy, Discussion in the Public Domain), *Aftab*, No. 10 (1380/2001), pp. 8–11.

"Jaye Khali-ye Nazariyeh-e Roshanfekri-ye Dini" (The Empty Place of the Theory of Religious Intellectualism), *Aftab*, No. 29 (1382/2003), p. 138.

"Jabejai-ye Eslahat az 'Arseh-e 'Omoomi be Qalamro-e Hokumati" (Replacing Reforms from the Public Domain to the Ruling System), *Nameh*, No. 1/16 (1381/2002), pp. 39–41.

"Daramadi bar Mabani-ye Nazari-ye Jonbesh-e Dovvom-e Khordad" (A Look at the Theoretical Principles of the Second of Khordad Movement), *Aftab*, No. 14 (1381/2002), pp. 6–7.

Roshanfekran-e Dini va Moderniteh dar Iran Pas az Enqelab (Religious Intellectuals and Modernity in Iran after the Revolution). Tehran: Gam-e No, 1382/2003.

"Tahavvol-e Soratbandi-ye Oposision dar Iran" (Changes in the Composition of Opposition in Iran), *Nameh*, No. 22 (1382/2003), pp. 36–37.

Peyman, Habibollah. "Jame'h Madani va Andisheh-ye Dini" (Civil Society and Religious Thought), *Aftab*, No. 13 (1380/2001), pp. 32–35.

"Chera Melli? Cher Mazhabi?" (Why Nationalist? Why Religious?), *Cheshmandaz-e Iran*, No. 20 (1382/2003), pp. 74–91.

"'Elm, Din va Zarorat-e Touse'h 'Aqlaniyat-e Modern" (Science, Religion, and the Need for Developing Modern Rationality), *Aftab*, No. 25 (1382/2003), pp. 92–7.

"Estebdad-e Roshanfekri" (Intellectual Autocracy), *Jame'h No*, Vol. 2, No. 14 (1382/2003), pp. 6–9.

"Roshanfekran Zir-e Tigh-e Naqd" (Intellectuals under Critical Blade), *Jame'h No*, Vol. 2, No. 15 (1382/2003), pp. 10–13.

"Rahbord-haye Pishro-e Mardomsalrai, Solh-Talabi" (Ways to Expand Democracy, Peacefulness), *Aftab*, No. 24 (1382/2003), pp. 8–15.

"Tangna-haye Nazari va Rahbordi-e Jonbesh-e Eslah-talabi" (Methodological and Ideological Shortcomings of the Reform Movement), *Aftab*, No. 34 (1383/2004), pp. 8–15.

Piran, Parviz. "Ta'sir-e Shebhe Modernism bar Jonbesh-haye Ejtama'i dar Iran" (The Influence of Pseudo-Modernism on Social Movements in Iran), *Aftab*, No. 16 (1381/2002), pp. 36–37.

"Shoresh-haye Tamam-e Khalqi 'Amel-e Taghirat-e Sathi" (Mass-Based Movements Causes of Superficial Changes), *Aftab*, No. 16 (1381/2002), pp. 36–39.

"Jonbesh-haye Ejtema'i-ye Shahri ba Nokati be Sharayet-e Iran: Jam'-bandiye Naha-ee va Nokati Chand dar Payan" (Urban Social Movements and a Few Points on Iran's Conditions: Final Analysis and a Few Concluding Points), *Aftab*, No. 27 (1382/2003), pp. 60–3.

"Za'f-e Nazari; Pashneh-ye Ashil-e Jonbesh-e Eslahtalabi" (Theoretical Weakness; The Achilles' Heel of the Reform Movement), *Aftab*, No. 33 (1382/2003), pp. 52–55.

Qabel, Ahmad. "Ba Din be Demokrasi Miresim?" (Do We Reach Democracy through Religion?), *Jame'h No*, Vol. 1, No. 11 (1381/2002), pp. 6–9.

Naqd-e Farhang-e Khoshunat: Khoshunat-e Siyasi va Taffakor-e Sonnati (Critique of Culture of Violence: Political Violence and Traditional Thought). Tehran: Saraee 1381/2002.

"Demokrasi ba In Qanun-e Asasi" (Democracy with this Constitution), *Jame'h No*, Vol. 2, No. 14 (1382/2003), pp. 14–15.

Qaderi, Hatam, "Naqd-e Siyasat-e E'tedal" (Critique of Politics of Moderation), *Aftab*, No. 11 (1380/2001), pp. 8–13.

"Naqd-i bar Roshanfekri-ye Dini" (A Critique of Religious Intellectualism), *Nameh*, No. 20 (1381/2002), pp. 42–44.

Qahari, Nezamolddin. "Shoura-haye Mardomi: 'Eyniyyat-e Kamel-e Mardomsalari" (People's Councils: Mirror Image of Democracy), *Aftab*, No. 22 (1381/2002), pp. 56–59.

Qane'irad, Mohammad Amin. *Tabarshenasi-e 'Aqlaniyyat-e Modern: Qara't-i Postmodern az Andisheh-ye Dr. Ali Shariati* (Geneology of Modern Rationality: A Post-Modern Take on the Thoughts of Dr. Ali Shariati). Tehran: Naqd-e Farhang, 1381/2002.

Qasemi, Ali Haji. "Eslahat; Ravandi baraye Hame Fosoul" (Reforms: A Process for all Seasons), *Aftab*, No. 33 (1382/2003), pp. 4–9.

Qazi Moradi, Hasan. *Dar Piramoun-e Khodmadari-e Iranian* (Concerning the Self-Centeredness of Iranians). Tehran: Akhtaran, 1380/2001.

Estebdad dar Iran (Autocracy in Iran). Tehran: Akhtaran, 1380/2001.

Qezelsofla, Mohammad Taqi. *Qarn-e Roshanfekran* (The Intellectuals' Century). Tehran: Harmas, 1380/2001.

Qoochani, Mohammad. *Bazi-e Bozorgan: Negari-e Jonbesh-e Eslahat-e Demokratik dar Iran* (The Elites' Game: Recording the Democratic Reform Movement in Iran). Tehran: Jame'eh Iranian, 1378/1999.

Do Gam beh Pish Yek Gam beh Pas: Vaqaye' Negari-e Jonbesh-e Eslahat-e Demokratik dar Iran (Two Steps Forward One Step Back: Recording the Democratic Reform Movement in Iran). Tehran: Jame'eh Iranian, 1378/ 1999.

Dowlat-e Dini va Din-e Dowlati (Religious Government and Government's Religion). Tehran: Saraee 1379/2000.

Yaqeh Sefid-ha: Jame'hshenasi-e Nahad-haye Madani dar Iran-e Emrouz (White Collars: Sociology of Civil Organizations in Today's Iran). Tehran: Naqsh-o Negar, 1379/2000.

Jomhuri-ye Moqaddas: Boresh-haee az Tarikh-e Jomhuri-ye Eslami (The Holy Republic: Pieces of the History of the Islamic Republic). Tehran: Naqsh-o Negar, 1381/2002.

Filsof-ha va Shoman-ha (Philosophers and Showmen). Tehran: Saraee 1382/ 2003.

Qoreishi, Fardin. "Tahrir va Tabyeen-e Bazsazi-e Indisheh-e Dini" (The Writing and Elaboration of the Reconstruction of Religious Thought), *Aftab*, No. 22 (1381/2002), pp. 70–77.

Bazsazi-ye Andisheh-ye Dini dar Iran (The Reconstruction of Religious Thought in Iran). Tehran: Qasideh Sara, 1384/2005.

Rahbar, Mohammad. "Hezbollah va Enteqad az Khod" (Hezbollah and Self-Criticism), *Jame'h No*, Vol. 1, No. 7 (1381/2002), p. 7.

Rahimian, Saeed. *Hoviyyat-e Falsafeh-ye Eslami* (The Nature of Islamic Philosophy). Qom: Bustan-e Ketab, 1383/2004.

Rahiminezhad, Morteza. "Negah-i Digar be Jonbesh-e Eslahat dar Iran" (Another Look at the Reform Movement in Iran), *Aftab*, No. 14 (1381/ 2002), pp. 66–67.

Rahmani, Mohtaram. "Roshanfekr Tolidkonandeh Ast" (The Intellectual Is a Producer), *Jame'h No*, Vol. 1, No. 9 (1381/2002), pp. 16–17.

"Aseeb-shenasi-ye Jaryan-haye Roshanfekri dar Iran" (Studying the Flaws of Intellectual Trends in Iran), *Aftab*, No. 27 (1382/2003), pp. 96–97.

Rahmani, Taqi. "Melli-Mazhabi, Nirou-ye Mobarez va Movvaled" (Religious-Nationalist, A Fighting and Productive Force), *Cheshmandaz-e Iran*, No. 18 (1381/2002), pp. 81–92.

"Moskel-e Tashakkol dar Iran" (The Difficulty of Organizing in Iran), *Jame'h No*, Vol. 2, No. 13 (1381/2002), pp. 18–19.

Naqqadi-ye Qodrat: Mavane'e Nazari-ye Esteqrar-e Demokrasi dar Iran (Critique of Power: Subjective Obstacles to the Establishment of Democracy in Iran). Tehran: Saraee 1381/2002.

"Nesbat-e Din ba 'Aqlaniyat-e Taqaboli ya Ta'amoli" (The Relations between Religion and Oppositional or Conciliatory Rationalism," *Aftab*, No. 20 (1381/2002), pp. 72–73.

"Goshudan-e In Gereh-e Forubasteh" (Opening this Internal Knot), *Aftab*, No. 25 (1382/2003), pp. 16–17.

Rahnema, Ali. *An Islamic Utopian: A Political Biography of Ali Shari'ati*. London: I. B. Tauris, 1998.

Rajabi, Fatemeh. *Eslahtalabi: Kandokavi dar Khwastgah va Ahdaf* (Reformism: An Exploration of Goals and Objectives). Tehran: Sobh, 1380/2001.

Rouhaniyyat Setizi dar tarish-e Mo'aser-e Iran (Anti-Clericalism in Contemporary Iranian History). Tehran: Amir Kabir, 1383/2004.

Rajabi, Mehdi. "Eslahtalaban bar Sar-e Dorahi" (Reformists at the Crossroads), *Aftab*, No. 25 (1382/2003), pp. 120–22.

"Barresi-e Tahlili-e Raftar-e Entekhabati-e Mardom" (An Analysis of the People's Voting Behavior), *Aftab*, No. 33 (1382/2003), pp. 16–23.

"Postreformism va Jonbesh-e Mardomsalari-Khahi" (Post-reformism and the Democratization Movement), *Aftab*, No. 34 (1383/2004), pp. 16–21.

Rajaee, 'Alireza. "Zaval-e Dowlat-e Estesnaee" (Destruction of the Special Government), *Aftab*, No. 10 (1380/2001), pp. 18–19.

"Arzyabi-ye Noirouha-ye Melli-Mazhabi dar Bastar-e Tahavvolat-e Ejtema'i" (Evaluating Religious-Nationalist Forces in Light of Social Changes), *Cheshmandaz-e Iran*, No. 16 (1381/2002), pp. 24–27.

"Payan-e Yek Nasl, Aghaz-e Roshanfekri-e Dini" (End of One Generation, the Start of Religious Intellectualism), *Aftab*, No. 14 (1381/2002), p. 25.

Rajaee, Farhang. *Andisheh-e Siyasi-e Mo'aser dar Jahan-e Arab* (Contemporary Political Thought in the Arab World). Tehran: Markaz-e Pazhohesh-haye 'Elmi va Motale 'at-e Estratezhik-e Khavarmiyaneh, 1381/2002.

Moshkeleh-e Hoviyyat-e Iranian-e Emrouz: Eefa-ye Naqsh dar 'Asr-e Yek Tamaddon va Chand Farhang (The Problematic of Contemporary Iranian Identity: Participating in the World of One Civilization and Many Cultures). Tehran: Nashr-e Ney, 1382/2003.

Ranani, Mohsen. "Tanasob dar Eqtedar" (Balance in Power), *Aftab*, No. 19 (1381/2002), pp. 12–17.

Rasaqi, Sohrab. "Jame'h Iran, Kodam Jeshmandaz" (Iranian Society, Which Perspective), *Aftab*, No. 25 (1382/2003), pp. 28–35.

Rashtian, Saeed. "Demokrasi-ye Irani" (Iranian Democracy), *Nameh*, No. 24 (1382/2003), pp. 5–7.

Razavi, Mas'oud. *Motefakeran-e Mo'aser va Endisheh-ye Siyasi-e Eslam* (Contemporary Thinkers and Islamic Political Thought). Tehran: Farzan-e Ruz, 1378/1999.

Jame'h Madani, Dovvom-e Khordad, va Khamati (Civil Society, Second of Khordad, and Khatami). Tehran: Farzan-e Ruz, 1379/2000.

Roshanfekran, Ahzab, va Manaf'e Melli (Intellectuals, Parties, and National Interests). Tehran: Farzan-e Ruz, 1379/2000.

"Chera-iye Yek Gosast: Hoviyyat-yabie Jonbesh-e Daneshjoee" (Analysis of a Rupture: The Identity of the Student Movement), *Nameh*, No. 24 (1382/2003), pp. 33–36.

Razavi Faqih, Saeed. "Fiqh, Maslahat va Hokumat" (Theology, Expediency and Government), *Aftab*, No. 2 (1379/2000), pp. 52–59.

"Nesbat-e Fiqh va Hekmat ba Hokumat az Nazar-e Farabi" (Farabi's View on the Relationship between Theology and Philosophy with Government), *Aftab*, No. 4 (1380/2001), pp. 68–73.

"Mafhoum-e Roshanfekri-ye Dini" (The Meaning of Religious Intellectualism), *Aftab*, No. 27 (1382/2003), pp. 78–79.

Razjo, Koshan. "Tarh-i baraye Taharrok-e Eslahat" (A Plan for the Reform Movement), *Aftab*, No. 22 (1381/2002), pp. 4–13.

Renani, Mohsen. "Soqut-e Sarmayeh-e Ejtama'i" (The Collapse of Social Capital), *Aftab*, No. 16 (1381/2002), pp. 26–35.

Rezaee, Amir. "Dindari-e 'Aqlani-e Elhami" (Rational Revealed Religiosity), *Aftab*, No. 33 (1382/2003), pp. 88–89.

Rezaqoli, Ali. *Jame'hshenasi-e Nokhbeh-koshi* (Sociology of Elite-killing). Tehran: Ney, 1377/1998.

Rohani, Hasan. "Mafhoum-e Jadid-e Hakemiyat-e Melli ya Farsayesh-e Hakemiyat-ha" (The New Meaning of National Sovereignty or Erosion of Sovereignty), *Hokumat Eslami*, Vol. 8, No. 2 (1382/2003), pp. 13–41.

Roodi, Zahra. *Naqd-e Yek Roydad* (Comment on an Event). Tehran: Ney, 1378/1999.

Baha-ye Azadi: Defa'iyat-e Mohsen Kadivar dar Dadgah-e Vizhe (Price of Freedom: Mohsen Kadivar's Defense in the Special Court). Tehran: Ney, 1379/2000.

Roshno, Nabiollah. *Zhe'opolitik-e Nokhbegan* (The Geopolitics of Elites). Tehran: Kavir, 1382/2003.

Rostami, Jalal. "Talash-e Dobareh Baraye Khod Mehvarsazi-e Roshanfekri-e Dini" (Another Effort for the Rationalization of Religious Intellectuals), *Aftab*, No. 34 (1383/2004), p. 122.

Rostami, Mas'oud. "'Aqlaniyyat, Demokrasi, Totalitarism" (Rationality, Democracy, Totalitarianism), *Aftab*, No. 34 (1383/2004), pp. 108–11.

Saber, Hada. "Melli-Mazhabi; Douran-e Vahdat dar Ein-e Tazad" (Religious-Nationalist; Time for Unity aginst Tension), *Cheshmandaz-e Iran*, No. 18 (1381/2002), pp. 34–42.

"Talash-i Rahbordi dar 'Arseh-e Ejtema'-e Dini" (Strategic Efforts in the Arena of Religious Society), *Cheshmandaz-e Iran*, No. 19 (1382/2003), pp. 54–67.

Sachedina, Abdulaziz Abdulhussein. *The Just Ruler in Shi'ite Islam: The Comprehensive Authority of the Jurist in Imamate Jurisprudence*. Oxford: Oxford University Press, 1988.

Sadeqi, Hadi. "Mardomsalari-ye Dini va Mardomsalari-ye Liberal" (Religious Democracy and Liberal Democracy), *Aftab*, No. 25 (1382/2003), pp. 116–17.

"Hekmat-e Mottahari ya 'Hekmat-e Mottahar'?" (Mottahari's Philosophy or Cleansed Philosophy?), *Aftab*, No. 34 (1383/2004), pp. 56–9.

Sadeqipanah, Hasan. "Emamiyeh va Siyasat" (The Imamate and Politics), *Aftab*, No. 25 (1382/2003), pp. 118–19.

Sadiqi, Nader. "Jomhuri, Eslami, Irani" (Republican, Islamic, Iranian), *Aftab*, No. 14 (1381/2002), pp. 8–9.

Sadri, Ahmad. *Mafhoom-e Tammadon va Lozoom-e Ehya-ye an dar 'Oloome Ejtma'i* (The Meaning of Civilization and the Necessity of its Restoration in the Social Sciences). Tehran: Harams, 1380/2001.

Sadri, Mahmoud and Ahmad Sadri. *Reason, Freedom, and Democracy in Islam: The Essential Writings of Abdolkarim Soroush*. Oxford: Oxford University Press, 2000.

Saeedi Rezvani, Hadi. "Vaqe'h-ye 'Ashura va Iran-e Mo'aser" (The Ashura Event and Contemporary Iran), *Aftab*, No. 33 (1382/2003), pp. 74–79.

Safar Dastgerdi, Mehdi and Hamed Haji Heydari. "Jomhuri-ye Doganeh" (The Double-Sided Republic), *Aftab*, No. 17 (1381/2002), pp. 120–21.

Sahebi, Mohammad Javad. *Andisheh-ye Eslahi dar Nehzat-haye Eslami* (Reformist Thought in Islamic Movements). Qom: Daftar-e Tablighat-e Eslami, 1367/1988.

Mabani-ye Nehzat-e Ehya-ye Fekr-e Dini (The Foundations of Religious Thought Revival Movement). Qom: Bustan-e Ketab, 1380/2001.

Sahhabi, 'Ezzatollah. "Marahel Takvin-e Qeshri-negari va 'Avarez-e Ejtema'i-e An" (Stages of the Appearance of Fanaticism and its Social Consequences), *Cheshmandaz-e Iran*, No. 15 (1381/2002), pp. 43–48.

"Arzyabi-ye Noirouha-ye Melli-Mazhabi dar Bastar-e Tahavvolat-e Ejtema'i" (Evaluating Religious-Nationalist Forces in Light of Social Changes), *Cheshmandaz-e Iran*, No. 16 (1381/2002), pp. 12–20.

"Arzyabi-ye Noirouha-ye Melli-Mazhabi dar Bastar-e Tahavvolat-e Ejtema'i" (Evaluating Religious-Nationalist Forces in Light of Social Changes), *Cheshmandaz-e Iran*, No. 17 (1381/2002), pp. 14–22.

Salar, Sara. "Eslahgari ya Shakkakiyat-e Luther ya Hume" (Reformism or the Skepticism of Luther or Hume), *Aftab*, No. 12 (1380/2001), pp. 52–53.

Salasi, Mohsen. *Jahan-e Irani va Iran-e Jahan* (Iran's World and the World's Iran). Tehran: Markaz, 1379/2000.

Salehi, Mohsen. "Tabo and 'Aqlaniyyat-e Modern" (Taboo and New Rationality), *Aftab*, No. 15 (1381/2002), pp. 58–61.

"Vorud-e Mafahim-e Modern" (Entry of New Concepts), *Aftab*, No. 22 (1381/2002), pp. 86–89.

Salehi Najafabadi, Ne'matollah. "'Aqlaniyyat-e Ideolozhik" (Ideological Rationality), *Aftab*, No. 27 (1382/2003), pp. 124–27.

Shahid-e Javid (The Eternal Martyr). Tehran: Omid-e Farda, 1382/2003.

Salimi, Hosein. *Kalbodshekafi-e Zehniyyat-e Eslahgarayan* (Anatomy of the Reformists' Mindset). Tehran: Gam-e No, 1384/2005.

Same'ee, Ahmad. *Doktrin-e Khatami dar Goftego-ye Tamaddon-ha va Farhang-ha* (Khatami's Doctrine on the Dialogue of Civilizations and Cultures). Tehran: Chekad, 1380/2001.

San'ati, Reza. *Mesbah-e Dostan* (Mesbah of Friends). Tehran: Homa-ye Ghadir, 1383/2004.

Saqafi, Morad. "Kodam Mardomsalari" (Which Democracy?), *Aftab*, No. 23 (1381/2002), pp. 34–35.

   "Rast: Ta'amol ya Taqabol" (Right: Corporation or Opposition), *Nameh*, No. 19 (1381/2002), pp. 6–10.

Sardarabadi, Khalilollah. "Jahani-shodan dar Qalamro-ve Siyasat va Farhang-e Siyasi" (Globalization in relation to Politics and Political Culture), *Aftan*, No. 20 (1381/2002), pp. 46–51.

Sariolghalam, Mahmood. *'Aqlaniyyat va Ayandeh-e Tose'eh-yaftegi-ye Iran* (Rationality and the Future of Iran's Development). Tehran: Center for Scientific Research and Middle East Strategic Studies, 1382/2003.

Schirazi, Asghar. *The Constitution of Iran: Politics and the State in the Islamic Republic*. Trans. John O'Kane. London: I. B. Tauris, 1998.

Seyyed Kabbari, 'Alireza. *Howzeh-haye 'Elmi-ye Shi'a dar Gostareh-ye Jahan* (Shi'a Seminaries throughout the World). Tehran: Amir Kabir, 1378/1999.

Shafifi, Shariyar. "Mabani-e Falsafi-e Jonbesh-e Eslahgari" (Philosophical Principles of the Reform Movement), *Aftab*, No. 33 (1382/2003), pp. 84–87.

Shafi'i, Naser. *Jame'h Madani, dar Kodamin Negah?* (Civil Society, From which Outlook?). Tehran: Honarsara-ye Andisheh, 1378/1999.

Shahbazi, Mahbob. *Taqdir-e Mardomsalari: Naqsh-e Entakhabat dar Ravand-e Demokrasi-ye Iran* (Democracy's Fate: The Role of Elections in Iran's Democracy). Tehran: Rouzaneh, 1380/2001.

Shahrestani, Bijan. "Demokrasi-e Dini, Naqd-e Yek Santez" (Religious Democracy: Critique of a Synthesis), *Aftab*, No. 24 (1382/2003), pp. 86–89.

Shakuri, Abolfazl. *Fiqh-e Siyasi-e Eslam* (Islamic Political Theology). Qom: Howzeh Elmiyeh, 1377/1998.

Shamsolva'ezin, Mashallah. *Yaddasht-haye Sardabir* (Editor's Notes). Tehran: Jame'h Iranian, 1379/2000.

   "Tamas Miyan-e Layeh-haye 'Aql-garye Do Jenah" (Contact between the Intellectual Sectors of Both Fronts), *Aftab*, No. 10 (1380/2001), pp. 16–17.

Sharfi, 'Abdolmajid. *'Asri Sazi-e Andisheh-ye Dini* (Co-Temporizing Religious Thought). Trans. Mohammad Amjad. Tehran: Naqed, 1382/2003.

Shariati, Ali. *Hobut dar Kavir* (Descent in the Desert). Tehran: Ferdowsi, 1361/1982.

   Baz-shenasi-e Hoviyyat-e Irani-Eslami (Re-Discovering the Iranian-Islamic Identity). Tehran: Elham, 1371/1992.

   "Aghaz-e Dobareh-ye Tarikh" (The Restart of History), *Aftab*, No. 261 (1382/2003), pp. 12–13.

Sharif, Mohammad Reza. *Enqelab-e Aram: Daramadi bar Tahavvol-e Farhang-e Siyasi dar Iran* (The Quiet Revolution: A Look at the Changes to Political Culture in Iran). Tehran: Rouzaneh, 1381/2002.

Sharif Musavi, Mohammad Hasan. "Sekularism az Manzar-i Dihar" (Secularism from another Perspective), *Aftab*, No. 14 (1381/2002), pp. 64–65.

Shayegan, Daryush. *Cultural Schizophrenia: Islamic Societies Confronting the West*. Syracuse, NY: Syracuse University Press, 1992.

Asia darbarabar-e Gharb (Asia Faces the West). Tehran: Amir Kabir, 1378/ 1999.

Bot-haye Zehni va Khatereh-ye Azali (Idols of the Mind and Perennial Memory). Tehran: Amir Kabir, 1381/2002.

Shayesteh, Fereydun. "Negah-i Digar be Jonbesh-e Eslahtalabi" (Another Look at the Reformist Movement), *Aftab*, No. 17 (1381/2002), p. 122.

Sheikhavandi, Davar. "Din-e Azadi-bakh Noushdaro-ye Mardom Ast" (Liberating Religion is the People's Antidote), *Jame'h Salem*, Vol. 8, No. 40 (1377/1998), pp. 10–12.

Sheikhfarshi, Farhad. *Tahlili bar Naqsh-e Siyasi-ey 'Aleman-e Shi'a dar Peydayesh-e Enqelab-e Elmai* (An Analysis of the Political Role of Shi'a Scholars in the Appearance of the Islamic Revolution). Tehran: Markaz-e Asnad-e Enqelab-e Eslami, 1379/2000.

Roshanfekri-e Dini va Enqelab-e Eslami (Religious Intellectuality and the Islamic Revolution). Tehran: Markaz-e Asnad-e Enqelab-e Eslami, 1381/2002.

Shils, Edward. *The Intellectuals and the Power and Other Essays*. Chicago, IL: University of Chicago Press, 1972.

Shoja'izand, 'Alireza. *Din, Jame'h va 'Orfi Shodan* (Religion, Society, and Secularization). Tehran: Markaz, 1380/2001.

"Din-e Ensan" (Human's Religion), *Aftab*, No. 15 (1381/2002), pp. 62–67.

Takapoo-haye Din-e Siyasi (Efforts of Political Religion). Tehran: Baz, 1383/ 2004.

Solhjou, Ali. *Gofteman va Tarjomeh* (Discourse and Translation). Tehran: Markaz, 1377/1998.

Soltani, Ebrahim. "Dinshenasi-e Abdolkarim Soroush" (The Religious Knowledge of Abdolkarim Soroush), *Aftab*, No. 1 (1379/2000), pp. 50–59.

Soroush, Abdolkarim. *'Elm Chist, Falsafeh Chist?* (What is Science, What is Philosophy?). Tehran: Sarat, 1368/1989.

Farbeh-tar az Ideolozhi (Healthier than Ideology). Tehran: Sarat, 1372/1993.

Hekman va Ma'ishat, Volumes I–II (Philosophy and Life). Tehran: Sarat, 1373/1994.

Ideolozhi-ye Sheytani (Satanic Ideology). Tehran: Sarat, 1373/1994.

Qabz va Bast-e Te'orik-e Shari'at: Nazariyyeh Takamol Ma'refat-e Dini (The Expansion and Contraction of Theory of *Shari'ah*: Analyzing the Evolution of Religious Knowledge). Tehran: Sarat, 1374/1995.

Hadis-e bandegi va Delbordegi (The Story of Slavery and Love). Tehran: Sarat, 1375/1996.

Darsha-ee dar Salsafe-ye 'Elm al-ejtema'a (Raveshe Tafsir dar Oloom-e Ejtema'i) (Lessons in Philosophy of Science of Society [Analytical Method in Social Sciences]). Tehran: Ney, 1376/1997.

Modara va Modiriyyat (Moderation and Administration). Tehran: Sarat, 1376/1997.

Raz-dani va Roshanfekri va Din-dari (Knowing Secrets and Intellectualism and Religiosity). Tehran: Sarat, 1377/1998.

Bast-e Tajrobe-ye Nabavi (Expansion of the Prophetic Experience). Tehran: Sarat, 1378/1999.

Sert-haye Mostaqim (Straight Paths). Tehran: Sarat, 1378/1999.

Nahad-e Naaran-e Jahan (The World's Tumultuous Nature). Tehran: Sarat, 1378/1999.

Siyasat-Nameh (Political Treatise). Sarat, 1378/1999.

A'in-e Shahriyari va Dindari (Rules of Sovereignty and Religiosity). Tehran: Sarat, 1379/2000.

Qomar-e 'Asheqaneh (A Loving Gamble). Tehran: Sarat, 1379/2000.

Taffaroj-e San' (The Pleasure of Creation). Tehran: Sarat, 1379/2000.

"Tose'h 'Elmi, Tose'h Siyasi" (Scientific Development, Political Development), *Kiyan*, Vol. 10, No. 54 (1379/2000), pp. 32–37.

Akhlaq-e Khodayan (The Morality of Gods). Tehran: Tarh-e No, 1380/2001.

Soroush, 'Abdolkarim. "Bi Rangi va Tabandegi" (Colorlessness and Illuminance), *Aftab*, No. 7 (1380/2001), pp. 66–73.

"Rang va Bi Rangi" (Color and Colorlessness), *Aftab*, No. 8 (1380/2001), pp. 40–47.

"Ayeneh-haye Bi Zangar" (Mirrors without Rust), *Aftab*, No. 9 (1380/2001), pp. 58–63.

"Bi Karanegi va Hesar-ha" (Openness and Fences), *Aftab*, No. 10 (1380/2001), pp. 62–69.

"Sekularism" (Secularism), *Aftab*, No. 11 (1380/2001), pp. 54–59.

"Mahdaviyyat va Ehya-e Din" (Divine Guidance and Religious Revival), *Aftab*, No. 12 (1380/2001), pp. 60–63.

"Din va Donya-ye Jadid" (Religion and the New World), *Aftab*, No. 13 (1380/2001), pp. 48–55.

"Eslam, Vahy va Nobovvat" (Islam, Revelation, and Prophecy), *Aftab*, No. 15 (1381/2002), pp. 68–79.

"Jame'h Madani, Jame'h Akhlaqi" (Civil Society, Moral Society), *Aftab*, No. 18 (1381/2002), pp. 68–73.

"Naqd-e Akhlaqi-e Qodrat" (Moral Critique of Power), *Aftab*, No. 23 (1382/2003), pp. 76–81.

Soroush, 'Abdolkarim. "Azadi-ye Bayan" (Freedom of Expression), *Aftab*, No. 24 (1382/2003), pp. 62–69.

"Azadi-ye Bayan, Haqq-e Ezhar-e Nazar va Ebraz-e 'Aqideh" (Freedom of Speech, the Right to Thought and Opinion), *Aftab*, No. 25 (1382/2003), pp. 74–79.

Soroush, 'Abdolkarim, *et al. Sonnat va Sekularism* (Tradition and Secularism). Tehran: Sarat, 1381/2002.

Andarbab-e Ejtehad (Concerning Ijtihad). Tehran: Tarh-e No, 1382/2003.

Soroush, Ali. *Shariati va Dialektik-e Mobarezeh* (Shariati and the Dialectic of Struggle). Tehran: Bozorgmehr, 1378/1999.

Soroush, Mohammad. *Din va Dowlat dar Andisheh-ye Eslami* (Religion and Politics in Islamic Thought). Qom: Howzeh Elmiyeh, 1378/1999.

Tabataba'i, Mohammad Hosein. *Osoul-e Falsafeh va Ravesh-e Re'alism* (Principles of Philosophy and Methods of Realism). Tehran: Sadra, 1362/1983.

Shi'a dar Eslam (Shi'ism in Islam). Qom: Daroltafsir, 1379/2000.

Zohour-e Shi'a (The Appearance of Shi'ism). Tehran: Shari'at, n.d.

Shi'a: Mozakerat va Mokatebat-e Professor Henry Corbin ba 'Allameh Seyyed Mohammad Hosein Tabataba'i (Shi'ah: Les Entretiens et les

Correspondances de Professor Henry Corbin avec 'Allamah Tabataba'i).
Tehran: Iranian Institute of Philosophy, 1382/2003.

Tabataba'i, Seyyed Javad. *Daramadi Falsafi bar Tarikh-e Andisheh-e Siyasi dar Iran* (A Philosophical Look at Political Thought in Iran). Tehran: Kavir, 1374/1995.

Mafhum-e Velayat-e Mutlaq dar Andisheh-haye Siyasi-e Sadeh-haye Miyaneh (The Meaning of Absolute Velayat in the Political Thought of the Middle Ages). Tehran: Negah-e Mo'aser, 1380/2001.

"Iran, Ayandeh-ee Motefavet" (Iran, A Different Future), *Nameh*, No. 24 (1382/2003), pp. 11–14.

Zaval-e Andisheh-e Siyasi dar Iran (Paucity of Political Thought in Iran). Tehran: Kavir, 1838/2004.

Tahmasebi, 'Ali. " 'Noandishi-ye Dini': Chalesh-haye Emrouz va Bohran-haye Farda" (Religious Modernism: Today's Efforts and Tomorrow's Crisis), *Nameh*, No. 16 (1381/2002), pp. 70–72.

Tajik, Mohammad Reza. *Tajrobeh-ye Bazi-ye Siyasi dar Miyan-e Iranian* (The Experience of Political Game among Iranians). Tehran: Ney, 1382/2003.

Daheh-ye Sevvom (The Third Decade). Tehran: Farhang-e Gofteman, 1383/2004.

Gofteman, Pad Gofteman va Siyasat (Discourse, Counter-Discourse and Politics). Tehran: Mo'asseseh-e Tahqiqat va Touse'h-e 'Oloom-e Ensani, 1383/2004.

Tajzadeh, Mostafa. "Chahar Rahbord-e Jonbesh-e Eslahat" (The Four Methodologies of the Reform Movement), *Aftab*, No. 11 (1380/2001), pp. 14–21.

Dar Defa' az Entekhabat-e Azad va 'Adelaneh (In Defense of Free and Fair Elections). Tehran: Farhang va Andisheh, 1381/2002.

"Emam Parchamdar-e Jomhuriyyat dar Iran: Naqdi bar nazariyeh-e Hokumat-e Entesabi" (Emam the Flagbearer of Republicanism in Iran: A Critique of Appointed Government), *Aftab*, No. 16 (1381/2002), pp. 8–13.

Siyasat, Kakh va Zendan (Politics, Palace, and Prison). Tehran: Zekr, 1381/2002.

"Enqelab Mashroteh va Rohaniyyat" (The Constitutional Revolution and the Clergy), *Aftab*, No. 25 (1382/2003), pp. 8–15.

Tavvakoli, Khaled. "Vafaq-e Melli va Hoviyyat-e Tahmili" (National Conciliation and Imposed Identity), *Nameh*, No. 17 (1381/2002), pp. 28–30.

"Demokrasi va Tamarkoz-zedaee Qomi" (Democracy and Tribal Decentralization), *Nameh*, No. 24 (1382/2003), pp. 39–41.

Tavvasoli, Gholamabbas. "Jame'h Madani, Qodrat-e Rant-khar va Sakhtar-haye Penhan" (Civil Society, Rentier Power and Hidden Institutions), *Aftab*, No. 34 (1383/2004), pp. 42–51.

Tavvasoli, Mohammad. "Hoviyyat-e Melli va Dini; Tekiyeh-gahe Tarikhi-ye Mellat-e Iran" (Religious-Nationalist Identity; Historic Support-base of the Iranian Nation), *Cheshmandaz-e Iran*, No. 18 (1381/2002), pp. 31–3.

Va'ezi, Ahmad. *Hokumat-e Dini: Ta'moli dar Andisheh-ye Siyasi-e Eslam* (Religious Government: A Look at Islamic Political Thought). Tehran: Mersad, 1378/1999.

Va'ezi, Hasan. *Eslahat va Foroupashi: Tashrih-e Tarh-e Bazsazi-shodeh-ye Foroupashi-e Shoravi dar Iran* (Reforms and Collapse: Surveys of a Reenactment of the Soviet-Style Collapse in Iran). Tehran: Soroush, 1379/2000.

Vahdat, Farzin. *God and Juggernaut: Iran's Intellectual Encounter with Modernity.* Syracuse, NY: Syracuse University Press, 2002.

Vahed-e Motale'at va Tahqiqat-e Farhangi. *Seyr-e Tafakkor-e Jadid dar Jahan va Iran* (The Path of Modern Thought in the World and in Iran). Tehran: Halal, 1382/2003.

Vahid, Madgid. *Siyasat-gozari va Farhang dar Iran-e Emrouz* (Policy and Culture in Iran). Tehran: Baz, 1382/2003.

Vali-Pourkalani, 'Ezatollah. *Shoukaran-e Eslah: Dar Botteh-ye Naqd* (Hemlock for Advocate of Reform: Under Critique), Qom: Zafar, 1380/2001.

Yarshater, Ehsar, ed. *Encyclopedia Iranica,* Volume I. London: Routledge & Kegan Paul, 1985.

Vasiq, Sheydan. *Laicism Cheest?* (What is Laicism?). Tehran: Akhtaran, 1384/2005.

Wright, Robin. *The Last Great Revolution: Turmoil and Transformation in Iran.* New York: Vintage, 2001.

Wuthnow, Robert. *Communities of Discourse: Ideology and Social Structure in the Reformation, the Enlightenment, and European Socialism.* Cambridge, MA: Harvard University Press, 1989.

Yaghmaian, Behzad. *Social Change in Iran: An Eyewitness Account of Dissent, Defiance, and New Movements for Rights.* Albany, NY: SUNY Press, 2002.

Yathrebi, Yahya. *Majara-ye Qamangiz-e Roshanfekri dar Iran* (Tragic Adventure of Enlightenment in Iran). Tehran: Danesh va Andisheh Mo'aser, 1379/2000.

Yazdani, Abbas. *Gofteman-e Hokumat-e Dini* (The Discourse of Religious Government). Qom: Farhang-e Teh, 1378/1999.

Yazdi, Ebrahim. *Se Jomhuri* (Three Republics). Tehran: Jame'h Iranian, 1379/2000.

"Mardomsalari va Roshanfekri-ye Dini" (Democracy and Religious Intellectualism), *Aftab,* No. 22 (1381/2002), p. 23.

"Mavane'-e Tahaqqoq-e Hoquq-e Bashar dar Keshvar-haye Eslami" (Obstacles to the Realization of Human Rights in Islamic Countries), *Aftab,* No. 22 (1381/2002), pp. 64–71.

"Roshanfekri-ye Dini va Chalesh-haye Jadid" (Religious Intellectuals and New Crises), *Nameh,* No. 20 (1381/2002), pp. 63–67.

"Demokrasi Farayandi Ejtenab Napazir va Ro be Roshd dar Iran va Jahan" (Democracy a Growing Phenomenon in Iran and the World), *Nameh,* No. 24 (1382/2003), pp. 15–19.

"Mabani-e Mashro'iyyat-e Hokumat: Qiyam-e Emam Hosein va Risheh-haye Hadese-ye Karbala" (Principles of Government Legitimacy: Imam Hossein's Rebellion and the Roots of the Karbala Event), *Aftab,* No. 34 (1383/2004), pp. 70–77.

Yusofi Eshkevari, Hasan. "Hokumat-e Demokratik-e Eslami" (Democratic Islamic Government), in Ali Mohammad Izadi, *et al. Din va Hokumat* (Religion and Government). Tehran: Rasa, 1377/1998, pp. 285–328.

Nogarai-ye Dini (Religious Reformism). Tehran: Qasideh, 1378/1999.

Shariati va Naqd-e Sonnat (Shariati and Critique of Tradition). Tehran: Yadavaran, 1378/1999.

"Avvalin Gami ke Bayad Bardasht" (The First Step that Needs to be Taken), *Cheshmandaz-e Iran*, Vol. 1, No. 6 (1379/2000), pp. 18–25.

Yad-e Ayyam: Roykard-haye Siyasi dar Jonbesh-e Eslahat (Remembering the Times: Political Developments in the Reform Movement). Tehran: Gam-e No, 1379/2000.

"Eslam, Azadi va Moderniteh" (Islam, Freedom and Modernity), *Aftab*, No. 9 (1380/2001), pp. 16–19.

Kherad dar Ziyafat-e Din (Knowledge in Service of Religion). Tehran: Qasideh, 1380/2001.

"Vafaq-e Melli Mabani-ye Nazari va Rah-e Kar-haye 'Elmi" (National Conciliation Theoretical Principles and Scientific Methods), *Nameh*, No. 17 (1381/2002), pp. 18–24.

"Roshanfekri-ye Dini va Chalesh-haye Jadid" (Religious Intellectualism and New Struggles), *Nameh*, No. 20 (1381/2002), pp. 63–67.

"Akharin Nazar-e Bazaegan: Beem-ha va Hoshdar-ha" (Bazargan's Last Opinion: Fears and Warnings), *Nameh*, No. 20 (1381/2002), pp. 68–70.

"Eslam va Mabani-e Qodrat" (Islam and the Principles of Power), *Aftab*, No. 14 (1381/2002), pp. 40–43.

"Mardomsalari-ye Dini" (Religious Democracy), *Aftab*, No. 22 (1381/2002), pp. 24–26.

"Roshanfekri-e Dini Momken Ast" (Religious Intellectualism is Possible), *Jame'h No*, Vol. 2, No. 17 (1382/2003), pp. 9–11, 34.

Ta'amollat-e Tanha-ee: Dibacheh-ee bar Hermeneutic-e Irani (Thoughts in Solitude: An Introduction to Iranian Hermeneutics). Tehran: Saraee 1382/2003.

"Tarhi az 'Omanism-e Eslami'" (A Plan for "Islamic Humanism"), *Nameh*, No. 23 (1382/2003), pp. 9–13.

Nameh-haye az Zendan be Dokhtaram (Letters from Prison to My Daughter). Tehran: Qasideh Sara, 1383/2004.

Yusofian, Ali. "Farhang-e Siyasi-e Iranian va Entekhabat-e Dorehye Haftom" (The Iranians' Political Culture and the Seventh Elections), *Aftab*, No. 33 (1382/2004), pp. 24–25.

"Bohran-e Roshanfekri va Tajdid-e Nezam-e Selseleh-maratedi" (Crisis of Intellectualism and Renewal of the Hierarchical System), *Aftab*, No. 34 (1383/2004), pp. 78–81.

Zahed, Sa'id. *Jonbesh-haye Ejtema'i-ye Iran-e Mo'aser* (Contemporary Social Movements in Iran). Tehran, 1382/2003.

Zahedi, Mohammad Javad. "Mafhoum-e Azadi dar Farhang-e Iran" (The Meaning of Freedom in Iranian Culture), *Andisheh-ye Jame'h*, No. 13 (1379/2000), pp. 19–21.

Zakariaee, Mohammad Ali. *Koy-e Daneshgah be Ravayat-e Rasaneh-ha* (University Dorm as Told by the Media). Tehran: Kavir, 1378/1999.

Gofteman-e Te'orize Kardan-e Khosoonat. (The Theorizing Discourse of Violence), Tehran: Jame'h Iranian, 1379/2000.

Zeidabadi, Ahmad. "Naqd-e Melli-Mazhabi-ha" (Critique of Religious-Nationalists), *Aban*, No. 150 (1382/2003), pp. 4–6.

Zibakalam, Sadeq. *Sonnat va Modernism* (Tradition and Modernity). Tehran: Rouzaneh, 1377/1998.

'Aks-haye Yadegari be Jame'h Madani (Memorial Photos with Civil Society). Tehran: Rouzaneh, 1378/1999.

Goftan ya Nagoftan (To Say or Not to Say). Tehran: Rouzaneh, 1379/2000.

Veda' ba Dovvom-e Khordad (Farewell to the Second of Khordad). Tehran: Rouzahen, 1382/2003.

Zinati, Ali. *Gofteman-e Roshangar darbareh-ye Andisheh-haye Bonyadeen* (An Illuminating Dialogue on Fundamentalist Thought). Qom: Mo'asseseh-e Amozeshi va Pazhoheshi-e Emam Khomeini, 1380/2001.